DIMENSIONS OF NATIONAL INTEGRATION :
The Experiences and Lessons of Indian History

DIMENSIONS OF NATIONAL INTEGRATION :

The Experiences and Lessons of Indian History

EDITED BY

Professor Nisith Ranjan Ray

PUNTHI-PUSTAK

&

INSTITUTE OF HISTORICAL STUDIES

CALCUTTA : : 1993

Published by :
Sankar Bhattacharya
PUNTHI-PUSTAK
International Book-sellers & Publishers
136/4B, Bidhan Sarani,
Calcutta : 700 004 (India)

●

Institute of Historical Studies
35, Theatre Road
Calcutta : 700017

First Edition. 1993

ISBN : 81-85094-62-4

Price

Printed By
Bilash Hazra
Modern Printers
61/B, Shyampukur Street
Calcutta : 700004.

CONTENTS

PREFACE

The Silver Jubilee Session (1986) of the Institute's Annual Conference which synchronised with the 39th Anniversary of India's Independence, chose "National Integration—The Experiences and Lessons of History" as the principal theme of discussion. This was both a response to a historical demand and a painful surprise at that. The element of surprise derives from the tacit admission that National Integration, the sine qua non of India's history through the ages, should appear in the present context, as an ideal phenomenon which requires to be re-examined and re-emphasised in practice. Unity and Integration have persistently held together the fabric of the sub-continent, known as Bharat-Varsha since ages past. Politically, as we know, India remained divided even in the days when the Britishers ruled, inspite of their claim to have effected for first time the political unification of this vast country. To concede such a claim is to negate the historical phenomenon of a 'Princely India' co-existing with a 'British India.' Geographically a close unit, but politically and administratively there remained within it two distinct units with differing status. In pre-British times, dating back to the days of remote antiquity, it was seldom that the whole of India formed one indivisible and cohesive unit owing allegiance to one single paramount authority.

This lack of political unity did not, however, connote, lack of integration. That integration is to be sought in the area of cultural concept and the people's allegiance to it, inspite of their differences—ethnic, linguistic, social, religious, economic and in ways of living. This unity fostered through acceptance of cultural norms, in many respects, different, from those followed elsewhere in the world at large, proved to be stronger than the unity forged through political agency. The latter inevitably carries with it an element of force or compulsion. So far as India is concerned, acceptance of a common distinctive cultural pattern and not conformity to political unity forcibly impored from above has been the real bond of unity among the people of India.

The first deviation from the historical lessons writ at large on her history was the partition of the country synchronising with the advent of Independence. However unavoidable it might have been in the context of political overtones, punctuated with so called religious fervour, it was nevertheless a negation of the trends and lessons of her history. The four decades that followed the advent of Independence, reveal that notwithstanding the country's remarkable progress in many spheres, traces of some basic weaknesses and even failure.

It would, however, a mistake to characterise the unfortunate symphonies of occasional communal disharmony, linguistic chauvinism and religious bigotry, as the growth of what may be termed as lesser nationalism, or sub-nationalism as pure emana- ties of the country's partition. The roots lie much deeper. The policy of Divide and Rule, for long pursued by the alien rulers, persistent economic disparities in the various regions of the country, the abomoniable negligence to educate the governed and the growing poverty which still continues to be a major scar—are all legacies from the British system of Govern- ment (or rather the lack of it). The vastness of the country has proved to be a source of both strength and weakness. The experiments in other multi-racial, multi-lingual countries have turned out to be ineffective and inadequate. But India has largely survived the challanges, so far, lending support to the belief widely held that the challanges to the nation's integrity are well on the way to be overcome.

But we must guard against complacency. A historian's task is to examine the experiences in depth and then to emphasise the lessons derived from experiences. This is what the present publication attempts to do. It comprises a corpus of 28 articles contributed by competent scholars and at least one jurist of great eminence, Mr. Justice M. H. Beg (who inaugurated the Conference). The volume treats the papers under 3 main divisions viz. (i) General Perception, (ii) Ancient and Medieval India's Experiences and (iii) Lessons from Modern Indian History. It is a study on aspects of the problem that faces the country to-day in the light of experiences, through the ages, presented, as far as possible, in regional environs. It is obvious that it is not a survey of all the constituent units of the Indian Union. Nor was it considered necessary since the problem has an overtone of regional bias from which the majority of constituent units are free.

We are deeply thankful to the contributors who have enabled us to present to the scholarly world, here and elsewhere, an intensive historical study on the most vital problem facing the country to-day. We regret that Mr. Justice Beg who not only inaugurated the conference but also contributed two learned papers did not live to see the volume in print.

Our grateful thanks are due to Professor Tarasankar Banerjee who not only bore with remarkable efficiency the onerous responsibility of the Local Secretary of the Conference but also generously helped in the editing of the text at great labour and with meticulous care.

We are under debt to Visva-Bharati University, in general, and the then Upacharya, Professor Nemai Sadhan Bose, in particular, for their kind help in enabling us not only to hold the Conference with success but also to bring out this volume.

Messers Punthi-Pustak' Calcutta have earned our deep appre-ciation for their co-operation in bringing out this volume. Thanks are also due to Shrimati Minati Chattopadhyaya, Registrar of the Institute for her assistance in connection with the production of the volume.

N. R. Ray

February, 1993.

LIST OF CONTRIBUTORS

1. Mr. Justice M. H. Beg, Chief Justice of India (Retd).
2. R. L. Raval, Department of History University School of Social Sciences, Gujarat University, Ahmedabad.
3. Dr. Tapash K. Roy Choudhury, Dept. of History, North Bengal University, Raja Rammohunpur, Siliguri, W. Bengal.
4. Mr. Ranabir Sammaddar, Dept. of History Gobordanga Hindu College, Gobordanga, W. Bengal.
5. Dr. K. Majumdar, Dept. of History, Nagpur University, Nagpur.
6. Dr. Gautam Sengupta, North Eastern Hill University, Shillong, Meghalaya.
7. Dr. G. P. Singh, Manipur University, Imphal, Manipur.
8. Dr. R. Venkatraman, Reader in Ancient History, Madurai Kamaraj University Madurai,
9. Dr. N. Jagadessan, Tagore College, Pondicherry.
10. Joseph Divien, Lecturer in History I. C. C. & C. E., Madurai Kamaraj University, Madurai.
11. Dr. V. Balambal, Reader in History Madras Universit, Madras.
12. Dr. J. B. Bhattacharya, North Eastern Hill University, Shillong. Meghalaya.
13. Dr. D. Nath, Lecturer in History, Dibrugarh University, Dibrugarh, Assam.
14. Dr. Rattan Lal Hangloo Dept. of History, North-Eastern Hill University, Shillong, Meghalaya.

15. Prof. D. A. Dalvi,—Principal Dnyanasadhan College, Thane, Maharashtra.
16. Dr. (Smt.) Sheela Raj, Bombay.
17. Dr. Mangubhai R. Patel, Reader in History, Gujarat University, Ahmedabad.
18. Mr. C. Paramarthalingam, Lecturer in History, Institute of Correspondence Cources, Madurai-Kamaraj University, Madurai.
19. Dr. Mani Kamerkar, S. N. D. T. Women's University.
20. Dr. Binod S. Das, Indian Institute of Technology, Kharagpur, W. Bengal.
21. Smt. Krishna Samaddar, Institute of Education, Chandernagar, West Bengal.
22. Mr. Dhurjati Prasad De, Gobordanga Hindu College, Gobordanga, W. Bengal.
23. Dr. Nirban Basu Dept. of History, Kalyani University, W. Bengal.
24. Dr. Ananda Gopal Ghosh, Dept. of History, North Bengal University, Shiliguri, W. Bengal.
25. Dr. D. R. Syiemlieh, Lecturer Dept. of History, North-Eastern Hill University, Shillong, Meghalaya.
26. Dr. E. Divien, Reader, Dept. of Indian History University of Madras, Madras.
27. Dr. B. B. Srivastava, Sagar University, Sagar, M. P.

PART—I

General Perceptions

I. JUDICIAL ROLE AND NATIONAL INTEGRATION

BY

Mr. Justice M. H. Beg
(Chief Justice of India (Retd.)

Importance of Judicial functions :

"The importance of the judiciary in political construction" wrote Henry Sidgwick in his "Elements of Politics", is rather profound than prominent. "On the one hand, in popular discussions of forms and changes of Government the judicial organ often drops out of sight ; on the other hand, in determining a nation's rank in political civilisation, no test is more decisive than the degree in which justice as defined by the law, is actually realised in its judicial administration, both as between one private citizen and another, and as between private citizens and members of the Government". Commenting on this observation, Harold J. Laski, in his "Grammar of Politics" observed : "Obviously, therefore, the men who are to make justice in the courts, the way in which they are to perform their functions, the methods by which they are to be chosen, the terms upon which they shall hold power, these, and their related problems, lie at the heart of political philosophy. When we know how a nation-State dispenses justice, we know with some exactness the moral character to which it can pretend".

If law is that part of culture or communicable knowledge which holds society together those who make it as legislators or administer it, either as executive or judicial functionaries, must understand how it does that. And, it is part of the judicial function to indicate and impress upon all of us how this happens. Here lies its importance for national integration which depends so largely on administration of justice according to law.

"Justice according to law" :

Although some people would prefer to say that law should be administered according to justice, or rather, according to the more fashionable term "Social Justice", without analysing the contents of either of these, yet, I have adhered to the time-honoured formula that justice should be administered according to law. My reason for doing so is that, whereas none can deny that concepts of justice change, and, with it, the meaning and administration of even the same laws, yet, judges cannot overstep the limits of their power to interpret statutory law. Of course, they may be able to indulge in some "judicial legislation", in consonance with justice, as they see it, when law is capable of being interpreted in more than one manner. There is also no doubt that, under the guise of finding the law, in countries following the "Common Law" tradition, judges have also made law, including "Constitutional law". This has been so in England where, as Dicey told us in his "Law of the Constitution", the fundamental rights of citizens were firmly established by declarations of courts of justice. Today, however, concepts of justice are sought to be incorporated so elaborately in written constitutions, such as ours, and, in statutes passed by legislatures, that the task of administering justice affords less scope for such "judicial legislation". It took place in England with the tacit approval of Parliament which has had immense respect for judges, except when it took the bit between its teeth and sought to punish judges, suspected of being royalists in Jay vs Topham, in an age when the struggle for political power, reflected in doctrines expounded in and by courts, between King and Parliament, was in full swing. That kind of situation cannot arise in England now.

Integrating Function :

Prof. Julius Stone tells us in his "Province and Function of Law" that law has displaced religion as "control of controls" today. In particular, our constitutional law, is meant to integrate the nation, through "Justice : economic, social and political". Judges when expounding this law and adjudicating on rights flowing from it are, therefore, expected to choose, out of two possible views, that which integrates the nation and upholds what has been described by Dicey as "Supremacy of the Constitution". This prevails in our country as in USA, as contrasted with "Parliamentary Sovereignty", which is a basic feature of the British Constitution.

Our Constitution and statutory laws are undoubtedly so advanced that, if they could be correctly interpreted and strictly enforced, there could be a lot better national integration than we see today with eruptions of wide scale lawlessness, with expressions of constitutionally abhorrent thoughts and sentiments, and with worse than bestial actions which disrupt and destroy lives of innocent people in our country in senseless bids to attract attention to actual or fancied grievances.

Under these conditions, it is not surprising that decisions of courts, from the highest to the lowest, are being treated with increasing disrespect. When the spectres of anarchy and disorder stalk the land, unless the decisions of courts, strictly uphold the law, as found in the Constitution and the statutory laws of the land, and laws are enforced unflinchingly by a strong executive authority backed by force, wherever needed, our country will face very grave and ugly anarchic prospects. Law and its strict enforcement, therefore, occupy a pivotal position for national integration.

Force, to back the correct decisions of law courts, can be both moral and physical. Moral backing is given by citizens voluntarily where the decision appears to them to be so just and impartial as to convince them that nothing better is possible, on the law as it exists, and, of course, physical force stands for what the police and the army can legally and reasonably do to meet either threats or use of violence. Ultimately, even the use of physical force can be effective only if its use is seen to be just and honest to enforce commonly accepted values, enshrined in the Constitution, as explained by the courts. Hence, I attach to what I may call the moral impeccability of decisions given by courts utmost importance in achieving the constitutional objective of national integration.

It cannot be denied that nothing is more integrating than a pervasive sense of justice. It implies rendering to each what is his or her due and treatment of each in accordance with a Constitution which enjoins upon the State equality of all persons before law and equal protection of laws. When the citizens see that they are getting this, they will vigorously fight and defend what the law unmistakably declares to be their birth right. This, at any rate, is the theory underlying our Constitution and what may be called a secular system of administration of justice which makes no distinction in rights between citizen and citizen on grounds of religion, race, caste, colour, region, or party. Hence in Virendra Singh's case (1954), Vivian Bose J, rather romantically declared : "At one moment of time a new order was born with its allegiance springing from the same source for all grounded on the same basis : the sovereign will of the people of India, with no class, no caste, no race, no creed, no distinction, no reservation".

Changing Tests :

It is true that the Constitutional could not, as Justice Bose's language suggests, suddenly dissolve all distinctions of class or creed, or regional prejudices. But, it did set up a powerful machinery of government to serve as a cementing force and provided, in the form of Fundamental Rights and Directive Principles of State Policy, excellent measuring rods for the courts to apply for judging what is and what is not "Justice, social, economic, and political". It is this kind of justice which has the effect of integrating the citizens. It follows that, where clear perception of the need and respect for effective administration of the laws in the Constitution and elsewhere, intended to secure justice, is wanting, dis-integrating trends of thought, feeling, and action develop. Lord Denning had this kind of perception of just treatment in mind when, in his "Road to Justice", he quoted a passage from Sydney Smith to illustrate how happy and contended people feel when treated justly by judges who could, in this way, remove the incentive for rebellion by doing justice in accordance with the law.

Of course, not all judgements, even of the highest courts of justice, are always correct or integrating in their effects. Not all judgements of courts bring out the correct philosophy underlying the Constitution and laws, Judges, like other human beings, are liable to err. They can reach differing conclusions even on interpretation of the same words. Thus, when Chief Justice Tanney, in the famous Dred Scott case, held that the Constitution of USA, based on the assumption that all human beings" are born equal", did not entitle Negroes to rights of citizenship, on the ground that they were sub-human, his philosophically and ideologically wrong judgment contributed powerfully to produce that rift or cleavage in thought and sentiment which led to a civil war between Northern and Southern States in U. S. A. We also know that later judges, interpreting the same constitution, held the negro entitled to equality given by law to him but accepted segregation or compartmentalised living as reasonable classification. In other words, in a different age, the claim of equality for the Blacks theoretically was conceded by courts in USA., but not for integration with the whites. The result was that Blacks got separation, as they have in South Africa even today, but not equality. A change in the philosophical and ideological climate bred by scientifically more advanced egalitarian education and laws ushered in what is known as the "Desegragationist" era. And, we find that the validity of law which gives even preferential treatment to the Blacks, in order to make up for the past wrongs and injustices suffered, was upheld in Bakke's case recently. Thus, even though the Constitution of U. S. A. did not change, the concepts of judges as to what equality of man, expressed by that Constitution, means, have changed considerably in the course of time with attitudes and approaches bred by changing philosophical, political and social ideas of each age.

How Integrating ?

In a book I read some time ago, entitled "How Courts Govern America", Chief Justice Neely, of a State Court in U. S. A. expressed the view that judges make the badly drafted laws of U. S. A. work by making their real intentions clear. The Chief Justice accused American legislators of deliberately enacting laws in vague terms for fear of offending vested interests. But, in his opinion, the Courts brought out the real intentions of the legislatures by making it very clear so that even ambiguous statutes become workable and effective. Courts are, therefore, keepers of the conscience of citizens and not seekers of popularity. They must be so upright as to place the dictates of their conscience above respect for any opinion whether of the public or of any person or body of persons in power.

It is a moot question whether judges in our country have

always followed the path of integration, as opposed to that of dis-integration, resulting from the philosophies underlying their judgments. For instance, in Keshavananda Bharati's case, the view which prevailed, by a narrow majority of one with a bench of 13 judges (I was one of them) the largest that the has ever sat in the Supreme Court, although, the majority opinion imposed the requirements of conformity to a "basic structure", culled out from the preamble to the Constitution, upon even amendments under article 368 of the Constitution, yet, this view could be said to produce anarchic and disintegrating results in as much as judges could decide very differently on what the basic structure meant. It is true that the basic structure, as explained by those who advocated it, rested upon highly integrating concepts of secularism, socialism, and democracy of a "Sovereign" republic, yet, these concepts are so wide and vague as to enable different judges to adopt differing versions of what constituted secularism, or socialism, or democracy.

Basic structure Doctrine :

It is true that, although, in the Rajasthan case and the Devraj Urs case, I have tried to limit the concept of basic structure to what is necessarily implied by constitutional provisions and is capable of being referred to constitutional provisions, yet, I wonder whether this attempt to narrow the sweep of the basic structure has been successful. I think lawyers could take differing views on the effects of this concept. Some may take the view that the concept of basic structure is bound to be used by judges only for purposes of upholding all the integrating values as embodied in the Constitution. Even if that be true, the sovereignty of the republic is certainly so diluted, upon the view taken by the majority of the judges of the Supreme Court in Bharati's case, that one could speak of the supremacy of the Śupreme Court. This dilution has resulted in what I consider to be an erroneous concentration of too much power in the Supreme Court making it virtually able to legislate. I have, therefore, felt that a Constitutional Court, representing all the three organs of the State, may be able to play a more integrating role.

It is interesting to notice that, recently, while the Speaker of Lok Sabha asserted the sovereignty of Parliament, a Member of Parliament, Mr. Swamy, kept on repeating that "the basic structure" was sovereign, another Member of Parliament said that the people are sovereign, and still another Member, Prof. Dandavate, is reported to have tried to divide sovereignty itself into legislative and judicial, into central and state spheres.

Sovereignty as an Integrating Concept :

Personally, I am inclined to agree with the proposition stated somewhat quaintly in Besanquet's "Theory of the State" "Sovereignty is a feature inherent in a genuine whole". Although, legal sovereignty is attributable to what stands for all the organs of the State, yet, its exercise, as I explained in Bharati's case, operates at different levels and in different forms, as the power of ultimate decision. The Supreme Court of India, in accepting the principle of legal "supremacy of the Constitution" repeatedly has given expression to this wholeness of the system of government set up by the Constitution. Its Preamble expresses the political fact that people of India had decided to set up a "Severeign Republic" in a legal document —the Constitution, to which all dignitaries of State and Judges and legislators swear allegiance, and which, as Chapter IV A of our Constitution clarifies, all citizens of India are also duty bound to uphold, stands for the unity and integrity of India.

The whole Republic and its organs, taken as a whole, and not merely parts of its, are legally sovereign. It is this sovereignty, which rests on the assumption of national integration and common citizenship of all citizens of India, irrespective of caste, creed, or region, which judges swear to interpret and uphold faithfully and truly, without fear or favour, affection or illwill. Their function is meant to be essentially integrating when they explain and expound its grand principles.

If the Constitution has the effect of integrating us, by securing acceptance of common principles of Justice "Social, Economic and Political", of which Liberty and Equality are only aspects or facets, adjudications on questions of right, in accordance with the Constitution and laws, are also meant to be integrating functions by redressing grievances, Courts must expound the true character of all integrating activities and obligations which are incumbent on all citizens of India as well as on all the organs of the State, whether executive, legislative, or judicial, in every region of India.

Friedmann's Observations :

I may quote here from Friedmann's "Law in Changing Society" on the role of the modern judge in a democratic system such as ours. He said :

> "The task of the modern judge is increasingly complex. Hardly any major decision can be made without a careful evaluation of the conflicting values and interests of which some examples have been given in the preceding pages. Totalitarian Government eliminates much of the conflict by dictating what should be done.
>
> The lot of the democratic judge is heavier and nobler. He cannot escape the burden of individual

responsibility, and the great, as distinct from competent, judges have, I submit, been those who have shouldered that burden and made their decisions as articulate a reflection of the conflicts before them as possible. They do not dismiss the techniques of law, but they are aware that, by themselves, they provide no solution to the social conflicts of which the law is an inevitable reflection".

"We live in an age of uncertainties and dangers, an age in which it is only too tempting to seek escape from the responsibility of decision in some kind of mythology. Millions have succumbed to authoritarian systems of government or emotional formulae which help to absolve the individual from decision and moral responsibility, and which afford an escape from the hard facts of life. In the administration of law it is also tempting to seek escape from the burden of decision. The law must aspire at certainty, at justice, at progressiveness, but these objectives are constantly in conflict one with the other. What the great judges and jurists have taught is not infallible knowledge, or a certain answer to all legal problems, but an awareness of the problems of contemporary society and an acceptance of the burden of decision which no amount of technical legal knowledge can take from us".

Correct Philosophy is the real test :

Whether the decision of a judge is integrating or otherwise depends, in my humble estimation, on his socio-economic and political philosophies. Correct orientation on issues raised here can no more be evaded by judges than by ordinary citizens of our land. National integration is a national objective whose service has to be common and compulsory on all of us whatever be our advocations in life. Our Prime Minister has rightly equated it with our duty to participate in national defence. Judges should be in the forefront and not in the rear of a disciplined march towards National Integration expounding faithfully and defending fearlessly what the Constitution stands for—the integrity and unity of our one nation.

Judges cannot shirk their duties to the nation by advancing any specious plea of a need for detachment. None of us can or should remain detached from his duty to the nation. Judges are not meant to function as disembodied ghosts hovering meaninglessly over the body politic. They are to articulate, as highly respected citizens, what binds or the "civil religion" which keeps together the secular polity. Toynbee, one of the most learned historians of our times, in his "Historian's View of Religion", spoke of a religion", in the sense of a binding force for men and women of each profession and avocation in life. If this be so, the "religion" of the forensic fraternity is the highest and the best. It is meant to soar above and integrate all religions whether traditional or vocational.

PART II

JUDICIAL ROLE IN NATIONAL INTEGRATION

Present Scene :

The present national scene is certainly depressing from the point of view of national integration. Those individuals who try to put forward integrating ideas are sought to be denigrated, maligned, and persecuted by those who want to put the clock back and to disintegrate the nation under pressures from domestic and foreign exploiters of religion and region and caste. Many politicians, instead of attempting to understand the implications of a secular polity from either judicial pronouncements on the subject or sound political philosophy, vie with each other in attempting to pander to popular prejudices and to fan irrational religious or regional frenzies to get votes. Many administrators too are infected badly by poisonous notions and befuddled and weakneed. Even religion, whatever its brand, could unite if its real essence could be understood and extricated from much rubbish collected round it by charlatans. It is much too often only a handmaid and prisoner of political and economic interests which misuse and pervert it. In such a situation, it should, in my humble estimation, be part of a correct judicial role to stand up firmly and fearlessly to indicate the integrating paths of socialism and secularism which a sovereign democratic Republic has to tread if it is to survive.

I quote from my own judgments in two out of a number of cases to illustrate how the judiciary has done its duty to show the road to national integration.

An Election Case :

In Z. B. Bukhari versus B. R. Mohra (S. C. C. Vol. II 1976 p. 17) upholding a judgment of the Bombay High Court in an election case, I said :
"38. The whole outlook revealed by the speeches of Bukhari is that of a medieval crusader who had embarked on a Jehad for extirpation of the heresy or 'kufr' which, in Bukhari's imagination, was represented by Chagla and his party. We do not consider such speeches to have any place in a democratic set up under our Constitution. Indeed, they have none in the world of modern science

which has compelled every type of religion, for its
own survival, to seek securer foundations than
child-like faith in an unquestioning conformity or
obedience to an invariable set of religious beliefs and
practices".

"39. We do not think that any useful purpose is
served by citing authorities, as the learned Counsel
for the appellant tried to do, to interpret the facts
of the case before us by comparing them to the
very different facts of other cases. In all such
cases, the line has no doubt to be drawn with care
so as not to equate possible impersonal attacks on
religious bigotry and intolerance with personal
ones actuated by bigotry and intolerance".

"40. As already indicated by us, our democracy can
only survive if those who aspire to become people's
representatives and leaders understand the spirit of
secular democracy. That spirit was characterised by
Montesquieu long ago as one of 'virtue'. It implies,
as the late Pandit Jawaharlal Nehru once said,
"selfdiscipline". For such a spirit to prevail,
candidates at elections have to try to persuade electors
by showing them the light of reason and not by
inflaming their blind and disruptive passions.
Heresy hunting propaganda on professedly religious
grounds directed against a candidate at an election
may be permitted in a theocratic State but not in a
secular republic like ours. It is evident that,
if such propaganda was permitted here, it would
injure the interests of members of religious minority
groups more than those of others. It is forbidden
in this country in order to preserve the spirit of
equality, fraternity, and amity between rivals even

during elections. Indeed, such prohibitions are necessary in the interests of elementary public peace and order".

What is Secular ?

"41. Learned Counsel for the appellant submitted that if we considered the substance of what was said by the appellant it would only amount to a plea that the voters should support one who opposes any change in Muslim personal law as against another who wanted to change it. It change of personal law is, it is suggested, only a secular matter, opposition to its change could not become an appeal on grounds of religion. To accept this argument would be to view the appeal to the voters after turning it upside down, or, perhaps, inside out. We are not concerned so much with the real nature of what is opposed or supported as with the grounds on which a candidate claims support over a rival. We have to primarily examine the cloak which the appeal wears to parade under and not only what lies beneath it".

"42. If all human activity in this world could be labelled "Secular", on the ground that it appertains to "this world" as against "the other world", all religious thought and activity could be described as "secular", as it takes place in this world. But, the term is not used so broadly. It is a convenient label to distinguish all that is done in this world without seeking the intervention or favour of or propitiating a superhuman or Divine Power or Being from that which is done professedly to please or to carry out the will of the Divinity. Secularism in political philosophy, is a system of utilitarian ethics, seeking to

maximise human happiness or welfare quite independently of
what may be either religious or the occult."

Primitive vs Modern Man

"43. Primitive man does practically nothing without
making it wear a religious garb because his understanding of the
physical world, of human nature, and of social needs and
realities, is limited. He surrounds customary modes of action
with an aura of superstitious reverence. He is fearful of depar-
tures from these lest he is visited by Divine wrath. Modern
man, with his greater range of scientific knowledge and better
understanding of his own needs as well as of the nature of the
universe, attempts to confine religion to its proper sphere : that
where he reaches a satisfying relationship between himself and
the Divinity he believes in so as to get an inner strength and
solace which enables him to overcome psychological crises or
fears when confronted with disturbing or disrupting events such
as Death, or their prospects. He does not permit his religion,
which should be essentially his individual affair, to invade what
are properly the spheres of law, politics, ethics, aesthetics,
economics, and technology, even where its administration is
institutionalised and operates as a social force".

The Secular State

"44. The Secular State, rising above all differences of
religion, attempts to secure the good of all its citizens irrespective of their religious beliefs and practices. It is neutral or
impartial in extending its benefits to citizens of all castes and
creeds. Maitland had pointed out that such a State has to
ensure, through its laws that the existence or exercise of a
political or civil right or the right or capacity for occupying
an office or position under it or to perform any public duty
connected with it does not depend upon the profession or

practice of any particular religion. Therefore, candidates at an election to a Logislature, which is a part of "the State" cannot be allowed to tell electors that their rivals are unfit to act as their representatives on grounds of their religious professions or practices. To permit such propaganda would be not merely to permit undignified personal attacks on candidates concerned but also to allow assaults on what sustains the basic structure of our Democratic State".

"45. Our Constitution and the laws framed thereunder leave citizens free to work out happy and harmonious relationships between their religions and the quite separable secular fields of law and politics. But, they do not permit an unjustifiable invasion of what belongs to one sphere by what appertains really to another. It is for courts to determine, in a case of dispute, whether any sphere was or was not properly interfered with, in accordance with the Constitution, even by a purported law. The validity of Section 123 (2), (3) and 3 (1a) has not been questioned before us. And, we have explained above what these provisions are meant for".

The State makes law in accordance with utilitarian principles to serve constitutionally enjoined objectives. Individuals and bodies concerned with religion in its conventional sense, on the other hand, occupy themselves with relations between themselves and what are assumed to be supernatural powers. The two spheres must not collide. Nor should one be allowed to control the other, although there can and should be harmony between the two. Neither can the State permit discrimination, persecution, lawlessness, or violence in the name of religion nor could religion be allowed to assume the control of law-making, administration, or adjudication in a Secular State even for sections of the citizens of that State. This is the principle underlying our Constitution, as explained by the Supreme Court of India in the case mentioned above.

Fundamental Rights and Directive Principles
(In Kesavananda Bharati vs State of Kerala
(4 SCC 225 at page 915, paras 1945 & 1846), I said :

"1800. The voice of the people speaking through Constituent Assembly constituted a new "Republic" which was both "Sovereign and Democratic". It no doubt sought to secure the noble objectives laid down in the Preamble primarily through both the Fundamental Rights found in Part III and the 'Directive Principles of State Policy' found in part IV of the Constitution. It would, however, not be correct, in my opinion, to characterise, as Mr. Palkhiwala did, the Fundamental Rights contained in Part III, as merely the means whereas the Directive Principles, contained in Part IV as the ends of the endeavours of the people to attain the objectives of their Constitution. On the other hand, it appears to me that it would be more correct to describe the Directive Principles as laying down the path which was to be pursued by our Parliament and State Legislatures in moving towards the objectives contained in the Preamble. Indeed, from the point of view of the Preamble, both the Fundamental Rights and the Directive Principles are means of attaining the objectives which were meant to be served both by the Fundamental Rights and Directive Principles".

"1801. If any distinction between the Fundamental Rights and the Directive Principles on the basis of a difference between ends or means were really to be attempted, it would be more proper, in my opinion, to view fundamental rights as the ends of the endeavours of the Indian people for which the Directive Principles provided the guidelines. It would be still better to view both fundamental rights and the "fundamental" Directive Principles as guidelines".

"1802. Perhaps, the best way of describing the relationship between the fundamental rights of individual citizens, which imposed corresponding obligations upon the State, and the Directive Principles, would be to look upon, the Directive Principles as laying down the path of the country's progress towards the allied objectives and aims stated in the Preamble, with fundamental rights as the limits of that path like the banks of a flowing river, which could be amended or mended by displacements, replacements, or curtailments, or enlargements of any part according to the needs of those who had to use the path. In other words, the requirements of the path itself are more important. A careful reading of the debates in the Constituent Assembly also leads to this premise or assumption. If the path needed widening or narrowing or changing, the limits could be changed. It seems to be impossible to say that the path laid down by the Directive Principles is less important than the limits of that path. Even though the Directive Principles are "non-justificable", in the sense that they could not be enforced through the Courts, they were declared, in Art. 37, as "the principles...fundamental in the governance of the State and it is the duty of the State to apply these principles in making laws". Primarily the mandate was addressed to the Parliament and the State Legislatures, but, in so far as Courts of Justice can indulge in some judicial law making, within the interstices of the Constitution or any Statute before them for construction, the courts too are bound by this mandate".

"1803. Another distinction, which seems to me to be valid and very significant is that, whereas, the fundamental rights were "conferred" upon citizens, with corresponding obligations of the State, the Directive Principles lay down specific duties of the State organs. In conferring fundamental rights, freedom of individual citizens, viewed as individuals, were sought to be protected, but, in giving specific directives to State organs, the needs of social welfare, to which individual freedoms may have to yield, were put in the forefront. A reconcialiation between the two was, no doubt, to be always attempted whenever this was reasonably possible. But, there could be no doubt, in cases of possible conflict, which of the two had to be subordinated, when found embodied in laws properly made.

"1804, Article 38 shows that the first of the specific mandates to State organs says :

"38. The State shall strive to promote the welfare of the people by securing and protecting as effectively as it may a social order in which justice, social, economic and political, shall inform all the institutions of the national life".

In other words, promotion of social order in which "justice, social, economic, and political" was the first duty of all the organs of the State".

"1805. The second specific mandate to State organs, found in Article 39, contains the principles of what is known as the socialistic "Welfare State". It attempts to promote social justice by means of nationalisation and State action for a better distribution of material resources of the country among its citizens and to prevent the exploitation of the weak and the helpless. It runs as follows :—

"39. The State shall, in particular, direct its policy towards securing—

    (a) that the citizens, men and women equally, have the right to an adequate means of livelihood ;

    (b) that the ownership and control of the material resources of the community are so distributed as best to subserve the common good ;

(c) that the operation of the economic system does not result in the concentration of wealth and means of production to the common detriment ;

(d) that there is equal pay for equal work for both men and women ;

(e) that the health and strength of workers, men and women, and the tender age of children are not abused and that citizens are not forced by economic necessity to enter avocations unsuited to their age or strength ;

(f) that childhood and youth are protected against exploitation and against moral and material abandonment".

ALLAHABAD CASES :

"1806. On the views stated above, it would be difficult to hold that, the necessarily changeable limits of the path, which is contained in the Directive Principles, are more important than the path itself. I may mention here that it was observed in one of the early full Bench decisions after the Constitution by the Allahabad High Court in Motilal & others, Vs. the Government of the State of Uttar Pradesh & others by Sapru, J. :

"I shall also say a few words about the directives of State Policy which, though not justiciable, may be taken into account in considering the constitution as a whole. These Directives lay down the principles which it will be the duty of the State to apply in the making of laws and their execution. Article 38 states that the State shall strive to promote the welfare of the people by securing and protecting as offectively as it may a social order in which justice, social, economic and political shall inform all the institutions of the national life".

"Article 39 lays down the principles which must inspire State Policy. Articles 40 to 51 concern themselves with such questions, inter alia, as, for example, the right to work, to education and to public assistance, the promotion of educational and economic interest of scheduled castes and the duty of the State to raise the level of nutrition and to improve public health".

"My object in drawing attention to the nature of these objectives is to show that what the framers of the Constitution were after was to establish, what is generally known now as the 'welfare' or the 'social service State', in this country. They had taken a comprehensive view of State activities and it is quite clear that they were not dominated by the laisseze-faire thought of the last century. So much about Directives. Now we come to Fundamental Rights".

"The object of these Fundamental Rights, as far as I can gather from a reading of the Constituion itself, was not merely to provide security to and equality of citizenship of the people living in this land and thereby helping the process of nation building, but also and not less importantly to provide certain standards of conduct, citizenship, justice and fair play. In the background of the Indian Constitution, they were intended to make all citizens and persons appreciate that the paramount law of the land has swept away privilege and has laid down that there is to be perfect equality between one section of the community and another in the matter of all those rights which are essential for the material and moral perfection of man".

"1807.   Indeed, in Balwant Raj VS. Union of India Dhavan, J., went so far as to hold that "the duty of the State" under Art. 37 to apply these principles in "making laws" was to be carried out even by the judiciary of the State whenever it had a choice between two possible constructions, that is to say, when it could indulge in judicial "law making".

Conclusion

Whereas the first part of this contribution was meant to elucidate certain general features of a judge's integrating commitment, by virtue of his oath of office, "to uphold the Constitution and the laws, without fear or favour, affection or illwill", the second part illustrated and elaborated more specifically the implications of this commitment.   The commitment, however, is not to any kind of partiality which would, in fact, operate as a disqualification.   It is to judicial freedom from partiality, even operating as "undisclosed premises", on grounds of creed, caste, race, religion or region.   Judges should set best possible examples to all citizens of a secular, socialist, democratic republic, of what is to be expected of them.

Essentially, it is the citizens of India who must discharge their integrating duties towards the nation by observing certain rules of conduct towards each other which these duties imply. Judges can only draw their attention to their fundamental duties as found in Part IVA of the Constitution and the laws of the land. Article 51 of the Constitution enacts these Fundamental Duties as follows :—

"It shall be the duty of every citizen of India :

(a) to abide by the Constitution and respect its ideals and institutions, the National Flag and National Anthem ;

(b) to cherish and follow the noble ideals which inspired our national struggle for freedom ;

(c) to uphold and protect the sovereignty, unity and integrity of India ;

(d) to defend the country and render national service when called upon to do so ;

(e) to promote harmony and the spirit of common brotherhood amongst all the people of India transcending religious, linguistic and regional or sectional diversities ; to renounce practices derogatory to the dignity of women ;

(f) to value and preserve the rich heritage of our composite culture ;

(g) to protect and improve the natural environment including forests, lakes, rivers and wild life, and to have compassion for living creatures ;

(h) to dovelop the scientific temper, humanism, and the spirit of inquiry and reform ;

(i) to safeguard public property and abjure violence ;

(j) to strive towards excellence in all spheres of individual and collective activity so that the nation constantly rises to higher levels of endeavour and achievement".

The integrating role of the judiciary consists in applying tests and safeguarding values enshrined in the Constitution and the laws. It does so on the ideological plane by a process of construction and interpretation of the Constitution and the laws. This, in itself, is an integrating role. It involves integration by either reconciliation of two seemingly conflicting principles contained in the laws, or, by rejecting the one which is opposed to the fundamental law in the Constitution and upholding that which can justly and reasonably be harmonised with it or flows from it. Similarly, on the practical plane, its task consists in either reconciling apparently conflicting claims or recognising and upholding one as legal and rejecting another as opposed to law.

Sir Henry Maine, writing in "Ancient Law" thought that the original of law itself was to be found in the judicial role of heads of families in primordial society giving decisions on problems encountered by members of the family in their dealings with each other and outsiders. These collections of verdicts, according to this theory, crystallised into custom venerated as supposedly divine in origin. Maine described these collections, woven into oral tradition, as "Themistes" from "Themis", the Greek Goddess of justice. The earliest notions of the king are also those of the judge and the law-maker rolled into one. Later, as society advanced and democratic aspirations developed, it was perceived that such a combination is the mother of tyranny and injustice.

The law contained even in ancient codifications, like the Roman XII Tables (This codification was the result of Plebian suspicions of Patrician magistrates so that laws may not be twisted to the disadvantage of Plebians), was transformed by judges who rationalised, secularised, and moralised it. They resorted even to fiction and then to Equity in order to harmonise law with justice.   Greek natural law or "Jus Naturale" and the rules of "Jus Gentium" common to all civilised nations in the ancient world operated through Roman praetors or magistrates, instructed by great jurists, to push forward the development of law towards greater justice, equity, reason and universality. The modern judge is in a more advantageous position.   He has to apply largely statutory laws which embody not merely basic notions of justice, but newer ones which answer the needs of a complex integrated society whose express object is : "Justice : Social, Economic and Political".   Judicial integrity, however, in applying the law, in consonance with principles of justice, remains an indispensable bulwark of national integration.   The law operating as the integrating force of society, through the secular state, has displaced religion as "the control of controls". Judicial integrity is a basic guarantee of preservation of secular polity and national integration.   It is the citizen's ultimate protection against unjustifiable discrimination and misuse of power of every kind.

Papers read of a Seminar in Hydrabad in 1984

EDUCATION FOR BETTER INTEGRATION

BY

Mr. Justice M. H. Beg

Evolving a National Persona :

The problem of national integration is one that requires to be approached from many directions. It implies the moulding of characters of individuals so that they become effective instruments for social cohesion and the progress and prosperity of the nation as a whole and not merely of sections of it. They must not become agents of disruption and disorganisation of parasitic individuals misusing their knowledge and capacities, nor, taking cover behind the pretence of religion or culture, should they exploit other individuals and damage the common good.

Now individuals in existing societies have been classified into three kinds by H. G. Wells : those with the "peasant persona" of the exploited and the downtrodden ; those with the "robber—baron persona" of the exploiter ; and, those with the "priestly persona" of the dedicated scientific investigator who works purely for the satisfaction or joy which acquisition of knowledge or service of others, irrespective of any other reward, and, possibly, the appreciation and approbation of others (if we allow introduction of a less selfless motive here) yield to one.

In general, those with the first type of persona try to cling to traditional ways, the second type often uses these as mass or means for preserving their privileged positions whilst the third, those with what H. G. Wells calls the "priestly persona", accept and respect tradition and religion so long as they are not used to block human progress but can rise above what may be traditional and yet obstructive and weakening.

It is the duty of this most valuable type of persona to propagate, if necessary, a new type of approach lying behind all that is called "religion"—one where we believe in the equality of human worth and dignity of all individuals irrespective of what their creed or caste may be called or the region they may reside in. Such a "religion", in the etymological sense of the term (from "religio" — to bind together) could be and should be, in my humble estimation, "a bond stronger than that of blood" which Mahatma Gandhi wanted. When we have succeeded in forging such a bond between all our countrymen we will have achieved National Integration. This would correspond to what Rousseau, a political philosopher, who believed in the nobility and goodness inherent in human nature, called a 'Civil Religion'. The purpose of education should be to bring out the higher side of human nature and to fix it in us as a part of a common persona of all of us as civilised human beings. This is what I mean by a "civil religion".

There is an obviously pressing need in our country for an educational revolution which will increase the number of those who can leaven the common bread, if I may so put it, of a secular culture and humanism on which the minds of our masses must be fed so that they too may get a taste of a world of thought and spirit freer and more elevating than what purveyors of conventional religion can provide for them.

National Integration, by definition, is a National objective. It cannot be viewed as just an elitist affair. It cannot be confined to particular groups or classes of people — whether social, religious, economic, political, or intellectual. Its objective has necessarily to be a super — persona or national character which transcends and binds together people of every type, profession, region, creed, caste, or race in the country into a single identifiable whole. There may be differences in basic approaches to it and in the relative importance one attaches to economic as distinguished from other factors in our lives and thoughts, in one's analysis and the proposals one may be able to make for strengthening national integration. I would, however, respectfully suggest that we should all be clear about the objectives we seek and what they mean or imply.

Politico-jural Philosophies :

Here, I think those who are expected to know something about the law and how it functions or is supposed to function in a world where, according to most jurists, law has "displaced, religion as the control of controls", can say something useful not only about what our Constitution, particularly its Preamble, says about the objectives set before themselves by the people and the ways in which these are to be attained – this, as I have tried to indicate elsewhere, provides the core of what I called our "Civil Religion"—but also something about what may enable us to see the three main bases of juridical and legal philosophies in the world of today. These not only determine the character of juridical thinking but also govern the lives and thoughts of people adopting them. They indicate what people of different countries have tried to use to build bonds stronger than those of blood.

The politico-legal or juridical philosophies of the world today may be divided into three broad types : Theocratic, Materialistic, and Natural Law philosophies.

The Theocratic is the most primitive because, as Sir Henry Maine indicates in his work on ANCIENT LAW, everything not fully understood, in early stages of human knowledge and experience, tends to be either divinised or assigned a superhuman source or origin. Even when reforming religions appear as strongly integrating factors the brief messages given by prophets, claiming to be sent by God, on moral, social and economic themes tend to be expanded into all-comprehending juridical and political philosophies reducing the solution of each problem, however novel and complex and unlike any that could have possibly arisen in the past, to the discovery of a religious, and supposedly divinely ordained formula given actually by a sacerdotal class, full of human error, frailties, and confusions of thought due to abysmal ignorance and lack of understanding of what they presume to pronounce upon. Indeed, if we examine the record of theocracies, in the course of human history, from the Spanish Inquisition and Calvin of Geneva to that of Khomeini of Iran today, men of real religion and saintliness may be horrified at the inhumanities and cruelties for which God and not human wickedness or perversity is made responsible. Such blasphemous transfer of moral responsibility to the Godhead may be very convenient and satisfying for theocrats, but it is fatal for the cause of national integration in a multi-religious, multi-cultural country like ours.

We take considerable pride in he secularism embodied in our Constitution, but, in fact, our masses seem still so largely swayed by those who have mis-educated them and who mislead and exploit them in the name of religion and culture, under the spell of theocratic or other similar narrow notions of caste and creed—notions which should have no recognisable claim in the world of law, politics, or economics of today. The task of the humanistic intelligentsia of our country in fighting these notions and their effects is not ended and can never end because the causes of humanism and justice and human equality and freedom will never cease to be in danger. Eternal vigilance is the price we have to pay to keep the dangers at bay. Indeed, we, who have had the very bitter experience of our country's partition, due to theocratic concepts and the political uses made of them, should become doubly vigilant when we find dangerous revival and use in international politics of such notions.

Theocrats find alliances with imperialists as well as with totalitarians and obscurantists of all kinds quite natural because their basic notions lead, quite logically, to both imperialism and totalitarianism, Hegel, who spoke of human history as the "march of God on earth" ended up by idealising the Prussian state. Hitler, who never failed to invoke the authority of God to support all that he did, waged a world war to establish the supremacy of the German race and destroyed Germany. It is evident that neither theocratic nor imperialistic nor totalitarian notions, which can be bracketed together for our purposes, can provide us with a bond stronger than that of blood.

The second school of thought is that of materialists, who consider human beings as so completely dominated by economic motives and drives that they are bound, willy nilly, to organise themselves, either consciously or sub-consciously, into two classes at war with each other perpetually—the exploiters and the exploited—between whom there can be no peace. In the end, according to this school of thought, the exploiting class, the expropriators, will be expropriated by the exploited or the expropriated class, so that there will be a classless society. For those of this view, religion, law, politics are really concealed forms of economic or materialistic activities and are instruments of domination.

All I would like to say here about such politico-legal concepts is that they are really parts of an economic or materialistic interpretation which relegates human volition and funds of human goodness, on which humanism relies, almost to a position of irrelevance. But, Communist countries, where the materialistic philosophy is sought to be embodied in socio-economic, political, and legal systems, have tended to use humanism or love of man for man (according to some this is a form of self-love) increasingly to work, to bolster, to support and embellish their own systems and cultures. In practice, the materialistic philosophy and not humanism is put in the background and not allowed to interfere with human bonds of the mind and spiri ?

Our conclusion should be that no dehumanising philosophy, be it theocratic or materialistic, could integrate the nation as a whole. Where can we then turn ?

I think, in order to find a satisfying and integrating politico-legal philosophy, both for domestic and international purposes, we will indeed, the whole world will have to turn more and more towards a natural law and humanistic philosophy, based on the natural needs of man as a social, rational, culture-building animal for bonds for human survival and for leading spiritually as well as materially richer human lives.

I cannot deal here with the views of those who deride or deny the validity of natural law philosophies of every kind. I cannot also dwell here on the differences of approach and opinion, in the juristic world, between those who believe in what appears to me to be a vague and nebulous kind of natural law, functioning in place of and above positive law, to be enforced by judges, those who share, as I do, the positivism and the pragmatism of Justices Oliver Wendell Holmes and Benjamin Cordezo, two great American judges who, whilst not rejecting natural law and natural rights' criteria, as tests of what ought to be, do not accept the doctrine that judges either have or ought to be presumed to have such judicial wisdom and power that they enforce their own notions of natural law against the clear meanings of what is positive law. I do, however believe in the ethics of a natural law based on human needs, on imperatives of the evolution of a human social order and what I, optimistically, believe to be human destiny.

Primitive & Modern Outlooks :

Primitive man had his limited stock of scientific knowledge in the application of which, at his level of technology, even he kept the spheres of the secular and matters of fact distinctly separate in his mind from the vast world of unseen powers, forces and beings his imagination conjured up (See : Malinowski in "Science, Religion and Reality") : He, however, often met, in his struggles with nature, with inexplicable failures and calamities. He was ignorant, weak, and full of fears. Therefore, he was disposed to see at every turn and corner the intervention of the unseen powers, He surrounded every activity of his with attempts to propitiate these powers in various ways (See : Sir James Frazer's "The Golden Bough") : His religion, consisting largely of mythology and ritual, dominated every aspect of his life – social, economic, political, legal, cultural, aesthetic, moral, and even technological – about which anthropologists have written so much.

The modern man, with his vast scientific knowledge and control over physical nature, tends to view religion as a matter of his personal beliefs about the relation with an Unseen Power or powers so as to guide his inner life of spirit and mind. He shares with primitive man his psychological need for religion as a prop and source of strength in times of stress and strain and in moments of emotional crises such as those of deaths and disaster. But, his religion is not the basis of social or political organisation. The sources of his laws are secular. His science, economics, and aesthetics are controlled by factors outside the sphere of religion. Even his morals and ethics are not tied to conventional religion but are based on principles and values whose validity is established by what is found to be right and just on grounds determined apart from those provided by particular religious beliefs or tenets. Hence, in truly secular social systems, whether in the East or in the West, differences in personal beliefs about the Unseen and in modes of worship do not regulate matters such as marriage and inheritance. In China, it is said to be not uncommon to find husband and wives, parents and children, brothers and sisters, living under the same roofs, as members of same families, professing different faiths. That is the kind of secularism in society we only dream of but rarely find. We seen to be still far from that "haven of freedom" into which our great national poet, Rabindranath Tagore, wanted our country to awake.

Secularism and Religion :

Secularism emerged in Western Europe as a movement of protest against the excesses, the massacres, and the wars waged in the name of religion. Its principles were derived from Utilitarian ethics (See Jeremy Bentham's "Theory of Legislation") which shunned what was based on prejudice and passion and sought to achieve human welfare by applying the scientific methods of induction and deduction to social realities. Society and its condition are, to the secular mind, the result of what men do and not of some Divine dispensation operating from above and outside man. All that exists is, according to it, the product of causes which can be ascertained. Injustice, wrong, oppression, exploitation of man by man, poverty, ignorance, disease, hunger, barriers of caste, class, and creed, are thus seen as man-made and not as the eternal and inescapable divinely ordained inflictions. By discovering and removing the causes of these, with the aid of science, conditions of human life can be improved. In Utilitarian ethics, which provided the philosophical foundations of secularism, human welfare and happiness are the tests of what is good and virtuous. Every activity and institution has to pass these tests to be acceptable. In this way, religion itself could be cleansed of its impurities and made to serve its true purpose.

There was a time when people in the West too murdered and burnt and crucified each other in the name of religion and believed that such acts, which were outrageously criminal and anti-social and evil according to the standards of Utilitarian or secular ethics, were modes of attaining Divine grace. Their conception of God was that of a monstrously cruel or vindictive being. If we find today an Anglican Bishop Robinson putting forward an altogether different conception of God, in his booklet "Honest of God," as a benevolent power working within us for our betterment and not as some unpredictable Being or Beings inhabiting space, it is the result of the secular and scientific thinking which characterizes western outlook on life today. He points out that even space, where these supernatural powers were supposed to reside, has no mysteries left now unknown to man.

Secularism is really a rational and scientific pursuit of individual as well as social welfare. In our organically interlinked world of modern science, the welfare of individuals and of social units or groups within a society, whatever the basis on which they are organised, and of nations, cannot be sought in isolation. Suffering, want, or ignorance and backwardness in any quarter has its repercussions on all others.

The problem of national integration in this country is largely one of bringing social realities in line with Constitutional theory and its implications. Formulation of a common civil code of personal laws applicable to all citizens uniformly may help ; but, if its principles are not, for any reason, generally acceptable, it may prove more irritating and frustrating than integrating. State action, through legislation, or, in cases of violation of the law, by appropriate proceedings in courts, will not suffice. Citizens must utilize their constitutional freedoms for building up a truly secular society in which the differences of class, creed, or caste cease to obstruct national unity and social solidarity. Are they doing this ?

Understanding Purposes of Religion :

If the real purpose of religion were understood by the mass of our people as a medicine for the troubled spirit or for cleansing and strengthening the spirit, differences in religion would cause no more dissension than the use of different medicines for physical ailments or different brands of soap to clean our bodies causes between us. Every individual could, in fact, benefit from whatever is good or cleansing or strengthening and elevating for the spirit in the teachings and precepts of any religion. Catholicity and tolerance in matters of religious beliefs is deeply embeded in Indian tradition. Bigotry and intolerance are foreign to it.

We turn, more and more with the passage of time, to the teachings of Gautama Buddha for a perception of the function of religion, both in individual and social life, as a means of attaining, without conflict with advances in scientific knowledge and truth, the eightfold path of self-mastery and virtuous conduct by a ceaseless and self-critical endeavour for : "right belief, right aspirations, right speech, right conduct, right mode of livelihood, right effort, right-mindedness and right rapture." Mahatma Gandhi, attempting to extract the essence of Hinduism as a religion, defined it as "a search after truth through non-violent means". In the famous Persian poet and Philosopher of Islamic Sufism, Jalaluddin Poomi, we find a synthesis between Vedantic philosophy and Islam. He declared that the great moral teachings and precepts, which he set forth in beautiful and moving verse with illustrative stories, were nothing but the "marrow" extracted from the Quran in Arabic, after casting away the "bones", served up in the Pehlavi language, Guru Nanak's teachings represent another liberal synthesis of religious ideas. Such broad and liberal concepts of religion ought to be popularised.

Much misunderstanding of the real teachings of the great religions of the world is caused by literal interpretations and unintelligent and unscientific study of passages contained in holy books torn from their contexts and divorced from their purposes. For example, the context in which the Prophet of Islam held out the pleasures of an after-life for the virtuous and his comparison of these to those of this earth, the language in which he described the damnation and sufferings of those who refused to accept the truths he taught, they duty of fighting oppression and wrong (jehad), which he talked about, was very special. He had the problem before him of civilizing an almost ferociously barbarous people who had to be both frightened into accepting and attracted by the restraints and discipline the Prophet succeeded in imposing upon them. The result was that, after assimilating a great deal that could be gleaned from the Roman Western civilization, the Arabs produced a brilliant civilization of their own of amazingly disciplined people who finally captured Constantinople, the seat of a Western Imperialism, and went on to threaten the West with conquest. The era of crusades and jehads by the clash of arms is long past. Our values and sense of right and wrong are very different today. Utterances which had a relevance in a different setting and historical context must be so explained to be properly understood.

In the modern world, the function of religion cannot be

to regulate politics, economics, law, or social organisation. Religion, in order to serve the psychological needs of man, in the age of modern science, must withdraw to its proper sphere that of personal beliefs about the Unseen and regulation of innor life as well as conduct of individuals in such a way as to promote human happiness and welfare of all. Differences of opinion and outlook in matters of religion, just like those in other spheres of life and thought, cannot be eliminated, But, conflicts between followers of different religions, of the kind we see from time to time, could be eliminated by secularization of life and thought which means that religion must be confined to its proper sphere and purpose.

Needed, Good Teachers and Guides :

If religion, like medicine, is meant to cleanse, heal, and strengthen the spirit, its administration should be in wise and expert hands, or, at least, under expert guidance, just as proper treatment of the body takes place under proper medical advice. The average teacher of religion, whether he is a priest, a Maulvi or Mulla, is so ignorant and so steeped in superstitions and prejudices that his own spirit needs cleansing and proper treatment before he can possibly impart good religious instruction. It would be better if the minds of the young and old in this country were not allowed to be infected and polluted by the very inferior substitutes for religion which they can serve. If religion is to be allied to and harmonized with science, its contents and the methods of imparting and administering it must change with the times. This has happened in Western countries. As an example of the ideas of good Christians on religion today I have already mentioned a booklet, "Honest to God" (SCM Series) by Bishop Robinson, one of the pillars of the Anglican Church in England. His last book, entitled "Truth is Two-Eyed", is meant to demonstrate that the highest teachings of Christianity resemble those of Vedantic philosophy.

We need not only an educational revolution in our country to cure the mental maladies with which our masses have been infected by the guardians of vested interests, but also sound guidance of such a revolution by an intelligentsia saturated with fresh and rational ideas such as those of men like G. B. Shaw and H. G. Wells in Britain whose writings and plays have moulded the views of older generations of the educated. They were products of the post-Darwinian revolution in thoughts and feeling in the Western world during the nineteenth century. Our great leaders of thought, such as Mahatma Gandhi and Rabindranath Tagore, were influenced by these world currents of thought. The late pandit Jawaharlal Nehru fully represented, and, indeed, spearheaded a revolution which could be described as "secularisation" of life and thought in this country. And, it seems to me that Prime Minister Indira Gandhi too did whatever she could in this direction.

The questions which I would like all of us to consider very seriously and answer are : What is the intelligentsia, in general, which could lead or mislead us doing ? What can it do and should do to propagate, inculcate, and promote objectives set before themselves by the people of this country mentioned in the Preamble to our Constitution ? Will it not be failing in its duty if it does not embark anew on a crusade to combat all that obstructs the progress towards these goals ? Could these objectives be breathed into all religion too so that religion, like law, could also become an effective means of cohesion and social, economic, and political transformation and real redemption of the masses ? Or, must all religion remain in an untochable domain and really act as an opiate for the masses meant only to exploit people and dominate them by instilling the fear of the Unseen into them ?

If these questions could be satisfactorily answered for us by our intelligensia or by whoever teaches, whether through formal or informal means in all vocations and professions of life, whether they are artists, scientists, lawyers, judges, doctors, or administrators or journalists and media people or professional teachers and specialists in imparting education, we would march more harmoniously towards our national goals.

HINDU SOCIAL COSMOLOGY AND NATIONAL INTEGRATION : SOME REFLECTIONS

R. L. Raval
Department of History
University School of Social Sciences
Gujarat University
Ahmedabad

This paper deals with the problems of national integration in the context of some of the broad assumptions underlying the concept of Hindu Social Cosmology, and the attempts made by the Indian Society to resolve contradictions arising out of the heterogenetic as well as orthogenetic challenges during its long history.

I

In this paper the term, 'national integration', is used in its wider connotation. This implies the muti-faceted cultural life of India and the sense of belongingness or the subjective realization of the cultural identity despite many apparent or real contradictions at horizontal as well as at vertical levels of the socio-cultural life.

In the Western sense the term, 'national integration', seems to heve its primary manifestation in the united political will of the people in the framework of the centre-periphery relationship thereby emphasizing, on the whols, the centripetal tendencies. The Indian experience tends to reject the need for any single or even uniform pattern of identities as essential requisite for the making of a nation-state. A civilization with its long tradition evolves a social cosmology which shapes its approach to the cultural identity till it exhausts itself to be replaced by a new social cosmology. Thus, in any society the reality always presents people with a given set of actions prone to be accomplished. However, which of these actions will be undertaken is thus determined by the conscious as well as unconscious structures of the human mind in the society. These in turn are more or less, similar for all men, albeit in the given spatio-temporal context. In order to understand the Indian social reality it is important to examine the broad assumptions underlying the Hindu social cosmology.

II

A social cosmology, is conceived of as "deep ideology" about all kinds of social and cultural things and how they relate to each other, implicit rather than explicit. In a way, if properly constructed it would define a complete social grammar.

The major dimensions of the Hindu social cosmology or for that matter any other social cosmology would include Space, Time, Knowledge, Person—Person relations, Person—Nature relations and Person—Transpersonal relations. The Hindu social cosmology was evolved by the cultural tradition of what was later on known as 'Hinduism' or a Hindu way of life, its religio-ethical values, the life-style and conduct-norms, shaped since Vedic time, and were lateron, formalized in the Epics.

If we examine briefly these dimensions of the Hindu social cosmology we find that the concept of social Space is not assumed as circular, in the sense that there is no one centre as such which would radiate its message expected to be received by the Periphery. In brief, the social space does not contain the ideology of expansionism as is the case with the modern Western social cosmology, in which the conversion and conditioning of the non-west is taken for granted. On the other hand, in the Hindu world-view the concept of social space is based on the principle of hierarchy. Thus it emphasizes the social space in vertical sense of the term. The principle of hierarchy was not only engrained in the system of Varna, caste and sub-caste stratification but also in the Hindu concept of triple human nature—*Sattva, Rajas* and *Tamas,* occupational life-cycle-four Ashrams, moral duties etc.

So far as the dimension of Time is concerned it is of cyclical nature. It implies the principle of continuity, which was symbolized by the idea of *Karma* and transmigration of soul. Therefore, the Western idea of progress based on linearity is absent in the Hindu social cosmology.

Knowledge as a third dimension of Hindu Social Cosmology was built on intuition or subjective insight, which, according to the Hindu tradition, was the fundamental and superior to the analytical objective type of knowledge, though the latter one was given due importance in the day-to-day life. The Hindu way of life and thought has special attraction for the holistic image of reality. As against this an empirical approach implies the grasping the nature of thing through its sub-divisions and fragmentations into the smallest parts or units and observed as related to each other mainly in a linear fashion, referred to as cause and effect. It is organized from a hard core of central propositions. Mastery of that hard core becomes prerequisits to command man and nature. This is one of the most important characteristics of the Western social cosmology. In this sense, mathematics becomes a tool mainly because it is contradiction-free ; while in the Hindu social cosmology it was chiefly meant to understand and appreciate the Infinite.

So far as Person—Person relations are concerned Hindu social cosmology's approach is holistic though it rests on the principle of hierarchy. Under this holistic approach, an individual, being a component of particular Varna, Caste or group, has to perform the duties assigned to him within the normative frame-work of that group, and thus his role as an individual is subservient to that of the group, caste or community. Thus, in the ideal situation, a person could earn his freedom while performing his duties within that group life, which itself was an integral part of the larger social life. Here, society is seen as an organic whole, and the basis of the relationship is duty rather than right, which if performed sincerely would create genuine social harmony. As against this, in the Western social cosmology the vertical social relations combined with the freedom of choice on the part of an individual creates a climate of struggle among the individuals, which is considered as normal and has taken an institutionalized form as competition.

The Hindu social cosmology takes the holistic view of the Person-Nature relationshipe. Ideally, there is no dichotomy between man and nature. He is a part of it. Therefore, he is expected to blend his economic cycles with nature's ecocycles in such a way that the two may become almost indistinguishable. But this is not the case with the Western social cosmology under which man is above nature and the latter is to be used for his aggrandizement.

In the Person-Transpersonal relationship the Hindu social cosmology works on the cardinal principle of transcendence implying thereby the progressive expansion of a person into universal as the ultimate meaning of religion. That is to say, society exists primarily as a manifestation of transcendental reality. At an empirical level, this reality is conceived in terms of an integrated Dhramic order, which attains equilibrium through proper performance of natural—*Swabhavik* roles. Thus the principle of trnascendence forms the basic concept contributing to integration as well as rationalization of the other value-themes of the tradition.   In the Western social cosmology, as also in the case of Islam and Judaism, Person-Transpersonal relationship is based on the Book-*Kitab*, and human beings are equipped with a soul capable of eternal life, and the problem is how to gain an access to this eternal life without losing the individual identity.   Thus, the principle of transcendence becomes almost a contradiction from the Western point of view.

III

If this view-point based on the Hindu social cosmology finds any justification it may logically follow that the Western approach is too narrow to comprehend and appreciate the problems of national integration.   This is because from Western point of view the principle failure of the Indian society through out its long history was its inability to function politically, to construct a viable political authority.   In short, the Indian society failed to build a centre, and therefore, it could be characterized as an apolitical society.   This view point is based on one of the most important characteristics of the Western World view, i.e., centre-periphery relationship.   While in the Hindu social cosmology, there is no such centre, therefore, if there is a circle it is without a centre.   This may sound absurd and contradictory from the Western point of view, which mainly strives for a contradiction-free programme for the society.

IV

If we go briefly, through the various phases of Indian history, we find that the Hindu society was primarily rooted in performing *dharma*.   This was characterized by hierarchical inter-dependence of several social roles and statuses based on the principle of transcendence. This attitude shaped ideally for the value-system based on tolerance, which in turn, helped the process of cultural integration. However, at a later stage, the Brahmin ascendancy based on scriptural authority and rituals smothered the process of the vertical social mobility in the Varna organization, which was expected to be based on *guna* and *Karma*, rather than on mere accident of birth.

A dissent movement initiated by Buddha and Mahavir, by way of questionning the established ideology, and belief-systems itself became a core of new ideology within the cosmology itself. The existing, folk and regional cultures, called 'Little tradition' by Milton Singer, continued side by side with the 'Great tradition', and gradually became a part of the common cultural consciousness shared by the people and expressed in essential similarities of mental outlook and ethos despite their apparent variant forms. Thus we find that even at later stage, most of the religious sects and new social groups, which emerged in the Hindu society, were the result of the processes of dissent and protest. And we have seen that these processes of change were, on the whole, orthogenetic in nature, as the categories of cultural innovations that were introduced through such sects and social groups were drawn from the cosmology itself. Thus, before the advent of Islam in India, as a political force, heterogenetic cultural influences were assimilated in the orthogenetic Hindu tradition.

V

When Islam came to India as a politico-religious force the Indian Society had to face for the first time the challenges of quite a different social cosmology. In contradistinction to the Hindu social cosmology, Islamic social cosmology was rooted into a strong centre, in the sense that it was purely monotheistic and messianic-historical in ethos. Being a nonhierarchical and simple in its basic tenets the cosmology of Islam tended towards the expansion of the periphery and the shrinking of the rest, explained in the terms of *Darul Islam* and *Darul harb*. Nevertheless, it had gone through many orthogenetic changes since it dominated the countries like Persia, Egypt, Syria etc. When Islam came to India the Hindu society felt a powerful jolt. As a consequence, the Hindu society tended to keep a low key profile, for, it found itself in a vulnerable position. It created its own defence mechanism, thereby making its tradition more rigid and using its doors for exit rather than for entry.

The withdraw syndrome of the Hindu society created a Bhakti movement, which in turn, became a movement of dissent. It was made up of saints coming from all strata of the society irrespective of caste or status. Being a multiregional in character it employed the medium of popular dialects and gave impetus to the regional languages and literature. Along with its Islamic counterpart in the form of the Sufi movement the Bhakti movement produced an atmosphere of cultural and emotional integration. As a result, many of the traditional traits of the Hindu culture crept into the Muslim society of India, as most of the converts hailed from the lower strate of the Hindu society, and many of the shrines of the Muslim saints became the places of pilgrimage for the Hindu also.

Though the Muslim rulers in India developed a dominant political style and an authoritative centre, their control of India was rather an exception than the rule, as most areas continued their cultural, economic and political autonomy with the village organization as its basic unit. Even the Muslim population living in the country side was found fit into this system with specialized occupation, and it also developed its own caste system.

Thus, despite the political and cultural influence of Islam the core-structure of the Hindu cultural tradition remained on the whole intact. Though differing on some vital points, both the Hindu and Muslim cultures with their traditional world-view existed side by side. But as mentioned above, more important aspect of their co-existence was their influence on each other leading to adaptation and cultural syncratism. In a way, Islam in India was indigenized and became a part of the Indian culture.

VI

As we come to the modern period we find that the British rule brought into Indian society the Western cultural tradition, which was in its ethos and structure fundamentally different from the traditional patterns of Hinduism. Rested on the Western social cosmology the British rule basically differed from its Indian counterpart. It was strongly wedded to the concept of centreperiphery relationship, therefore, it created a sense of dichotomous attitude among the newly educated urban middle class. The British administrators claimed that by establishing a central authority they could unite the Indian Society, which in their view, was more divisive and fragmented. In a sense, this claim was not without foundation. The Hindu intellectual elites of the first and second generation of the nineteenth century welcomed new progress in all walks of life symbolizing an ever expanding hope in the Indian destiny under *Pax Britannica*. The reform movement, first in the socio-religious sphere and at later stage in the political sphere enthused the social and political leaders with a feeling of nationhood and quest for liberty and freedom. Nevertheless, the nationalistic consciousness of these leaders was oriented towards the Indian tradition, and the co-existence of entirely two different cosmologies was rather uneasy.

The rise of the Hindu rivivalism in the last decades of the nineteenth century created an intense urge for the search for the cultural selfhood, and a tendency to defeat the West with its own cultural weapons grew strong. Dayanand Saraswati wanted to introduce the concept of a centre and the authority of the Book, i. e., the Vedas. While Swami Vivekanand introduced new vitality to the concept of Vedant. Activism rather than escapism became his dominant note. According to him, social accountability was to be demonstrated by serving the lowest of the lowly. Dayananda's appeal was ironically based on the model of the West ; while Vivekanand superbly interpreted the Hindu social cosmology by refuting the fallacy of dichotomy between the infinite and finites, through Vivekanand the modern world for the first time could appreciate the message of one of the greatest representatives of the Hindu social cosmology, namely, Ramkrishna Paramahamsa who demonstrated that there were different paths to the same Truth (Yatamat tata path). Vivekanand tried to understand the Western values of material progress in right spirit as there was no dichotomy between the material and spiritual progress.

Tagore and Gandhi were the product of this ethos of new cultural federalism and universalism. However, most of the liberal intellectuals, both the Hindus and Muslims, were attracted by the Western model of the nationalist movement. But these remained an inherent contradiction in their nationalist thinking because it reasoned within a framework of knowledge based on the Western social cosmology, where representational structure corresponded to the very structure of power that the nationalist thought sought to reject. Gandhi could see this contradiction as the British colonialism had imperceptibly colonized the minds of the intellectuals by releasing forces within the society to alter their cultural priorities once for all. Gandhi refused to play the game according to the rules laid down under the impact of the Western social cosmology. He gave priority to the programme, which could make the Indian mind uncolonized. Thus, Gandhi worked simultaneously for the double revolution, the political and social, however he did not want to separate one from the other. He wanted to apply the holistic approach to solve the problems of the Indian nation. His concept of a free India, his solution to racial, caste and inter-religious conflicts and his concept of human digiuty were free from the constraints of history. His emphasis was on economic and political decentralization. In that context the role of the state was expected to be minimal. In the socio-religious sphere, for Gandhi the cleansing of filth and the cleansing of soul went together. Only this approach, in his view, could wipe out socio-cultural inequality. No doubt, Gandhi's task was stupendous and his personality traits were complex. But he tried to give a meaning to India's future breathing the essence of the Hindu social cosmology.

VII

An almost paranoid concern with the politico-cultural stability of India, particularly after the Partition, seems to be the result of the impact of the Western social cosmology. There is no denying of the fact that the concern for this stability is more imperactive when a new nation like India has to face fissiparous tendencies because of external as well as internal forces. Perhaps the right clue for such an integration may be found in the indigenous cosmology itself under which the process of integration may radiate from the periphery itself. To be consistent with this approach the developmental models based on centrism would not be workable at least within the frame-work of this paper. In the polycentric society of India it would be very difficult to have one uniform blue-print for the whole nation. Indian society is like an Osceanic circle in which the inner circles may be allowed to command the necessary autonomy and authority to perform most of the socio-economic and political tasks.

The true spirit behind the national integration that the Hindu, in fact the Indian social cosmology is expected to achieve is expressed in the Rigveda "Let noble thought come to us from every side." Gandhi echoed this in his characteristic style when he said, "I do not want my house to be walled on all sides and my windows stuffed. I want the cultures of all the lands to be blown about my house as freely as possible. But I refuse to be blown off my feet by any". And the same spirit is reflected in the poetic genius of Tagore who put it in the most succinct way, "I love my Maker because He has given me the right to deny Him".

REFERENCES

Ahmad Aziz, *Studies in Islamic Culture in the Indian Environment* (Clarendon Press, Oxford, 1964).

Akram S. M., *Muslim Civilization in India* (Columbia University Press, New York ; 1964).

Chatterjee Parth, "Gandhi and the Critique of Civil Society", in Guha Ranajit (ed.), *Subaltern Studies*—III (Oxford University Press, 1984).

Galtung Johan, Erik Rudeng and Tore Heiestad, "On the Last 2500 Years in Western History", in *The New Cambridge Modern History*, XIII, Campanion Volume (Cambridge University Press ; 1979).

Galtung Johan, "On the Dialectic Between Crisis and Crisis Perception", in *International Journal of Comparative Sociology*, Vol. XXV., Nos. 1-2 (1984).

Gandhi M. K., *Hind Swaraj* (in Gujarati) (Navjivan Publishing House, Ahmedabad, 1969).

Gandhi M. K., *Gandhi Shikshan* (in Gujarati) Vols. I-XII (Bombay ; 1923).

Gibb H. A. R., *Modern Trends in Islam* (Chicago University Press, Chicago, 1945).

Gupta Krishna Prakash, "Sociology of Indian Tradition and Tradition of Indian Sociology", in *Sociological Bulletin*, Vol. XXIII, No. 1 (1974).

Heimsath Charles H., *Indian Nationalism and Hindu Social Reform* (Oxford University Press, 1964).

Kothari Rajani, *Politics in India* (Orient Longman Ltd., 1970).

Kripalani J. B., "Gandhian Thought and Its Effect on Indian Life", in *Studies in the Cultural History of India* (UNESCO Publication, Agra, 1965).

Majumdar R. C. (ed.), *British Parampuntcy and Indian Renaissance*, Part II (Bharatiya Vidya Bhavan, Bombay, 1965).

Nandy Ashis, *The Intimate Enemy* (Oxford University Press, New Delhi, 1983).

O' Malley L. S. S. (ed.) *Modern India and the West* (Oxford University Press, London, 1941).

Panikkar K. M., *Hindu Society at the Cross Road* (Bombay, 1955).

Radhakrishnan S., *Our Heritage* (Hind Pocket Books, New Delhi, 1973).

Radhakrishnan S., *The Hindu View of Life* (10th impression, George Allen and Unwin Ltd., New York, 1957).

Rao M. S. A., "Themes in the Ideology of Protest Movements," in Malik S. C. (ed.), *Dissent, Protest and Reform in Indian Civilization*, Institute of Advanced Study, Simla, 1977).

Singh Yogendra, *Modernization of Indian Tradition*, (Thomson Press, India Limited, Publication Division, Delhi, 1973).

Thapar Romila, "Dissent and Protest in the early Indian Tradition," in *Studies in History* Vol. I., No. 2. (New Delhi, 1979).

Young India (June 1, 1921).

DIMENSION OF NATIONAL INTEGRATION :
An X'ray of Experiences and Teachings of Modern Indian History

Dr. Tapash K. Roy Choudhury
Department of History North Bengal University
Raja Rammohunpur West Bengal

The question of nation-building and state formation, with which the issue of national integration is closely related, was tentatively answered in Indian history in a rather unilinear process. A broad trend of political integration through conquests and cultural assimilation has been the most common syndrome in all the different periods of Indian history to which the 'primordial' power had always resorted. Consequently, centricism of the political power had more often emerged as a trend in the political culture of this sub-continent, and all other forces which lay dormant had never come up for closer examination either for their structural necessity or for functional importance. So, what was achieved in the process were (i) a sense of geographical unity, (ii) administrative unity and (iii) affiliation or apparentation of some little nationalities with the metropolitan culture. But the forces of integration released by the sources of political power too were not functioning without interruption, as the dynasties fell and foreign invaders came to political power. As a result, two significant socio-political developments were observed. On the one side greater nationalities having emerged as an organised system from weilding political power in previous decades or centuries, and later removed by foreigners from political control, had perpetuated their existence through challenge or response to the new metropolitan culture. On the other, the large number of little nationalities which had existed outside the frame of the previous metropolitan cultures had either succumbed to the new political forces or remained a *cul-de-sac* as ever. All that followed from the type of integration analysed in the prefatory passage were incidents of accommodation dictated by political opportunism. Presumably, repeated assertions of regional powers with the fall or dissipation of the central authority was the inevitable consequence of our state system throughout history. The impact of such cultural and political cessation was so immense that whatever cultural unity that could survive the political crisis manifested in ethno-centricism. The greatest casualty in the process are the senses of geographical unity or one statehood which the universal empires had somewhat made tangible. All these tendencies of disunit would obviously prompt one to ask whether the nationhood in India was not achieved by the coalescences of all the different forces of culture and tradition, or that the stateformation process remained incomplete.

We intend, in the following pages, to study the crucial issues which are rulated to the genuine state-formation process, and had been neglected over centuries either on account of the motivation of the 'primordial' public to introduce a monoculture, or due to inadvertance, Nationhood, integration of different components of nationality and state-formation are inter-related aspects of a political process, and the appropriate degree of maturity understandably may be attained on the basis of the degree of maturity attained in the first two stages i.e., growth of nationhood and cohesion of nationalities in multinational states. India being a multi-national state its success as a state for all practical purposes depends on the integration of the political and socio-economic forces of the multiple nationalities. India's experience during the colonial era, to which we intend to apply our analysis, remains to be one of wrongly placed emphasis on priorities determined by colonial interest.

I

The issue of national integration in the context of our present political behaviour wilfully admits that either the process of integration has not been completed, or that it has been placed on wrong footing needing rectification. The experience of the pre-colonial era is somewhat expressed by the cliche 'unity in diversity', unity obtained, till the fall of the Hindu and the Buddhist rule, by the process of 'Sanscritisation' of India since the arrival of the Aryans. But this process, whatever be its merits or lapses, was seriously disturbed by the arrival of the Muhamadans and their emergence as the political power in India. Though they had repeated the process of achieving political and administrative unity of India by 'Islamisation' success remained to be half way through; the cultural unity that was achieved during the pre-Muhamadan era was perceptibly disturbed by the introduction of a new element in the Indian cultural horizon. They might have influenced each other as they did, but it was not towards syncretism at the metropolitan level that the thrust was percevied; rather it was in the localisation or regionalisation of the ethnic aspects of culture, or in other words through ethnocentricism a more or less tangible unity was retained whose influence at the national level was never very profound.

What has happend as a consequence were the (i) emergence of a second metropolitan culture supported by political power and an organised egalitarian religion and (ii) the resumption of the regionalisation process at the political level after the fall of the Muhamadan universal empires. Besides, the concept of the geographical unity of India was submerged in the urgency to establish linguistic-religious kingdoms virtually reversing the state-formation process. This was the politcal scenario of India when the East India Company assumed political power In their colonial interest the servants of the Company followed almost the euristic model of expansion through conquests and annexation at the early stage of their rule.

After the completion of the conquests the state-formation process was revived by generating some fresh integrative forces. The number may not be legion, but some of them which indeed exerted profound influence on the socio-political life in the sub-continent are (i) secular approach to political life, (ii) introduction of common law, (iii) construction of the railways and (iv) the application of the western science and technology. Christianisation of the Indians ran as a parallel stream and was conducted with impetuosity and over-enthusiasm by the missionaries, though its importance as a substitute to the existing organised religions as a state-building force was limited.

(i) Secularisation of the political life in India was one of the major integrative forces which successfully brought a large number of little nationalities within the fold of the greater nationality that was emerging out of the ruins of the previous centuries. Indian political life had always had a theocratic bias with one great religion or the other prescribing for the social ethics and political behavious. The colonial administration, instead of replacing them by Christianity, started with a secular approach which, among other things, helped to create an able bureaucracy—an important structural component of a stable state order. Pre-colonial bureaucracy was dependent on the ruling families, subsisted on wages in kind and cash and consequently never enjoyed the liberty which money economy provides. Therefore, it had never had the opportunity to act as a great unifying force. Absence of secularism, persistence of tribalism in our culture and the prevalence of inept money economy caused the pre-colonial Indian bureaucracy to be virtually inactive in the state-formation process.

But the full potential of this very vital structural component of a state, even during the British period, could not be realised because of the racial policy of the colonial administration and for its resistence against proper Indianisation of the bureaucracy. So, inspite of being professionally competent the bureaucracy remains to be dis-functional with reference to its structural necessity in the state-formation process. The absence of the Indian element in the bureaucracy, during the colonial era, to the extent it was needed, destroyed its organic character *vis-a-vis* the Indian mass and so remained to be superimpositional.

Another important aspect of the secularisation process was the introduction, of course in a limited scale, the constitutional system of government which initiated the process of representing different nationality interests. Constitutionalisation of some vital aspects of Indian political life resolved partially the identity crisis which encouraged the propensities towards all forms of regionalism in the past. But the system could not come full circle, as the communal awards having started with the Morley — Minto reforms became a part of the constitutional development in India till the Act of 1935, notwithstanding the fact that the secular spirit of the system would be visibly destroyed in the process. The partition of India in 1947 on communal ground was the nemesis to which this sub-continent had succumbed for stifling the process of constitutionalism in a secular spirit. It is understandable that the prime motivation of the colonial power was not to stabilise a state in India through the integration of different nationalities but to tender utmost effort for exploitation. Therefore, the objectives of colonialism and the attainment of a stable nationhood through a well developed state system were never identical. Introduction of secularism in the Indian polity by the colonial administration turned out, in the final analysis, to be the product of a spasmodic application of the utilitarian philosophy. It started with a promise but ended in confusion.

(ii) In the course of secularisation and for an urgency to establish the rule of law the British government introduced a body of common laws in India to settle all disputes arising out of various transactions. No doubt it was alien law that was introduced, but its merit lies in the fact that it was the product of a sense of justice and secular morality rather than being conducted by the *dharmasastras* of the Hindus or the *shariat* of the Muslims. Consequently, it could have brought more people, respectfully honouring its different provisions, under its wings. Hindu or Muslim laws having originated from their respective religious systems had assumed a somewhat personal character and could be enforced on the believers of the two faiths in a compartmentalised way. So, their acceptance was neither universal nor wilful, and as a result when the Muslims came to power the Hindu subjects succeeded to make their personal laws being recognised by the rulers to regulate their problems of succession and inheritance. True, Akbar intended to have a set of common laws for both the communities, but they were not continued by his son and great-grand son, as *Fatawa-i-Jahangiri* and *Fatwa-i-Alamgiri* virtually reversed the process.

The urgency to establish the rule of law had induced the colonial authority to introduce British common laws in India, and they started to apply them through the Supreme Court of Calcutta at the begining. The initial stage of this process was not very hopeful for the Indians, for it caused confusions and resulted in controversial judgements as in the case of

Nandakumar. But gradually it gained ground and eventually it became the nucleus for all common laws enacted in India. The only place where the jurisdiction of the common laws were restricted were in the areas of marriage, succession and inheritance which were allowed to be conducted by the customs and usages, or in other words the personal laws of the Hindus and Muslims. Later, they were suitably codified for all practical purposes. This was an act of compromise, and compromise was possible here because of the inocuous character of the laws as far as the colonial administration was concerned.

Though the acceptance of some aspects of the personal laws of the two major communities of India had again provided stimulus for the perpetuation of the communal character of the nationalities and so activated the disintegrative forces that were sought to be arrested by the common laws, common laws had more success than many other measures to integrate the varied and diverse elements in India. Its strength laid in the fact that being secular it was impersonal in nature and hence resistence against it by the Indians was of marginal character. On the contrary, it stimulated some social reformers amongst the Indians like Raja Rammohan Roy and Iswar-chandra Vidyasagar to organise a few successful movements to reform some oppresive and irrational aspects of Hindu personal laws and customs and push them within the fold of common law for the perpetuation of the rule of law. Besides, the common laws could have partially integrated at the legal level the numerous tribal communities where they could be successfully applied through the British courts. The racial discrimination which laws were made to entertain in the interest of colonial administration only affected the relations of the Indian communities with their British rulers. An indirect result of this discriminatory policy of the ruling power was the growth of nationhood feeling which could temporarily subdue all inter-communal or inter-nationality differences towards a common objective of consolidated nationhood.

(iii) Another important integrative force released by the British government was the construction of a net work of railways. Road and river ways were the channels of communication in the pre-British days, but they were never comprehensive nor all weather worthy for quick and large traffic. So, majority of the Indians remained sedate, localised and were not exposed to the wider public and their culture. Besides, their perception of the geographical unity of India could not grow beyond what they have learnt from the epics. Absence of cartographic illustration of the Indian physical geography necessarily deprived them of any visual aid to their vague and legendry oriented knowledge. Diversity of languages and scripts deepened the crisis. The combined effect of all these factors was perceived in the growth of segrigativeness amongst the Indians in multiple directions.

The railways achieved a break through in the exclusiveness of the localised life of the majority of the Indians. Movement became faster and in the erstwhile unknown regions, and the quicker mobility of persons and goods from one corner of India to the other had unfaillingly resulted in (a) creating a perception of geographical unity and (b) a feeling of national heritage by establishing relations of identity with the relics of the past all over India and with the living cultures of the peoples living outside their respective regions. Further, due to the mobility of goods and traffic gradual cosmopolitisation of Indian life started correspondingly to transform local and regional ties or loyalties into national loyalty through the process of identity and the perception of togetherness. The process thus started too could not complete the circle, because a new horizon was opened to the Indians through English education.

British metropolitan culture conveyed through the English education and spread by political power created new opportunities and hence provided an alternative area of loyalty which turned out to be an anti-thesis of the process initiated by the new communication system. It is largely true that the English language by itself, like the railways, was a great integrating force performing the act of a common language for all regions and all linguistic groups. But its benefits never filtered down to the mass, and besides, being the language of the ruling community those amongst the Indians, mostly the urban folk, who were drawn to it developed a new perception about India divorced from the emerging consciousness of its cultural moorings. It developed a new tension area in Indian society, which it had never had in the past, in the form of competitive assertions of tradition and modernity, the later being closely identified with westernism in the absence of any indegenous connotation of the term 'modernity'. Consequently, an area of separate identity had developed amongst the English educated Indians whose closeness to the 'primordial' elite, on that account, had induced them to revise identity. This phenomenon is persisting till now, as long as the English education will not spread amongst the masses. The feeling of a privileged class among the exploited community had spoilt the cohesiveness which the integrative forces released by the railways and the English education could have materialised.

(iv) Transfer of western technology which started during the colonial rule too had some potential to integrate the Indian society through the stronger elements of diversities. The place where it could have touched the cord of Indian life is to change gradually their consumption policy to achieve unity and a perceptible identity. The consumption policy of the erstwhile society was largely dictated by the diverse production technology and varied raw materials available on localised basis.

Transport remaining slow and hazardous the localised character of the consumers goods helped to render some attitude orientation to the consumer communities. Consequently, diversities again became prominent causing minimisation of the more basic but inarticulate forces of identity.

Western technology supported by colonial policy had created a market force for the western comsumers' goods in India. Its influence, though limited and particularly confined to the urban centres at the initial stage, had gradually spilt into the hinterland part of the countryside. As a result, new consumers' goods being raised to the status of dignity and social repectability by their ruling elite clientel had exerted a profound influence among the English educated urban Indians. Acquisition of these western commodities by the Indians accentuated the process of cultural amalgamation of the urban Indians into the metropolitan culture of the ruling community. This has strengthened the bonds of identity for the English educated Indians from all over India among themselves on the one hand ; on the other, it had facilitated the way for different cultural orientations that had distinguished them from the general mass in terms of coreperiphery relations.

The general implication of this value diversification was to introduce a new element of disunity amongst the Indians, who were basically rooted to their tradition. The wave of consumerism had touched only the fringe of the society, and as long as the new consumers' goods remained limited in circulation they hardly succeeded to help the forces to convert the entire community to the ethics of the challenging consumption. The new consumers' goods became the cultural symbols of urbanism and neo-elitism. One of the consequences of this elitism was to cause a serious structural disorder in the Indian society by replacing the traditional sources and symbols of power and elitism which used to have the advantage to function in the organic or natural leadership role in the society. It is arguable that this leadership was more personal, being based on patron-client relationship, than institutional which the new political culture tried to introduce. But the Indian political behaviour being conducted by patriarchal aptitudes, as all other relations in our society, has deeper roots and wider acceptance amongst the mass than its replacement by formal institutions.

II

On the whole, the Indian experience regarding national integration during the colonial period was a mixed bag of certain expectations being raised by the measures mentioned above remaining unfulfilled and some emphasis having been placed on priorities which would suit the purpose of colonial administration but not for India as a unified politico-cultural entity. The reasons why the state formation process remained incomplete and the issue of national integration remained an open sore were multiple of which I intend to deal with the following which I consider to be essential for the development of a successful nationhood.

(a) The primary objective of the colonial administration was not to activate the state-building forces but to achieve a superficial administrative unity for their convenience. Secularism, constitutionalism and common law philosophy were, therefore, used as appropriate tools to augment sufficient social forces to perpetuate the British rule in India. The administrative principles were alien and their application was ensured by superior military might, and so whatever feeling of togetherness was brought about by it remained to be superimpositional rather than being originated from the structural cohesiveness of this feeling with the political institutions, or from an innate

urgency of functional necessity. The laws and political institutions of India about which the Indians gained experience
and treated them as symbols of national unity had not been
assimilated into the new body of laws or systems of governments. While the political institutions were totally rejected in
the new system the laws could only partially survive assuming
a personalised character being totally disabused of all potential
for national integration.

Whatever praise the British common law might have earned
for their secular content the fact remains that the prime motivation for the British to introduce this law was to benefit the
colonial administration. One of the forces which can stabilise
the state system is the legal ethics of the people to which they
can refer for protection and for an ideal which can be realised
in their political behaviour. Such a system of law should grow
indegenously through the assimilation of all the common
elements of legal ethics in a multi-community country. The
emergence of such a body of laws provides one of the
appropriate tools to identify different components of multiple
community with each other to the satisfaction of individual and
communal psyche. The colonial administration had purposively
ignored this very vital aspect of Indian life. The treatment of
the indigenous laws as only the personal components of their
new legal system had accelarated the process of disintegration
and stifled the growth of a feeling of one nationhood in our
multi-community state. Consequently, the state-formation
process remained not only incomplete but very much crippled.

(b) The second important factor for ideal nation building
is to minimise the economic differences between different classes
and communities. The exploitative nature of the colonial
economy not only enhanced the deprivation of the disadvantaged
communities but it created multiple divergences in the core-
periphery relations. The inevitable consequence was the
disunity of the nation.

Removal of property by wealth generation, equitable distribution of income and man-power resource utilisation have been discussed by professional experts and they are as well applicable here to narrow down income gaps and to lift the immiserised population in India above the subsistence level. This is a very important measure for national integration, but what I consider to be equally important is the measure by which each nationality and region may be made to develop a feeling of mutual trust and dependence on the other on the basis of active participation in the process of economic regeneration. Colonial economy has localised production centres, took situational and raw material availability advantages and conveniently ignored to involve all the nationalities and regions of India in the production process. As a result, a large part of India remained dependent, neglected and underdeveloped. Though this policy has been partially modified after 1947 the legacy of the colonial era still persists.

National investment policy is partly guided by the anticipation of quick returns, and so areas which got scanty attention from the colonial administration are still struggling for capital and know-how to develop infrastructure for contributory production. Therefore, many of the regions suffer from a feeling of being neglected by the persons in power. The comparatively organised regions which have already had a place in the map of national economy, on the contrary, nourish a feeling of being overburdened to support the non-productive regions. Obviously, the argument that every rupee invested in developed sector or regions gives more return than from the undeveloped sectors holds good for an exploitatative economic policy, but it is counter-productive in the long run. The inevitable consequence of mutual recrimination and absence of resiprocal dependence is cessationism.

So, a proper program to develop overall economy may serve three purposes viz. (i) it can involve meaningfully all the regions of India and their manpower resources in the totall economic regeneration of India, (ii) it can equalise the level of economic growth and can achieve a correspondance between the national level of growth with the regional variations and finally (iii) it can remove the feelings of neglect or burden-someness by a healthy feeling of mutual dependence for the growth of the national economy. Obviously, core—periphery relations either in economic sector, or in the administrative and cultural sectors will undergo suitable modifications to develop a climate of equality and kinship. All these changes could be achieved only by replacing the traditional patron-clientel out-look of the feudal society by institution-alising the instruments of growth and development.

(c) One aspect of the British colonial policy was the dislo-cation of the Indian society. But it also caused serious struc-tural disorder by introducing a *comprador* community which sustained itself by being close to the centre of power and, ironically enough, remained to be structurally irrelevant to the society at large. Because, this structure in a highly stratified society had not grown out of the functional necessity of the society itself. Hence, its absorption in the Indian society did not take place in the natural order of things, as long as the economic background of the Indians would not change. Con-sequently, it remained to be eufunctional, if not totally disfunc-tional, in the context of the mores of the Indian society. Society, as a result, became more diversified, hierarchical and disunited.

Besides, it introduced a new dimension in the concept of core-periphery vis-a-vis the traditional Indian society. Core and periphery categories had always been determined in the Indian society on the basis of 'great' and 'little' traditions. It is true that the 'great' traditions might have often emerged through the process of the assimilation of some 'little' traditions, but some 'little' traditions or cultures had always remained autonomous and opted out to remain outside the frame of the 'great' traditions. Core, therefore, in the traditional Indian society was determined, as in many other identical situations, by the nucleus which released the cultural forces and those which were assimilated into it to help the total culture to emerge as a mighty stream. For pre-British India Hinduism and Islam remained to be the nucleus which had released all the mojor forces to develop 'great' traditions. Those 'little' cultures which were not assimilated into them were always treated as peripheries of the cultural tradition. The social hierarchy too had developed on that basis giving the place of 'primordiality' to the core mostly in the form of ritual status. Either for holding political power or for being identified as superior on racial grounds, understandably on account of military might of the intruders, this superiority was somewhat accepted by the Indian society. The 'primordial' community in turn practised a form of endogamy either to preserve blood or to protect the exclusiveness of their 'primordiality'.

The new strata which the colonial administration had introduced in the Indian society could not be explained presumably in terms of any tradition developed in India. The 'primordial' elite remained to be the Britishers and the Indians could grasp it in no time, as soon as the political power was seized by them. But the confusion arose about the location of the new class of Indians in the traditional society, who in their outlook and training were more close to their British masters than their kinsmen. The 'primordiality' which they intended to enjoy was partially transferred to them by their master for their administrative convenience. This was true as far as their localisation in the administrative structure was concerned but their potential to release authentic forces to create a 'great' tradition was not admitted by the Indians in general. They did not strongly believe it themselves either. Because, many of them had later relapsed into Indianness after a sudden wakefulness in westernism. The realisation of the innate limitation of the role of a *comprador* had brought about this change, and so, their new perception about the 'great' traditions of India had been always marked by a quest for identity.

The 'great' tradition that had tentatively grown out of the British rule and its political manifestation in the neo-Indian nationhood consequently remained to be a conglomeration of 'little' nationalities being presided over by British military might and their comsumerism. The 'great' tradition thus born did not represent any indegenous element, nor could the 'little' nationalities in India identify themselves with any of the components of this new tradition. The consumerist culture, either in terms of western commodity consumption or values which provided the new symbols of unity and integrity were treated as elitist in nature. And, in fact, the Indian clientel who were converted into this culture considered it to be their exclusive preserve. The mass, therefore, remained outside its influence.

The political nationalism that finally erupted into freedom struggle was initially born of an urge toreact against the political and social discriminations of the British rulers, and eventually, in the course of its own logic, it had proliferated into economic and cultural nationalism. To wage this struggle new political idioms to highlight national unity and integrety were sought, and in the absence of secular instances religious symbols from the 'great' traditions were used to serve the purpose. For convenience the different communities in India had chosen symbols from their own religions which consequently gave to them a communal overtone on religions line. Presumably, for this reason, the communities could not tender their loyalty to those symbols on universal basis. The attempt made by Gandhi to unify the symbols from the two 'great' traditions i.e., Hinduism and Islam was to integrate the ideas of *satyagrha* and *khilafat* in the Non-cooperation movement. But this arrangement eventually fell through, because the loyalties of the two communities did not cut across the boundaries of their respective community ethics. Besides, what was more important was that an integrated nationhood was not preparing itself in the entire struggle to confront another tradition. Rather, it was just the other way round, the logic of the struggle necessitated a compromise effort to lead the struggle to a successful conclusion. This objective, unfortunately, could not be realised ; and what had happened was the accentuation of the divisive forces culminating in the partition of the country on communal ground. If this incident clearly demonstrates that there is no iota of integration among the 'great' traditions themselves it also hints at similar disunity between the 'little' traditions and between the 'great' and 'little' traditions, even after their assimilation into a composits culture.

(d) In disregard of the fact that for genuine state-building integration of the nationalities needs to be suitably accomplished without causing any identity crisis for them the Indian mind has always confounded on this issue in the last few decades. While the Congress position regarding the nationality issue was that India had always been an one-nation state the assumption remained to be basically *a priori*. The others who argued in favour of cultural autonomy of the nationalities or self-determination for them had ignored the facts that (i) the process of integration which had started, however imperfectly, due to India's historical situation would be seriously disturbed and (ii) the nationalities, particularly the 'little' ones by themselves cannot grow into full fledged state system through the principle of self-determination. Because, many of them did not have the autonomy character, either culturally or politically, which could have helped to generate state-building forces. Besides, if a country has gained some experience of cohesiveness, however imperfect, its maintenance ought to be the basic reponsibility of the political leadership. Demand for cessation by some regions on ground of being neglected by the central authority has one meaning and can be combated by the removal of the grievances, but if cessation is being used as the *modus operandi* for gaining political power by some ambitious persons, even at the cost of national interest, the answer would be different. On the whole, it has been observed that as long as the central power remained militarily strong in India divisiveness always remained in a subdued state, if not totally eradicated. This lesson, significantly enough, remains to be true even today.

All the differences at the superficies between the cultures of different nationalities may not lead to separatism, but separatism, however disliked by nationalists, is always rooted in the basic difference of the socio-economic mores of nationalities 'great' or 'little', unless such differences are partially resolved by developing areas of common interest and loyalty. The freedom struggle in India, among other things, examplifies a case of hesitant rejection of an alien tradition by the indegenous and compiting traditions. Perhaps, one manifestation of this hesitancy now is to invite wilfully the intellectual domination of the west in the name of 'development'. Similarly the Pakistan movement before independence and many other cessationist movements in India after independence strongly suggest that inspite of all claims for single nationality in India the two 'great' traditions did not amalgamate in any important sector of their religions or cultures to make the single-nationality concept materialise in one political system. The 'little' nationalities which have been incorporated either culturally or politically within the frame of the Indian statehood too remained irreconciled. To argue that all of them are anti-national and that a foreign hand, though ubiquitous, had induced them to do this mischief would be a dangerous act to refuse to face the facts. Facts, for all practical purposes, have to be faced, howsoever unpleasant they may be, if the national interest has to be served. So, the premise has to be reformulated that most of the so-called cessationists are equally nationalist as their overjelous nationalist counterparts ; the only factor which distinguishes the former from the latter is that the latter is in the periphery and all their peaceful efforts to revise this peripheral status have failed to bear any fruit.

IV

In conclusion I arrive at the following points that (i) the Indian mind has to be made up to accept the fact that India is a multi-national state, (ii) the economic integration always remains to be one of the most powerful of the nation-building forces, and economic integration is not quantifiable unless the national average of growth has correspondence with regional variations. Each region has a right to share national wealth in as much as each region should be made to feel proud to have contributed to the growth of national wealth by being involved in the economic process, (iii) investment for quick gains may be an act of merdantilism but national integration cannot be achieved by the shortsighted profit motivation which the mercantilist philosophy implies, (iv) a representational culture system just as a representational political system would answer appropriately to the needs of the day, but it can be done by developing areas of common loyalty both in language and script and partially, if not in full measure, homogenising our culture inspite of multiplicities and (v) a conceptual change to determine 'primordiality' in a society in new terms has to be introduced in the emerging social order ; 'primordiality' ought to be determined now on the bsis of actual contributions by individuals or classes to national growth instead of assumption of or closeness to political, economic or religious powers, by any class. This will help to revise the concept of 'periphery' as well. It has to be realised that geographical periphery of a state and its cultural frontiers may not coincide, and therefore introduction of mobility by a dynamic economy will change (a) the location of core areas and (b) hypertrophisation of 'primordiality' in old terms. Not to need them will be collosal national *faux pas.*

IN SEARCH OF THE MAKING OF A NATION :
The Quest For A Paradigm

Mr. Ranabir Samaddar
Department of History, Gobordanga Hindu College
Gobordanga, West Bengal

Consider the time when Suren Banerjee wrote on the making of a nation and searched conscienciously what could be the reasons, the perspective and the story of it.[1] If that was the occasion when such a search had begun, when nationhood could be the object of an enquiry, today the wheel has come full circle. The idea of nationhood, national integration etc. has become dominant today and enquiry today is directed at the objective factors that attack this dominant concept. So, we are again at the beginning, again involved in search of the making of a nation. A quest for a paradigm.

My point is basically political. As I see, the perennial search for a paradigm among historians and political sociologists as an explanation to the making of a nation has been basically determined and guided by political factors. There have been two parallel processes, both involving conflicts and contradictions : One, the real life process of the nation, the other the conceptual build-up around it, in short the ideological process of nationalist thought. My endeavour will be to dissect the concept of national integration, to deconstruct the structure of thought, to unravel the intermingled elements of myth and reality embedded in the concept. In other words, this is a search into the search of the making of a nation. We have to see, whether it has been a false search of a false problematic. It is thus a critique in the domain of ideology. I could make only one more introductory comment. In the euphonia of nation-building, we saw only the dominant trend—the trend towards homogenization of different structural elements of a nation, it was a case of dancing the foxtrot. But now academicians are aghast, that what they had thought dominant, might not be so much after all. The flaming tango has shocked us, the world around the national integrationists is falling apart. As I see, it is the pull down of the ideological world of nationalism too, where myth had played not an inconsiderable part in deluding the myth makers.

II

With these few introductory remarks, I can now straighatway jump into the matter. I shall be brief and hence it need not be elucidated that the structure of what we have called the Indian nation is structure of numerous interpenetrating elements— elements which overdetermine each other. These elements are, as we all know, various social solidarities like nationalities, castes, classes, religions etc ; apart from social solidarities, there is a production mode, a certain culture, ideology too. Clearly these elements are in a relation of domination of one over another. The dynamics of one influences the other. Indeed, the dynamics of one structural element—its position, situation, strength etc., is determined in relation to another. In other words, the whole structure is in constant motion, tension, historical specificity. This is what I have tried to suggest by the interpenetration and overdetermination of the structural elements of Indian nationhood.

But if the feature of interpenetration and overdetermination is the secular law in the making of the nation, the fact remains that this secular law was clouded by many things and observers, according to and prompted by political exegencies, chose to emphasise only the unity and not the tensions or contradictions that in a certain state of balance went into making that structural unity. The classic case is of course Nehru's Discovery of India. But examples are many.[2] At certain other times, observers have overemphasised the reverse aspect, i. e., the contradictions. Here again the classic case is Myron Weiner's analysis of Indian polity.[3] To me, it seems that the ideological world too has been similarly structured. The material world has excelently reproduced itself in the thought process.

Politics has played a very vital part here. I shall show that while a liberal politics produced the vision of Suren Banerjee to Nehru, a particularist politics has produced the opposite vision of Ambedkar etc. By a structured concept, I mean that dominant and dominated ideologies and values, a holistic and a particularist tendency, a teleological outlook where by all the elements appear as necessarily leading to nationhood and a contrasting atavistic outlook which takes the particularities to be historically eternal—these are allembeded in that concept. Since Social realities are rarely self-evident, the dominant politics of an all-India nature has found it convenient to gloss over the realities and use the mystifications in positing a dominant nationhood as absolutely natural. Today, when the material reality of a nation is being subject to challenges emanating from below, that ideological axioms too are being challenged. And the ruling class is finding itself increasingly difficult to peddle the half truth of a 'beneficial', 'spontaneous', 'well established' nationhood. It is in this sense, I have asked whether our search into the making of a nation has been a false search, our paradigm a false paradigm.

III

Let me be more concrete. The indigeneous bourgeoisie had all along fought for a pan-Indian market, a pan Indian polity,

This was true during the colonial period and all the more true in post colonial times. Thus to it, a nationhood was a necessity as well as a natural outcome of its station in Indian society. This was the class which had accepted liberalism as its raison de'tre since inception ; one can get a living document of its economic ideas in Bipan Chandra's book on economic nationlism or still better in the writing of Aurobindo, Gandhi ; what did this liberalism signify ? If in political field it signified the rise and access of an all India middle class to the political levers of power and the active role of bourgeoisie as the representative of the entire society against the old order and an alien rule, in the field of thought this signified that the dominant class or classes wanted to conceive of and fashion the destiny of the country according to its own ideas. Thus, an Ambedkar, a Periyar, a Jogen Mondal seemed an aberration, a hindrance to national unity. This liberalism signified a modernisation immersed in westernisation ; a utopian ironing away of all discrepancies and varieties ; a desire that there be no 'we' 'they' thought in social thought process. Hence, apropos to the phenomena of nationalities, tribes, religions or even castes, it exhibited an amazingly naive outlook. The present kicks are hence a justified reward. But the more pertinent point is, this ideological naivity was the alter ego of the desire of the dominant class to impose a certain standardization or homogenization upon the society.

Consider certain examples. Take the question of tribes. Nehru on the advice of Verrier Elwin took again a typical liberal stand. While tribes, he said, could not be protected in a hothouse fashion, he argued that they need not be necessarily Indianized.[4] What did that mean ? On the one hand, the armed forces were sent wherever and whenever there was a strong assertion of identity, on the other hand it was thought that their presence could be ignored and the Indian juggernaut could roll on according to its own momentum. If Risley could be accused of stoking up a pandora's box, no less guilty in a reverse way are our liberal rulers who think that a right dosage of liberalism, some state spon-sored welfare schemes, some elitist development within the tribes would take account of the tribal question. The very nature of our political system must be kept in mind. It is parliamentary as well as federal—a rare example of bourgeouis liberal political system, which means that accomodation is provided for at both the levels—centrally as well as regionally, vertically as well as horizontally. This is thus an accomodative system, which Myrdal characterised as soft State. But which is absolutely necessary for the ruling bourgeoisie to extend its economic hegemony over the country. It cannot deny the particularist existences, nor can it admit that its own hegemony is precisely based on this denial or on the absorption of these particularities in the system. This is thus deliberately a competitive arrangement—political concessions to achieve economic hegemony. When that arrangement fails and the sub-levels of social formation start kicking, the liberals are aghast that the tribes have been so inconsiderate as not to appreciate the magnanimity of majesty. Mean—while, a wholesale campaign has systematically been conducted regarding the tribal nature of a social solidarity. Pray, what is a tribe ? Does the constitution say anything on that ? Is it an anthropological animal ? The constitution only enjoins that certain tribes are scheduled, lays down the modus operandi for scheduling some other, but does not tell, what is a tribe ! A different social formation, a different production mode waits at the historical alter of a stronger social formation and mode to be vanquished. Ideologically it is conquered by being attested with the label of tribe—an exotic concept come at the behest of colonial anthropologists. A stronger name has been added—there are autochthonous agglomerates, who must now be nationalised, that is homogenized by the standard of a bourgeois liberal polity.[5]

A similar example can be given with reference of nationality. Gandhi had clearly fought a losing battle against the dominant outlook when he pleaded for a plural polity. The rise of middle class, a prosperous peasantry—more specifically kulaks and the growth of regional bourgeoisie have pushed the nationality question to the forfront. The 1956 linguistic reorganisation of states has proved inadequate and the same secular law that pushed to the force the nationality question, has been pushing the subnationalities too. It would be too mycopic to treat this phenomenon as merely one version of 'sanskritization'. We shall be missing the real essence i.e., the trend towards assertion of self identity of peoples. The subnationality question has taken us a back with its ferocity, unmindful as we were with the effects of an expansion of capitalist production relations among the lower social levels. The best insight that we gain is from Amalendu Guha's account of Assam or Handgraves account of Tamil Nadars, where of course a caste question was intermingled with nationality question. It is for all these complexities, I am really scary and wary of so much hullaballo about national integration, for I feel that by suppressing their urge of self identity, a nation cannot come into being ; only by a free will of them, such a thing may come. And however, a liberal smokescreen is raised about combatting sectarianism and narrowness, this will ultimately fail. But meanwhile, the dominant cultural apparatus in our country— the tv, newspaper, radio etc. is trying to nail it into our head that such an assertion is harmful to people, that there are gifted people in Delhi who know what is best for whom. But have our political scientists, our legal experts, our constitutional historians paused to think whether the present political framework is sufficient to give play to these 'we' ness of different peoples ?

In what sense this 'national integration' a historical event ? In what framework of political knowledge can it be defined ?

In Indian case, it means a unified market, structure and polity tied to certain interests, at a certain juncture of space and time. This is its historicity. But it is an evidence of success of state leadership in India that it has been able to turn a historically specific category into a an ahistorical, idealised religion—a singular metamorphosis of the idea. It has duped us with that, we have taken naturally to the idea that 'separatism' is to be fought with 'integration'. We have now to deconstruct the two categories and in order to do so we have to posit them in their historical specificity which means the specificity of the political struggles for power.

In order to deconstruct, as I have argued, we have to break the 'myth' of integration. Though the rabble rousers will not be wanting in accusing me of separatism, that myth must be broken. Incidentally, what is after all a myth ? Sorel and said, myth is the conviction of a group in finding its own identity and history. It is prehistory serving the history of today. The myth around nation had to be treated, strengthened and perpetuated to serve the needs of the dominant class in our country. Such a myth falsified the events, minimised the plurality of the movements in colonial times, negated the uprisings of the lower levels and presented a homogenous picture of national awakening. The Hindu regeneration today like the Bharatmata Yagna, Ekatimata Yagna, etc. etc. has further strengthened that myth. The nation was conceived of indirectly familiar religious language. With the aid of religion, the myth remains and has become an integral part of our political culture. Its sole utility lies in providing legitimacy to the rule *over* the nation, by making it appear as the rule *of* the nation. If a cool retional race like the Britons could survive on the myth of Nelson or a myth of Dunkirk or of Falklands, it is all the more likely for an anthropological race like us to believe in the myth of national hemogenlity and integration !

IV

You will have noticed that one of my targets of criticism has been excess of anthropology in historical and political analysis. And I see a still more false search in the making of nation, which solely concentrates upon the group dynamics of the social structure. A famous anthropologist had said with reference to oriental countries like ours—History For us, Anthropology For you ! According to such an anthropological outlook the modern Indian society never reached a total entity, but has always remained fragmented between competing group interests. In history thus you find Anil seal or Broomfield's classic study of elite conflicts in a plural society ; in sociology the line taken by Hunter, O' malley, Risley ; in political science Myron Weiner. Philip Spratt and others. Basically, this is an anthropological outlook so popularised in twenteth century by Malinowski, where with a liberal outlook of respecting indigenous culture you fix your attention upon a backward group or people as a homo sapien specie, but never care to look upon thyself. I have lost count of recent studies along the line of social anthropology and could not also, even if I had kept a regular track of that, so varitable is the deluge of such studies. The mushroom growth, always inspired by Ford, Rockfeller and Cambridge etc. has only one aim ; it is to distort, the historical and political specificity of Indian nationhood in a reverse way, in fact to deny it altogether by an excessive emphasis on group psychology. Thus Tamil nationality is only a non Brahmin revolt, the Satara uprising of 1942 an inter-mediary caste uprising, the Tamluk revolt a Mahishya movement, the Bihar agrarian struggles a result of Ahir-Harizan clash etc. I could go on multiplying such examples. Take the example of a study on Gujrat : the migration of seasonal labour from Maharashtra is, as Jan Breman puts it, an exploitation of Halpattis. And if you consult the writings of Luis Dumont, you will simply be astonished at the ignorance of such celebrated brains regarding the secular laws of society. It will seem from a study of the developmental school of thought,[6] either the groups are competing for power (a variant of power—approach), or the contradictions within the structure would appear a result of the interaction of different groups (a variant of behavioural approach) or even, you would feel that Indian nation is nothing but a system where the inputs are predominantly 'anthropological' in nature (a systems-approach). Though such a particularist outlook no doubt reveals a truth hitherto ignored by the liberals, this is only a partial truth and misses the wood for the trees. I feel that such an attitude has corresponded with the rise and growth of regional bourgeoisie in various parts of India ; as well as, it has been stimulated by the imperialist concern to lay bare the sources of tensions in Indian society and plug the loopholes. Though such an anthropology ostensibly purports to restore to the groups and sub-groups tribes and aboriginals, nationalities and sub-nationalities, and all such levels and sub-levels the dignity and status of sovereign existence, as Fei. Hsiao Tung commented in his proposition on "Toward A People's Anthropology", such an anthropology betrays an ignorance of the basic laws guiding a society.[7] Hence, this too has been a false search, based on a false paradigm and the huge facts of material life of people unearthed by the diligent sociological and anthropological researches during investigation and observation have been set a limit in way of their proper utilisation because of a distorted view of national politics.

I will give you an example. At the end of 1984, when general election was declared, pundits came out with so many calculations based on caste, region, religion etc, in short what we call political arithmatic. Then the nationwide swing astonished us. Pundits were proved obsolete in outlook, the

6

masses proved their advanced politics. Then the psephologists, if you remember the t. v. of those days, started discussing the extent and uniformity of waves, swings, pendulum, etc. It was an instance of wisdom after the theft by cat. How could such a nationwide swing happen transcending all 'anthropological' barriers ? This was typically a peasant indictment of local rule, whereas so many peasant historians have informed us, the peasantry identifies with central authority in castigating the tyranny, disorder and chaos that beset their life at a *concrete, material, immediate,* hence local level and thinks, a strengthening of the Raj can save themselves from a despotic disorder. It is typically an ambivalent attitude to authority, uniform in hystenical applause and savage denunciation. The martyrdom of a leader brought out the peasant nature of our society in one singular event.[8] Which is then a greater anthropological truth in the life of our nation : a peasant society submerging the various islands of particularities, or, a collective society composed of different popular solidarities with a mutual 'we', 'they' relationship ?

V

Some have thought, radical anthropology is the answer. They say, that a radical historiography can learn more and more from anthropology—an anthropology which concentrates upon man at his real, material level, which as these subaltern historians say, restore to the subject of an oppressive rule the dignity and prestige of his own destiny—maker ; an anthropology which does not reduce the science of man to a science of 'barbarians'. In this sense, radical anthropology challenges the dominant ideology of national integration in a far more effective way, brings out the social tensions and contradictions inherent in nation-making in a plural society, exposes to light how the authority above could impose a nationhood upon the society in cooperation and contradiction with its subjects. Such a radical anthropology informs us how even a single nationality is formed by utilising and then superceding the essential peasant character of the awakening of a popular solidarity. Sumit Sarkar's account of 1905 movement of Bengal, Partha Chatterjee's analysis of Bengali baboos,[9] Gail Omvedt's account of Maratha awakening, Gyan Pandey's account of the rise of Congress in U. P. are all necessary materials in the understanding of the making of our nation. Even political studies have taken an anthropological turn in a radical way. Foremost comes to my mind the example of Rajni Kothari.[10]

But a radical anthropology has also missed a very vital point, which I shall put briefly this way : Granted, that the objects of history have been restored the status of subject, but do we not in the process exaggerate it, over romanticise it in all contravention of the operation of those secular laws, which made possible the making of a nation — of which I have been so incessantly harping ? Let the sub altern levels be duly recognised, but is it not true that their acceptance of national leadership was the key to later's legitimacy and the overall unity of Indian social formation based upon their consent led the nation into being ? What is that Gramsci implied by passive revolution ? It is a revolution, where masses stop half way in revolt. Where revolution is completed from above to check and thwart the revolution from below. The making of Indian nation is certainly such an instance where all the structural elements have been incoportated, but not amalgamated, where the precapitalist elements survive to serve the dicktats of a nation developing from above. It is a nation, where the people must not be allowed to become the sovereign masters of their destiny. They must surrender, capitulate and obey the collective will imposed from above. Our radical anthropology has missed out this vital reality. It suffers from populism, for such an approach has been contemporary to and the intellectual birth product of a populist politics of sixties and seventies.

VI

The mystification of nation, which is the essence of 'national integration', depends as an ideological process upon a real life-process : the standardization and homogenization of the component elements. Towards that understanding, the role of modern technology is one fascinating area of study. Consider the growth of t.v., newspapers, magazines, radio, cinema and other mass media, based particularly on electronic technology and at once the process of nation making assumes a new significance. Not only in the field of economics or politics, in culture too you find that a deomnant technology only reinforces a dominant ideology. The NAMEDIA or Joshi Report on t.v. for instance, shows how a Delhi programme passes on as a national programme. How a north Indian character like Lallu. I am speaking of Hum Log, becomes an Indian archetype. How the Punjabi variety of Buniyad masquarades as the partition tragedy in easter part also. The Seventh Plan envisages a phenomenal expansion of t.v. — with that a simultaneous projection of the dominant profile as the national profile. Or, take the example of newspaper today, photocomposing based on electronic technology enables the major newspapers become a common ownership Unit, i.e., a chain. How else, the Times of India could enter Patna, Amrita Bazar Patrika Lucknow, Indian Express Madurai or Cochin ? How else could you have India Today, Illustrated Weekly etc. in all major corners of India dishing out a distorted image of what constitutes national politics or culture in a plural country ? The archetype is set up : The Punjabi is hard working but hot headed felow, devoid of grey matter ; the Tamil a conservative ritualistic man ; the Bengali an essential baboo — lazy, lethargic and quarrelsome. The archetype Indian, only busy in scrambling to go above the ladders of social recognition.

VII

In conclusion, I repeat what I had said at the outset, it is this dominant concept, which we must lay bare to grasp the historical specificity of it. But the key to that specificity is the specificity of political relationships. This means, we have to take into account the practical factor of state in the propagation and strength of such a concept.[11]

Hitherto classical political studies had taught us that a nation aspires to be a state or it is only a half nation which is not a nation—State. But today the roles are reversed. The state aspires to be a nation. To gain legitimacy it must become synonymous with nation. If there is no nation, then it must create such a nation, impose it from above. Such is the novelty of social engineering. The numerous studies on modern Africa have proved it and I think that a far more evident process is operating in India. The colonial state had initiated such process and after 1947 we are witnessing a vigorious continuation of it. Today, the innerlying agency ares are thrown open to national fortunes and vicissitudes a standard law replaces customary laws, a straight jacket of capitalist industrialization is put forth everywhere, the process of planning brings a national economy into functioning, all India services provide the steel frame of country-wide administration, paramilitary troops become the backbone of law and order : in short, a standardised political process is initiated and takes root everywhere. There is state sponsored politics, culture, propaganda, ethics — everything. To break the mystification around nation, you have to break the mystification of state. As the physiologist would say — "Cut open the corpse, you will see light".

Note :

1. I am indebted to Partha Chatterjees introductory comments in "Bengal 1920-47 Land Question," 1984. Calcutta.

2. An emphasis on parts is the crux in the developmental school of thought, whether in contradictions or in accomodation. An early version can be found in Morris Jones, who spoke of multiplicity of political languages—modern, traditional, Saintly.

3. What is a paradigm ? This is basically an issue of methodology, kuhn is "Structure of Scientific Revolution," 1962, defined paradigm as "universally recognised scientific, achievements, that, for a time, provide model problems and solutions to a community of practitioners". But can the concept of paradigm be accepted in social sciences ? See "The structure of scientific Theories," ed. frederick suppe, Chicago, 1977.

REFERENCES

1. Surendranath Banerjee : A Nation In The Making : Being the Reminiscences of Fifty Years of Public Life. (Calcutta, 1963).

2. The History And Culture of The Indian People, Bharatiya Vidya Bhavan Series, (Bombay, 1960).

3. Myron Weiner : Party Politics In India, (1957).

4. Verrier Elwin : Philosophy of NEFA, (Shillong, 1957).

5. Nirmal Sengupta : General Aspects of Nationality Problem In The Central Tribal Belt, (Pune, 1985.)

6. A classic exposition of this school, Morris Jones : The Government and Politics of India, (London, 1964) ; Politics of Developing Areas, Ed by Almond and Coleman, Introduction by Coleman, (1960).

7. Fei Hsiao Tung ; Towards A People's Anthropology (Beijing, 1982).

8. Partha Chatterjee : On Swings, Waves, Landslides and Other Metaphors, (Calcutta, 1985).

9. Chatterjee, Bengal Rise and Growth of A Nationality, Social Scientist, Vol. 4, No. 1 (1975).

10. Rajni Kothari's Introduction to "Caste In Indian Politics" : Ed by Rajni Kothari, (New Delhi, 1970).

11. Politics And State In The Third World : Ed by Harry Gouldbourne (London, 1979).

NATIONALISM VERSUS SUB-NATIONALISM :
The Historian's Dilemma

Dr. K. Majumdar
Professor, Department of History
Nagpur University, Nagpur

The most worrying problem in contemporary India is the increasing emotional disintegration of its people amidst closer administrative integration of the country. A growing spirit of separatism seems to undermine the very fabric of the country's federal polity. India now offers a classic example of a union without unity.

Fight against foreign rule had nurtured the Indian unity ; fight among fellow citizens of the country today tends to destroy that unity. Nationalism, an accomplished fact at the end of the foreign rule, is now just a flickering ideal smothered by the pressure of sub-nationalism and regionalism. The intensity of the pressure is so great as to cause misgivings about the relevance of the ideal to the present situation in the country. No doubt, with all the appurtenances of modernism India would scamper into the twenty first century, but the fear is if in the process the nation would leave its soul behind— and that irritrievably. A people without an ideal to inspire them is like a ship without a rudder to guide it through a rough sea.

The historian is troubled by this phenomenon, this seeming irreconcilability between the ideal of nationalism and the pressure of sub-nationalism, for he knows that sub-national forces need to be contained before they could do further damage to the emotional unity of the Indian people. However, the historian could at best diagnose the malady in the national life and warn of the serious consequences if it is not cured in time : it lies with the political decision makers to heed the warning and take effective measures to tackle the national problem.

Sub-nationalism represents the feeling of self-awareness, self-identity, self-expression and self-assertion on the part of units and elements composing a political, social and economic structure. The feeling originates in and feeds on a sense of deprivation and denial of what is fondly cherished as just claims to political power, economic position and social status. The feeling may lie dormant and subdued through the ages until a change in the existing situation allows its expression.

The intensity of the feeling and the virulence in its manifestation in the present day Indian context seem to have had a direct relation with the political configuration in the country in the last two decades and the political othos of those who have wielded power in the same period. Power has often been so exercised in recent years and so manipulated as to help further anything but national interests ; this has bred jealousies and rivalries between different regions of the country and different socio-economic groups. In fact, power in post-independence India has tended to concentrate in direct proportion to the widening of the scope of state activity and increasing devolution of the Government's responsibility for public welfare. A democratic political structure without a democratic spirit operating it is like a fabric, imposing from without but hollow within.

It is the emotional confidence of the people which keeps a country united and strong, not just its constitution nor its political parties. And contemporary India is afflicted by the crisis in the confidence of the people that they could stay united for long when sub-national and regional forces are threatening to tear them apart.

Sub-nationalism in India expresses itself through the feeling of identification with and loyalty towards one's own region, own community, own caste and own linguistic group. Such a feeling is really unexceptinable and but natural in a plural society as the one India. But then, the fear is when the feeling breeds an insular mentality in some people and chauvinism in others which find vent in violence towards those who refuse to share the feeling. Such chauvinism and violence have a chain reaction and a natural tendency to spread. This is procisely what has happened in India in recent years.

II

The historian, like all others, is acutely conscious of the need for a deft adjustment of the national needs and sub-national expectations if the socio-economic aspirations of the Indian people are to be realised, and if the balanced development of all the constituent units of all the constituent units of the federation are to be achieved.

But the historian himself finds the adjustment rather hard to bring about, and this gets reflected in his own works. For example, in his studies on the history and culture of the country as a whole, he is likely to emphasise only the integrating forces in the national ethos, while writing about his own region, his own community, his own caste and own linguistic group, he might diligently identify only those elements and forces which are patently regional in nature. He might seek to establish that sub-nationalism had been a far deeper sentiment in the country's history than the national spirit, and that meeting the growing sub-national demands today was the only means to promote the national cause. The historians problem is how to reconcile what he regards as his national obligation with what he is keenly aware of as his sub-national commitments. He cannot forget the national priorities any more than he can ignore regional pressures. He might even be required to write different kinds of history to suit different purposes. The historian today is a split personality, though not a spoilt one.

III

The best example of how sub-nationalism has influenced the historian is afforded by the micro-treatment of Indian history, a distinctly post-independence trend in Indian historiography. Such treatment is at times the result of sub-nationalism and at others its distinct indicator. Micro-history has occasioned a change in the very concept of history, its content, its focus and its purpose. It has resulted not only in the enlargement of the areas of research but in the exploration and examination of new source materials : in the treatment of the latter too there has developed a new attitude. Even the use of well known materials has yielded results quite different from the earlier ones based on the same materials. With the change in perspective and change in the purpose of history, facts have no longer to speak for themselves : historians would make them speak the way they want.

Micro-treatment of events and issues signifies a new approach to the art of writing history itself ; it represents a new technique too. Nither to great places, great events and great men had been the subjects of history. But now the focus is on small events influencing great issues ; small places sustaining the great ones : and small men working silently behind great leaders of movement. Today the historian studies not only the great forces shaping the national life but the small, apparently diffused and disparate currents which together make up the forces themselves.

This trend of Indian historiography is indicative of a new awareness, of a new determination to project the images of areas and individuals whose importance in history had either not been at all or inadequately recognised earlier. For individuals to crave for the limelight is but a natural desire ; so is to for regions to find a high place in history.

One happy result of the trend has been the very minute and intimate study of facts hitherto ignored or held either irrelevant or inconsequential ; there has been new interpretation of known issues of regional interest ; also demolition of the conclusions hitherto held definitive and incontrovertible. The areas of research on regional life and culture have widened ; many dark recesses of the life have been illumined ; clash of views on many a knotty problem has added new dimensions to the existing knowledge of men and matters in history. Thus the rewriting of Indian history has involed a continuing process of the re-examination of facts, re-interpretation of issues and re-assessment of characters. In the process links have been established between regional incidents and national events ; national issues have been explained by the need to accommodate regional demands ; and many activities of nationalist leaders have been found to clearly reflect their inability to get over their caste and community prejudices.

IV

The best examples of micre-history are the numerous studies on various regions of the country and their political and administrative sub-divisions. The emergence of sub-nationalism and regionalism has been explained by social and economic factors affecting the inter-relations between communities and groups with distinct affiliations in terms of caste, language and religion. The studies on different castes and sects, on communalism, on the non-Brahmin movement, the Dalit movement, the peasant movement, the labour movement and the tribal movement, for example, have revealed a clear correlation between the changing political condition in different regions and the growth of the spirit of identity and assertion on the part of elements who having so long endured and envied power are now determined to enjoy it. These elements are the heroes of today's grass root history or history from below.

Of particular significance are the historical works on the social and economic development of the many regions of the country. They have shown how regional politics had always been but a reflection of the rivalry between local socio-economic groups. The emergence of that social group which became later the ruling elite and its exploitative tendencies, the maladjustment of the economic interests of various social groups, and particularly the simmering discontent in the peasantry and the industrial proletariat, not to mention the disparity in the economic development of various regions of the country— all these are emphasised in many regional studies with their focus on the local socio-economic problems. These studies no doubt help us account for the unease and unrest in the present society and to understand the background to the present feelings of deprivation and denial of just rights in several regions of the country. Sub-nationalism and regionalism have grown out of these feelings, and the present political discontent and signs of separatism have indeed their socio-economic roots in the country's historical past.

Studies on the Indian freedom movement at various levels —erstwhile provinces, revenue divisions, districts, taluks, towns and villages—provide another example of "regional sub-nationalism" as it has influenced historical scholarship in post-independence years. The trend was set by the need to rewrite the history of the Revolt of 1857 as the first great challenge to the British rule. The numerous monographs that have appeared over the last forty years have clearly brought out the regional variation in the nature of the uprising, the variation to be attributed to the fact that the motivating impulses were not identical everywhere. Although an anti-British feeling was common to all regions, neither the circumstances which caused the feeling to grow nor its manifestations was uniform at all places. And that was because of the varying political, social and economic situation in different regions. The ramification, the intensity and the duration of the uprising depended on whether or not it had a mass base ; and enquiries into this question have brought to light the socio-economic problems in different areas. The historian studying the Revolt of 1857 in its national perspective and seeking to project it as a national movement has indeed to weave a pattern out of its regional variations in course, causes and character.

Regional studies on the national freedom movement initially sponsored by state governments have been followed up by professional historians and academics attached to universities and research institutions. Courses in history have been res-tructured to foster local interest in studying the contribution of the local people to the country's struggle for independence. This has served a good purpose indeed. Many local characters have been salvaged from oblivion, not to speak of the many source materials which have been brought to light and made good use of. Of such materials particular mention should be made of government papers which for years lay buried under dust heaps in collecorate record rooms and in municipalities and corporations where many a local leader had their political apprenticeship.

Researchers now rummage through old copies of hitherto neglected local newspapers and cull bits of information from regional literary works. Local leaders have recorded their reminiscences of bygone days for the reconstruction of the history of their own regions, own communities and own socio-economic groups. So has grown in recent years oral history which is being increasingly used to write, revise and rewrite regional history. Oral history is indeed the best tool to fathom the intensity of sub-national feelings though the ages. The feelings may have had no historian to record them for posterity, but they had been recorded in the memory of the local people. However, it needs emphasising that public memory is often clouded with popular passion. In fact, the historian could make such use of the local oral history as to contribute to regional gratification or foster regional passion.

Sub-nationalism is not a wholly political phenomenon ; it has acquired a cultural dimension too. Micro studise on Indian culture are a recent trend in the cultural historiography of India. A voluminous literature has come up on historical monuments in different regions, several forms of art and architecture, schools of painting, contres of literary and such other creative activity as music and dance. Not the constituents of the regional sub-cultures alone but their makers at different strata of society have been the themes of recent works on Indian culture. The economic base of the sub-culture and the political climate that reared it have been explored to underscore the cultural aspect of the present problem of sub-nationalism. It is found that elements constituting an integrated political set up are asserting their cultural identity and emphasising their cultural distinctiveness. Cultural historians at regional levels seek to establish the greatness of their respective regions by showing how different the local culture had been through the ages from culture in other areas till the sub-cultures merged in an "Indian culture" through a relentless process of political integration.

V

On both the need and worth of regional history as such there is no dispute but the way it is to be written and the purpose it is to serve are the two points on which there is room for discussion and difference of opinion. If the object of history be the portrayal of the intricate pattern of the socio-economic life of the people, then one has to figure out the elements which together make the pattern. If the cultural mosaic of the country is to be projected in its history, then each individual facet of the culture needs identification and under-standing in its intimate detail. This would bring out in sharp relief the conglomerate character of the Indian society and the complexity in its culture. The historian wishing to emphasise what he considers to be the Indian genius would no doubt show the compositeness in the Indian culture evolving through the variegated material life of the Indian people. On the other hand, the historian tracing the roots of sub-nationalism would see this life reflective conflicts and contradictions between socio-economic groups and a sordid tale of demination by a few and deprivation of the many.

But then, while micro history is welcome, its danger lies in the auther's developing a micro outlook. His hunt for the trees in the wood might result in his missing the view of the wood itself. Not unoften does one find the glorification of the region as the main purpose of writing its history ; and in so doing not unoften does the author exaggerate and embellish facts which suit his own predetermined conclusions, and underrate or ignore those which donot. He distorts issues and stretches his imagination far and wide. Even this is not to be deplored so much as another tendency : to debunk and denigrate historical characters of "other regions" and to underestimate the achievements of "other peoples" of the country. And all this is done with the loud declaration that the object of history is to ascertain the truth or at least what appears to be the truth on a careful study of all available facts. Ignorance of or inability to see the truth is far less blameworthy than the refusal to admit it.

The very character of regional history would be different if the focus is on issues rather than on events, and the emphasis is on forces rather than on individuals. As for the object of regional history, it should be to trace the evolution of the community rather than to project the exploits of personalities and the importance of places. The spirit of much history should be one of critical understanding of the problems of the region in the context of selfsame issues in other regions. A region should be studied not as though it were an isolated political unit but as an element in the continuing process of the social, economic, political and cultural evolution of the country as a whole.

The real purpose of regional history is not so much to emphasise local identity as to bring out in clear life the underlying unity of the country despite regional diversities. Events in different regions should be treated as contributing to the national mainstream of social evolution. This calls for a change in the mental framework of the writer of regional history and adjustment of his perspective. He should break away from, what Toynbee calls, the "prison walls of the local and short lived accounts"; he should take a unified view of history; a sense of national stake should take precedence over his regional commitments.

The task of tracing the evolution of the social, economic and cultural life of a region would call for academic cooperation among scholars of the region itself, and then a critical assessment of the result of this academic exercise by reviewers not necessarily belonging to the region. For an intimate knowledge of the local language and local events and issues is as much important for writing local history as the objective analysis and interpretation of the events and issues – and it is here that the suggestive comments and helpful criticisms of reviewers could provide the needed restraint on the natural tendency of local scholars to paint local history all too brightly by either playing up or playing down events and personalities. Some detachment in out look helps in placing events and characters in their proper perspective.

Writing regional history should be a purposeful academic exercise ; the cause of national integration, for example, would be served better by tracing the local people's life and their relations with people of other regions than by highlighting the wars fought between regions and territories conquered by local ruling dynasties. All that involved the people on mass – farming and agriculture, trade and commerce, religion and cultural tradition – need to be stressed to make local history really meaningful. Regional interdependence in social, economic and cultural evolution of life merits sharper focus than regional wars and political conflicts. Such a change of vision would bring out the fact that diversity and disparity in the political growth of different regions had not very much impaited their close relations in non-political aspects of life. Lut history be viewed as an evolution of social structure, of economic adjustments through a process of conflicts and concessions, and of cultural exchange and adaptation on the part of peoples having a varied political experience over a long period of time. This would widen the historians mental spectrum which would enable him to take a comprehensive, ecumenical view of his subject.

VI

Nationalism is hailed as a lofty spirit, sub-nationalism is telerated as a natural feeling, but regionalism is deplored as a disintegrating force. It has assumed, in the context of the recent political developments in the country, a dreaded connotation. It is commonly believed that the national feeling is but a fusion of sub-national sentiments, and national ethos is the aggregate of sub-cultures in a conglomerate society. But regionalism, in its present virulent form, not only tends to swamp nationalism but to destroy it altogether.

In this context, therefore, the demand for correcting regional imbalances in respect of political power, more equitably distributing the national economic resources among regions, and providing greater opportunities to the traditionally handicapped social groups appear as manifestations of centrigugal tendencies in these who are determined to promote their sectional and sectarian interests at the cost of the national ones.

Such a situation has put the historian on the horns of a dilemma ; he could neither forsake his cherished ideal of nationalism not ignore the weightly regional claims and just sub-national feelings in the people around him. Not unoften, therefore, does the historian develop an ambivalent attitude while explaining the current national issues in their historical perspective. People around him expect him not only to reflect in his work the sub-national feelings and regional senti- ments but to interpret them in such a way as to foster the local demands for concessions from the power wielders at the national level. The involvement of some historians in the raging disputes between state governments is a pointer to the role assumed by them as the moulders of the local public opinion.

The historian's agreements to promote the cause of his "own men" and "own region" are often influenced by the data he collects from past history which convince him of the injustice and wrongs "his region" and "his men" had suffered in the past at the hands of "other regions" and "other men". His study of the experience of his forbears in the past might influence his assessment of present events involving his own men and his own region. Past events could be seen by his through the haze of present day obsession, passion and projudice. Relations between regions, religious communities and social groups in the past could be interpreted in the light of the existing state of relations between them today. The result is that some contemporary socio-economic history, in particular, in its regional context appear to be indistinguishable from political propaganda stuff.

In such a situation the historian is not just a faithful chronicler and an objective narrator of past events ; he is also a commentator of current issues ; his object could be to pander to local and sectional passions and reap political harvests therefrom. Political considerations not only influence his thoughts but even at times dictate his creative activity, depending on his proximity to the centre of political gravity in his "own region" and among his "own men".

VII

None for sure would dispute that to foster the spirit of emotional integration in the peoples of the country, it is necessary to study and write its history on correct lines. But what these correct lines are is a point on which there is no agreement among historians themselves. And this disagreement has of late become acute due to the increasing politicisation of the country's academic life, and political decision makers' bid to get history rewritten by those who believe in the dictummake hay while the Sun shines. In such circumstances, the very object and purpose of the study of history today is different from what it was before independence. Unlike then, history today is no longer a quest for truth, sweet at times and bitter and hurtful at others. History now is a means to that definite socio-political end as determined by political end as determined by political decision makers. Indeed, history has now become a handmaid of politics. The time capsule episede and the ban on some history text books for stating facts which had been accepted as true for generations but now feared as incompatible with the national policy are examples too patent to need any reiteration.

For history to serve a national purpose, it need not suffer any patent distortion, not should it be glaringly tailor-made. In fact, preindependence Indian historiography too promoted a great national cause just as its post-independence variant is required to do. Indian historians before independence emphasised the glorious tradition of the country, thereby contributing immensely to the growth and sustenance of Indian nationalism. The sense of pride in the country's heritage generated through their works formed a strong base of the nascent nationalism.

True, more than ever before, history today needs to be socially relevant and purposeful ; and this does call for rewriting it and reinterpreting many an event and issue. But then, the spirit of national integration could rather be promoted better by identifying the historical roots of the current trends of sub-nationalism than by the officially favoured policy of either underplaying or ignoring them. Some historians too seem to believe that the present relations between various religious communities and socio-economic groups in the country would be further impaired if the old scars in their past relations are opened by an incisive enquiry into their origin and an analysis of their effect on contemporary society and polity. This clearly is not an academic argument but a political necessity which obliges the historian to suppress facts and sometimes to distort them for the sake of promoting what is held out as the national cause.

But then it bears recalling that a plural society, as India's has always had centrifugal political, social and economic forces in varying stages of effectiveness at different periods of the history of the country. But nevertheless, the cultural unity of the country, in the broadest sense of the term, had remained unimpaired. If the stages of the evolution of the society as at present are to be traced in a historical work, the many conflicts and contradictions in the course of the evolution have to be clearly brought out. Through the ages men had indeed been accustomed to identify themselves with particular communities, groups, castes, creeds, sects and clans, and yet there had never been as grave a threat to the emotional integrity of the country as there has been in recent years.

So long, historians in admitting this fact had not been accused of deing any harm to the national interests whatever, but now they are being ridiculed as "reactionaries" if they donot give up what is condemned politically as rather conventional, and so unacceptable, view of Indian history. In fact, however, the historian who traces the roots of the present malady of the country serves it the same way as the physician does his patient good by warning him of his ailments. Today that historian is dismissed as a communalist who does not hide facts or distorts them in the name of reinterpretating historical events for the sake of establishing the officially supported contention that throughout the course of history relations between communities had been perfectly harmonious. The historian's problem is whether to state facts as he finds them or to interpret them in conformity with what the political decision makers want.

It is, in fact, fatuous to expect to reinforce the integrative forces in the country by suppressing the bitter truth in the name of rewriting history. History rarely, if at all, shapes the course of events ; it only records the course for the posterity to take lossons from. The truth is, that there does exist a causal relation between the growing threat to the country's emotional integrity and the current political others of the country. No sense of emotional unity in the people could be generated by any history written on officially approved lines when the political system of the country itself encourages people to assert their distinctiveness of caste, community, language and religion. The contrifugal forces cannot just be wished away by any made-to-measure history ; the political culture of the country needs to be changed if the traditionally latent sub-national forces are not to assume any graver proportions to endanger the foundations of the country's political integrity. It is this warning which the honest historian has to convey through his works.

It is as futile to ignore to the sub-national and regional forces in a plural society as it is dangerous to succumb to them with a view to furthering the selfish ambition of the political power brokers. Any historian worth his salt should explain the growth and intensity of the forces through the years while warning against such political action as tends to encourage them. Emotional disunity of the people is the surest sign of the political disintegration of the country. Let the historian mince no words to convey this truth to the political decision makers at various levels of the country's administration.*

*[This is a revised and enlarged version of the author's paper published in *The Quarterly Review of Historical Studies,* No. 1, Vol. XXV, and bearing the same title].

NORTHERN AND EASTERN INDIAN ELEMENTS IN THE ART OF SOUTH-EASTERN BENGAL
A Two-Way Interaction

Dr. Gautam Sengupta
North Eastern Hill University Shillong

I

Most of the recent works on early Indian art-history are characterised by an increasing concern with the regional and / or local dimensions of art-traditions. Elsewhere, we have discussed how this concern is linked up with the growing awareness about the linguistic, ethnic and cultural identities.[1] Historians of Indian Art are preoccupied, more than ever, with categories like region, sub-region and centre. This new trend has certainly expanded the horizon of art-historical studies, but, in the process, the distinctiveness of regional art-tradition is often over emphasised. There is no denying the fact that geographical factors and historical developments lend special character to a regional art-tradition. One cannot, however, overlook great degree of commonness among different regional traditions. Which was made possible by sharing of common myths and symbols, widespread use of textual sources, net-work of pilgrim centres, movement of artists and craftsmen and a host of other factors. This explains how a Mahabalipuram Mahisamardini panel was copied with little variation at a Karnataka monument ; or a Mathura Bodhisattva model emulated, at Buddha-Gaya. Examples can be multiplied. Most of the *silpa* texts have drawn upon diverse sources and despite the regional variation, certain common elements can always be recognised. This possibly accounts for the use of a particular method of bronze-casting, enumerated in a Kerala text of the 16th century A. D., by the image-makers of Nepal.[2] Vincent.

A. Smith's observation beautifully sums up the position"...
These *śāstras* are the common property of Hindu artisans,
whether of northern or southern India".[3]   A regional art-
tradition cannot be viewed in isolation, it becomes viable
through interaction and inter connection with other regional
tradition.   It will be our endeavour in this essay to assess the
impact of northern and eastern Indian art-idiom on the growth
and development of the art of South-Eastern Bengal.

II

Three geographical regions are involved in this essay, viz
Northern India, Eastern India and south-Eastern Bengal.
Admittedly, the terms are somewhat loosely used in the absence
of precisely defined nomenchtures.   Without trying to elaborate
upon this, let us put up our point straightforeward.   Northern
India, in this context, stand for north Indian plains spread
between Mathura and Varanasi.   Beyond Varanasi lies Eastern
India ; an aggregate of Bihar.   West Bengal and parts of
Bangladesh.   South-Eastern Bengal is more difficult to define in
precise terms.   Frederick. A. Asher equates it with Samatata
and describes its geographical limits. "The mountains of Tripura
and the Chittagong Hills stands to the east, while the Bay of
Bengal flanks the southern boundary......To the north, the
Meghna river sets off the region, while to the west the Meghna
is joined by the mighty Padma".[4] But the geographical extent
of the region cannot be fully appreciated without reference to
another term, viz *Harikela* which was widely used between the
7th and the 13th centuries A. D. B. N. Mukherjee sums up the
limits of Harikela in the following terms"...the name Harikela
denoted by c. 7th century A.D. only the Chittagong area
of Bangladesh. Later ..the name was extended, perhaps with
the expansion of the power of the Chandras, from their
base in Harikela to the areas of Samatata and Srihatta.
There are reasons to believe that at least parts of Tripura,

including its Belonia subdivision, were also incorporated in Harikela. The inclusion of these territories within Harikela gave it fairly well-defined natural frontiers. It had Bay of Bengal on the south, hill tracts of Chittagong, Eastern most Tripura and Cachar and Lushai Hills on the east Khasi and Jaintia Hills on the north, joint streams of the Padma and the Meghna, the Meghna and perhaps another river (probably the Surma in the western area of the Sylhet district and in the eastern section of the Mymensingh district) on the west".[5] The South-Eastern Bengal, an aggregate of Samatata and Harikela, thus possesses well-defined geographical limits which renders a distinctive regional indentity and tends to evolve its own cultural ethos.

III

An outlying (*pratyanta*) region in the 4th century A. D,[6] South-Eastern Bengal was nevertheless exposed to the historical developments of Northern and Eastern India through a combination of factors. Its history must be viewed in relation to main currents of events and ideas in the sub-continent. The extension of authorities of extra-local powers like the Imperial Guptas, Gauḍas of Western Bengal, Khadgas of Eastern Bengal, opened up the possibilities of effective contact with the rest of India and the out-side world.[7] A number of local powers, who succeded them, not only made use of this contact, but shared most of the ideas and symbols associated with Kingship in other parts of the country. The Phraseology of the Copper-plate charters of S. E. Bengal is reminiscent of the standard formula prevalent in Northern India. But more than the dynastic scenario, trade and religion further buttressed the links with the neighbouring and distant territories. Because of its geographical location, South. Eastern Bengal emerged as a viable trading zone. The decline of the port of Tamralipta hardly left any alternative for the merchants of Eastern India but to explore the ports of this region. Available evidence tends to suggest that from the 7th century A. D,[8] the region controlled much of the traffic and sea-borne trade to South East Asia. No wonder, its ports and marts attracted merchants. Along with the merchandise, they must have brought with them the cultural traits of other areas which were absorbed and re-interpreted in the art-traditions of the region.

Monastic establishment is another important force which sustained and shaped the art-achivities of the region. The network of monasteries, spread all over India, contributed much to the exchange of ideas and icons among monks and devotees of different parts of the Country. No wonder, Viryendra, an inhabitant of Samatata and a resident monk of Somapura Vihara of North Bengal, dedicated a Buddha image at Buddha Gaya,[9] evidently carved in the prevailing 10th century idiom of Bihar. Prosperous Buddhist establishments like Bhavadeva Vihara (Mainamati, Comilla district), Pandita-Vihara (Jhewari ? Chittagong Hills) became the melting pots of diverse artistic and cultural traditions. The monks and the lay-worshippers from different parts of India and South-East Asia converged into these monasteries. In their trail came the artisans and craftsmen trained in different ateliers who were either commissioned by the monasteries or supported by the devotees. The composite nature of monastic population is clearly indicated by the Paschimehag Copper-plate charter of Srichandra.[10] It alludes to among other thing. Shrines (matha) specifically marked for the outsiders (Desantaniya) as against those meant for the local (Vangala) devotees. The evidence cited above relates to a Brahmanical establishment, but it seemed to have been the general pattern. A monastic establishment thus became the centres for dissemination of diverse cultural traditions.

IV

One must not, however, loose sight of the specific regional elements in the cultural history of South-Eastern Bengal. The first set of image, like elsewhere in Bengal, were in all probability imports from Mathura as would be clearly evident from Silhua Yaksa (?) figure.[11] Unmistakably related to the Colossal type Mathura statuary of c. 2nd-3rd centuries A. D. it certainly had its origin beyond the region. But by the 7th century A. D, the region evolved certain distinctive elements— some of which were later used in the ateliers of Eastern India. In the Sarvani image (Fg 1) of the time of Deva Khadga[12] (C. 675 A.D), an important innovation is made. The Central figure is placed within an oval shaped rim-aureole with multiple arms projected like struts which in turm link up the goddess with the rim. This local innovation was tried with great success at Manirtal (24 pargana) Mahasthan (Rajshahi District) Nalanda, Buddh Gaya and Kurkihar.[13] Again, a number of bronze images from Mainamati (Comilla District) datable to c. 8th century A. D. are characterised by a pedestal type which is without parallel in Eastern India.[14] The iconographic features of two stone plaques recovered from the same site underscores the distinctive iconic tradition prevalent in the region.[15]

But, there is little substance in the assumption that 'the independent character of Samatata art came to end when the region was for the first time in its history, brought into a larger political fold'[16] under the Palas. Elsewhere, we have tried to show how historians of Indian art tend to overemphasize impact of political history on artistic developments.[17] Much before the imposition of Pala rule in South-Eastern Bengal around the 10th century A. D, the region was exposed to the main currents of artistic developments in Northern and Eastern India.

The art-activities of the region wavered between two ends-articulation of local perception in form and in content as well as accomodation of northern and eastern Indian idioms percolating into the area through merchants, monks, pilgrims and itinerant craftsmen. As noted above, 7th century A. D. saw the emergence of distinctive regional elements in the art of South-Eastern Bengal, but parallel to this was a conscious attempt at absorbing elements from other sources. The terracotta panels of Mainamati illustrates this in no uncertain terms. The stratigraphic evidence revealed by 1967-68 excavation, show that the terracotta tradition had its beginning at Mainamati sometime in c. 8th century A. D.[18] Mainamati terracottas offer a wide range of themes and motifs-much of which emerged out of a common artistic and religious heritage and can be traced with marginal variations at Nalanda (Temple site No. 2. Dado panels)[19], Antichak[20] and Paharpur.[21] Motifs like Kinnara beating the time with his hand, Gandharva playing on a damaru, Vidyadhara carrying a garland, makara, Vyala and goose emitting out the pearl necklace, cannot be explaned without a reference to the artistic experience of the Gupta and post-Gupta periods. Similarly some of the cognizable stylistic elements like sweeping lines and rounded limbs witnessed in the plaques are definitely derivative of the Gupta idiom. The impact of Mainamati is felt further east in the recently discovered terracotta plaques of Pilak in Tripura. A powerfully rendered wild boar and a Kinnari (Fig 2) examplify the extent of influence Mainamati had exerted in this area[22].

The stone sculptures, produced in the region, draw heavily upon experiences of Sarnath and eastern Indian ateliers. It had been the perpetual concern of the artists of the region to accomodate this experience in their own works. Carved out of a local variety of coarse-grained sandstone, a number of sculptures of Pilak and Jolabari, two tiny hamlets in Southern Tripura[23], exhibit this concern in varied degrees.

A notable feature in many a figures is a slim and compact torso supported by tall and slender legs resulting in a sense of weightlessness and reduction of volume. The artist must have worked from a Sarnath prototype. An Avolokitesvara is a typical example. Although its columnar legs comes very close to that of Deulvadi Sarvani. The date of the figures canno be ascertained with precision. They owe much to the late Sarnath model and combines in them features essentially local in character. Most probably, the figures are assignable to C. 8th century A. D.[24]

By the 9th century A. D, the artist is more closely dependant on the Sarnath model. This phase is best illustrated by a badly damaged Buddha of Pilak. Its rounded modelling, transparent drapery and serene contemplative expression clearly underscore the association. Even the details are faithfully copied.[25] Some of the pieces, like Surya, Narasimha and Andhakasuravadha murti of Siva, are characterised by sturdier build and powerful physical features. It is in these figures, (Fig 3) all significantly of Brahmanical affiliation, one discerns the impact of Eastern Bihar and Nothern Bengal statuary.[26]

The use of coarse-grained sandstone remained localised in Southern Tripura and Comilla districts for above two hundred years. By the 10th century A. D, black basalt was introduced. Not many stone-sculptures are known from the region, but among the scanty finds are a few inscribed pieces bearing dates in the regnal year of Pala and Chandra king. Whether black-basalt was introduced into the region because of the extension of Pala rule is inconsequential ; what is of significance is the fact that the first set of blackbasalt images were ·caused to be installed by merchants.[27] Whose connections beyond the region must explain this change. These pieces indicate the historical context of the radiation of early mediaeval idiom of Eastern India in South-Eastern Bengal. The inscribed sculptures of the region range in date between c. 940 A. D. to 1932 A. D.[28] Recovered mostly from the Comilla district (including erstwhile Tirperah district) and Udaipur sub-division of Southern Tripura, these black-basalt sculpture share all the features in common with Standard early mediaeval sculptures of eastern India. The configuration of the stela, rathaka arrangement of the base, decorative scheme, stances, and gestures bespeak of common stylistic and iconographic sources. Visnu image from Baghaura (Fig 4) is illustrative of this[29] Not only do we notice standardised features, but such smaller details as the crossbar with intricate floral motif along the shoulder of the god is also reproduced. Again, the Palgiri (Comilla district) Nataraja image is almost indistinguishable from those discovered in Dacea district.[30] Similerly, the Udaipur sculptures are totally dependant on the eastern idiom not only in the choice of material but also in their mode of representation Mask-like facial expression, taut surface and metallic finish make the pieces completely indistinguishable from the Sena period products.[31]

This raises two important questions—whether the sculptures were carved by the local artist who came to identify the dominant eastern Indian idiom as his own or an itinerant group of artist commissioned by local patrons with eclectic taste ? Admittedly, there cannot be a.definitive answer. It is, however, to be noted that almost all the blackbasalt sculptures are known from a small area-for sometime the core area of South Eastern Bengal with a number of important political and religious establishment within its fold. The greater part of the region remained, as it were, indifferent to the new medium. Secondly, metal sculptures, not stone, enjoyed a kind of general sanction all over South Eastern Bengal and outnumbers the stone sculptures by an impressive margin. Thirdly, sculptures in black-basalt almost inevitably depict Brahmanical pantheon, while the bronzes, by and large, relate to Buddhism.

Can it be so that black-basalt sculpture found acceptance within a particular area, because it was closer to eastern Bengal and thus, more strongly influenced by its artistic tradition ? Nevertheless, the introduction of blackbasalt statuary made South-Eastern Bengal an integral part of Eastern Indian art-tradition of the early mediaeval period, but it must be viewed as a cultural event independent of the political vicissitude.

Compared to the terracotta and stone sculptures, bronzes of South Eastern Bengal are much more distinctive regional products. Beginning with the Deulvadi Sarvani, through Maina-mati and Jhewari bronzes, the metal sculpture tradition to a great extent, evolved its own character-both in style as well as in content. But even here, one can hardly overlook the elements imbiled from other areas.

The Surya image discovered, along with the Sarvani at Deulvadi, is illustrative of this trend.[82] Ascribed to the 7th century A. D, its simple, unadorned and bold torso couple with full and oval face of the sungod bespeaks of its indubitable relationship with the standard Gupta idiom. The aureole format, solid, oval and topped by a flame funial, is very much different from what one observes in the Sarvani image. It retains much of what has already been achieved in late Gupta tradition in Bihar and Bengal.

The Mainamati bronzes of c. 8th-9th century A. D perpe-tuates the tradition laid down by the Deulvadi Sarvani. Their slender body and pedestal type can certainly be distingui-shed from those of Nalanda-Kurkihar bronzes. But, as one turns from details to broad stylistic perimeters, one can hardly deny that a group of Mainamati figures, described as refined images by the excavator,[83] is markedly dependant on the Nalanda idiom. Of special importance is fully rounded breast of Tara and easy grace of Manjsuri-which cannot be explained without a reference to the Nalanda experience. Another bronze from the area-Sitapatra of Tipperah[84] is marked by an elaborate pedestal and accessories associated with Mainamati figures, but its overall appearance has much in common with the Tara images of Nalanda datable to the 9th century A.D.[85] Similarly, the bronze Lokanatha from Bandarbazar (sylhet district) is unmistakably derived from Nalanda archetype. It is a tall and slender figure and the sense of height is emphasised by relatively longer legs supporting a sensitive torso. Its overriding simplicity springs from the stylistic idiom of the 9th century A. D. at Nalanda and diffused therefrom through a network of religious and commercial institutions.

But more significant is the radiation of Nalanda or eastern Indian idiom in the coastal Chittagong area along with the distinctive regional idiom. Three stylistic groups can be worked out from among the Chittagong bronzes mostly recovered at Jhewari.[36] (a) Some of the bronzes are clearly related to Nalanda or eastern Indian idiom so much so that some scholars have even suggested that they were metal versions of East Indian stone sculptures[37], (b) a number of bronzes are cast following the distinct regional tradition and (c) a few display features reminiscent of Burmese statuary. But, much of the compositional and iconographic elements discernible in each group have their origin in Nalanda imagery. The extent of Nalanda impact is clearly seen in a Vasudhara whose physiognomical features are inconceivable without reference to a 9th century A. D.[38] Tara of Nalanda. A standing Buddha in diaphanous robe is stylistically very close to the Sarnath type.[39] But for the open eyes, protruded usnisa, raised urna sign, and certain physical variations like brooder shoulder and narrower waist, this metal Buddha from Jhewari could have been easily placed with the Sarnath group. "For here, too, we find the same plastic abstruction effected by minimising the variations of the plane in the treatment of body surface that glows and vibrates beneath the monk's robe which is translucent. Elegantly poised this Buddha exhibits a rare sense of dignity and being more awakened from the classical meditative type, it sets forth the basic psychology for the East Indian Buddha—types".[40] The Sarnath elements must have percolated through Nalanda and reached Chittagong around the 10th century A. D.

Tripura bronzes, like their counterparts at Comilla. Sylhet and Chittagong, responded to the eastern Indian idiom in varied degrees. A ninth-century standing Buddha from Pilak-Jolaibari (South Tripura) is based on Sarnath Kurkihar archetypes, but somewhat less refined in its appearance. A group of Avalok-itesvara and Taras, on the other hand, show articulation of distinctive elements even when these are rooted to the eastern idiom.[41]

V

This account, a somewhat summary treatment of the interconnections of regional art-tradition, seeks to reiterate the premise from which the essay took its start. A regional art-tradition assumes significance through a long-drawn process of interaction with other traditions. In South-Eastern Bengal, a distinctive art-idiom did emerge by the 7th century A. D. and continued to exist till c. 12th century A. D. A number of factors—its geographical setting, religious environment, mercantile enterprise, royal patronage and ethnic composition-can be cited to explain the emergence and development of art-activities in the region. The exposure to other traditions contributed to the enrichment of regional art-idiom, which, in turm, offered important elements to the neighbouring art-styles.

South-Eastern Bengal's experience must not be viewd in isolation. Throughout its history, regional art-traditions in India have borrowed from each other, shared their experiment and innovations, drawn upon a common heritage of themes, motifs, symbols and even mode of representation. This is an important segment of India's past-and we can hardly afford to ignore it.

REFERENCES

1. Gautam Sengupta. Trends. In Early Indian Art-History since 1947 in T. S. Banerjee (ed) *Indian Historical Research Since Independence,* Calcutta, 1986. pp. 135-138.

2. Asok, K. Bhattacharya. A Study In Technique *in* S. K. Mitra (ed) *East Indian Bronzes,* Calcutta, 1979, p. 64.

3. Quoted by S. Hadway Architecture and Sculpture of Mysore, the Haysala style. *Indian Antiquary,* vol XLIV, 1915, p. 91.

4. Frederick M. Asher, The Effect of Pala Rule ; A Transition In Art. *Journal of The Indian Society of Oriental Art New* Series, vol. XII-XIII, 1981-83, p. 1.

5. Keynote Address (mimeographed). *Seminar on Harikela In Early Medieval Times* Calcutta, 1982, pp. 1-2.

6. Samatata is mentioned as a *pratyanta* power in the Allahabad Pillar Inscription of Samudragupta.

7. For a dynastic history of the region, see A. Choudhury, *Dynastic History of Bengal,* Dacca, 1967.

8. The most important evidence on trade is furnished by a continuous series of Harikela coins discussed by B. N. Mukherjee. A Survey of Coinage of Harikela in J. P. Singh & N. Amed (ed) *Coinage and Economy of North-Eastern States of India,* Varanasi, 19 pp. 17-24.

9. D. C. Sircar. *Select Inscriptions bearing on Indian History & Civilization* vol. II. Delhi, 1983 p. 59.

10. D. C. Sircar, *Ibid.* p. 98, v. 42.

11. Nurul Islam Khan (ed) *Noakhali,* Bangladesh District Gazetter, Dacca, 1977. plate facing page 82,

12. N. K. Bhatlasali Some Image Inscriptions From East Bengal *Epigraphia India,* vol. XVII. pp. 103-105.

13. For photographic representation of the figures see. Frederick M. Asher. The Art of Eastern India, 300-800, Oxford 1980 pl 230 ; 2131 (Mahasthan) pl 252, (Barisal), for Bihar bronzes, S. K. Mitra (ed) *op. cit,* Figs 4 (Kurkihar) 5 (Nalanda) 105 (Manir Tat), and 61 (Deulvadi Sarvani).

14. Asher ibid, plates 247-251.

15. Asher ibid, Plates 111-112.

16. Asher, *JISOA,* p. 5.

17. Sengupta *Op. cit,* p.

18. *Pakistan Archaeology* No. 5, 1968, p. 169.

19. V. S. Agarwala and Krishna Deva. The Stone Temple At Nalanda, *Journal of the U. P. Historical Society,* vol XXIII, pp. 198-212.

20. Bhagawant Sahai Terracotta Plaques From Antichak. *Journal of the Bihar Research Society,* vol. Lvii, pp. 57-76.

21. K. N. Dikshit, *Excavations at Paharpur, Bengal,* MASI, No. 55, Delhi, 1938.

22. Gautam Sengupta. Early Sculptures of Tripura *in* J. B. Bhatta-charjee (ed) *Studies in the History of North East India,* Shillong. 1986 pp. 4-5, Fig 5-7.

23. Sengupta *ibid.* pp. 2-3

24. For a discussion on the dated sculptures see, Suan. L. Huntington, *Pala. Sena Schools of Sculpture,* Leiden, 1984.

25. Huntington, *ibid.*

26. First International Congress on Bengal Art (Souvenir).

27. Sengupta. Early Sculptures of Tripura, pp, 3-4 Fif 3-4.

28. Asher. *The Art of Eastern India,* 300-800 pl : 114.

29. A.K.M. Shamsul Alam, *Mainamati,* Dacca, 1975, pp. 57-58.

30. Asher, *ibid,* pl. 251.

31. S. K. Mitra (ed) *op, cit,* Fig 69.

32. Asher, *ibid,* pl. 253.

33. For an exhaustive account of Jhewari bronces see Debala Mitra, *Bronzes from Bangladesh,* New Delhi, 1982.

34. Nihar Ranjan Ray, *Bangalis Itihasa* (in Bengali) Calcutta, 1980, p. 979.

35. S. K. Mitra (ed) *op. cit,* Fig 69.

36. Ashok K. Bhattacharya. A Study in Style *in* S. K. Mitra (ed) *op. cit,* p. 25. Fig 28.

37. Ashok. K Bhattacharya *ibid.*

PART—II

Ancient and Medieval Indian Experiences

THE CONCEPT OF NATIONAL INTEGRATION IN ANCIENT INDIA

Dr. G. P. Singh.
Manipur University,
Imphal, Manipur.

It is really very difficult to justify the application of the term, national integration, as such, in ancient Indian context for manifold reasons. The data available in the sources at our disposal are too meagre to project a distinct picture of the subject under discussion. There is a good deal of controversy among the scholars with regard to the emergence of the concept of national integration in ancient India. The use of the appellation 'Rashtra' by ancient Indian classical writers in varied context further creates confusion and misunderstanding in our minds. However, on the basis of Slender thread of evidence furnished in the literary texts, classical treatises on India, the general historical records and other contemporary sources, we can prove it with certain amount of confidence that the said concept was not totally absent in ancient India and there were few attempts at the political unification of the country.

The modern concept of national integration finds expression in the form of national consciousness, which was conspicuously present among the Vedic Aryans. This can be amply substantiated through the impartial examination of the ideas contained in the hymns of the Vedas. From the vedic literature—the Yajurveda (Vajsaneyi Samhita)[1], the Rgveda[2] and the Atharvaveda[3] it transpires that the concept of one nation had emerged among the indigenous Aryans of Bharatavarsha. This finds confirmation in their invocations to gods for the unity, stability and prosperity of a nation, and solicitation to their kings to guard the nation against aggressors, hostile forces and so on. They were also familiar with the concept of 'Swarajya', which they wanted to maintain at every cost. The Brahmanical lirerature (Tattiriya Samhita, 7. 5. 18 and Tattiriya Brahmana, 3. 8. 13) also provide some references to the national awakening in contemporary India. But the authenticity of this particular evidence furnished in the Brahmanas is not beyond question.

The Rastra or nation comprising several countries and the duties and responsibilities of a king to defend the integrity and maintain the unity of the country also find little reflection in the secular literature, i.e. the Smritis and the Dharmasutras. The Manusmriti,[4] the Yajnavalkya Smriti (1.321), Vishnu Dharmasutra (3. 4. 5) and Kamandakiya Dharmasutra (4. 50-56)[5] have slightly touched on the ideas connected with the ways and means for making the Indian Nation strong and prosperous in ancient times.

The loyalty of ancient Indian rulers to the nation, called Bharata and their patriotism as reflected in the Bhisma Parva[6] of the Mahabharata fairly attest to their intense feelings for keeping the country bound together. The sense underlying the early Vedic hymns in this regard finds its echo in this Epic. The ancient Indian historical traditions also confirm the truth that the ideas connected with the oneness of the country were visualised both by the potentates and populace of early India. Actually, they had a well-established tradition of looking upon their another land as one nation, which further inspired the Indians. Thus in the twilight of the literary evidence it can be established that the very concept of national unity had germinated in the ancient India of pre-christian era.

Here we must take note of the fact that prior to Persian and Macedonian invasions of India no such event took place, which might have posed a threat to the unity and integrity of the country. Hence there never arose any necessity for the ancient Indians to think in terms of integrity of nation to that extent, which we do to-day. Inspite of diversity of race, language, religion and culture the country remained united till the beginning of the 6th century B. C. without losing its any part and retaining the age-old geographical identity and political boundary. The country in the real sense of the term, was never found on the verge of disintegration. Therefore, the said concept of national integration made slow progress. In view of the facts stated above we don't find a fair scope to apply this concept in such a way that it could suitably match the modern one.

In pre-Mauryan Age (650-321 B. C.) India had been politically, parcelled out into a multitude of petty states (some powerful monarchies and some tribal republics), whose rulers and heads were continuously fighting among themselves for supremacy or building up imperial states and owed no allegiance to any overlord. The political rivalries and wars shattered the unity of the country. Before Alexander's invasion (326 B. C.) of India, there was no paramount authority to maintain the unity and integrity of the country, whose geographical boundary extended up to Ariana. Both from the literary and classical (Graeco-Roman) sources it appears that the political conditions of both North-western India and Gangetic valley were not conducive to the growth of the feeling of unity. However with the said invasion, the history of India took a significant turn.

It is worthy of remark that Alexander's invasion proved to be a boon in disguise for India. In fact it constituted a milestone towards the political unification of India. **Prof. R. K.** Mookerji has correctly stated that "Alexander's invasion promoted the political unification of the country. Smaller states which handicapped unity were now merged in the larger ones, such as those of Paurava, Abhisara or Taxila. These conditions were favourable for the rise of an Indian Empire to be shortly founded by Chandragupta. It swept away internal barriers which prevented the unification of the lands concerned. The con—federacies of other tribes which had maintained their proud-Isolation from other political system were utterly broken. Smaller principalities were swallowed up in a realm such as those given by Alexander to the Paurava. This, no doubt made it simpler for the Mauryan king, who few years later took these countries in his great Indian Empire."[7] H. C. Raychaudhuri has also, more or less supported this view. To quote him, "It helped the cause of Indian unity by destroying the power of the petty states of North-West India, just as the Danish invasion contributed to the union of England under Wessex by destroying the independence of Northumbria and Mercia."[8]

Alexander's creation of vast empire comprising Punjab and Sindh marked the beginning of disintegration in ancient India. The Macedonian occupation of North-Western India for about eight years hurled a challenge to the integrity of the country. But fortunately, the political anarchy and convulsions, which ensued following the death of Alexander in 323 B. C., led, to the disruption or dismemberment of the empire carved out by Alexander on the North-western frontier. The whole area was the theatre of war and the provinces were about to turn into independent kingdoms. Taking advantage of the emerging situation Chandragupta, the first historical founder of the great Mauryan Empire decided to liberate India from a foreign yoke, unify it with the help of northern states and thereby restore its fallen glory. He also resolved to restore India to a geographical position held in pre-Alexandrian period extending as far as Ariana. The political unification of the country achieved during his time (321-297 B. C.) constitutes a solitary example of an attempt at integration of India in ancient times. Admittedly, it was during this age that the whole of India was politically united for the first time under one head and rule. Further the uniform system of administration helped keep the country well-knit together.

Chandragupta placed himself at the head of the Indian, who were smarting under the frustration caused by the foreign rule, and, after Alexander's departure defeated his generals, exterminated the Macedonian garrisons, drove away the Greeks from Punjab and Sindh and finally consolidated his imperial authority over these provinces by 321 B. C. The classical writers have also acknowledged the importance of the role played by Chandragupta in the political unification of India in the fourth century B. C. Justin says that he "shook the yoke of servitude from neck of India"[9] and gave liberty to it after Alexander's retreat. But his explanation that he "soon converted the name of liberty into servitude after his success subjugating those, whom he had rescued from foreign dominion, to his own authority"[10] is not a reasonable one. Because, he had to do so for tying them into a single thread of unity. Plutarch's[11] view, that he subdued not only Punjab but the whole of India, is perfectly justified.

The task of integrating the country was accomplished at much later stage. Seleucus Nikator, one of the ablest generals of Alexander after having obtained possession of the Asiatic dominions of his master and establishing his supremacy over large area extending from Western Asia to Afghanistan proceeded to take possession of Punjab. His ambition was to carry out the designs of his great commander Alexander but it was never fulfilled. The presence of overwhelming force, which Chandragupta had deployed on North-West Frontier to defend its integrity, was enough to strike terror in the heart of Seleucos. Neverthless, a conflict took place between Chandragupta and Seleucos sometimes between 305-302 B. C. in which the latter was ignominiously defeated. Consequently, the Indians occupied some of the countries situated along the Indus, which formerly belonged to the Persians. They also obtained a larger portion of Ariana, which Alexander deprived of them and established there settlements and provinces. Thus during this period India again obtained possession of eastern Iran, which she had lost few centuries earlier to it. The country which Seleucos ceded to Chandragupta comprised the four Satrapies beyond the Indus called, Aria (Herat), Archosia (Kandhar), Gedrosia (Baluchistan) and Paropanisadae (Kabul).[12] The inclusion of Kabul Valley within the Indian empire can be testified to by Asoka's inscriptions in Greek and Aramaic found on a rock at Shari-Kuna near Kandhar in Afghanistan, four Edicts found in the vicinity of Shalata and Qargha in province of Laghman in Afghanistan bearing inscriptions in Aramaic and Prakrit in Kharoshthi script, etc.

Thus the empire which he established embraced the whole of Northern India lying between the Himalaya and Vindhya mountains together with that portion of Afghanistan which lie south of the Hindukush, North-western India comprising the trans-Indus regions, Western India including Kathiawar and Saraushtra, Central India including the regions of north of the Narmada river, Gangetic Valley and far-south including Tamil land and Mysore. Thus he not only organised his empire in Punjab keeping numerous petty Chieftains under his controlling authority, but provided unity to the country stretching from the bank of the Sindhu to the mouth of the Ganga.

As a matter of fact, India emerged for the first time in ancient India—as a unified country under the banner of Chandragupta Maurya. The analysis of the facts warrants us to admit that the political unification of India was achieved during his time through the establishment of an empire over the whole of Hindustan and the Punjab. The empire was not merely composed of a number of provinces brought together under a single sceptre, it was a real unit based on the principle of uniformity of rule and the welfare of the people, at large. Chandragupta had a clear vision of the unity of the country. Historically it will not be fair and accurate to hold the view that his attempt was only at the establishment of an empire and not the integrity of the nation. Actually, the consolidation of the empire was the media for achieving his end that was to provide stability to the country. F. W. Thomas has aptly remarked that "the establishment of a single paramount power in Hindustan embracing a part even of the country south of the Vindhya mountains and standing in relation to the still independent areas, supplies a unity which previously was lacking and which in fact was rarely realised in later ages".[13]

The success or failure achieved in the field of integration of a country should be judged not by applying the modern concept of national integration but by taking in view the changing concept of unity and integrity in the contemporary situation. Chandragupta's concept of national unity after being put on the touchstone of several changes effected in the political system of the country in course of passage of time may, of course, be taken to-day as a concept of imperial authority, but viewed in the perspective of exigencies of the situation which he faced, the danger of disintegration which he averted and the success which he achieved in maintaining the unity of the country extending from Afghanistan in the north to far south, it appears that this concept was basically a concept of unity and integrity.

With the emergence of several poltical regions, kingdoms, empires, etc. in the Indian sub-continet during the period C. 200 B. C.—A. D. 300, the process of disintegration started.

The foregoing treatment of the subject gives us the impression that the concept of national integration never remained static. It had to undergo transformation according to needs, changes and situation. From the Vedic Age down to the 6th century B. C. the unity and integrity of the Indian nation remained intact because of geographical barriers and other impediments. Moreover, the ancient Indians did not face any problem of disintegration during this period. They had a clear concept of the unity of India. But as a result of the Persian and Macedonian invasions India lost greater parts in the North-western Region. But Chandragupta during the reign of twenty-four years made every possible efforts to unify the country by recovering all the lost possessions. Actually it was he who saved India from disintegration. He restored India to its pristine glory by giving her back, which she lost between 6th and 4th century B. C. His was the first and the last attempt at the political unification of the country in ancient times.

REFERENCES

1. Original Sanskrit Text with parallel Hindi Trans. by Pt. Shree Ram Sharma Acharyya (Bareilly, 1974), 22. 22 ; See also Vasudeva Sharana Agrawala, ITIHASA—DARSANA (Varanasi, 1978), pp. 101-2.

2. Shree Ram Sharma Acharyya (Trans.—Bareilly, 1974-75), Vol. 2, 4. 42. 1 ; 5. 66. 6 ; Vol. IV, 10. 173. 1 & 5 ; 10. 174. 2 ; See also Pt. Viseshwar Nath Reu, Rgveda Par Ek Itihasik Dristi, (Delhi, 1967), p. 209.

3. Shree Ram Sharma Acharyya (Trans. Bareilly 1973), Vol. 2, 12. 1. 8. 12. 1. 14 ; See also P. V. Kane, Dharmasastra Ka Itihasa, (Lucknow, 1982), Vol. 2, pp. 639-642 and Acharyya Priyavarta Vedavachaspati, A Study in Vedic Polity, (Merrut, 1983), pp. 18-21, 656-59 (for study of Bhumi Sukta of Mandala—12).

4. Original Sanskrit Text trans. and annotated by H. G. Sastri and edited by Gopala Sastri Nene (Varanasi, 1970), IX. 251 ; See also V. S. Agrawala, India as Described by Manu, (Varanasi, 1970), pp. 46-47.

5. Quoted in P. V. Kane, Op. Cit., p. 639.

6. Trans. and Edtd. by Shree Pada Damodar Satvalekar and Shree Shruti Shila Sharma (Pardi, Gujarat, 1972), IX. 5-9.

7. Hindu Civilization, pp. 294-5.

8. Political History of Ancient India, (Calcutta, 1953), p. 263.

9. Watson's Trans. pp. 142-43 cf. H. C. Raychaudhuri, Op. Cit., pp. 272-73 ; See also J. Talboys Wheeler India from the Earliest Age (Delhi, 1973), Vol. III, p. 176.

10. Justini Hist. Philipp Lib. XV, Chap. IV. cf. F. Maxmuller, A History of Ancient Sanskrit literature (Varanasi, 1968), p. 246.

11. Life of Alexander, LXII ; See also his Vita-Alexandri C-62, Vide, Maxmuller, Op. Cit. p. 248.

12. Paul Masson-Qursel & C. Ancient India and Indian Civilization (London, 1934), pp. 36-37 ; E. J. Rapson, Ancient India (Varanasi 1981), p. 53 ; W. W. Hunter, M. Elphinstone, E. B. Cowel & C ; Ancient India (Varanasi, 1983), Ch. IX, p. 90 ; R. G. Bhandarkar, A peep into the Early History of India (Varanasi 1978), p. 5 ; Romila Thapar, A History of India (Middlesex, 1966), Vol. I, pp. 70 ff ; V. A. Smith, The Oxford History of India (Delhi, 1981), p. 52 ; See also W. W. Tarn, The Greeks in Bactria and India, Cambridge, 1938. p. 100 and Ind. Ant. Vol. VI, pp. 114 f.

13. Vide E. J. Rapson (ed.), Tne Cambridge History of India Vol. I. Ancient India (Delhi, 1962), p. 420.

THE TAMIL SIDDHA CULT :
A Product of Pan-Indian Cultural Integration

Dr. R. VENKATRAMAN
Reader in Ancient History
Madurai Kanaraj University
Madurai—625021

The compositions ascribed to the Siddhas of Tamilnadu form one of the most fascinating pages in the culture of the Tamils, whose contributions to the treasures of human civilization are many and variegated. These Siddha compositions still form one of the darkest and almost unknown chapters in the history of Indian thought. Opinion among scholars about these Siddhas differ greatly, even radically. Some hold that theirs was "a monolithic puritan creed"[1] and 'they formed the noblest order who viewed the Vedanta and Siddhanta alike'[2]. Others hold that 'most of them were plagiarists and imposters...Being eaters of opium and dwellers in the land of dreams, their conceit knew no bounds'[3]. Many Tamil scholars, unaware of a pan-Indian cultural mileu, think that these Tamil Siddhas are a set of free thinkers unique to the Tamil Country.

This paper attempts to show that the Tamil Siddhas are a group of Tantric Yogis and their cult is 'one of the most important and interesting off-shoots of the pan-Indian Tantric Yoga movement'[4]. Further, such cultural traits never get themselves confined to any single region. Like art, they transcend the regional barriers and grow into a much complex phenomenon incorporating the different regional strands either in their original or modified forms.

Though tradition holds that the total number of Tamil Siddhas is 'eighteen' ('Patinen Siddhar'), investigations show that this tradition is as unhistorical as the tradition of the 'Eighty Four Siddhas' of North India. The origin of the said Tamil tradition (of 'Eighteen') 'seems to be as recent as the 19th century'[5].

Investigations further show that at least three groups of authors are lumped together under the term 'Eighteen Siddhas'. The three groups are : (i) the Sanmārga Siddhas, (ii) the ñāna Siddhas and (iii) the Kāya Siddhas.

The first group has its origin in Tirumular (c. 10th century A. D.)[6] whose only authentic work, the *Tirumandiram*, is a compendium of the Siddha cult, containing *in nuce* almost all the features of the cult. (The Tiruppanandal Mutt edition is followed in this paper).

The second group considers the world as well the physical body unreal. It yearns for a mystical union with the ultimate, called Sivam, through deep devotion and *laya yoga*. In many respects it shows a striking similarity with the Indian Sufis.

The members of the third group are primarily Śāktas and a few of them follow *vāmācāra*[7] practices. Unlike the second group, which is pessimistic about the body and the world, this group aims at physical immortality, perpetuation of youth and acquistion of occult power, all with a view to enjoy life, especially the sex act. For this purpose they search for the elixir of life and make extensive experiments in Yoga, medicine, magic and alchemy. They often employ alchemical symbols to describe their Kundalini Yoga.

This paper confines itself to the first group, especially the *Tirumandiram*. Until recently the historians of Tamilnadu did not investigate this cult seriously. So this cult gets a very superficial treatment even in works[8] dealing with the social life of the medieval Tamil Country, where it prevailed. While some reputed scholars hold that the history of this cult 'is rather obscure'[9], majority of the rest ignored it completely. So, to many Tamil scholars this cult appeared as 'most perplexing'[10] or as 'an enigma'[11].

The real position is that the Tamil Siddha cult, like any other, is the product of an evolution and a fruit deriving from different roots. The period of evolution would go back to proto-historic times. The roots are diverse belonging to different soils and periods. So, the nourishment had been qualitatively different. What ultimately cropped up, as a result of these in the Tamil Country, is the Sanmārga Siddha school in the 10th-11th centuries, and after a pause settled down as the Tamil Siddha cult around the 15th-17th centuries.

Of these different roots, four seem to be important and identifiable, showing the criss-cross fashion in which the cultural fabric of India took shape. They are : (i) the proto-historic native beginnings, (ii) the Kāpālika cult, (iii) the Tāntric Buddhism and (iv) the Nātha Siddha cult.

The resultant fruit, or the Tamil Siddha cult, is, thus, a blend of Yoga and magic representing a very archaic modality of spirituality aiming at an ecstatic self deification for magical powers. This cult has all the basic components and features common with the North Indian Tantric Siddha Yoga. So, this cult is certainly not an isolated and unique one, as claimed by many, but an integral part of a pan-Indian tradition, the essential feature of which as will be shown, is that it finally completes the synthesis among the various elements of Buddhist Tantrism, Saivite Tantrism and the 'holy seeking of the lower strata, especially the Dravidas in South India'[12]. This pan-

Indian Tantrism appeared as a distinct stream around 4th century A. D., and spread all over the country from about 5th century onwards.

The Native origin : Tantrism may be traced back to the proto-historic Harappan culture[13], and more certainly to the 'holy seeking' of the ancient Tamil tribes who worshipped their god Muruga with bacchanalian dances at which he was impersonated by 'Velan', a medicine-man holding a spear (*Vel*), whose frenzied dance was called 'Velan Veriyāḍal'[14]. It is a ritual dance in which the Velan was believed to have been possessed by Muruga. This ecstatic self deification was an important component of Tantrism or Siddhism, which, for similar end, employed also Yoga, *yantras*, *mantras* and even *ganja* (Indian hemp).

The Kāpālika origin of Siddhism : The Kāpālikas were ascetics who aimed at a mystical communion with Bhairava (a terrific aspect of Siva) by means of Tantric rituals for gaining superhuman powers, or *siddhis*[15]. Due to its striking similarity with the 'Velan Veriyāḍal', Lorenzen thinks that this cult too 'originated in South India or the Deccan'[16]. It appears probable that the Kapalika cult was an important channel, which having assimilated the ecctetic tribal cults of the South, influenced many religious schools of the North like the Sahajya Siddhas, and the Natha Siddhas. Kanhapada, the famous Sahajya Siddha elevates the Kāpālikas to the rank of perfect yogins[17]. It is said that 'many of the Tantric practices of the Natha Siddhas resemble those attributed to the Kāpālikas'[18].

Tantric Buddhism (Vajrayāna and Sahajayāna) : Though it is still debatable as to the time of the Tantric intrusion into Buddhism, around the 7th century A. D., the Tantric tendencies culminated in the rise of Vajrayāna school of Buddhism. According to it the union of man and woman was a great yoga, and the pleasure thereof was considered symbolic of 'Mahāsukha', which is the positive aspect of *nirvāṇa*, a negative concept of earlier Buddhism[19]. Vajrayāna developed all its esoteric practices around this 'Mahāsukha', her important innovation.

The unethical elements in Vajrayāna gave rise to a new school of protest from within, and it was called the Sahajayāna school, a least known branch of Buddhism. It was started towards the end of the 8th century in eastern India by Rāhulabhadra, also know as Sarahapāda. Most of its authors including Rāhulabhadra were inhabitants of Bengal or adjoining areas during the reign of the Pala dynasty (8th-12th centuries). Most of them were connected with the Vikramaśīla University[20]. The basic features of the Sahajiyas are :

(i) They revolted against orthodoxy of any kind—Brahmanical or Buddhist.

(ii) Revolting against the *varna* system, they espoused the cause of the humbler castes.

(iii) They stressed the realisation of *sahaja*, a state of the highest bliss (as against the 'Mahāsukha'), which can only be intuited in a perfectly non-dual state of mind. Its nature, like the Upanishadic Brahman, is ineffable.

(iv) Being against any ritual, they said, the shaja can be realised only within the body by bringing about a union of (not man and woman but) 'Iḍa' and 'Pingala' with 'Suṣumna' by means of 'Prāṇāyāma'[21].

(v) The human body is the epitome of the whole universe.

(vi) Devotion to the 'Guru' is indispensable for realising the '*sahaja*'.

(vii) Their Caryapadas and Dohas employed mystical symbols meaning various things at various levels—objectively, subjectively and mystically[22].

The Natha Siddhas : Nathism, a pan-Indian Śaiva Tantric movementdeveloped in North India simultaneously with Tantric Buddhism. It represents the synthesis of Buddhism and Saivism, especially in the works of Matsyendranath, who in his *Akula-Vīra Tantra* identified sahaja, on the one hand with Siva, and on the other, with Arhanta Buddha[23]. Many Natha Siddhas were claimed by both the sects. Thus Jalandhara appeared in Western India as a Natha Siddha, and in Eastern India as a Buddhist Siddha[24]. Further almost all the main teachers of the Natha sect are mentioned in the lists of Buddhist Siddhas preserved in Tibetan texts[25].

Since the school of Matsyendranath, like the Vajrayāna school, smacked of sexual laxity[26], his disciple Gorakhnath started a strong movement against the master enjoining complete celebacy. Like the Sahajiyas he internised the sexo-yoga as follows : Sun, the destructive femal principle (called 'Kuṇḍalini') in the 'Mūlādhāra', when risen to the 'Sahasrāra' to cohabit with Siva, the Moon, a state of bliss is attained. It results in the secretion of *amṛta* (nectar) from the Sahasrāra. Drinking this by means of 'Khecarī Mudrā', the Siddha attains immortality of the body or Kāyasiddhi, which is the *summum bonum* of the Goraknathis[27].

The means advocated by Gorakhnath is the 'Hatha Yoga', involving the purification of the *nāḍis* through Asanas, Pranayama, Mudras etc. He adds that during the 'Kuṇḍalini Yoga' (lifting the 'Kuṇḍalini'), the Yogi 'hears some musical sounds in his head'[28].

Though the revolution of Gorakhnath seems comparable to

the Sahajya reform, the former makes a compromise with sexo-Yogism. Accordingly he advocated that during *mudra* (Yogi's cohabitation with a woman) the restraint on the flow of seminal fluid and its elevation in the body makes one's body strong and adamant[29].

The Gorakhnathis bury the dead Yogi, making the corpse sit cross-legged as in meditation. A *linga* is installed on the grave (*samādhi*) and the dead Yogi is supposed to remain in trance (also called *samādhi*) indefenitely[30].

Siddhism in the Tirumandiram : The actual evolution of the Tamil Siddha cult begins with Tirumular's Tirumandiram (10th-11th century A. D.). It has all the features of the Buddhist Tantrism and the Natha Siddha cult outlined above. In its unmitigated use of obscure symbolic terminology too it is in full agreement with the pan-Indian Tantric usage. It has all the other basic components which distinguish the pan-Indian Tantric Siddha schools[31]. the quest of perfect health[32] and immortality in this life[33] ; the basic *hatha yoga* techniques[34] ; and the development of *siddhis*[35]. The other important features peculiar to North Indian siddha schools found in the Tirumandiram are :

(i) The worship of Bhairava[36], basic to Kapalikas and Natha Siddhas.

(ii) The revolt against the Brahmins[37] and espousing the cause of the humbler castes[38].

(iii) The stress on the realisation of Śivahood[39], which is akin to the Sahaja state of Sahajyas and the Brahman of Vedanta.

(iv) The sexo-yogism of Buddhist Siddhas and Natha Siddhas is graphically described in a chapter called Pariyanka yoga[40], meaning 'Bedstead yoga'. It emphasises the concept, peculiar to Gorakhnath, that the downward flow of the seminal fluid must not only be restrained but also that it should be elevated in the body for 'Kāyasiddhi'[41].

(v) The Kuṇḍalini yoga of Gorakhnath and Tirumandiram are strikingly similar both in technique and nomenclature. The following is a sample : The union of the 'Sun' in the Mūlādhāra with the 'Moon' in the Sahasrāra[42] of the yogi and the 'drinking' of the 'nectar' by means of 'Khecarī Mudra' for Kāyasiddhi, the *summum bonum* of the Gorakhnathis is well described in the Tirumandiram[43]. Similarly there is a striking similarity between the two not only when they describe the Yogic physiology – the 72,000 *nāḍis*[44] in the human body—but also about the musical sounds a yogi could hear during the Yoga Praxis[45] and the mode of burying the corpse of a yogi[46].

(vi) The mention of *Sivabodhi*[47] in the Tirumandiram reminds us of the synthesis of Buddhism and Saivism found in the Natha Siddha works[48].

(vii) Above all, the Tirumandiram accepts the *nava* (nine) Nathas[49] as the foremost leaders in the path of Yogic penance.

(viii) The realisation of a final stage of effulgence as being the other side of the three fold 'Sunya' which the Sahajiya Siddhas stressed[50] constitute one of the basic features of Tirumandiram, to which the effulgence is 'Sivajyoti'[51] and the three fold Sunya is 'Muppāl'[52]. It is to be noted that it says the 'sahaja marga' is the highest level of attainment and to its adherants no more penance is needed[53].

(ix) Like all the Northern Siddha cults, Tirumandiram also stresses the grace of the Guru as indispensable for the realisation of this effulgence[54].

One of the most essential qualities of the pan-Indian siddhism is its capacity to synthesise various religious philosophic, theistic and cult elements cutting across the barriers of regions. If Nathism synthesised Buddhist and Saivite Tantrism in the North, Tirumular in the Tamil Country synthesised Vedanta, pan-Indian siddhism, Kashmir Śaivism and the theism of the Nāyanmars, and thus sowed the seeds for Saiva Siddhanta, which is one of the finest and proudest products of the Tamil region.

Kashmir Saivism and Tirumandiram : Tirumandiram, predominantly concerned with the nature of the Self, the nature of the Ultimate and the means of the former realizing the latter, is much influenced by the theistic obsolutism of Kashmir Saivism[55]. Like the former, the latter too accepts the concept of the three *malas* (or 'impurities' such as *āṇava, karma* and *māya*) which the Absolute (Śiva for both) voluntarily accepts as a self limitation owing to Its (His) sportive nature[56]. This influence is equally pronounced in the latter's concept of liberation[57] and its means called saktipāta or saktinipāta[58].

Conclusion :

From the foregoing discussion it is clear that Tamil Siddhism is not an isolated and unique cult as supposed by some, but it is an integral part of a pan-Indian Tantric tradition. As in the North, in the South too it has successfully displayed its genius to integrate various cultural traits from different regions. The path of integration laid by the Tirumandiram acted as a great cultural force in the subsequent centuries too. Thus in the 15th-17th centuries the ñānasiddhas of Tamilnadu acted as a synthesising agent between Tamil siddhism and sufism, and in the recent centuries Thayumanavar (18th century) and Ramalingar (popularly known as 'Vallalar meaning 'the Venerable Philanthropist') (19th cent.) both being great mystic poets of considerable reputation reconciled in their poems the different contending philosophis and theistic schools, and thus transcended all narrow barriers. The 'Vallalar' called his school as 'Samarasa Sanmārga', or the 'Reconciling True Path'. Subrahmanya Bharati, the Nationalist Tamil poet par excellence of this century was highly inspired by the Tamil siddha songs. All these show that siddhism still has the inner Capaciy to act as an integrating force and that it has a great contemporary relevance, as for as its this attitude is concerned.

REFERENCES

1. K. A. Nilakanta Sastri, *Development of Religion in South India,* Orient Longmans, 1963, p. 95.

2. M. S. Purnalingam Pillai, quoted by K. V. Zvelebil, *The Poets of the Powers*, Rider and Co, London, 1973, p. 8.

3. M. Srinivasa Iyengar, quoted by K. V. Zvelebil, *Idem.*

4. K. V. Zvelebil, *The Poets of the Powers,* p. 16.

5. M. Arunachalam, "Tirukkuralum Urudipporulum" (Tamil), a paper (unpublished) presented in a seminar on the Tirukkural, in Madurai Kamaraj University, in April 1978, p. 4.

6. This date has been controversial ; the generally held date being 5th or 7th century A. D. This author has tried to place him in the 10th century : R. Venkatraman, "The Date of Tirumular—A Reassessment", *Proceedings of the 38th session of the Indian History Congress,* pp. 100-106.

7. Meaning 'left hand practice', it is a branch in Śakti workship with wine and woman in its orgiastic rituals.

8. e. g., T. V. Mahalingam, *Administration and Social Life* under Vijayanagar, Part II, Madras University, 1975 (2nd ed.), pp. 194 f.

9. K. A. Nilakanta Sastri, Loc. cit.

10. K. V. Zvelebil, *op. cit,* p. 7.

11. M. Arunachalam, *Tamil Ilakkiya Varalaru (14th century)*, (Tamil), Gandhi Vidyalayam, Mayuram, 1969, p. 339.

12. Max Weber : *The Religion of India ; The Sociology of Hinduism and Buddhism,* The Free Press, New York, 1967, p. 295.

13. The Harappan seal with a Yogi-like figure on it surrounded by animals may be taken as a proof of it.

14. *Ahanānūru* : 22, 8-11.

15. David N. Lorenzen ; *The Kapalikas and Kalamukhas : Two Lost Saivite Sects,* Thomas Press (India) Ltd., New Delhi, 1972, pp. 94 f.

16. *Ibid.,* p. 53.

17. S. B. Das Gupta, *Obscure Religious cults,* Firma K. L. Mukhopadhyaya, Calcutta, 1969 (3rd ed.), pp. 57 f.

18. D. N. Lrenzen, *op. cit,* p. 35.

19. S. B. Das Gupta, *op. cit.,* pp. 32-34.

20. *Ibid.,* Introduction, p. xxxiii.

21. *Ibid.,* p. 89.

22. Herbert V. Guenther (ed.), *The Royal Song of Saraha*, University of Washington Press, Seattle, 1969, pp. 23 f.

23. *Kaulajñāna Nirṇaya*, P. C. Bagchi (ed.), Calcutta 1943, Introduction, p. 55.

24. Bhupendranath Dutta (tr.) *Mystic Tales of Lama Taranath*, Ramakrishna Vedanta Math., Calcutta, 1944, p. 26.

25. Buddha Prakash, *Aspects of Indian History and Civilization*, Agra, 1965, p. 26.

26. *Ibid.*, p. 294.

27. *Gorakṣa Vijaya*, quoted by S. B. Das Gupta *op. cit*, p. 223.

28. G. W. Briggs, *op. cit*, p. 200, cf. *Tirumandiram* 606 f.

29. Buddha Prakash, *op. cit.* p. 300, *Gorakhbani* (Hindi), P. D. Barthwal (ed.), Prayag, 1943, p. 49.

30. G. W. Briggs, *op. cit.* pp. 39-43, cf. Tirumandiram, 1910-1922.

31. K. V. Zvelebil, *op. cit.* p. 29.

32. *Tirumandiram*, 724-739.

33. *Ibid.*, 764 and 807.

34. *Ibid.*, 553-639.

35. *Ibid.*, 671-711.

36. *Ibid.*, 1291-1296.

37. e. g., *Ibid.*, 1860, 519.

38. *Ibid.*, 7th Tantra, 13th chapter is called 'Maheśvara Pujai', which until very recently meant 'feeding the lower castes'.

39. *Ibid.*, 1750, 1816, 1823, 1963 etc.

40. *Ibid.*, 825-844.

41. *Ibid.*, 828, 834 and 841.

42. *Ibid.*, 852, 853 and 862.

43. *Ibid.*, 803-809 cf. *The Gorakṣa Śataka*, 64 f.

44. *Ibid.*, 729. cf. *The Gorakṣa Śataka*, 25.

45. *Ibid.*, 606 f. cf. *The Gorakṣa Śataka*, 101.

46. *Ibid.*, 1910-1922, cf. G. W. Briggs, *op. cit.*, pp. 39-41.

47. *Ibid.*, 79.

48. *Vide*, f. n. 26 above.

49. *Tirumandiram*, 3067. There is a tradition of Nava Nathas among the Natha Siddhas, S. B. Das Gupta. *op. cit.* p. 206.

50. S. B. Das Gupta, *Ibid.*, p. 196 f.

51. *Tirumandiram*, 2054.

52. *Ibid.*, 2496 and 2497.

53. *Ibid*, 1632.

54. *Ibid.*, 2054.

55. C. V. Narayana Ayyer, *Origin and Early History of Saivism in South India,* University of Madras 1939, (Repring 1974) p. 208.

56. See. L. N. Sharma, *Kashmir Saivism,* Bharatiya Vidya Prakashan, Varanasi, 1972, pp. 325-332. cf. *Tirumandiram* 2548, 432, 391, 396 etc.

57. R. Venkatraman, *Origin and Evolution of the Tamil Siddha Cult,* Ph. D thesis (unpublished) submitted to M. K. University, Madurai, 1980, pp. 94-99.

58. L. N. Sharma, *op. cit.* pp. 341-348 ; *Tirumandiram*, 1514 ff.

ŚRĪ VAISHṆAVISM
—A case study in Integration

Dr. N. Jagadeesan
Tagore College, Pondicherry

While identifying the forces generating integration in the pre-British India, the emergence of Śrī Vaishṇavism as a unifying force is too conspicuous to be missed. Rāmānuja (1017—1137), the founder of Śrī Vaishṇavism, combined in it centuries of Indian thought enshrined in North India and in South India, in Sanskrit and in Tamil, and in the pre-Christian and the post-Christian eras. This fusion was original in its conception, superb in its fabrication and unparalleled in the socio-religious plane of Indian life. Rāmānuja's deft handiwork in designing Śrī Vaishṇavism as a chrysalis of integration was prefaced with a long historical development of religion in the Indian subcontinent from the Vedic time downwards, a resume of which is as follows :

More than three millennia ago, when the early Āryan immigrants of North India fanned their way into the Punjab and the Indus Valley, their society was governed by a polity a special feature of which was the worship of gods of the open sky like Indra, Varuṇa and Agni. The early phase of the Āryan religion, which lasted from the Rig Veda to the Brāhmaṇas, consisted in the propitiation of their gods by the performance of Vedic sacrifices by the Purohits (Brahmanical priests).

The second phase dawns with the advent of the Upanishads containing abstruse metaphysics and speaking of the impersonal Supreme Being (Brahman) and God-man relationship.[1] The

Upanishadic period more or less coincides with the Age of
Buddhism and Jainism. These famous heretical sects talked in
a vein unfamiliar to the rituals of the early Vedic period and a
metaphysic of the later Vedic period. When the dryness of the
former and the abstruseness of the latter were attacked by these
heresies and attempted to be replaced by human ethics (understood and appreciated by the masses), the real danger faced the
Brahmanical orthodoxy.

Now occurred an event which turned out to be a turning
point. It was the Gīta. The Gīta professes to be orthodox,
Vedic and Brahmanical. It supports the Varṇāśrama Dharma.[2]
But it surpasses the Vedic and the Upanishadic texts and says
that the 'unknowable' Brahman is easily attainable by Bhakti.
The Gītāchārya calls Himself Vishṇu (magnified beyond Vedic
proportions) and calls upon the Jīvan (mortal) to surrender
himself unto Him. By prescribing Bhakti, the Gīta suggests
that the elaborate rituals of the Vedic period are not necessary
for introduction to and acceptance by God, surpasses the Karma
prescribed in the Sūtras and the Sāstras, and cuts short the
Upanishadic adventure in the realm of search for God. In
other words, the Gīta subordinated the two methods prescribed
for reaching and comprehending God till then *viz* the performance of Karma and intellectual understanding, to the third
viz Bhakti. Thus, by the time of the Gīta, there were three
ways open for a seeker after salvation : (1) the performance of
sacrifices and scrupulous observance of rituals, (2) intellectual
speculation and (3) the performance of normal Varṇāśrama
duties with faith in and love for God.

Of these three, the first was knocked out by the Buddhist
teachings ; the second was always beyond the masses ; and the
third alone was capable of linking the past with the future,
connecting Karma with ñāna providing thereby a synthesis.

10

In this way, the Gīta brought the Vedas and the Upanishads to the level of the masses and surpassed the popularity of the Buddhists ; by greatly altering the texture of the Brahmanical teaching, it gave a new birth to orthodoxy ; by the fascination which the glamour of Bhakti gave to the people, it dealt a blow (which in course of time proved fatal) to Buddhism and Jainism.

In short, the post-Gīta Hinduism stood on a tripod of Karma, ñāna and Bhakti, represented respectively by the Vedas, the Upanishads and the Gīta.

The earliest phase of Bhakti in the Tamil country (in fact, in all India in that advanced form) is to be seen only in the hymns of the Ālvārs, collectively called the Nālāyira Divya Prabandhas. How the Bhakti of Vāsudeva – Krishṇa percolated to the South and influenced the Ālvārs is a mystery. "We have lost the historical link between the early Bhakti movement of the North and the movement in the Tamil country", says K. A. Nilakanta Sastri.[3] But it is just possible that it was an independent development though not perhaps absolutely so. Nevertheless, the two sources of Bhakti tradition—the Sanskrit Gīta and the Tamil Ālvār—were equally respected.

The Bhakti movement become so strong, especially in the Tamil country (led by the Vaishṇava Ālvārs and the Śaiva Nāyanmārs), that by the time Sankara was on the scene, it looked as if the Vedas and the Upanishads were to function as merely backdrops while Bhakti was to be the main operative force in Hinduism. Hence the anxiety of the philosophers to reconcile the three legs of the Hindu tripod. So, Sankara chose the Brahma Sūtras as the common point.[4] Although his was the first major attempt to reconcile these three, Karma suffered at his hands because of the Māya principle and Bhakti was debilitated because his theism was weak. The intellectual path led to strange conclusions resembling the Nirguṇa Brahmam which was next door to the Buddha's non-God.

The Visishṭādvaita philosophy of Rāmānuja, associated with Śrī Vaishṇavism[5], came later than the exposition of Advaita by Saṅkara. But, Rāmānuja's mission was to reconcile the three different traditions into one movement and one thought – in short, into one way of life. It was not impossible for him to prove that a common way of life could be evolved by integrating the teachings of the inerrant Vedas, the philosophy of the Brahma Sūtras, the principles of the prestigious Gīta and the mystic Bhakti of the Ālvārs. Everything seemed to be moving towards a confluence in Rāmānuja who stood as a symbol of unity.

Like every other Hindu, Rāmānuja took his stand on the Vedas. Interpreting the Tatvamasi statement to suit his philosophy, he was really commenting upon the Brahma Sūtras and, at the same time, was actually building up a philosophical edifice on the foundation of Bhakti as enunciated by the Tamil Ālvārs.[6] He spoke of the Ubhaya Vedānta, treating the Sanskrit Vedānta and the Tamil Prabandhas of the Ālvārs as of equal value.[7] This equality, germane to and a speciality of Śrī Vaishṇavism, is a corroboration of the celebrity and the sanctity of the hymns of the Ālvārs acclaimed as the Bhagavat Vishayam. And then, the special Vaishṇava Paribhāsha and the peculian Maṇipravāla style of writing were the natural consequences of Rāmānuja's joint use of Tamil and Sanskrit[8].

Rāmānuja reconciled the different traditions by personally writing the Śrībhāshya (commentary on the Brahma Sūtras) and by giving a strong support to the doctrine of devotion therein. Thus he combined the Vedic teaching and the Ālvār Bhakti. The already existing link between the Gīta and the Ālvārs was a useful bridgehead. And he wrote a commentary

on the Gīta too. Having himself attended to the northern
Sanskrit texts (by commenting on the Brahma Sūtras and
the Gīta), he appointed one of the ablest of his disciples,
Tiruk-kurugaippirān Pillān, to comment authoritatively on
Nammālvār's Tiruvāymoli which is the cream of the Ālvār
Prabandhas. This reconciliation was further cemented by his
open acknowledgment of indebtedness and gratitude to the
Vedic seers and the paurāṇikas by naming two of his infant
contemporaries after Parāśara and Veda Vyāsa[9].

That unity which Rāmānuja emphasised, implanted and
reared in Śrī Vaishṇavism was fostered by him until his last.
To carry forward his mission after his lifetime and to spread
it in all directions, he appointed seventy-four Simhāsanādhi-
patis (apostles). But, what was the final outcome of Rāmānuja's
sustained efforts ? Śrī Vaishṇavism failed to spread throughout
India. It could at the most become one of the multifarious
sects under the banner of Hinduism. Ultimately it split,
manifesting 'a house divided'.

This anticlimactic turn poses a vital question : Were the
forces harmonised by Rāmānuja so disparate that permanent
fusion was impossible ? Historical processes are inevitable in
the sense that later historical events cannot but be influenced
by the earlier events. That is how after Rāmānuja's epic
attempt at reconciliation of Karma, ñāna and Bhakti, with
implied emphasis on Bhakti over the other two, his successors
were not all agreed on this emphasis. Some of his successors
held the view that the śruti of which Rāmānuja spoke did not
exclude Karma as determined by the Dharma Sāstras, the
Grihya Sūtras etc,, while others held that in the face of Bhakti
every other means of salvation, including Karma and ñāna,

would retreat. This was the basis for the Schism in Śrī Vaishṇavism, denoted as the Vaḍakalai—Tenkalai split.

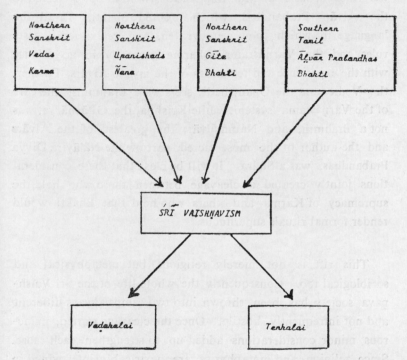

Delineation of the different traditions integrated by Rāmānuja in Śrī Vaishṇavism which eventually split

| Northern Sanskrit Vedas Karma | Northern Sanskrit Upanishads Ñāna | Northern Sanskrit Gīta Bhakti | Southern Tamil Ālvār Prabandhas Bhakti |

ŚRĪ VAISHṆAVISM

Vaḍakalai   Tenkalai

The words 'Vaḍakalai' and 'Tenkalai' literally mean northern culture and southern culture respectively. Inferentially, 'Kalai' means the language which manifests the culture. Naturally the northern language is Sanskrit, known in Tamil as 'Vaḍa Sol' or 'Vaḍa Moli'; and, Tenkalai is Tamil[10].

The Vaḍakalai, or the northern school, appropriately so called because the Vedas were born in the North. Sanskrit was the northern tongue for the Tamils, and the Dharma Sāstras and the Grihya Sūtras were written by the northern seers. The Tenkalai, or the southern school, also appropriately thus

called because the Ālvārs were born in the South and Tamil
is the southern language. The Vaḍakalai held that the Vedas
and their ancillary texts in which Karma held a dominant
place, Sanskrit the language in which the Vedas were written,
and Manu and other Dharma Sāstras which rigidly laid down
the rules of caste and its implications were to be preferred to
the Ālvān Prabandhas which exalted Bhakti, Tamil the
language in which they were written, and relaxation of caste
rules and the Varṇāśrama Dharma generally in accordance
with the experience and teachings of the mystic Ālvārs, Further,
the Vedic and the Upanishadic seers were Brahmins – the core
of the Varṇāśrama system, while Krishṇa, the Gītāchārya, was
not a Brahmin, and Nammālvār, the greatest of the Ālvārs
and the author of the most sacred part of the Nālāyira Divya
Prabandhas, was a Sūdra. It will be clear that these considerations jointly created a cleavage between those who held the
supremacy of Karma and others who held that Bhakti would
render formal rituals superfluous.

This rift is not merely religious but metaphysical and
sociological too. Consequently the whole life of the Śrī Vaishṇava society has been thrown into two camps always different
and not infrequently hostile. Once the cleavage started, numerous minor considerations added up to strengthen each cause.
Since religion and metaphysics are inextricably intertwined in
Hindu thought, the differences were based on religio-philoso-
phical considerations to begin with but later were extended to
the purely social field[11].

'Release' on the basis of complete devotion was predicated
by Rāmānuja's system which by implication suggests social
equality by total removal of caste distinctions. This egalitarian
trend is a signal contribution to Hindu sociology. Did it bring
about "social integration"? There are certain well-known

instances of Rāmānuja and some of his immediate associates breaking the rules of caste.[12] However, except within a very short range of close disciples and relatives of Rāmānuja this reformation seems to have had little effect. That his reformation has not met with permanent success does not disprove Rāmānuja's sincerity of efforts but only proves the extraordinary vitality of the Varṇāśrama system. Rāmānuja's efforts to uplift the 'lower' castes succeeded in the strictly religious sphere but failed in the purely social sphere.

REFERENCES

1. The language and the contents of the Upanishadic teachings are so obviously different from those of the Vedas that it seems to be incredible that the Upanishads merely repeat what already has been said in the Vedas. The historian therefore will consider the Upanishadic teachings to a later point in the evolution of the Brahmanical religion from the Vedic time downwards.

2. In its supreme call for everyone to do his duty, the Gīta means the Varṇāśrama regulations by the duty.

3. Development of Religion in South India, P. 39.

4. The Brahma Sūtras were but a peg on which these philosophers hung their own ideas. Max Mueller states that "Saṅkara and Rāmānuja pay often less regard to the literal sense of the words and to tradition than to their desire of forcing Bādarāyana to bear testimony to the truth of their own philosophical theories" (Six Systems of Indian Philosophy, P. 191).

5. Both in Vaishṇavism and in the Visishṭādvaita metaphysics, there are many forms. The Śrī Sampradāya (Śrī Vaishṇavism) in the school of Rāmānuja and its philosophy is Visishṭādvaita. Mādhva (Ananda Tīrta) founded the Brahma Sampradāya and its philosophy is Dvaita (Dualism). Vishṇuswāmi and Vallabha founded the Rudra Sampradāya, and Nimbārka the Sanaka Sampradāya. The last two have the Suddhādvaita and the Dvaitādvaita as their philosophies. Chaitanya's system is known as the Chaitanya Sampradāya. It adopts Achintya Bhedābheda and is considered to be a branch of Mādhvaism. Visishṭādvaita itself is not necessarily Vaishṇavite. It can be Śaiva Visishṭādvaita or Vaishṇava Visishṭādvaita. The Śaiva Visishṭādvaita is the system enunciated in the Śrīkanṭha Bhāshya by Śrīkanṭha Śivāchārya. The only difference between the two is that Śrīkanṭha substituted Śiva for Rāmānuja's Vishṇu.

6. The essential contribution of Rāmānuja to Indian thought was to have developed a coherent philosophical basis for the doctrine of devotion to God based on the hymns of the Alvārs in sharp contradistinction to Saṅkara's Advaita.

7. P. N. Srinivasachari, Mystics and Mysticism, P. 199. According to M. Monier Williams, Sanskrit literature "is the only key to a correct knowledge of the opinions and practices of the Hindu people" (Indian Wisdom, Introduction, P. xv). This is clearly not true at least so far as the Śrī Vaishṇavas are concerned because their opinions and practices are governed equally by the Alvār Tamil Prabandhas.

8. *Vide* N. Jagadeesan, Śrī Vaishṇavite Written and Spoken Tamil, Journal of Kerala Studies, Vol. I, pp. 159 ff.

9. The Śrī Vaishṇava tradition relates the fascinating story of the triple message of the three closed fingers of Alavandār (Yāmunāchārya) to Rāmānuja as providing the necessary motivation for the latter's religious activities. Rāmānuja had always wished for meeting and becoming a disciple of Alavandār. So, he left for Śrīraṅgam. But, by the time he reached Śrīraṅgam, Alavandār passed away. He noticed the three closed fingers of the deceased Alavandār and understood their triple message. He then set about the mission of carrying out Alavandār's behests. Accordingly he wrote the Śrībhāshya (commentary on the Brahma Sūtras), made Tirukkurugaippirān Pillān write the Aṟāyirappaḍi (a commentary of six thousand granthas on Nammālvār's Tiruvāymoli) and named the two sons of Kūrattālvān after the ancient seers Parāśara and Veda Vyāsa. The story seems to be apocryphal to one who is not emotionally involved in the religion ; and, it merely represents Rāmānuja's anxiety to channelise in one large stream what had flowed through various tributaries and provide a common basis for the Śrī Vaishṇava social and religious life.

10. The words 'Vaḍakalai' and 'Tenkalai' are mentioned in the songs of Tirumaṅgai Alvār, but they refer only to Sanskrit and Tamil languages and some early inscriptions also refer to 'Vaḍakalārya' and 'Tenkalārya' meaning Sanskrit and Tamil respectively, but they do not ever distantly mean the shismatic difference.

11. V. Rangacharya says that "it is evidently after these doctrinal and ritualistic differences became rigid and stereotyped that social differences came into existence". (The Successors of Rāmānuja and the Growth of Sectarianism among the Śrī Vaishṇavas, Journal of Bombay Branch of Royal Asiatic Society, Vol. XXIV, p. 1331).

12. Pāmānuja attained immense reputation for having pronounced in the hearing of a multi-communal crowd and from the top of the Tirukkoṭṭiyūr Perumāl temple the Praṇava. He explained his courage by saying that he would prefer to be consigned to hell himself if he could secure the salvation of so many others. He permitted the Pañchamas, whom he designated the Tirukkulattor (auspicious community), to enter the Melkote temple in Mysore. He fed Tirukkachchi Nambi, a saintly non-Brahmin, in his house as if he were a Brahmin. He used to return home leaning on Pillai Uṛaṅgā Villi Dāśar, his non-Brahmin disciple, after bathing in the Kāviri. Peria Nambi, who performed the Pañcha Samskāras (initiation) to Rāmānuja, is renowned for having performed the funeral rites to Māraneri Nambi, a Chaturtta, braving the orthodox opposition. Similar is the ease of Tirumalai Nallān Chakravartti, who cremated a Chaṇḍāla's dead-body which came floating in the river near Kāñchipuram. The experiences of Peria Nambi and Tirumalai Nallān Chakravartti shaw the social attitude of the Brahmins in those days and that exceptional men had dared to defy orthodox public opinion even then.

NATIONAL INTEGRATION IN INDIAN HISTORY AS REVEALED THROUGH BHARATI'S WRITINGS
—A Case Study Of Select Aspects.

Joseph Divien
Lecturer in History I. C. C. & C. E.,
Madurai Kamaraj University.
Madurai—625 021.

In this paper an attempt has been made to examine the concept of national integration. The first part of the paper purports to give an over-all view of the Indian historical writers' attitude towards national unity and solidarity.

In the second part of the paper, the various disruptive elements of national integration such as caste, religion, language, communal feelings and regional bias have been elaborately dealt with. It also discusses the various efforts made by the Indians to overcome them. Special reference has been made about poet Bharati's writings. For, Bharati believes that we are all citizens of the Indian soil—the soil which spoke the language of fruits, flowers and trees and not Marathi, Punjabi, Bengali or Tamil. Bharati happens to be one among the pioneers to see India as a whole—India the Mother. Bharati's writings reflect that he is above the barriers of caste and communal feelings. He foresees clearly that national integration is possible only by negating all differences of caste, creed, religion, language, regional and sectarian feelings.

In this paper an attempt has been made to examine the concept of national integration. It means the realisation of the basic unity of the country ; it implies doing away with inter-state, inter-linguistic, inter-religious and inter-cultural prejudices and of fostering a spirit of tolerance, respect and appreciation of the view point of those belonging to other states or linguistic, religious and cultural groupings. Even-though the central theme has been to expouse the concept as expounded by the national poet, C. Subramania Bharati, yet it may not be out of place here, to give as clear a picture as humbly possible of India's national unity as depicted by the historical writers.

Indian historians did not attach much importance to politi-cal unity, but to cultural unity, because India during the pre-British period had never been a single political expression, except during a few periods, for example, undar Mauryas and Guptas. Indian unity is largely the creation of the British rule, a by-product of the Pax-Britannica. Writers like Radha Kumud Mookerji, K. M. Panikkar, Tarachand etc. have all contributed to the growth of national sentiments.

Still there is lacuna. Because these writers, still, could have paid little more attention to the problems of national integra-tion, because their writings did not anticipate many problems of integration, which the country is facing today. But their contribution is much more significant and praiseworthy than what they had by chance omitted to mention. Apart from these distinguished historians there are chauvinistic historians like RL. Oak. The latter's concept is nothing but "India for the Hindus". This kind of regional and chauvinistic attitude is bound to weaken the basis of national integration. So long as these 'isms' are not removed from the minds of our contry-men, India is always open to danger. In other words history may repeat itself and India may be parcelled into several antagonistic states.

Though we have not had serious breaches of peace in the recent past, the memories of the border disputes between some southern states and the regional clashes that followed them bring back a tinge of uneasiness, uneasiness about the future of the country. It is the duty of the historical writers that they should take care to ensure that history does not become a sphere of petty politicking or a hot-bed for intrigues by communal or ideological zealots.

Again, the Marxist interpretation of history. The Marxist historians do have an integrated and even an international outlook. But their area of study is too narrow, biased and they do not always join the main stream of the historical writings on national integration. For instance, the influence of the Marxist or Leftist approach to the writing of history has been so profound that the 'Events of 1857' have been described as the 'Peasant Revolt'. Karl Marx was wrong in labelling it so for the rural people never took a serious part in the incident.

One more factor that has marred the progress of history is racial feeling which must be abhorred. As will and Ariel Durant rightly point out, "It is not the race that produces the civilization ; on the other hand it is the civilization that makes the race"[1]. Hence, the history of India has to be written from Kanyakumari to Kashmir as one, instead of quite unnecessarily dabbling over the Aryan–Dravidian problem. A critical analysis regarding the origin of the race is indeed essential while writing the history of India Coherently, but too much emphasis can be considered redudant.

Yet another drawback which one quite often comes across in Indian historical writings is the hero-worship. In the words of K. K. Munshi, "Hindus looked up to Rana Pratap and Shivaji as their heroes ; the Muslims admired Mohamed Ghazni and Aurangazeb ; in this antagonishic outlook lay the seek of

Pakistan"[2]. The division of Hindustan into India and Pakistan was the high price paid by the Indians for their failure to bring about Hindu—Muslim unity. How can Indians form one nation when they cannot even have common national heroes ? A nation can be evolved by creating identical or similar ideals for all sections, classes and communities and by inspiring equal pride in them for real and imaginery past deeds, achievements and heroes of the country.

One is able to derive a lesson from the Time capsule buried at the entrance of the Red Fort on the Independence Day in 1973. The Capsule contains a 10,000 word document purporting to give an account of the happenings in India from 1947 to 1972. "The then Union Minister Dr. P. C. Chunder told the Lok Sabha on April 10, 1974, "authenticity and accuracy are a grave casuality in the document."[3]

Miss Manibhen Patel, daughter of Sardar Patel, dismissed as far back as December 27, 1973, the document as a "father and daughter business intended to glorify Jawaharlal Nehru and Mrs. Indira Gandhi"[4]. So long as pride and prejudice dominate historical writings, there is no possibility for an integrated out-look in the works.

National integration depends on certain fundamental factors involving all Indians and not one which revolves around a few heroes worshipped by some of these historians. Heroes do shape national sentiments but too much hero-worship undermines the foundations of such sentiments. Moreover, history deals not only with the individuals, but also with the society. There are some historical writings on some heroes who have contributed to the growth of national unity and solidarity. Poet Bharati is one hero, who at the initial stage shaped our patriotism and national integration. Earlier, I spoke that there must not be too much of hero-worship. My paper, hence while mirroring the significant contribution of Bharati towards national unity, is not at the same time attempting to magnify the same as one singular achievement of the national bard.

The role of history in shaping national unity cannot be under-estimated. But history can be rised also to present a distorted view of the past and as a vehicle of propaganda. As Nietzsche rightly puts it, "History can be inspirer of rashness and fanaticism".[5] Hence the historical writers must be alert and cautious and should make use of 'Clio the Muse' to present facts without passion or prejudice which alone would make history scientific. The historical writers with scientific temperament must avoid Krishna basin bias or Ganges Valley bias and instead must have, like Bharati, a national outlook embracing the whole of India.

C. Subramania Bharati (1882-1921) popularly known as Bharati[6] was the first Tamil poet to propagate the concept of integration among the Indians living in different parts of the country[7]. He insists that national integration is basic to the survival of our society. He warns his countrymen to transcend the disruptive forces of casteism, communalism, regionalism, linguistic chauvinism and sessionism and forge not merely a political unity but the unity of the minds and the hearts of all people living in India. He aroused national consciousness among his countrymen through his revolutionary writings. His was indeed a timely message in the context of our present day problems which poses a threat to our hardwon independenc. This is evinced from his immortal song, "she has thirty crores of faces, but her heart is one ; she speaks eighteen languages, yet her mind is one"[8].

It is firmly believed that one among the factors that retards India's progress is caste system which has been labelled as the curse on Indian national life. For petty political gains, the leaders of the country invoke casteism and bank, upon communal prejudices of the illiterate electorate. In many cases, party tickets are alloted, not on the merits of the candidates, but on the basis of his influence with members of his caste or community." Narrow communalism is often rampart in India. In the first popular cabinet in Mysore headed by K. C. Reddy, not only were the ministers chosen on a caste basis, but each had a secretary from his own sub-sub-sub caste"[9]. It has been rightly remarked that caste considerations have coloured the very texture of Indian politics. It used to be a slogan that no votes of the Vanniyar caste were to be cast, in favour of others. As Joseph Chailley very rightly puts it, "Caste bars out altruism, unity and patriotism and that its rules render social life and progress impossible".[10]

The greatest evil of caste system is untouchability. It is untouchability with all its subtle forms that separates the Indians from one another and makes life itself unlovely and difficult to live. This has been very aptly summarised by James Forbes thus : "The pooleahs are not permitted to breathe the same air with other castes, nor to travel on the public road—yet debased and oppressed as the pooleahs are, there exists a caste called parians, still more object and wretched. If a pooleah by an accident touches a Pariar, he must perform a variety of ceremonies and go through many ablutions before he can be cleansed from the impurity".[11]

To-day all our activities are caste-centred. This is perhaps the only bitter fruit that our Tree of Independence has borne since 1947. Long before Gandhiji appeared on the scene, Bharati sang about the liberation of untouchables with gusto. As Eugene

F. Irshick rightly points out, "Bharati was a smartha Brahman, but he was extremely liberal in his views and never hesitated to criticise the maintenance of a caste system which had out lasted its usefulness and tended to produce only inequality and bitterness."[12] Specifying the prominence of untouchable and other oppressed castes, Bharati Sings of their deliverance thus. : "The Pariahs, pooleahs, paravas, Kuravas, Maravas and others should enjoy the succulent fruits of the hard-won freedom".[13]

Bharati's vision of an united India is devoid of religious and caste differences, a republic in which the principle of equality will be finally realised. To quote, "all are of the same caste ; all are Indian people ; all of the same tribe, weight and value ; all are kings of this country"[14]. Not merely caste oppression, the very system of caste earns his ire. He asserts that there is absolutely" no caste and it is indelible to talk of high and low castes"[15]. The only superiority he recognises is that which is based on "intellectual and moral acquisitions"[16]. Like Bharati, Rowe also feels the same. In his book, '*Everyday Life in India*', the latter writes thus ; "The very essense of caste lies in the degradation of others"[17].

Bharati never hesitated to move with the Harijans and with people of other castes. As early as 1907, Bharati imagined that the Pallas, a Harijan Caste, singing a Pallu (a kind of folk song) in celebration of the achievement of political and social liberation. Affirming that the days are gone when the Brahmin was revered for his birth, the Pallu continues : "Freedom is the talk everywhere ; equality is ensured for one and all. Let us blow the conch of truimph and broadcast this to the whole world"[18].

The national poet's dream of a casteless society is yet to become a reality. In this context, let us look into the

11

observation made by V. B. Kulkarni in the Indian Express of August 22, 1973 ; "not a day passes without reports about the persecution of Harijans including physical assaults, murder, looting and burning of their property"[19].

Bharati visualised a society above its class that will refuse to demean itself into visions of caste, that will respect the tiller and toiler, a society where virtue shall be strength and earnest endeavour seek to promote the abiding good.

No doubt, there are difficulties in eradicating caste from our social organisation. As M. N. Srinivas very rightly puts it "caste is an institution of prodigious strength and it will take a lot of beating before it will die. Buta realization of this difficulty should not prevent us from taking all possible steps to preare the ground for the disintegration and final collapse of the institution of caste"[20].

Regionalism is another disintegrating force in our country. More than a majority of the people living in the South belong to the Dravidian race whereas the people living in the North belong to the Aryan. Although, there has been a great intermixture resulting in the disappearance of pure racial characteristics, yet there is a feeling of superiority among the people, belonging to the Dravidian race. Bharati advises his countrymen that there is absolutely no difference as Aryans and Dravidians. He points out that in spite of many regional differences, there is a common thread running in our ways of living which is unique to our country.

Religion, more than any other factor can play a vital role in strengthening the feelings of oneness among the Indians. It can also supress those narrow prejudices which tend to divide them into exclusive cells. But, unfortunately in our country, religion has been used atleast for some decades now, not for constructive purposes, but for raising artificial barriers between the various religious groups, with the result that they view each other with suspicion, distrust and hostility. In other words, religion has been often used as an instrument to serve political ends.

National integration means first and foremost inter-religious amity, especially Hindu-Muslim unity. Bharati could champion this cause with a sense of dedication because he was entirely free from religious sectarianism. He respected other faiths while revering his own. In the words of S. Ramakrishnan, "He lived up to the Rig Vedic Maxim, *Ekam Sat, Viprābahutā Vadanti* (Truth is one though sages call it by several names."[21])

Bharati warns that all religious factions are a product of the narrow mentality of adhering to one particular form of God, and of denying all others and propagates the meeting of all religions. "The Brahmin saluting the fire, the Muslim turning towards Mecca while praying and the Christians bowing to the Cross are only affirming God's omnipresence. Why, then, the meaningless division between religion and religion"[22]

Bharati says that there are many religions in this world. But their meaning is the same ; sense is only one. In this context, he points out that, "Religion is the one thing where confirmity is more dangerous than in any other. But in the service of the Motherland, we are all one creed and one religion, one caste and one creed, one aim and one ideal.[23].

One's language has an emotional appeal which few other things can equal. The issue of language has been a perennial problem to Indian national leaders. It led to ugly demonstrations involving repressive action in Assam in 1961 and in Madras in 1965[24]. In the words of Jawaherlal Nehru, "One of the most shameful episodes that deserve our bitterest condemnation has been enacted in Assam where in the name of·language, innocent people had been butchered and widespread demonstration wrought. If India is to remain a united democratic state, wedded to the highest concept of socialism, we have to do away, completely, with narrow and illogical linguistic theory[25]. Thus linguistic chauvinism began to gain more strength and it manifested itself in almost every state. In Punjab, it assumed the form of an organisation for a Punjabi-speaking state[26].

In Bihar, it showed up indiscrimination against the linguistic minority of Bengalis. These disturbances in many parts of the country in recent years have tarnished the fair name of India before the eyes of the world. This kind of destruction of life and property could have been very well avoided, if the Indians had faith and belief in national integration.

Long long ago, Bharati advised his countryment, that they need not attach undue importance to a particular language, instead they work for the consolidation of an integrated India. National integration in a country as diverse as ours is possible only by mutual respect for each other's language. Though Bharati says that Tamil is the most beautiful and supreme language like Telugu, which for example, he eulogises as a "Sweet Telugu language"[27].

Bharati wants the various language speaking people of India to have a common understanding so as to unify the Country. This has been aptly put forth by the national poet in the following words : "Singing songs in sweet Telugu, with lovely girls of Kerala, we'll row our boats and rollick on the soft moon light in the river Sindhu. Let us exchange the wheat grown on the banks of the Ganga for the tender betal leaves on the banks of the Cauveri"[28]. It is hoped that national integration is not going to be jeopardised by language differences.

Today, inter-river disputes between some states are there and this should be put an end to.[29] There must be mutual understanding between the states, so as to strengthen the unity of the country. Being a true national poet, Bharati firmly holds that Nature's gift such as rivers are common to all people to make use of. This is explicit from his song : "With the excess of water that flows in Bengal, let us raise crops in the mid-lands."[30] Thus, Bharati, in his poem after poem, celebrated this concept, this living reality of an integrated India. As V. Sachithanandan points out, "The poet's imagination spans India from east to west and from south to north and brings together whatever is between them.[31] Jawaharlal Nehru in his magnum opus, "The Discovery of India" writes, "The Discovery of India—what I have discovered" ?...Today she is our hundred million separate individual men and women, each differing from the other, each living in a private universe of thought and feeling—yet something has bound them together and binds them still. India is a geographical and economic entity, a cultural unity amidst diversity, a bundle of contradictions held together by strong invisible threads.[32]

Like Karl Marx, the greatest exponent of socialism, Bharati believed in the concept of a classless society. In his essay, "The Coming Age" (May 21, 1915), Bharati warns his countrymen that, "so long as the principle of competition holds sway over the structure of human associations, men are bound to behave worse than brutes in their economic relations at any rate."[33]   Bharati makes a brief explanation of the cause of the French Revolution : "There was a widespread demand that equal justice should be meted out to both rich and the poor and law should make no discriminations on the basis of wealth".[34] The national poet insists that discriminations of all type should be dispensed with and all men should be treated as equals.

To-day, the threat to India's unity has come mostly from internal forces. The forces of subversion from within are identified as regionalism, communalism, linguistic chauvinism and sessionism. The slogans of "Greater Andhra", 'Samyukta Maharashtra' or 'Punjabi Subha' have had their own disintegrating effect on the growth of Indian nationalism. The result is that national solidarity has received a setback in recent years. The simple lesson that the Indian have to learn from the past is that they have to develop a sense of oneness which Bharati puts it thus : "A nation's glory depends not on its natural wealth, but on the connected efforts of its people"[35]. Thus if the Indian people can shed off the silly notions such as casteism, communalism, linguistic chauvinism, seasionism and feel that they all belong to one Motherland (Bharath) and are all children of the same soil, this may be the greatest tribute they can pay to the greatest poet of all times, who like Bankim Chandra is also of the view that, 'Indians are weak not because of any inherent frailty, but because they have no sense of unity or national pride ; and there can be no sense of unity interpreted by Indian historians."[36]

REFERENCES

1. Will and Ariel Durant, *The Lessons of History*, Simon and Schuster, New York, 1968 p. 18.

2. K M Munshi, *Warnings of History*, Bharatiya Vidya Bhavan, Bombay, 1963 p. 8.

3. V B Kulkarni, *History and National Unity*' Indian Express, 10 April, 1974.

4. Ibid Indian Express, 10 April, 1974.

5. Quoted in E. H. CARR, *What is History*, Penguin Books Ltd., England, 1964 p. 27.

6. Subramanian was the name given by his parents. The title "Bharati" meaning a learned and talented person, was conferred upon him by the Tamil scholars of the court of Ettayapuram in recognition of his poetic talents.

7. But Kamil Zvelebil seems to think otherwise—"Bharati, let us have the courage to admit it, does not belong to the greatest. He is not a Vyasa, nor a Valmiki, nor a Kampan, not even a Tagore."
   Kamil zvelebil, *The Smile of Murugan* (E. J. Brill, Leiden, Netherlands, 1973, p. 286—87).

8. Kavitaikal (collected poems of Bharati) (Aruna pattippakam, Madurai, 1960) p. 25.

"முப்பது கோடி முகமுடையாள் உயிர்
மொய்ம்புற வொன்றுடையாள் – இவன்
செப்புமொழி பதினெட்டுடையாள் எனிற்
சிந்தனை ஒன்றுடையாள்".

9. K. K. Pillay, *Studies in the History of India with special Reference to Tamil Nadu*, (A publication of the Author, Madras. 1979) p. 403.

10. K K Pillay, op cit. p. 401.

11. Quoted in Percifal Griffths, *Modern India—A Brief History*, (Jaico Publishing House, Bombay, 1962) p. 19.

12. Eugene F Ivshick.—*Politics and Social Conflict in South India, The Non-Brhmin Movement and Tamil separatism 1916-1929* (University of California Press Ltd, London, 1969) pp. 286—287.

13. Kavitaikal, p. 257.

    "பறையருக்கும் இங்கு தீயா புணையருக்கும்
                        விடுதலை; பரவரோடு
    குறவருக்கும் மறவருக்கும் விடுதலை"

14. Kavitaikal, p. 46.

    "எல்லாரும் ஓர்குலம் எல்லாரும் ஒரினம்
    எல்லாரும் இந்திய மக்கள்
    எல்லாரும் ஓர் நிறை எல்லாரும் ஓர்விலை
    எல்லாரும் இந்நாட்டு மன்னர்".

15. Kavitaikal, p. 169.

    "சாதிகள் இல்லையடி பாப்பா! குலத் தாழ்ச்சி
    உயர்ச்சி சொல்லல் பாவம்"

16. Kavitaikal, p. 21.

    "நீதி நெறியினின்ற பிறர்க்குதவும்
    நன்மையவர் மேலவர்கள், கீழவர் மற்றோர்".

17. Quoted by K K Pillay, op. cit. p. 381.
18. S. Ramakrishnan,—*Bharati—Patriot, Poet, Prophet* (New Century Book House Private Ltd, Madras 1982) p. 50.
19. Quoted by K. K. Pillay, Op. Cit. p. 381.
20. Quoted by K. K. Pillay, Op. Cit. p. 404.
21. S. Ramakrishnan Op. Cit ; p. 43.
22. Prema Nanda Kumar—*Bharati* (Sahitya Akademi, New Delhi 1978, p. 48).
23. C Subramania Bharati—"*Agni and other poems and Translations and Essays and other Prose Fragments*", (A Natarajan) Madras, 1980, p. 89.
24. In Madras, the year 1965, saw the outbreak of anti-Hindi agitation and the debacle of the congress party. The Dravida Munnetra Kazhakam, a regional party came to power.
25. B. M. Banerjee—Choicest Essays (Khanna Brothers, Ambalacantt, 1967, p. 69.

26. The problem in Punjabi is yet to be solved. The incidents that took place in the Golden Temple at Amritsar bears ample testimony to this fact.

27. Kavitaikal. p. 32.

" சுந்தரத் தெலுங்கினில் பாட்டிசைத்து "

28. Ibid. p. 82

" சிந்து நதியின் மீசை நிலவினிலே
சேர நன்னட்டினாம் பெங்கட்டனே
சுந்தரத் தெலுங்கினில் பாட்டிசைத்தத்
தோளிகளோட்டி விளையாடி வருவோம்
கங்கை நதிப்புறத்தக் கோதுமைப் பண்டம்
காவிரி வெற்றிலைக்கு மாறு கொள்ளுவோம் ".

29. In recent times, one has witnessed disputes between Tamil Nadu and Andhra, Tamil Nadu and Karnataka over the sharing of river waters.

30. Kavitaikal, p. 31.

" வங்கத்தில் ஓடிவரும் நீரின் மிகையால்
வையத்து நாடுகளில் பயிர் செய்குவோம் ".

31. V. Sachithanandan,—*The Impact of Western Thought on Bharat* (Annamalai University Publication, Annamalai Nagar 1970) p. 80.

32. Nehru 'J—*The Discovery of India* (The Signet Press, Calcutta, 1946) p. 28.

33. C. Subramania Bharati op. Cit p. 98.

34. V. Sachithanandan Op. Cit. p. 131.

35. R. A. Padmanabhan—*Chitira Bharati*—Amutha Nilayam Madras 1957, p. 19.

36. V. C. P. Chaudhary—'*Indian Historiography as the tool of Ruling Class Interest—A general survey from Canning to Moraji Desai*', (Proceedings of the Jourteenth Session, Indian History Congress, Summit Sarkar New Delhi, p. 698).

INTEGRATION IN ANCIENT INDIA (Upto 1206)
A Myth or Reality ?

Dr. V. Balambal
Reader in History, University of Madras

Not even a single text book on Indian History fails to mention that there is unity in diversity in India. Regarding the physical features of India, it has lofty mountains, flat plains and fertile river valleys.

There are perennial rivers and deserts where not even a single blade of grass grows : Every kind of climate exists in India—the scorching heat of Rajasthan desert ; the arctic cold of snowy heights of the Himalayan ranges, dry rocky table land of the Deccan. Moist tropical luxuriance of Bengal and Malabar, etc.

Regarding rainfall, India enjoys equally wide range. It has the world's highest record of rainfall, while the tracts of land in Rajasthan are noted for scanty rainfall. Amazing variety of latitudes and altitudes, temperature and moisture produces a corresponding variety in flora and fauna. India possesses most of the types of flora and fauna known to natural sciences. The physical diversity led to the growth of different kinds of animals and vegetables.

There are many races of people in India—the jungle tribes, the Aryans, Dravidians, Greeks, Sakas, Kushans, Huns, Mongolians, Arabs, Turks, Tartars, Afghans, etc. Today India has the primitive tribesmen as well as the polished inhabitants of cities.

Regarding languages, there are 14 main languages and each has its own literature. There are more than 150 dialects spoken in India. India is the birthplace of many religions like Hinduism, Jainism and Buddhism. Indians have accepted the foreign religions such as Islam, Christianity and zoroastrianism, etc. There are many sub-divisions in these religions too.

There are differences in the social status, habits, dress and diet of the Indians.

All these differences have made it difficult to establish an all India empire. There was no political unity in Ancient India. It was never ruled by a single ruler. India was disintegrated into various chieftaincies.

After the advent of the Aryans and the establishment of 16 kingdoms in North India too, there was no political unity among Indians. Each ruler was trying to establish his suzereignty over others and nobody bothered about integration. Even after conquests, the feeling of difference was intense in the minds of both the conqueror and the conquered.

Many kingdoms and dynasties flourished from time to time. The nature of the Governments differed. Many were monarchies, some republics and few dictatorships. Most of them were from time to time brought under the subjection and integrated into an extensive empire by powerful rulers like Chandragupta, Maurya, Asoka, Samudragupta, Harsha, Pulakesin II, Rajaraja I, Rajendra I and Vikramaditya VI. But none of these rulers exercised their sway over the whole of India. Even though the above mentioned emperors ruled somewhat bigger regions, and tried to establish uniformity in their administration, it was not possible for them to buildup a

United India. When internal weakness and disorder or foreign invasions or both shattered their empires, India relapsed again into political disunity. These were periods of anarchy, misuse and darkness.

India has been mostly governed by her local provincial dynastics. Infact, India had never enjoyed supreme political unity till 1947. Politically, a popular national feeling was almost absent. Calamity of a neighbouring province did not rouse much sympathy and support in the people of another province. They had no urge to unite even in the face of common enemy or danger. It fostered growth of varieties of Indian culture and civilization, but retarded also seriously the political progress of the country and hindered India from becoming a nation. When Cyrus, Darius and Xerxes invaded India the rulers of the north could not defeat them. The invasion of Alexander was resisted only by Porus while Ambi surrendered to him. Had the rulers of North India united against the Persians and the Greek invader, further invasions of the foreigners could have been easily averted.

The important dynasties which ruled parts of India in ancient times were the Sisunakas, Nandas, Mauryas, Sungas, Kanvas, Satavahanas, Guptas, Mankaris, Vardhanas, Chalukyas of Vatapi and Kalyani, Rashtrakutas, Yadavas, Kakatiyas, Silaharas, Kadambas, Gangas, Pallavas, Cholas, Cheras, Pandyas and the Hoysalas. The foreigners who made inroads into India were the Persians, Greeks, Sakas, Pahlavas, Kushans, Huns etc. Did any one of these rulers integrate India politically ? Some of the scholars opine that an All India Empire was first accomplished during the Maurya and Sunga period to a great extent. This view is to be questioned. Chandragupta Maurya, with great hardship and assistance of Chanakya founded the Maurya dynasty in the North. Though nothing is specifically known about his son and successor Bindusara, the boundary of the Mauryas extended farther south during the reign of Asoka. But it is very clear that Asoka fought only one battle—the Kalinga battle—in his life time. Hence the southern conquests were made by Bindusara only. But still the Chera, Chola, Pandyas and Satyaputras were ruling in the south as contemporaries of Asoka is known from his Rock Edicts. In the north also some regions were not under the control of the Mauryas. Hence political integration was a myth during the Maurya period. Anyhow, it cannot be denied that the Mauryas were the first ones to establish a bigger empire in India, if not an All India Empire.

During the Sangam age, the Tamil country was under the control of the Chera, Chola, Pandyas and many other chiefs. There was constant warfare among these rulers. Though some Sangam works refer to the fact that Imayavaramban Nadunchera-latan and few others had marched as far as the Himalayas and imprinted their marks, it is certain that they had not consolidated their victories. There was always enmity between the rulers of the north and south and it was referred to in many literary works and epigraphs.

Samudragupta's Allahabad inscription gives a detailed account of his victories in the North and South. But it is clearly stated that the southern conquests were never consoli-dated by him. Vindhya and Satpura continued to be the strong barriers between the north and South. The north western part of India was occupied by foreigners and tribal people. Unification could not be dreamt of.

In South India, Pulakesin II, the Western Chalukya ruler conquered Harsha of Kanouj on the banks of Narmada and Mahendrapallava of Kanchi. But he had not occupied the regions beyond Narmada and he was avenged by Nara-simha Pallava, the son and successor of Mahendra I. As there were strong regional and dynastic feelings, it was not easy for the people of the conquered regions to regard the conquerors.

The Rashtrakutas who succeeded the Chalukyas fought constantly with their neighbouring rulers. There was triangular struggle for the possession of Ganga-Jamuna Doab and the lands adjoining among the Prathiharas, Palas of Bengal and Rashtrakutas of Malked. The Rashtrakuta rulers Dhruva, Govinda III and Indra III crossed the Narmada and waged successful battles with the Prathiharas and the Palas but they had to return to their country to look into the local problems.

There were mere expeditions and conquests to show their valour but no ruler was capable of establishing a unified and integrated empire. Similarly Krishna III defeated the Cholas and went as far as Rameswaram but soon after his return, the Pandyas and the Cholas re-established their power in their res-pective territories. As each part of India was under the control of one particular dynasty or chieftain, integration was not at all possible.

Rajaraja I, the Chola ruler conquered the Cheras, Pandyas, Gangas, Nolambas, Vaidumbas, a part of Ceylon, Vengi, and 12000 islands of the sea. But there is no mention of his northern conquests. His notable son and successor, Rajendra I, enriched the Chola power by conquering Gangetic region, Kadaram, Sriviyaya, Ilamuridesam, Manakkavaram and other regions. Again it is a great controversy whether the consolidated his northern and foreign conquests. The feeling of one nation was totally absent.

The ideal of great rulers of India in various ages has been to become 'Chakravarti' or to rule the whole country. But in reality they merely assumed the title without conquering or consolidating or ruling the whole country. For instance most of the rulers had high sounding titles like Chakravarti, Trilokyamalla, Tribhuvanachakravarti, Ekrat or Samrat, when they were not even the rulers of three districts. Hence the remarks of some learned scholars that Chandragupta Maurya, Asoka and Samudra Gupta established their power over the whole of India could not be accepted as a historical fact. Assuming titles and performing Yagas alone did not show their conquests.

It is very sad to note that even from time immemorial, regionalism has been playing an important role in social life. Specific region was ruled by a particular dynasty and the ruler and people of that region identified themselves with that area. This has led to serious warfare. Though caste differences were not very much felt during the early Vedic period and the Sangam age, later they have become the curse on the Indian Society. In such circumstances, integration is a misnomer. The plight of the Chandalas and the untouchables was pitiable and horrible.

There were fundamental differences in their food habits, shelter, dress etc. based on the regional and climatic conditions. Regarding their languages, though Prakrit, Pali, Sanskrit and Tamil were used in literary fields, various dialects were used in different parts of the country. In course of time, there grew many regional languages and the rulers of those regions patronised the respective languages (e. g.) Chalukas – Kannada : Eastern Chalukays—Telugu ; Cholas—Tamil ; Palas and senas —Bengali. This widened the gap and integration and unity were unachievable ends.

Inspite of the absence of political and social integration in ancient times, it is interesting to note that there is religious and cultural unity in India. There is an undercurrent of religious unity among the various religious sects in India. All the sects and creeds believe in the majesty of the spiritual life. Worship of Siva, Vishnu, Subramanya though under different names, is widespread in the North as in the South. There are temples for Siva, Vishnu, Subramanya, Ganesa, Kali, Durga, etc. all over the country. Ramayana and Mahabharata are known to Indians. The cow, the Vedas, the Puranas and other scriptures are respected equally throughout the country. Immortality of the soul, reincarnation, karma, deliverance or *Moksha, Nirvana* etc. were doctrines believed in and followed by all the sects prevailing in the country. Indians have faith in Unseen Reality and a sense of sacredness of all life, charity and tolerance. Religious rites and rituals had almost the same uniformity throughout the land. Saivites, Vaishnavites, Jains and Buddhists have their sacred places all over the country. Badrinath in the north, Dwaraka in the West, Puri in the east and Rameswaram in the South are the unifying religious centres of the Hindus and they speak of India being one land. The daily prayer of a Hindu includes the names of all the main rivers of the North and South. It breaks the narrow, parochial, provincial and religious sentiments and inculcates broad cultural and religious views.

There has been a basic unity of literary ideas, philosophy, conventions and outlook upon life throughout the country. The cultural unity is reflected in the social ceremonies, the religious rites, festivals and modes of life which are the same in North and South India. The sanctity of the family, the rules of castes, the *Sanskaras*, the rite of cremating the body, cleanliness of the kitchen etc. are common to all the communities and sects. *Kumbamela* at Hardwar, Allahabad and

Ujjain, and Mahamaham at Kumbakonam are attended by all people. Deepavali, Dasara, Holi, Rakshabandan etc. are celebrated throughout the country.

Sages, saints, missionaries and pilgrims are the agents fostering fundamental unity and uniform culture. They are selfless and hence the cultural unification is possible whereas the emperors tried to establish their individual power and strength whereby they failed to establish political integration. Hermitages of sages were centres of learning and holy cities were visited by people. Though the sages had to face some ordeals, they were not persecuted or disrespected totally. Sri Sankara went as far as the Himalayas to spread Saivism and his name and fame would remain ever green in the cultural history of India.

It is interesting to note that in Vishnupurana and some other religious literature of later origin, India is called by the single name BHARATA VARSHA or the land of Bharat. (The country that lies north of the ocean and south of the snowy mountains is called Bharat, for there dwell the descendants of Bharat). This view is definitely questioned by the Dravidians who could be pacified with the explanation that this nomenclature is used only in religious literature and not in a historical document.

Compared to North, South India is noted for its continuity and stability in social organisations and unity of its culture. It was not much affected by foreign invasions too. The Chera, Chola, Pandya, Tondaimandalams were in fact geographical units which had an established and continued cultural and political existence. On the contrary, in North India, the history was based largely on dynasties. The South therefore could provide definite contribution. Even though the Aryan elements are found in early Tamil literature, Aryananisation of South India may be regarded as essentially a process of adaption, because some of the cultural elements in the South are of Aryan character, while a few others are distinctly traceable to pre-Aryan times.

In view of the above statements it may be concluded that political integration of India was a myth in ancient times whereas India was culturally integrated inspite of the existence of different religions, habits and practices and pouring in of foreign culture. In a vast country like India with many diversities, unity and integration seem to be a myth but it is necessary that every Indian should realise the differences and the need and necessity for unity and integration. It could be achieved only with toleration and better understanding among the Indians.

REFERENCES

A. EPIGRAPHS   :   (1) Epigraphia Indica
                              (2) South Indian inscriptions.

B. LITERATURE   :   (1) *Ettuttogai*
                              (2) *Muvar ula*
                              (3) *Pattupattu*

C. BOOKS   :

(1) Altekar, A. S.   : Rashtrakutas and their times.
(2) Gopalachari, K.   : Early History of Andhra country.
(3) Gopalan, R.   : History of the Pallavas of Kanchi
(4) Krishnaswamy Iyengar : Ancient India
(5) Lunia, B. N.   : Life and Culture in Ancient India.
(6) Majumdar, R. C. (Ed) : The Classical Age
(7) Majumdar, R. C. (Ed) : Age of Imperial Kanouj
(8) Mookerji, R. K.   : Ancient India
(9) Nilakantasastri, K. A. : History of South India
(10) Nilakantasastri, K. A. : The Cholas
(11) Nilakantasastri, K. A. : The Pandyan Kingdom
(12) Sircar, D. C.   : Successors of the Satavahanas in the Lower Deccan
(13) Smith, V. A.   : Early History of India.
(14) Smith, V. A.   : Oxford History of India.

INDO-ARYAN ELEMENTS IN TRIBAL STATE FORMATION PROCESSES IN MEDIAEVAL NORTH EAST INDIA

Dr. J. B. Bhattacharya.
North-Eastern Hill University,
Shillong.

The State as a collection of individuals in a specific geographical area connected by a complex system of relations had emerged from the indigenous tribal bases at a very early stage of Indian civilisation. The researches of Surajit Sinha[1], Hermann Kulke[2], Romila Thapar[3] and many others in recent years have brought to focus certain common elements in the process of tribal state and polity formations in ancient and mediaeval India like the role of property, social stratification and the impact of Brahmanical Hinduism, drawing largely from the observation of Engels that "At a definite stage of economic development, which necessarily involved the cleavage of society into classes, the state became a necessity because of this cleavage"[4]. These studies at the same time have focused on the fact that in Indian context the role of Brahmanical Hinduism, or its protestant variant, that is, Buddhism, had been crucial in the state formation processes in early times and that these states experienced the twin processes of cultural assimilation and economic interaction.

Our studies on the Hinduised tribal states in North East India do suggest the following common elements in the state formation processes in the region : (i) the tribal society transformed itself with the emergence of private property, when such societies were stratified in terms of differentiated land-holding and the extent of political dominance that strengthened the position of the traditional institutions at clan/tribe level ; (ii) the sphere of dominance of a chief was extended either by subduing the neighbouring tribes/clans/communities or by direct territorial conquest or by their voluntary submission to his protective authority : (iii) the authority was further strengthened by leading the people in war path either for offensive or for defensive purposes and it continued to be unquestioned, at least at the formative stage, in cases where the state came into existence through military adventures ; (iv) the ruling chiefs succeeded in developing a centralised administration with an elaborate defence structure and the means to appropriate surplus through a hierarchically organised political order ; (v) the introduction of more sophisticated agricultural technology to ensure increased production, and the production control on the part of the ruler, could be an essential precondition for a centralised state authority ; (vi) the families with traditions of administrative proficiency and the artisans and peasants were induced to immigrate from Bengal and the adjoining areas of eastern and northern India and settle in the territory ; (vii) the process of Hinduisation/ Sanskritisation and the role of the Brahmins in establishing the divine origin of the ruler helped the legitimation of the assumed status of the latter and its consolidation, and the myths that were created in the process resulted in the universalisation of culture ; (viii) the adoption of the language and religion of the majority in the territory's population by the ruling family and the aristocracy enlisted loyal support of the dominant revenue paying group ; (ix) the rulers emerged as the champions of their new faith (i.e. Hinduism) and the patrons of the language (Assamese/Bengali) and culture of their subjects ; (x) the matrimonial connections with the ruling houses of neighbouring states with similar ethno-cultural traditions evoked mutual complementality and raised them in the estimation of their subjects ; and (xi) the deplomatic relations with more powerful neighbours served as essential instruments either to guarantee political existence by reckoning the expanding influences of such neighbours or to pacify the disgruntled elements within the state.[5]

The important Indo-Aryan elements in the tribal state formation processes in the north-east, as noted above, are (a) Brahmanical Hinduism, (b) Sanskrit and Assamese/Bengali languages, and (c) the immigrant Indo-Aryan population. In this paper, we propose to examine the role of these elements in five mediaeval monarchies viz. Assam, Cachar, Tripura, Manipur and Jaintia.

Assam

The Ahoms, who belong to the Tai race, came to Assam in the 13th century. The chronicles insist on the heavenly origin of their progenitor. It is said that *Indra*, the lord of Heaven, had two sons who descended on the earth by a golden ladder and that one of them became the progenitor of the Ahoms. Sukapha, the military leader, who became the first Ahom king in the Brahmaputra Valley, belonged to the *Chao-pha* or celestial clan. His two counsellors, namely, *Burhagohain* and *Bargohain*, also belonged to two special clans, viz. *Chao-Frongmung* and *Chao-Taomung* respectively. These three lineages had three corresponding priestly lineages, viz. *Bailung*, *Deodhai* and *Mohan*. This provided the basis for the growth of Ahom political organisation in which all important offices were linked to either of the lineages. The number of lineage groups increased in course of time due to social and spatial mibility as well as fissions. The proliferation occured during the state formation processes. In fact, the divine origin of the ruling clans was upheld by the newly created Brahmanical myths during the Hinduisation process in the Brahmaputra valley since when the Ahom king became populer as *Swargadeva* or the 'Lord of heaven'. The Brahmins and the temples were highly respected by the Ahom rulers. They made several *Devattara* and *Brahmattara* land grants. The inscriptions and coins issued in the Ahom state had Sanskrit-Hindu legends in Assamese/Bengali script and were dated in *Saka* era. In course of time, the Ahoms adopted Hindu religion and Assamese language. The Assamese language and literature flourished under their patronage. The Brahmins. professionals, artisans and peasants from Bengal and the neighbouring regions immigrated and settled down permanently in the state under royal patronage. These immigrants contributed to the restructurisation processes and prosperity of the state as well as cultural assimilation and integration[6]. As Guha puts it[7].

A new phase of intensified Brahmanical influence started with the reign of Suhummung Dihingiya Raja (1497-1539). He annexed Habung (an ancient Brahmin settlement) in 1512, a Chutiya dependency until then. Thereafter, the whole of the Hinduized Chutiya Kingdom and parts of the present Nowgong district, then ruled severally by the *barabhuyans* and the Dimasa king, were gradually annexed to the Ahom kingdom. Since then resettled *bara-bhuiyan* chiefs and their relations began to be absorbed as scribes and warriors in the lower echelons of the growing state mechinery. By 1539, the Ahom territory became at least twice as big as what it was in size around 1407. More important, its Assamese-speaking Hindu subjects were now more numerous than the Ahoms themselves. This resulted in the availability of a wider range of artisan skills as well as a greater scope of division of labour within the kingdom. This expansion to new territories and populations, fully or partly Hinduized, had its impact. The King assumed the Hindu title of *Swarga-narayana* (god of heaven) and came to be addressed since then as *Swarga-deva* in Assamese. Suhummung introduced the *Saka* era in place of the old system of calculating dates by the sixty-year Jovian cycles. According to some chroniclers, he also started striking coins to mark the coronation. The hereditary nobles (*Chao*) were now allying themselves with the Brahmin literati with a view to forming an expanded ruling class. The Ahoms, themselves, being traditionally stratified into the high and low, there was no difficulty on their part to come to a compromise with and respect the rigidities of the Assamese caste society within their kingdom. State power was now, for the first time, also backed by fire-arms that had come into use in the wake of the Turko—Afghan invasion of Upper Assam in 1532.

One dimension of the Hindu impact was the grafting of Hindu myths on Ahom legends with a view to identify all principal Tai-Ahom deities with gods of the Hindu pantheon, as for example, Lengdon with Indra. It is now impossible to say when this first happened. According to Gait, this might have been the result of the early exposure of the Tais to the Hindu colonizers in southeast

Asia. However, the attempt in some chronicles at tracing the Ahom king's origins to Indra's intimate relations with a celestial woman (vidvadharii), in her human incarnation as a tribal woman, was surely a much later phenomenon. Instead of associating the Ahom royal lineage with *Surya* or *Chandra Vamsa* (Solar or Lunar dynasty) as was expected of them, the shrewd Brahmins accomodated the Ahom legends to the extent of describing it as *Indra-Vamsti* and this manipulation found its way into the chronicles. They also expanded the theory of divine origins to uphold the sacre-d ness of the person. Any blemish or wound on it was hence forth viewed as a disqualification for his office. This is how the Brahmins helped legitimize and validate the dynastic rule of the Ahoms in the eyes of their Hindu subjects.

Cachar :

The life and condition in the Barak Valley has been influe-nced by the developments in Bengal as this Bengali-speaking area was included in Srihattadesha and covered by the state formation processes in South-East Bengal in ancient and medi-aeval times. The modern Cachar segment of ancient Srihatta passed under the Tripuri rule around 13th century A.D. the Khaspur State came into existence in 16th century, and finally, in the 18th century it was integrated into the Dimasa State. However, the Dimasa sphere of control covered a small portion of Cachar Valley since 16th century and this segment of their principality substantially influenced their state for-mation processes in Brahmanical Hindu lines which they had experienced in a rudimentary way even earlier. An off-shoot of the Bodo race, the early phase of the Dimasa state formation processes was in the Brahmaputra Valley when their capital was in Dimapur. The sack of Dimapur by the Ahom in the beginning of the 16th century occasioned the transfer of the capital to Maibong in the North Cachar Hills since when the Dimasa state formation process entered into its crucial inter-mediate phase with the occupation of a small portion of the Cachar Valley. A tradition suggests that after his expulsion from Dimapur the Dimasa ruler came under the influence of a Bengalee Brahmin who helped him in organising his govern-ment in Maibong and that this Brahmin was given the status of his *Guru* by the king. The fact of Brahmanical influence in the Dimasa court in Maibong is also known from various historical sources. The royal court was adorned by a galaxy of scholars from Sylhet, who translated some of the *Puranas* into Bengali. They also composed some of the master-pieces of mediaeval Bengali literature and a few of the Dimasa Rajas contributed songs and poems to Bengali literature. Some Bengalee settlements of artisans, professionals and Brahmins like Kumarpara, Kumarpara, Dhamadir Haor, Brahmanpara etc. came up in Maibong. Where as the Dimasa rulers in Dimapur had tribal names (e.g. Khunkara, Khora-pha, Dersong-pha, Detsung etc.), in Maibong they started taking Hindu names (e.g. Nirbhoyanarayana, Meghanarayana, Josonarayana, Pratapanarayana etc.) The traditional Dimasa deity *Kachai-kati* now came to be known as *Ranachandi*. Like in the Ahom state, the coins and inscriptions had Sanskrit-Hindu legends in Assamese/Bengali script, and dated in *Saka*. The official records were maintained in Bengali. *Deyattara* and *Brahmattara* landgrants were made by way of patronage to the Brahmins and the deities. The process of Hinduisation was reinforced with the shifting of the capital from Maibong to Khaspur in the Cachar plains in the final phase of state formation. The royal clan and the members of the Dimasa aristocracy came to be known as 'Barman'. They were proclaimed by the Brahmins to be *kshatriya* in the *varna* system. The Brahmins also found that the royal clan descended from Ghotutkacha ; the son of Bhima and Hirimba *rakshashi*. The kingdom was, therefore, named as 'Heramba-rajya' after Hirimba. The *Dharmadi-Guru* or the *Raj-Pandit*, who was always a Bengalee Brahmin, exerted considerable influence in state politics. He was the chief advisor to the Raja and the sole intepreter of Hindu Law. The ministers and officers of the state were appointed from among both the Dimasas and the Bengalees. The Bengalee population in the plains increased further by the immigration of the Brahmins, peasants and artisans from Sylhet.[8] As we observed elsewhere.[9]

> The transformation of the Dimasa political system from its indigenous tribal formation to a monarchical state was reached mainly through syncretic adoption of the symbols of Hinduism by bringing the tribes within the broad Hindu-base civilisation of Aryan India generated through the Bengal plains. The Brahmanical myths gave the ruling tribal clan a divine descent which added status and respectibility to the leadership of the tribal pattern and strengthened its base to integrate not only the cognate clans and bordering tribes but also the culturally and technologically more advanced Bengalees, universalising, in the process, their *Kachai-kati* cult through *Sakta* cult of the Hindus and offering, in return, the Brahmins, settled in and around the capital, a dominating position in regulating the state affairs by manipulating the court politics.

The process of state formation reached its crucial stage in Maibong, and at a time when in the whole of the north-eastern region of India similar development took place ; viz. Cooch Behar, Assam, Jayantia, Manipur and Tripura, due mainly to the induction of a confronting situation inspired by the Ahom expansionism with superior military skill. The Dimasas had passed through initial experiments in state building earlier in the Brahmaputra Valley and the archaeological evidences testify the formative experiences at Dimapur where considerable Bengal influence has been noticed. The emergent leadership was legitimised through the Brahmins and its authority was further strengthened in the war path when the masses looked upon the Raja as the protector of their persons and the means of production.

Tripura

Tripura is situated on the frontier of Bengal and the state in its hey days covered a large chunk of the Bengali—speakings plains. The life and condition in the area, therefore, as in case of Cachar, had been influenced by the developments in South-East Bengal. In fact, the Tripuris, who belonged to the Bodo race and had been the inhabitants of the Kapili Valley in Assam, experienced the early phase of state formation processes in Cachar Valley when their capital was in Khalangma near Silchar. They passed through Sylhet and Comilla, over which they ruled with capital in different places in South East Bengal, and finally, reached present Tripura where they eastablished their capital at Agartala. It was during their rule in South East Bengal that they adopted Hindu religion and Bengali language, and the state system that they developed over the centuries was influenced by Brahmanical methods. When

Sylhet and Comilla passed under Turko-Afghan rule in 15th century and the independent Khaspur state came into existence in Cachar Valley in 16th century, the Tripuri state became limited to present Tripura and the adjoining areas of Bangladesh. Ratna Manikya in 16th century is believed to have first assumed the Hindu name, and he was given the title 'Manikya' by the Sultan of Bengal. The Brahmins and other castes, artisans and peasants, professionals and solders were encouraged to immigrate from Bengal. As in Assam and Cachar, the coins and inscriptions had Sanskrit-Hindu legends in Assamese/Bengali script. The impact of Hinduism on the Tripuris was so great that stratification occured in the society virtually in caste lines.[10] As we observed elsewhere,[11]

A study of the history of the Tripuri state formation reveals the factors and processes that helped the elevation of the political system from a tribal base to a well developed monarch. The leadership of the tribe had passed into the hands of a single personality on hereditary line during the migrations and attempts at establishing a principality of their own. The initial settlement in the wet rice cultivation area predominated by the Indo-Aryan Bengalees exposed the tribe to Hindu influences that resulted in social stratification and legitimization of the status of the ruler by the Brahmins who established divine origin of the royal clan and thereby enlisted the loyalty of the people. The military support received from the neighbouring larger state of Bengal enabled the ruler to overcome any possible opposition to his assumed authority and to subdue the bordering hill tribes and in extending the boundary of the state. The leadership in war against neighbouring imperial forces and war like chieftains strengthened his position further and helped develop an adequate defence system. The protective position of the ruler and his universalised social status helped him in organising an elaborate hierarchical order suitable in sustaining the structure and in planting artisans and professionals from other territories without any opposition from the members of his tribe or indigenous population. The support and loyalty of the more productive non-tribals were enforced by the Raja's projected role as the champion of his new faith and their cultural and linguistic assimilation with the majority group in the state. The sustenance came in the form of surplus extraction in terms of tribute and taxes and personal service and the Rajas themselves indulging in profitable trades.

Jaintia

The Jaintia or Jayantia kingdom had its origin in the Jaintia Hills, but the state formation process assumed appropriate proportion when a portion of the Sylhet plains was brought under it in 13th century and the capital was shifted from Sutnga to Jaintiapur. The Bengali-speaking plains division of the state formed the economically core area of the state in which the capital was also located, and, as a result, this division exerted considerable influence in the state affairs. The members of the royal family and the aristocracy adopted Hinduism, Although the tribals in the hills continued to adhere to their traditional religion, Hinduism made some impact there as well. The royal court in Jaintiapur was adorned by a galaxy of Sanskrit-Bengali scholars. The coins and inscriptions in this state also had Sanskrit-Hindu legends in Assamese/Bengali script, and the official records were maintained in Bengali.[12] As Pakem observes,[13]

......there was an amount of Brahmanical influence in Jaintia State by the end of the 15th Century throught the Jaintia rulers who bore Hindu names since the 13th Century. It took about 200 years after the annexation of Jaintia Plains in 1250 A. D. for Brahmanism to have finally found its place among the family members of the Rajah and nobles. Thus, when *Syiem Sutnga* became the Rajah of Jaintia, he was found to be a patron of Brahmanism of the Sakta Sect. The Rajah was surrounded by the Upper Caste Hindus such as the Brahmans, the Kshatriyas and the Kayasthas. They acted as his advisers not only in religious matters, but also in secular matters. Unlike Christianity and Islam, because of the caste structure of Hinduism, the Brahmins of the day could not place the Rajah in any proper caste hierarchy except to regard him as an orthodox Sudra. Gradually, the influence of Brahmanism, though faintly, reached places as far as Nartiang, Sutnga and Yale Falls and thrust very deep into the interior of Jaintia Hills. However, the Rajah of Jaintia Plains acting as the *Syiem* of Jaintia Hills, still maintained his loyalty to the tribal gods and goddesses including the deities of the sacred groves, the spirits of the hills, rivers and forests, and the ancestral spirits. That was why the principle of succession to the throne of Jaintia State was strictly followed through the nephew and not the son. Even if there were no more nephews and relatives the next Rajah should be the hill man through the process of tribal divination. This is the Brahmin model, if there is such a model, or call it the model of acculturation if not Hinduisation and Sanskritisation.

Manipur

The state formation process in Manipur was also influenced by Brahmanical Hinduism. The Hindu influence penetrated into the Manipur valley in early times through Cachar. In mediaeval period the Ramanandi Vaisnava saints initiate the Raja to their faith. But it was finally the Gauriya Vaisnava Goswamis of Bengal who made it a mass religion among the Manipuris. The Brahmins who went to Manipur from Bengal ultimately became Manipuri Brahmins by adopting the local language and the way of life. A new form of caste system reinforced the social stratification process essential for state formation. The Meitei language was now written in Assamese / Bengali script. The coins and inscription had Sanskrit-Hindu legends, and the Radha-Krisna cult became the principal theme of Manipuri literature and its internationally acclaimed dance form.[14] As Saha puts it,[15]

In the period before the acceptance of vaishnavism the tradititonal Laining (i. e. Meitei religion) was the religion for all and all people paid their regard to Maibas and Maibis. From religion point of view there was no differentiation amongst the people. This was the theme in Vashnavism also. Gareeb Niwaz (1709-1748) was impressed by this religion and he accepted theRamanandi Sect of Vashnavism. He also forced his subjects to accept the same. But he failed to make it state religion. Maharaja Bhagya—Chandra (1763-1798) was in frequent contact with the Goswamis of Bengal on political ground. He became prone to this religion and under his sponsership Gouriya Vaishnavism became very popular in Manipur. But he did not allow each and everyone to accept this religion. But first allowed those who were structurally close to the king and then the commoners to accept this Vaishnava religion. He, however, did not allow the degraded to accept Vaishnavism. The value was that those who accepted Vaishnavism became pure and those who did not accept it were impure and those who accepted it earlier had the higher status than those who accepted it later. The Brahman became the preceptors and priests. The Brahman gave ritual service to the palace and thereby attained the highest status. The Bishnupriyas after the acceptance of Vaishnavism performed lalup and were lebelled as commoners. The outcaste group Yaithibi were declared untouchables. Though the Brahmin attained the highest status by applying the value of purity and impurity, this new value of purity and impurity could only strengthen the existing order in the hierarchy.

Summing-up

The Indo-Aryan elements, namely, (i) religion, (ii) language, and (iii) population played vital role in the tribal state formation process in mediaeval North East India. These states undoubtedly emerged from their indigenous tribal bases through stratification method eversince the emergence of private property in the erstwhile egalitarian society, which created the basis for social inequality over a long period of time as an essential precondition for the rise of the state. The much misinterpreted caste system during the hinduisation process served as an instrument to uphold and reinforce the extant inequality in the

13

society. The myths created by the Brahmins regarding the divine origin of the rulers contributed towards the legitimation of their assumed status. The authority of the Brahmins as experts of scriptures could be invoked by these rulers to find justification for all their actions. The new found religion infused elements of commonalty among the people and impelled upon them to abide by the sanctions of the scriptures which they came to know only through the Brahmins. As the authority of the king was unquestionable, it was possible for him to enact laws, to control the means of production and distribution, and to extract and appropriate the surplus. The emerging state systems, therefore, represented noticable identical features, in ideology, form and content, between themselves and those in other regions of the country, with minor regional variations due mainly to ecological influences. As in rest of the country, Sanskrit language and the Saka era served as great unifying forces. The symbols and legends in inscription and coins were equally effective in promoting integration. The form and contents of the inscriptions and coins as well as the objectives, terms and conditions of the landgrants to the Brahmins, temples and officials had been the same as prevalent in any other part of the country. The adoption of Assamese and Bengali languages and script perpetuated the smooth functioning of the states and the social and cultural assimilation. The immigrant Indo-Aryans with various social and professional background enforced technological and occupational change and mobility and economic self-sufficiancy of the emerging states. The Indo-Aryan elements thus generated influences towards the revitalisation of the indigenous systems, institutions and cultures. In the process, the diverse communities in the region were integrated in India's composite social milieu without losing their own ethnic or cultural identity as, in Indian context, every stream enjoyed the status of a main stream and shared a common heritage which they themselves collectively procreated.

REFERENCES

1. Surajit Sinha, "State Formation and Rajput Myth in Tribal Central India", *Man in India*, Vol. 42, No. 1, January-March, 1962, pp. 35-80.

2. Hermann Kulke, "Early State Formation and Royal Legitimation in Tribal Eastern India", cf. R. R. Moser & M. K. Gautam (ed), *Aspects of Tribal Life in South Asia I : Strategy and Survivals*, Bernasia, 1978.

3. Romila Thapar, *From Lineage to State*, Oxford University Press, Bombay, 1984.

4. Friedrich Engels, *"The origin of the family, private property and the state*, London, 1972, p. 232.

5. J. B. Bhattacharjee, "State Formation in Pre-Colonial Tribal Northeast : A Case Study of the Dimasa State", *The North-Eastern Hill University Journal of Social Sciences and Humanities*, Vol. II, No. 3, July-September, 1984.

6. Edward Gait, *A History of Assam*, 3rd edn, Gauhati, 1967 ; p. Gogoi, *The Tai and the Tai kingdom*, Gauhati University, 1968 ; Suniti kumar Chatterji, *The Place of Assam in the History and Civilisation of India*, Gauhati University, 1955.

7. Amalendu Guha, "The Ahom Political System : An Enquiry into the state Formation Process in Mediaeval Assam : 1228-1714", Occasional Paper No. 64, CSSS, Calcutta, 1983, pp. 27-28

8. Upendra Chandra Guha, *Cacharer Itibritta* (Bengali), Dacca, 1911 ; Surya Kumar Bhuyan (ed.), *Kachari Buranji* (Assamese), DHAS, Gauhati, 1936.

9. J. B. Bhattacharjee, op. cit, p. 21.

10. N. R. Roychoudhury, *Tripura Through the Ages*, Agartala, 1977 ; Surya Kumar Bhuyan (ed.), *Tripura Buranji* (Assamese), DHAS, Gauhati, 1939 ; A. C. Choudhury, *Srihattar Itibritta* (Bengali), Sylhet, 1317 BS.

11. J. B. Bhattacharjee, "Tripuri State Formation in Mediaeval Tripura", *Proceedings of the North East India History Association*, Third Session, Imphal, 1982, p. 69.

12. Sayeed Murtaza Ali, *History of Jayantia*, Dacca, 1954 ; Surya Kumar Bhuyan (ed.), *Jayantia Buranji (*Assamese*)*, DHAS,

Gauhati, 1936; J. B. Bhattacharjee, "Sources of the History of the Khasis and Jaintias", cf. S. P. Sen (ed.), *Sources of the History of India,* Vol. II, IHS, Calcutta, 1979, pp. 205-221.

13. B. Pakem, "State Formation in Pre-Colonial Jaintia", *The North-Eastern Hill University Journal of Social Sciences & Humanities,* Vol. II, No. 3, July-September, 1984, p. 57.

14. J. Roy, *History of Manipur,* Calcutta, 1967 ; L. Mangi Singh & L. Mani Singh (ed.), *Vijay Panchali* (Bengali), Imphal, 1967 ; J. B. Bhattacharjee, "Sources of the Late Madieval and Modern History of Manipur", cf. N. R. Ray (ed), *Sources of the History of India,* Vol. IV, IHS, Calcutta, 1982, pp. 439-456.

15. R. K. Saha "State Formation among the Meitei of Manipur", a paper presented in the workshop on Tribal Polities and State Systems in Pre-Colonial Eastern and North-Eastern India, CSSS, Calcutta, July 1981, (Mameographed) pp. 19—20.

INTEGRATION OF NORTH-EAST INDIA IN THE FIRST HUNDRED YEARS OF KOCH RULE

Dr. D. Nath
Lecturer in History
Dibrugarh University

The rise of the Koches, one of the aboriginal tribes of North-east India[1], as a political power on the ruins of the Kamata kingdom in the early part of the 16th century is an important event in the history of north-eastern region. While assuming political power in the western Brahmaputra valley in the early 16th century, they exercised for a time, their sovereignty over almost the entire north-east. They made a significant contribution towards the progress of civilisation and culture of the Brahmaputra valley in particular, and of north-east India in general. Bisu, later known as Biswa Singha, the adventurous Koch chief, organised the strength of his tribe following the invasion of the Kamata kingdom by Ala-ud-din Hussain Shah (A. D. 1493-1519), the Sultan of Bengal, in A. D. 1498. He laid the foundation of his kingdom in about A. D. 1515 on the ruins of the Kamata kingdom. His son and successor Naranarayan (A. D. 1540-1587) was not only the greatest of the Koch kings, but was also one of the illustrious rulers of his time. His long reign of nearly half a century formed a landmark in the history of the Brahmaputra valley. With the help of his able brother Chilarai, who was also his general, he brought most of the neighbouring States under the Koch hegemony and by greatly patronising various cultural pursuits as well as the Neo-Vaishnavite movement, helped in the opening of a new chapter in bringing about the process of integration in this part of the country.

Contemporary Political Situation :

Contemporary political conditions in the entire north-east India during the hey day of the Koches (16th century) was one of utter confusion and witnessed smaller political divisions. In the eastern Brahmaputra valley, the Ahoms, a branch of the famous Shan tribe of the Mongoloids formed a state and had already resisted the Muslim invaders successfully in 1527-1533, and meanwhile subjugated the Chutiyas, another branch of the same Mongoloid stock, who were ruling over the extreme north-eastern part of the region. Amidst strong resistance in form of popular revolt and protracted fight their territory too was annexed to the Ahom kingdom by king Suhungmung, the Dihingia Raja (1497-1539) in 1527.[2]

It was not only the Chutiyas who had to bear the brunt of Ahom inroads, but the Kacharis also faced the same situation.[3] These tribe, a section of the Bodos, had been ruling during the time of the Ahom consolidation in Upper Assam, over the region from the Dekhow to the Kalang river on the south of the Brahmaputra and included the valley of the Dhansiri and also the present North-Cachar Subdivision.[4] But since the beginning of the 16th century, the Ahoms began vigorously extending their territories at the cost of the neighbouring kingdoms including that of the Kocharis. As a result, by 1536, they occupied the region of the Dhansiri valley and brought under control the area as far as Dimapur.[5] As such in face of heavy opposition from the Kacharis, their kingdom was reduced to extent of covering the regions of North-Cachar and the Kallong valley in present Nowgong district, when in the meantime the Koches rose to power in the west.

These apart, the *Darrang Raj Vamsavali*[6] the genealogical work of the Koches, testify to the fact that the whole of north-east India was divided into a number of smaller states at the time of the formation of the Koch state in the Lower Brahmaputra valley. These included the kingdoms of Manipur in the present Manipur area, and the Jayantiya which then consisted of the Jayantiya hills and the plains tract south of it and the area to the north of the Surama or the Barak river. The kingdom of Tripura, the abode of the Tippera tribe covered the areas of the entire Barak valley, and a considerable portion of Sylhet and Comilla districts of present Bangladesh. In the beginning of the 16th century they annexed a part of Cachar[7] resulting in the tense relations between the two neighbouring tribal states. Meanwhile relations were established between the kings of Tripura and the Sultans of Bengal which often turned hostile. It appears that a portion of Tripura was conquered by Sultan Jalal-ud-din of Bengal (1418-1431) in the early part of the 15th century when Mahamanikya (c. 1400-1430) was ruling in Tripura.[8] Although Dhanyamanikya (1490-1515) conquered some portions of Bengal when Ala-ud-din Hussain Shah (1493-1519) was ruling there, the latter also occupied a portion of Tripura as evidenced by the *Sonar Gaon Inscription* of A. D. 1513.[9] Such hostile relations between Tripura and Bengal often resulted in border clashes which continued till the Afghans were succeeded by the Mughals in Bengal. This political confusion continued till when the Koches began the process of territorial integration in the region. As recorded in the *Vamsavali* there existed by this time another tribal principality of Khairam located to the north of Jayantiya kingdom besides Sylhet (Sirath) to the north of the Kusiara river which was then under the suzereinty of the Bengal Sultans. The source under reference further records that there was another tribal state of Dimarua on the south of the Brahmaputra near Guwahati whose chief was a Garo.[10] This in brief is the political fragmentation of the north-eastern region at the time of the advent of the Koches in the Lower Barhmaputra valley.

Besides these tribal states, there were a large number of Bhuyan landlords scattered hither and thither controlling a major part of the economy of the valley.[11] It now becomes clear as to what was the exact situaion of north-eastern region in the beginning of the 16th century and to what extent the Koches confronted it if they at all desired to bring about an integration of all this.

Territorial Integration :

The Koches in the personality of Naranarayan however, faced the situation effectivey ; and as we shall see Chilarai, the brother-general of Naranarayan successfully subjugated all the ruling tribes one after another and brought them under one central control. The Ahoms had been first subjugated in 1562 and forced to accept Koch vassalage by paying taxes and sending important persons to the Koch court as hostages.[12] Chilarai also brought with him some artisans, scholars and poets from the Ahom kingdom.[13] Thus was laid the first step towards political integration of the whole Brahmaputra valley which subsequently opened the way for cultural unity of the regions. With the subjugation of the most powerful tribe of the time i.e. the Ahoms, the other powers gave way very soon with or without fight and the Koches brought besides the Bhuyans, all the tribes under control as mentioned earlier. In Cachar, Chilarai also established a colony of the Koches (called *Dehan*)[14] which not only remained there for a long time, but also brought about Koch-Kachari relations of a permanent socio-cultural importance. The Cachar campaign concluded within a short time. The *Vamsavali* states that after the conquest of Cachar, Naranarayan and Chilarai sent *Katakis* or ambassadors to the king of Manipur demanding his submission.[15] The Manipuri king – possibly one Muktawali Singha (1561-1579), having heard of the victorious campaigns of the Koch king in the kingdom of Assam and Cachar, submitted of his own accord and agreed to pay him annual tribute.[16] The king of Jayantiya who was either Bargohain (1548-1564) or Bijoy Manikya (1564-1580) although preferred to challenge the Koches and entered into an armed conflict with them, in the battle the Jayantiya king was slain. The son was installed on the throne on condition of fidality and was permitted to issue coins (without the king's name) so that trade pursuits in the region do not suffer.[17] As stated earlier, the political confusion in Tripura provided a gaining factor for Chilarai. The Tripura king was slain in the field and as many as 18,000 of his soldiers massacred. The king's brother was placed on the throne on his having consented to pay an annual tribute of 9000 gold coins.[18] It is further stated that after occupying Tripura Naranarayan built there ramparts and excavated tanks.[19] Such astounding victory naturally terrorised smaller kings like that of Khairam who submitted without fight. Naranarayan installed him as a tributary king and was also allowed to mint coins at the name of the Koch kings.[20] The ruler of Sylhet, *Patsa* of the *Darrang Raj Vamsavali*, gave stiff resistance to the invading Koch forces so that Chilarai, after three days of hard fight had to search for new and more vigorous means to compel the *Patsa* to succumb to death.[21] King Naranarayan appointed the king' brother Asirai the *Patsa* of Sylhet after obtaining from him the assurances of paying all kinds of gratitude and obeissance. After the conquest of Sylhet the Koch forces returned via Guwahati and on the way at Dimarua south of the Brahmaputra, vanquished its chief and compelled him to be fidal in future.[22]

It should be noted here that all the powers not only accepted Koch vassalage but also entered into socio-cultural and economic ties with one another in times to come. This is how a tiny power growing in a corner of Goalpara district of Assam, gradually grew in power, and it was through its seer dint of effort and influence that it successfully established greater political relations with the neighbouring states and brought about an effective territorial integrity to help grow the present concept of north-east region as a geographical entity.

Integration Through Cultural Activities :

The Koch kings were great patrons of education and literature, music and dance and art and architecture. Their rule synchronised with the introduction of the Neo-Vaishnavite movement launched by Sankaradev and his apostle Madhavdev. This movement, which gained wonderful popularity among the masses within a short time and opened a new chapter of cultural progress in then Assam, received active patronage from the Koch kings. The Koch rule thus has a special place in the cultural integration of the north-eastern regions.

During the period under discussion, in north-eastern India there existed a number of heterogeneous sects and beliefs.[23] The non-Hindu tribals worshipped in their own ways without any interference from the others. Hinduisation till then was mainly confined to the ruling families or to certain areas, usually in the neighbourhood of the capital cities. The Koch kings, for political purposes, patronised both Brahmanic and tribal worship, although they themselves accepted Hinduism and were elevated to the status of *Kshatriyas* by the Brahmin priests. But in spite of this, there was brought to the society a major change by the Neo-Vaishnava movement whereby people from all quarters assembled in a single platform to develop among themselves a sense of brotherhood and equality under the banner of the same Koch kings ; and it was under this Vaishnavite banner that unity of thought and action to a great extent was achieved from east to west and from north to south which the society carries till today.

The Neo-Vaishnava movement in Assam was a response to the Indian Bhakti movement ; but it was not a mere replica of the latter. Under the prevailing conditions of north-eastern region, when ignorance and superstitions were widely rampant, there was no doubt, the need for rationalising men's religious attitude. But at the same time there was also the need for uniting the heterogeneous tribes and different communities through the bond of a common faith and create conditions for their harmonious living. The repeated attack from the Turko-Afghans resulting in the conquest and inauguration of Muslim rule in Kamarupa-Kamata or western part of the Brahmaputra valley intensified the feeling for the need of such a unity. The Koch kings felt the gravity of this need and it was through the Neo-Vaishnavite Movement which they largely encouraged, that they tried to achieve it. The teachings of this Neo-Vaishnavism was based principally on the *Bhagavat Puran*, and emphasised solely on one Supreme God for which reason it was also known as *Ekasarana Bhaga-vati Dharma.* The new creed. marked by a sense of broad humanism and wide democratic sentiment, had a universal appeal. It did not accept any distinction of caste or creed. In the fraternity of devotees of this faith there were one Govinda, a Garo ; one Paramananda, a *Miri* (Mishing) ; Narahari, an Ahom ; Jayram, a Bhutiya : Chandsai, a Muslim ; and Damodar-dev and Bhattadev both Brahmins.[24] Among others mention may be made of Madhav of Jayanti village who was a *Hira* by caste and Sriram (*Ata*) and Bhobora Das who were of *Kai-varta* and *Baniya* castes respectively.[25] In his *Nam-Ghosha*[26] Madhavdev refers to the acceptance of the new religion by people of *Garo, Bhot* (Bhutiya), *Yavana* (Muslim), *Miri* (Mishing), *Asama* (Ahom) and Kachari origin[27] who were till then remained outside the pale of Hinduism.

The other important aspect of this movement that had accelarated the process of integrity amongst the masses was the beginning of the translating of religious Sanskrit scriptures into the Vernacular and thereby rendering them comprehensible to all people which privilege had hitherto been virtual monopoly of the Brahmins. As a result the new creed became gradually popular among the masses. Further, its democratic outlook and the emphasis on community feeling soon appeared to be a threat to the Ahom monarchy even in its growing stage, whose principles of administration were based on despotism and crushing of the individual liberty of the subject population. But the Koch king Naranarayan, even after understanding all this fully well, established Sankardev by appointing him as the *Gomosta* or the administrative officer and gifted him lands to establish *Satra* at Bheladunga (later known as Madhupur),[28] near the Koch capital at Koch Behar. Besides, Naranarayan issued a declaration permitting free propagation of his teachings among his population.[29] His brother Chilarai got his initiation from Sankardev and became an active patron of the new creed. With such royal patronage, people from all walks of life became converts to the new creed and within a short time Neo-Vaishnavism became religion of the people from Sadiya in the east and Koch Behar in the west.

It is now in both the hills and the plains that major part of the people including the tribes follow Vaishnavism and use to assemble at a single platform—the *Namghar* forgetting their mutual differences. This sense of unity derived during the Vaishnava reforms of the times of the great Koch kings still prevail amongst the people ; and tribes non-tribes and Hindus still sit together to discuss of matters of mutual relations. This is particularly applicable in the lower echelons of the society. It should however be mentioned that the Koch kings did not alienate the other sects also, and Brahmins and tribes who did not like each others beliefs and customs, were made to live in complete amity by permitting them to live in their own way. The *Darrang Raj Vamsavali* contains sufficient reference to this wherein it is recorded that Naranarayan allowed the Brahmins of his kingdom to practice Brahmanic law in the region to the south of the *Gohain Kamala Ali,* and at the same time the Kacharis to practise tribal ways to its north.[30] Patronage to harmonious development of all castes and creeds made the days of the Koches unique and it is due to this that while Naranarayan and Chilarai built the Sakta shrine at Kamakhya, they also simultaneously patronised Vaishnavism. While Brahmin pandits were facilitated to cultivate literature and learning in the court, adult education for *Sudras,* women and tribes had been permitted to be imparted at the *Namghars.*[31] This is how there is no contemporary evidence to show that any popular revolt had occurred during the hey day of the Koches unlike the Moa-mariya revolt that took place during the Ahoms in a later period.

ECONOMIC INTEGRATION

One of the major steps undertaken by the Koch kings to integrate the north-eastern region was pursuits of commercial activities through all kinds of encouragements accorded to the traders. It is the Koches who reorganised the existing tribal economy of the region and developed commercial enterprises not only among the states of north-east but also between the Koch kingdom and the other neighbouring Asiatic countries of the time. The vallies and the hills of north-east were always rich in forest and animal products. Industrial goods in the Koch kingdom had been extensively and qualitatively produced. All this not only encouraged the native merchant class to persue commercial transactions in the north-easter states,[32] but also attracted foreighners to carry on trade with the region. The underlying idea herein was to establish both political and economic harmony of the neighbouring territories.

Trades developed among Bengal, Asam (Ahom kingdom), Bhutan, Tibet, China and also with Mughal India. Mountain passes provided the passages to trade with the hilly countries like Bhutan, Tibet and China. It should be noted that inter state and international centres of commercial enterprises developed during this period and people from all the neighbouring countries traded there like members of one community and one country. Referring to such an important tradecentre, Karampatan or Kararpatan in the north of the Koch kingdom the *Tabaqat-i-Nashiri* observes as follows :

> ...and every day, at daybreak, in the cattle market of that city, about one thousand five hundred horses are sold ; and all the tangahan horses which rich the Lakhanawati country they bring from that place. The route by which they come is the *Mahanmah-i-(or Mahanmha-i)* Darah (pass), and this road in that country is well known ; for example, from the territory of Kamrup to that of Tirhut are thirtyfive mountain passes by which they bring tangahan horses into the territory of Lakhanawati.[33]

The Koches also developed trade with neighbouring kingdoms like Bengal, Cachar, Sylhet, Jayantia and Manipur. The capital city at Koch Behar itself became such a centre of all India importance. The Portuguese traveller Stephen Cacella writes that large boats from Gaur frequented the capital at Koch Behar and moved on up and down for the whole year.[34] It should be noted that Naranarayan permitted the kings of Jayantiya and Khairam to mint coins so that trade relations

with these countries as well as with Bengal would not suffer.[35]
It was under their rule that big traders used to form temporary
partnership to trade in distant lands.[36] The *Katha Guru Carit*
mentions how one Bhabananda Kalita had traded with seven of
his companions in Bengal, Bhutan, Garo Hills and the Ahom
kingdom under the instruction from king Naranarayan.[37] Thus
it was under the Koches that the whole of north-eastern region
had been connected through a commercial network that
developed subsequent to the political unity achieved through
their large-scale conquests. Trade routes—both over land and
water had brought about easy communications between the
north-eastern states. In the market places and trade centres—
people from both the rich and the poor sections and from hills
as well as plains gathered together to trade in their respective
items. It is as a result of these enterprises that people from all
the present states of the region have a history of ethnic and
cultural relations from ancient times. The policy of moneti-
sation of north-eastern economy had further helped in developing interdependence of the states in those 16th-17th
centuries.

Matrimonial Policy as a Factor of Integration :

Like many other famous dynasties of ancient and medieval
India marriage played a major role not only in moulding
politics of the time, but also in binding different ethnic and
political groups into mutual relations. The *Darrang Raj
Vamsavali* records how the founder Koch king Biswa Singha
married eighteen wives from different countries like Gaur,
Kashmir, Nepal and Kamrup. It was Chilarai's marriage with
Kamalapriya, the niece of the Vaishnava reformer Sankardev
that helped in bringing about an attachment between the
Kayasthas and the Koches. The *Ahom Buranjis* contain innumerable references to the marriage relations between the
Ahoms and the Koches. It is very interesting to note that it

was due to the matrimonial policies of the Koch-Ahom rulers that the present day people of Assam can not claim, unlike in other parts of the country, a fidal ethnic identity completely distinguishable from other ethnic groups. The concept of *Asamiya* (Assamese) grew from it. Many fundamentals of present Assamese culture are Koch countributions ; and these still inspire integrity among the people from Koch Behar to Sadiya. It was Naranarayan who first introduced the process of worshipping the image of Goddess Durga in the north-eastern region ; and the Ahom rulers who sent their own artisans to Koch Behar for special training in the art of making images, had introduced it second.[38] The present *Durga Puja*, therefore, which is celebrated in the whole north-east and where the masses still actively participate forgetting all their mutual differences, had a lasting impact in the integration of the society.

Conclusion :

The first hundred years of Koch rule which saw the rise, climax and disintegration of their power, was marked by important changes in the political, socio-economic and cultural life of this part of the country.   In the political field, they succeeded in bringing about a political integration at least in those areas which were under their direct administration.   It had its impact in the autonomous territories also. The large militia with which Naranarayan and Chilarai carried on their extensive conquests were drawn not only from the areas under their direct administration but also from those under the autonomous rule of the Bhuyans, the tribal chiefs or the feudatory rulers. These soldiers in course of their fairly long period of military expeditions, obviously came into contact with the people of other parts of the region. This mobility and mutual contact, although for purely military purposes, had undoubtedly influenced the social relations of the heterogeneous tribes and communities of the region and thereby helped the process of political and cultural integrity. Besides, there had always been a threat of invasion from the western neighbour—the rulers of Bengal—which had intensified the need of political integration.

In the social life the period saw significant changes brought about mainly by the Neo-Vaishnavite movement which received direct patronage of the Koch rulers. Sankardev himself in the *Bhagavat Puran* states that the new creed built a society where the "Kiratas, the Kacharis, the Khasis, the Garos, the Miris, the Yavanas, the Kankas, the Goalas and others"[39] had become the members of one Vaishnava fraternity. In fact, it was this movement which had unified the diverse tribes and communities under a common Vaishnava fold and gave them a common *lingua-franca* in the form of Assamese, a common cultural pattern and thereby a common cultural identity. This socio-cultural integration was a supplement to the political integration, and it strengthened the bonds of unity among the people. The advocacy of the path of devotion as the way of salvation for all castes including the *Chandalas* or untouchables and the ideal of "universal social brotherhood" of the new religion greatly helped the creation of harmonious atmosphere and bridged the distinction between the Brahmins and Sudras.

The creation of a vernacular literature in form of Assamese brought about a new society in which the Sudras, Brahmanas and even wowen could read and write. Naranarayan, who had sheltered Sankardev, worked hand in hand with the Vaishnava saint in getting not only the Sanskrit religious texts translated into Assamese but other works as well. His noble objective is clear from his own words uttered before the scholars whom he had summoned for the purpose. "These translations will first

14

be read by women and Sudras and after sometime by the Brahmins as well."[40] The translation of original Sanskrit texts made their contents open to all people high or low. Thus the development of a common literature in a common language for all classes of people had started to break the social distinctions among people, and that led to an integrated society where people thought of common good and welfare.

It is true that inspite of all this, the process of integration was not complete. Repeated Muslim invasions from the west in the 17th century leading to the disintegration of the Koch kingdom itself and reactionary forces behind all the social reforms had slowed down, and even blocked the process. Limitation in the process of Hinduising or Sanskritising the tribes, opposition to the Vaishnava reforms by some sections in subsequent times had led to this. But the weight of negations measure less than that of achievements. The ethics of the time : "Kirata Kachari Khasi Garo Miri Yavana Kanka Goal, Asama Muluka Rajaka Turuka Kuvaca Mleccha Chandala" still have a sense of equality and brotherhood in the north eastern region which is possibly a unique social character of the region.

REFERENCES

1. H. H. Risley, *Tribes and Castes of Bengal*, Calcutta, 1891, p. 492 ;
   E. T. Dalton, *Tribal History of Eastern India*, Reprint, Delhi, 1973.
   p. 89.
2. See G. C. Baruah, *Ahom Buranji*, Calcutta, 1930, pp. 58ff.
3. *Ibid*, pp. 52ff.
4. E. A. Gait, *A History of Assam*, 2nd edn., Reprint, Gauhati, 1981,
   p. 248.
5. *Ibid*, p. 301.
6. *Darrang Raj Vamsavali*, (ed), N.C. Sarma, Pathsala,1973, vv. 318-496
   (Henceforth referred to as DRV).
7. J. B. Bhattacharya, *Kachar Under British Rule In North-East India*
   Delhi, 1979, p. 4.
8. R. C. Majumdar, (ed), *History and Culture of Indian People* : The
   Delhi Sultanate, Vol. VI, Bombay, 1967, Reprint, p. 209.
9. Cf. N. R. Raychoudhury, *Tripura Through the Ages*, Agartala,
   1977, pp. 27f.
10. DRV, v. 445.
11. D. Nath, 'The Bhuyan land-lords and their Role in the Economy
    of medieval Assam,' *India Past and Present*, 1986 Vol. III, No. 2,
    p. 243.
12. *Deodhai Asam Buranji*, (ed), S. K. Bhuyan, D. H. A. S., Gauhati,
    Reprint, 1962, pp. 46ff ; *Ahom Buranji*, p. 87 ; *Purani Asam
    Buranji*, (ed), S. K. Bhuyan, DHAS, Gauhati, Reprint, 1977, p. 51.
13. *Ahom Buranji*, p. 87 ; *An Account of Assam*, by J P. Wade (ed),
    B. Sarmah, North Lakhimpur, 1927, p. 205.
14. J. B. Bhattacharyee, *op. cit.*, p. 4
15. DRV, vv. 405-406.
16. *Ibid*, vv. 412-413.
17. *Ibid*, vv. 416-420.
18. *Ibid*, v. 428.
19. *Ibid*, v. 431.
20. *Ibid*, v. 43>.
21. *Ibid*, vv. 475-477.
22. *Ibid*, v. 445.
23. Gait, *op. cit.* p. 58.
24. *Amulya Ratna* (MS) ; *Katha Guru Carit*, (ed), U. C. Lekharu,
    Nalbari, 1952, pp. 140, 255.
25. M. Neog, *Sankardeva and His Times*, Gauhati University, 1965,
    p. 369.

26. *Sri Sankara Vakyamrita* (*Namghosha* Section), (ed), H. N. Datta Baruah, Second edn, Nalbari, 1967, vv. 473, 501.

27. *Ibid,*

28. *Katha Guru Carit*, p. 252.

29. *Guru Carit* by Ram charan Thakur, (ed), H. N. Datta Baruah, 3rd edn, Nalbari, 1978, vv. 3507-3508.

30. DRV, v. 337.

31. *Katha Guru Carit*, p. 446ff.

32. *Ibid.*, p. 109.

33. *Tabaqat-i-Nashiri* by Minhas-ud-din Shiraj, (tr.) H. Raverty, Reprint, New Delhi, 1970, Vol. I, pp. 567f.

34. C. S. J. Wessels, *Early Jesuit Travellers in Central Asia*, The Hague, 1924, pp. 128f.

35. DRV, vv. 419, 439.

36. A. Guha, 'Medieval North-East India : Polity, Society and Economy (1200-1750 A. D.), occasional paper No. 19, CSSR, Calcutta, p. 17.

37. *Katha Guru Carit*, p. 107.

38. *Asam Buranji Sar*, (ed), P. C. Choudhury, Gauhati, 1964. p. 24.

39. Sankardeva's *Srimad Bhagawat*, II, (ed), H. N. Datta Baruach, Nalbari, 1948, v. 474.

40. DRV, vv. 604-606.

KASHMIR AND MUGHAL INDIA :
A Study of Medieval Linkages *

Dr. Rattan Lal Hangloo
Deptt. of History,
North-Eastern Hill University,
Shillong-793014.

To question the finality of Kashmirs accession to India is an unparadonable attack on India's integrity but why then calls of this sort are heard ?

Was it in one sweeping move that India gained control of her strategic asset (Kashmir) and embarked on an irreversible step forward ?

Does it demonstrate the beginnings of the crisis of confidence among Kashmiris ?

In seeking answers to these questions raised at the very outset, one can do no better than begin from the mughal conquest of Kashmir (in 1586) which marks a turning point in strengthening Kashmirs linkages with the rest of India.[1] Knowing that the attribution of the process of integration, in Indian nation building activity, to mughals, (as done by Yasin earlier) will prove a deceptive approach and merely create an unusual historical situation,[2] we therefore only sketch the nature of affairs as stemmed from the mughal occupation of Kashmir.[3] From the last quarter of fifteenth century one finds that no steady progress had been made from the promising beginnings made by Sultan Zain-ul-Abidin (1420-1470) of Shahmir dynasty.[4] Civil wars, fratricide and increasing incompetence of kings deteriorated the central authority. The growth of coercion and degeneration of administration paralleled the unrest among the masses.[5]. Sultan Hassan Shah's reign (1472-1484 A.D.) with all the attendent evils depleted the state treasury to the extent of leaving it utterly resourceless and ultimately he choose to debase the currency. Srivara the director of Hassan Shah's musical department noted, "owing to the exhausted state of the treasury, the old copper *Pancavimsatika* was somewhat reduced in weight."[6] The successive regime of sayyids did not stop the increasing lawlessness, promotion of corruption, oppression of peasantry and women.[7] The frequency of feuds among various factions of nobility whose material strength came from land and its revenues, the series of *Shia-Sunni* conflicts with the occassional hits on Hindus (though unmotivated by theological reason) represents perhaps the most brutalising, though certainly not a unique, impact on the overall social format of Kashmir.[8] The institution of nobility was not powerful and united in defence of its interests but was bitterly divided. It were probably these inner divisions which upset them in any confrontation. In most of such instances it were the peasants whom nobles utilised for they constituted the only military strength readily available. The state was not sound enough to provide necessary security in times when famine, war, pleague and geographical limitations created harsh existence that people could cope up without attending to their fields appropriately. How the increasing demands of the secular and religious aristocracy could be met in these conditions can only be seen from the extreme misery of peasantry and craftsmen.[9] In 1534 A. D. the scarcity of food became so much acute that a *Kharwar* of *shali* (paddy) could not be procured even for ten thousand *dinnars*.[10] This volume of mortality and migration thouched highest magnitude. Our chroniclers do not provide any statistical information to supplement this argument but we are persuaded by the frequency of literary evidence to support these statements. Not surprisingly therefore, Kashmiris refused to recognise their future as something different and preferred mughal rule to their regional sovereignty.[11]

Now our starting point is with emperor Akbar the founder of mughal rule in Kashmir. On June 28th 1586 Qasim Khan *Mirbhar* was sent to Kashmir with the instructions, to practise enlightenment, justice, nonsuffrence or wickedness, and the accepting of apologies and the chastisement of evil.[12] To this statement here various interpretations are permissible but it is indeed not plausible to argue that the mughal occupation of Kashmir was carried out in accordance with the strict instructions of Akbar and was therefore devoid of any military destruction. The nature of reality under scrutiny reveals that some of the factions in Kashmiri nobility were no less anxious than their mughal counterparts, not to amaze the world with their might but to capture the court life which offered limitless access to riches and moments of intoxicating splendour. Though they worked hard at task but such an aura was not achieved and the total submission to mughal authority was ensured in 1586.[13]

However, by any historical standards no immediate ameloration to these aforesaid conditions could be expected at the hands of mughals but this mughal occupation did set in motion a series of socio-economic, political and cultural processes which contributed significantly to Kashmirs links with the rest of India. Akbar formulated long term goals which facilitated concrete progress of social transformation in Kashmir. The most significant elements of this process appear to have been the restructuring of the agrarian system and the expansion of handicraft production. The status of mughal *subhah* was extended to Kashmir by bringing it under the mughal adminis-

tration and for futher administrative purposes the territories
of Kashmir were made into various *sarkars*. Five member
team of Sheikh Faizi, Mir Sharif Amuli, Khawaja Muhammad,
Hussain, Khawja Shams Khafi and Kanwar Man Singh were
sent to formulate the pattern of land revenue assessment and
to determine the nature and volume of collection.[14] After a
thorough evaluation, the team fixed the land revenue at one
third (1/3) as the state share.[15] This was further subject to
the changing nature of harvest—a step very rarely conceeded
by sultans. Possibly the rulers must have kept in view the
serious ecological limitations to Kashmir's agrarian economy.
Apart from these measures the oppressive taxes of *Baj* and
Tamgah were also abolished.[16]. Jahangir is said to have
abolished the *Rasum-i-Faujdari* as well.[17] The other features
of administrative reorganization also included the payment of
cash salaries to the soldiers instead of kind.[18] Abul Fazl
remarks, "cash transactions not being the custom of the
country, some part of *Sair Jihat* cesses however, are taken
in cash. Payments in kind and coin were estimated
in *Kharwars* of *shali* rice although 1/3 was rate but in actual
practice 2/3 are taken......The cesses of *Baj* and *Tamgah* were
altogether remitted by his majesty which produced a reduction
of 67824 1/2 *Kharwars* equalent to 898400 *Dams*. For
additional relief of husbandmen, five *Dams* on price of a
Kharwar were thrown in."[19]

To what degree these various administrative regulations
were observed to the benefit of the peasantry will be clear
from the statement of Irfan Habib (who scrutinised the revenue
and administrative records to the best satisfaction of History).
"......in Kashmir Akbar's administration found the demand to
be set in theory at one third but amounting in reality to two
thirds. Akbar ordered that one half should be demanded."[20]

From all these pieces of evidence it becomes amply clear that after passing into the hands of mughals there was a change in administration and these measures must have effected changes in the land based relations between various classes of society. Though these changes were aggressively encouraged by the other representatives of mughal government as well but these measures did not effect the conditions of peasantry other than changing their condition for worse. The increasing expansion of agrarian bureaucracy helped the mughals in controlling the large proportions of surplus in the form of land revenue and in ensuring the application of what J. N. Sarkar calls the uniform administrative type throughout the length and breadth of the mughal empire.[21] This was a subtle mechanism of setting up a common transferable machinery for all their dominions. Besides the agrarian structure was a matter of comprehensive interest affecting all classes of society. It helped the mughals in containing the conflicting interests of local nobility within the restructuring process.[22] Because their (Kashmiri nobles) strifes would otherwise have aroused all antagonisms and acted as a brake in the process of growing incorporation into the Indian system. The more interesting and probably sometimes highly informative discussion on this aspect fallow from our analysis of expanded handicraft production and trade.

From remote past artisanal production supplemented agriculture and therefore formed a significant aspect of Kashmir's economy. Agriculture was carried out only from four to five months a year, for the rest the land remained under snow when no cultivation was possible. To go without work for almost half the year, posed serious threat to the sustenance. In these circumstances craft production was the lone alternative, attracting attention of Kashmir from ages past.[23] Abul Fazl also observed, "There are artificers of various kinds, who might be deservedly employed in greatest cities. The bazar system is little in use-as brisk traffic is carried on its places of business."[24] However, it was with the mughal occupation only that encouragement of trade and promotion and expansion of artisanal production with combination of internal freedom and external protection was vigourusly enforced. Akbar took very keen interest in shawl industry from the very begining of his rule. Here it is important to note that the other industries were also paid serious attention but shawl industry attracted his immediate attention, probably because of large social division of labour involved therein. He personally dictated the designs in manufacturing process and even determined the colouring pattern. This interest of Akbar is recorded in *Ain-i-Akbari*, "His majesty improved this department in four ways. The improvement is first visible in *Tus* shawls which are made up of wool of an animal of that name......people generally wear it without altering its natural colour. His majesty has had it dyed......secondly in *Safid Alchas* also called *Tarahdars*, in their natural colours. The wool is either white or black. The stuffs may be had in three colours, white, black or mixed...his majesty has given the order to dye it in various ways. Thirdly in stuffs as *Zardozi*, *Kalabatun Kashida*, *Qalgha Bandhunn*, *Chint*, *Alcha*, *Purzdar*, to which his majesty pays much attention. Fourth an improvement was made in the width of all stuffs his majesty had the pieces made large enough to yield the making of a full dress......His majesty encourages in every possible way, the manufacturers of shawls in Kashmir".[25]

These measures of Akbar promoted trade between Kashmir and other parts of mughal India. There is a large body of evidence to suggest that merchants from Kashmir visited various parts of India very frequently and Indian merchants also established their business establishments in Kashmir. Mughal India received large supplies of Kashmiri products such as zeera, paper, shawl, papermachine-articles, baskets, honey, forest products, saffron, ragpaper, fruits and woolens. Kashmir exported saffron to Agra and other parts of India entering into competition at Patna with saffron brought from Nepal. In return it imported salt paper, opium, cotton, yarn etc.[26] Infact to ensure the security of increasing trafic between Kashmir and various parts of India Jahangir constructed the main highway (Mughal road) which connected Kashmir with various parts of Punjab and indeed India.[27] It freed Kashmiri life from two serious limitations. (a) Its seclusion from the wider world and (b) the scale on which men thought of distances. Marts in mughal India beyond Kashmir became accessible and consequently what had seemed distant seemed near. Kashmiri merchants travelled as far as Bengal to sell their articles and import salt. Henry vanistart has very keenly observed the advancing of money by Kashmiri merchants at Sundarbans in Bengal and their providing to *Malangies* to work salt pans. His estimate of duties on salt amounts to thirty thousand rupees and as he noticed, this process had been going on for years.[28] This evidence restores the impression that such dealings of advancing money must have involved wider and more enduring contractual procedures which in course of time added a new element of strength and stability to an already existing process of reciprocity. These developments further broke the relative isolation of Kashmir and introduced a process of articulating Kashmirs economic activity with a kind of generalised Indian economy.

Since Kashmir's economy was not predominantly given over to agriculture like other parts of India (except the north eastern belt and some portions of present Himachal) expansion of market seems to have provided a massive response to growth of craft production and the expanding social differenciation created a mass of wage receiving occupations. In course of time these occupational groups recognised their social position and served to the legitimacy of mughal ruling class for promoting the kind of economy suitable to their needs. W. C. Smith has observed that the mughal empire was allied to the middle class commerce as a secondary and very important basis of income, its primary base being land.[29] But in case of Kashmir both the sectors appear to have been equally important. Here it is necessary to mention that the services of stock raisers, cattle rearers and horse keepers were no less significant in maintaining the growing volume of these commercial relations. Besides these occupations, by the very nature of their relationship with the market economy, linked the interior of Kashmir with the rest of the country, such measures would not have been possible without bringing in the integration of the processes of production and giving rise to a class of people highly dependent on Indian goods and predisposed to accept the new idealogical influences contributing to the erosion of the concept of regional sovereignity. The community of merchants from within beyond Kashmir had to associate with the ruling classes to ensure the safety of their establishments, and help the growth of an administrative system managing their responsibility. They must have also sought allies locally and in political institutions to achieve monoply over the public opinion for controlling the market economy from time to time. Thus the intrusion of Indian merchant goods broke the regional self sufficiency of Kashmir and proved conducive to their economic dependence and psychological emancipation.

Linkages were further advanced by granting the Kashmiri nobiliting positions of power and material strength within the mughal administration and by encouraging matrimonial relations. Qazi Nurullah and pandit Totaram were the *Peshkar* (deputy) of Mirza Yusf Khan (1587-93), Pandit Mahadevan was the *peshkar* of Ali Mardan Khan.[30]   Fazil Khan (1698-1707) is said to have recommended a large number of Kashmiris for *mensabs*.[31]   Inayatullah was the first Kashmiri *mansabdar* who rose to the *Zat* rank of 4000 and became the imperial revenue master in 1717 A.D.[32]   Qazi Khan a Kashmiri by birth held the office of *Qazi-ul-Quzzat* under Aurangzeb,[33] Mohammad murad a Kashmiri attained the position of a *Haft Hazari* with *suwar* rank of ten thousand.   He was in charge of the *Sarkar* of Muradabad.[34]

To bend further the loyality of Kashmiri nobles to their new credo, the mughals entered into matrimonials with them. Akbar married Shams Chaks daughter during his first visit (in 1589) to Kashmir.[35]   The daughter of Mubarak Khan Chak and Hussain Chak were married to prince salim.[36]   During Shah Jahans reign prince Murrad married the daughter of maliks of Shahabad.   Unfortunately our chroniclers have accounted only a few cases which seemed to them more important from the point of view of their affiliation to the Mughal court.   But our oral tradition reveals that many more relations were fostered between merchant families and other social groups. "The descendants of Mughals may now be found among Mirzas, Begs, Mirs, Buchh etc".[37]   Since there was no feeling aganist the inter-marriage this also must have been an effective means of ever widening totallity of affairs.   In these circumstances, the nobility, the merchants and most of the urban groups, whose sustenance was directly linked with the other parts of mughal India and who exercised a paramount influence over entire Kashmiri society, must have functioned to create a climate to strengthen this process.   A more serious consequence must have been the natural inclination of all those involved in these relations of commerce from both the sides, to absorb each others cultural package for their personal advancement.   Hence the economic forces were no longer alone in producing the lasting degree of ties with the Indian strecture because the mughal occupation of Kashmir put the varied means of enterprise within the reach of Kashmiri society, more so to their own advantage.

Before dealing with the post mughal phase, there is an interesting evidence relating to inclusion of two frontier territories of Ladakh and Kishtwar, within the mughal dominion. Jahangir occupied Kishtwar (1618) and Shah Jahan invaded Ladakh.[38] Both the territories were strategically important. Besides ladakh had been an entreport of trade between India on one hand and Central Asia and China on the other, without emerging from stone age. Kishtwar equally lacked the necessary elements of state appratus where King did not collect the land revenue and still there existed the regulation of manpower.[39] There was very little in their arts that mughals did not regard with admiration but both these areas had provided refuge to the representatives of Kashmir's political legacy from early times. This clearly demonstrates the urgency of mughals in containing these territories for fixing the mughal dominion in Kashmir. Here it deserves to be noted that it was for the first time only after the mughal occupation that both the territories of Ladakh and Kishtwar were brought permanently under one political system with varied ethinic and cultural base.[40] In these territories, what the successive rulers did was merely the reassertion of the mughal authority.

When the disintegration of mughal empire tookplace, the links between Kashmir and others parts of India had been so conceretly cemented that Kashmiris did not choose to settle their political separateness but continued to be under the Afghan Indian rule (1753-1819).[41] The representatives of Afghan Indian government persued their policies with an ironical design. Without effecting any improvements in means of production they went on securing the tax base of the mughals. Over and above the existing ones, they levied the new taxes of *Zari-Niyaz.* (presentation tax) *Zariashkhas* (property tax) *Zarihubub* (grain tax) *Zari-Dudah* (religious tax on Hindus) and *Dag Shal* (tax on Shawl weavers).[42] However, the bruden fell more heavily on the peasantry and artisans. But the artisans appear to have tried their best to compensate by putting in more additional labour and artisanal production emerged as an important area of resources for the strength of Afghan rule in Kashmir. The Afghan Governors massively appropriated the agricultural surplus that made feasible the existance of various urban centeres. These measures not only maintained the earlier established trading links with India but even permitted Kashmiri merchants to participate occassionaly in the world market in Central Asian belt. George forester mentions, "In Kashmir are seen merchants and commercial agents of most of the principal cities of Nothern India, also Tartary, persia and Turkey, who at the same time advance their fortunes and enjoy the pleasure of fine climate and country over which are profusely spread the various beauties of nature."[43] The Afghan nobilitys quest for power in Kashmir pre-occupied them with the expansion of tax apparatus, possibly some times without the legal consent of the state. This posed a serious threat to Kashmir's hadicraft production for importing the necessaries of life. To this attitude of Afghans the general population was not passive some protests took place.[44] Consequently there emerged anti systemic forces by breakaway movement within the nobility as well and facilitated the occupation of Kashmir by Ranjit singh in 1819.[45]

By this time the European entrance into the trading world of Asia had made tremendous progress by gradual colonization of India. Kashmir too could not escape the British attention being an economic and strategic asset to Indian sub-continent for long centuries. It was in 1846 that British took over Kashmir from

Sikhs. They handed over Kashmir to Maharaja Gulab Singh for carrying out administration in strict accordance with the pattern laid down by them.[46] In order to strengthen further the already established pattern the British included Jammu with Kashmir and carved it out as a state of British Indian Empire, thus completing the long movement from regional system to over all Indian system. With the completion of British packup in India the Kashmiris found themselves so deeply immersed into over all Indian strecture that they looked to India for solutions.

Now keeping in view the nature of affairs before us Our eonclusions remain hasty because we have not been able to take an account of cultural, psychological, religious and some other aspects which were involved in this long drawn process of Kashmir's links with India. In course of our analysis we have found that from the mughal occupation Kashmir became primarily dependent on India for her sustence despite the immensity of distances. The re-organization of administration, the matrimonial relations, the increasing expansion of trade and commerce and various other mutual persuites nourished a new environment without distressing their identity. Hence to yelid to the tempetation to nible at the nature of Kashmir's accession to India (whether final or otherwise) is a share excrecence on their identity.

NOTES AND REFERENCES

* I thank Professor T. S. Banerjee whose ideas made it remarkably easy while writing this paper. I also thank my all colleagues and my wife Sharika for some of the useful suggessions which strengthened my argument.

1. Infact Kashmir's strong ties with the rest of India from early ancient times can not be ignored but what persuades us to choose the medieval period is that it occupies the Central terrain in the whole process.

2. Yasin Mohammad ; *Akbar and Indian nationalism,* Srinagar, 1965.

3. On closer scrutiny one learns that a series of issues were involved in the mughal occupation of Kashmir. It was in 1561, When Akbar sent his first expedition to Kashmir under the command of Mirza Kara Bahadur, whose qualification for carrying out the task was his close acquaintance with Kashmirs topography and political affairs apart from military skill. Since no progress was registered in first instance, then Akbar sent Mirza Mnqim Isfahani and Mir Yaqub as his envoys to Hussain Shah Chak's court in 1568. The later's attitude to these envoys makes it clear that Akbars might was recognized when the Hussain shah offered his daughters in marriage to prince Salim along with other valuable gifts to Akbar. But Kashmiri nobility had always benefited from the country's political crisis they spoiled the friendly atmosphere and Akbar was forced to choose military action in 1586—not much against the wishes of common man there. Abul Fazl ; *Akbar nama,* (persian) English translation by H. Beveridge 3 vols. Delhi 1972 (reprint) vol. II. P. 198. Badauni Abdul Qadir ; *Muntakhab-ut-Tawarikh,* (Parsian) English translation by W. H. Lowe 3 vols. Patna 1973 (reprint) vol. II. pp. 128-129. Chadura Haidar Malik ; *Tarikh-i-Kashmir* ; Persian manuscript (unpublished) Research department library Kashmir University Srinagar ; P. 56.

4. Sultan Zain-ul-Abidin was the seventh sultan of this dynasty which ruled Kashmir from (1339-1540) of all the rulers produced by Shahmir dynasty zain-ul-Abidin was the only Sultan who initiated administrative reorganization and showed keen interest in the welfare activities of his subjects by promoting the craft production. Zutshi N. K ; *Sultan Zain-ul-Abidin of Kashmir.* Lucknow 1976 Parmu R. K ; *A History of Muslim rule in Kashmir,* Delhi, 1969, pp. 132-173.

5. Parmu, *op. cit.* 175-206.

6. Srivara Pandit, *Jaina Rajatarangini*, (Sanskrit) English translation by J. C. Dutt under *Kings of Kashmir.* 3 vols. Calcutta, 1935, Vol. III p. 228. Apart from heading the musical department Pandit Srivara has left a detailed record of Kashmirs history from (1459-1486) though full of traditional bias.

7. *Ibid,* Vol. III p. 252-270. A detailed reference to these measures also occurs in (Anonymous) *Baharistan-i-Shahi* (unpublished Persian Ms.) Research department library Kashmir University Srinagar. Folio's 68. 71a.

8. The *Shia Sunni* differences cropped up in Kashmir only after the arrival of Mir Shams-ud-Din Iraqi (1484) the founder of *Nurbakshiya* Order in Kashmir Shustri N. Qazi ; *Majalis-al-Muminin* ; Tehran A. H. 1299. pp. 315-316. But the real violent clashes of *Shias* and *Sunnis* which involved Serious loss of men and materials took place after the arriaval of Mirza Haider Dughlat who ruled Kashmir (1540-1550) Dughlat ; Mirza Haider ; *Tarikh-i-Rashidi* (Persian) English translation by Sir E. Denison Ross with introduction by N. Elias. London 1895. pp. 435-437. *Baharistan-i-Shahi* ff. 111-112. See also Koul N. A. ; *Tarikh-i-Kashmir* (1710) (unpublished Persian Ms.) Research department library Kashmir University Srinagar ff. 58-59.

9. From the very beginning Kashmiri peasant has been endowed with a peculiar Geography which does not permit the peasant to go in for a regular agriculture throughout the year and leaves farming to a Short Summer during which the peasant had also to fullfil heavy military and other obligations of the state and content himself with extreme sufference.

10. In those times 1000 *dinnars* were equal to ten *dams* (81/4 of a rupees) but still by all estimates it was beyond the common mans capacity to correspond to this price hike. Suka Pandit and Prajabhatta: *Rajvalipatika* ; Sanskrit. English translation by J. C. Dutt entitled *Kings of Kashmir* ; (1486-1513), Calcutta 1935. Vol. III. pp. 372-374.

11. A careful study of the sources reveals that from the very beginning, the mughal occupation was not resisted strongly because there was never nay popular protest. Infact when Yaqub Shah Chak the last ruler of Chak dynasty fled to *Kishtwar*, a suggestion was made to him by his nobles to submit to mughal authority much arlier. Possibly this suggestion seems to have emanated from

the lack of mass support. Besides the frequent visits of Kashmiri nobles to Akbar's court also suggest strong discontent and disatisfaction among masses. Abul Fazl ; *Akbarnama* Vol. II, 769. Suka. *Op. cit.* p. 407 *Baharistan-i-Shahi* ff. 184a-184b.

12. Abul Fazl ; *Akbarnama* Vol. III. p. 753.

13. It was on 16th of October 1586 that Akbar was declared the sovereign of Kashmir. *Ibid.* p. 770. Suka. *op. cit.* p. 47.

14. Abul Fazl ; *Akbarnama* ; Vol. III. 830-32.

15. Abul Fazl ; *Ain-i-Akbari* ; Vol. II. pp. 366-367.

16. *Baj* was a kind of toll tax and *Tamgah* was demanded over and above the usual land revenue ; *Ibid.* Vol. II. p. 363. The inscriptional evidence has been misinterpreted *by* R. K. Parmu for asserting the total abolition of forced labour in Kashmir but the incription on the main gate of *Nagar Nagar* fort refers to non-utilization of forced labour for construction of fort but that does not establish the total abolition of forced labour in other economic activities. The original persian text of the inscription reads :

"Bani Qali Nagar Nagar bud

ba ahde padshahe dadgustar,

Shahi Shahani Alam Shahi-Akbar.

Taalla Shana ha Allah Akbar.

Shahanshahe Kidar alam misalash

Na bnd ast-n-na khahad bud bigar,

Karore-o-dah lakh az Makhzan Firistad

Dh sad nrtadi Hindi Jumla Chakar

Na kardah hech kas begar anjah

Tamame Yaftand az makhzanash zar

Chihil-o-chahar Julnse padshahi

Hazar-o-shash ze tarikhe paigambar"

Translation :

"The foundation of fort town of Nagar Nagar

was laid in the reign of just sovereign,

King of Kings, unique among past and present

sovereigns of the world. One Carore and

ten lakhs were sent by him (Akbar)

from Central exchequer with two hundred

master builders and their servants—

No one was seized on begar (forced unpaid labour), all received

their remuniration in the 4th year of his accession corresponding to 1006 of the prophet i. e. 1006A, H" (1597 A. D.) Parmu ; *op. cit.* p. 301.

17. Sufi G. M. D ; *Kashir* 2 vols.   Lahore 1949, Vol. I. P. 262. Also Gladwin. F ; *The History of Jahingir.* Madras, 1930, p, 92,

18. Suka, *Op, cit,,* P. 418,

19. Abul, Fazl ; *Ain,* vol, II, pp, 366, 367.

20. Irfan Habib, *Agrarian System of Mughal* India ; Bombay, 1963. pp. 215-216.

21. For details see Sarkar J. N. *Condition of Kasmiri People under, Muslim rule.* Delhi, 1949. Bamzai P. N. K ; *A History of Kashmir.* Delhi 1962. pp. 385-386.

22. In this process of administrative recognization it is not possible to believe that every body became an *amil, mansabder, mirbakshi* or even a village level revenue official but the growth of commerce did provide a chance to earn their sustenance. Apart from taking to agriculture some of the nobles must have taken to horse keeping and other allied persuits which were equally essential for this kind of economy.

23. Even *Nilmatapura* refers to various kinds of artisans in early 6th Century A. D. Nila, *Nilmata Purana* Sanskrit, English translation by Ved Kumari Gai. 2 vols. Delhi, 1973 Vol. I, p. 138.

24. Abul Fazl ; *Ain* ; Vol. II. p. 353.

25. *Ibid* ; pp. 97-98.

Shawl Industry was one of the important source of subsistance both to rural and urban sections of Kashmir's population. With Mughal occupation the expansion of market for shawls in various parts of India strengthened and further expanded the social division of labour involved therein. By middle of 19th century when some of the European travellers and some local historians unveiled the nature of labour involved in shawl making, there were around seventeen persons whose labour was appropriated at various levels in producing a   single shawl for the market. For details see ; vigue G. T ; *Travels in Kashmir, Ladakh, Iskardu, countries and the mountain courses of Indus and Himalayan, North of Punjab* ; 2 vols. London 1842 vol. I. pp. 127-130. Moorcraft. W. G. Trebeck ; *Travels in Himalayan Provinces of Hindustan and Punjab, in Ladakh and Kashmir.* 2 vols. London 1971 (reprint) vol. II. pp. 167-200. Moorcraft. W. *Tour Diary Ms.* EURD-265.

Indian Office Library, London, pp. 30-117. Among the local historians see. Saif-ud-Din *; Akbarat* Persian Ms. 13 vols. (1846-1856). (Unpublished) Available with the author in microfilm.

26. Irfan Habib *; op. cit.* p. 87.

27. Sufi *; op. cit.* vol. I. p. 87 and vol. II. p. 654.

28. Vanistart. Henry *; A Narative of Transactions in Bengal (1760-64)* 2 Vols. Vol. II. pp. 165-70.

29. Quoted from Sufi ; *op. cit.* vol. I. p. 294.

30. *Ibid ;* vol. I. p. 272.

31. Parmu ; *op, cit,* p. 327, Fazl khan was the Mughal Governor of Kashmir from (2698-1710) it is interesting and important to record here that during the governorship of Fazl Khan the (*MoiMubark*) Sacrid Hair of prophet Muhammad was brought to Kashmir in 1699 by Khawaja Nur-nd-Din Ishabari from Bijapur (Deccan). It clearly illustrates that the traders even had visited parts of Deccan, Dedmari, Mohd, Azam ; *Wakiati-Kashmir ;* (Persian Ms. unpublished) Research department library Srinagar, pp. 155-156.

32. Sofi *;* Vol. I. p, 288. *Cambridge History of India,* Vol. IV. p. 337,

33. Parmu, *op. cit,* p. 327.

34. Irvine ; William *; Later Mughals* ; edited by J. N. Sarkar, Delhi 1971 (Reprint) vol. I. pp. 340-42.

35. Abul Fazl ; *Akbar nama* ; Vol. III. p. 958.

36. *Idid,* p. 958.

37. Khan M. I., *Perspectives on Kashmir ;* Srinagar, 1983. p. 129. Dr. Khan's statement is firmly based on reliable sources. Dr. Khan has raised some interesting questions while analysing the mughal occupation of Kashmir in this work, but we only offer our apologia for not touching upon them in this paper, a detailed attention is paid to them in my forthcoming monograph on "Pre-colonial social formation in Kashmir".

38. Jahangir Padshah, *Tuzki—Jahangiri ;* English translation by A. Rogers and H. Beveridge 2 vols. London 1914, pp. 137-139, see also Khan. M. *Iqbal nama-i-Jahangiri,* Calcutta 1915. pp. 142-147.

39. Elliot H. M. and Dowson, J. *History of India as told by its own Historians* 8 vols. London 1877. vol. VII. pp. 62-63. Bamzai ; *op, cit ;* pp. 394-397.

40. Infact Ladakh, Kistwar and Kashmir have nothing in common other than the political system. Only some areas of Kishtwar speak language which is slightly similar to Kashmiri and that is only because of their border with Kashmir.

41. Sufi ; *op. cit.* vol. I, p. 308.
42. Parmu ; *op. cit.* p. 364.
43. Quoted from Khan M. I. ; *op. cit.* pp. 49-50.
44. A protest should not be taken to imply only a revolt against the system. Various strata of society protest in various forms at different times. The large scale migration from Kashmir to various parts of north India, under Afghans should also be considered a nonviolent form of protest against Afgan rule, Fauq. M. D ; *Tarikh-i-Aqwam-i-Kashmir* 2 vols. Lahore, 1919, vol. I. p. 379.
45. Shamat Ali ; *The Sikhs and Afghans.* Lahore, 1983, p. 22.
46. Lawrence H. M. *Transfer of Government to Maharaja Gulab Singh,* Section C. 28 January 1848 file Nos. 33-44 unpublished, Jammu Archieves.

THE ROLE OF SAINT-POETS IN SOCIO-RELIGIOUS INTEGRATION OF MEDIEAVAL MAHARASHTRA

Professor D. A. Dalvi.
Principal, Dnyanasadhan College,
Thane, Maharashtra.

The saint-poets of medieaval Maharashtra had been the torch-bearers of religious and social enlightenment during the most critical period of its history. Through their devotional songs, poetic works, upright character and dedication they preserved cultural and historical traditions and saved the socio-religious structure from virtual degeneration. Their efforts were mainly responsible to creat among the Marathi speaking people a strong bond of unity, love, compassion and ethnical bearing. The literary and poetic compositions of saints have moulded the Marathi mind with its peculiar features of simplicity, tolerence and perseverance. The period of their activity largely synchronizes with the loss of political freedom owing to Muslim invasions of the Deccan till the formation of Swarajya by Chatrapati Shivaji. From 13th century A. D. to the end of the seventeenth century Maharashtra produced a galaxy of the outstanding personalities who wrought a miracle in the life pattern of the people. By granting them a distinct philosophy and a practical approach through the Bhagwat Dharma.

The role played by saint poets in preserving religious and social integrity marks a distinct achievement and has few parallels elsewhere. We come across several saints on the b road canvas of Indian History such as Basweshwar, Ramanuja,

Purandardas, Chaintanya, Kabeer, Mirabai and Tulsidas who stand supreme in their individual performance and literary contribution. But the significance of Marathi Saints is at once unique and different as it paved the way for the beginning of a well co-ordinated and continuous mass movement that finally emerged as the Bhakti movement culminating into Varkari Sampradaya. The Varkaris or itinerant volunteer devotees spread the spirit of intense devotion and purposeful life to the nook and corner of Maharashtra binding the people together by unfailing bond of love, compassion and brotherhood.

The achievements of saint poets have been interpreted in different manners by different scholars, historians and literary authorities. Justice M. G. Ranade, in his masterly work, 'The Rise of Maratha Power' first focussed the attention on the role of saints in preparing ground for sound socio-religious order that finally led to the foundation of Swarajya under Chatrapati Shivaji. According to Ranade the saints were primarily responsible for bringing socio-religious unity and harmony in Maharashtra. (1) In the light of Ranade's observations several other scholars such as Lokmanya Tilak, L. R. Pangarkar, V. K. Rajwade, Rajaram Shastri, Bhagwat, Datto Waman Potdar and N. R. Phatak have explained and interpreted the achievements through different angles and meanings. Modern critics including S. G. Tulpule, B. R. Sunthankar, S. D. Pendse, G. B. Sardar and P. G. Sahasrabuddhe have tried realistic and down to earth analysis and assessment of the contribution of saint poets. All of them admit invaluable meta phisical and theological significance of the poetic thought but at the same time dispassionately analyse the fact that how best the saints could have participated in socio-religious mobilization in the hour of crisis. G. B. Sardar is of the opinion that the activities of saints had socio-economic repercussions and it had been an attempt through mass-movement to inculcate spirit of integrity equality and socialism. (2) In the light of the above, one has to agree that the Bhakti Movement under the saints was not merely a religious or literary experiment but it proved to the most effective and comprehensive force of regional integration and spiritual solidarity. The present paper is a humble attempt to explain how far the activities and works of saint poets of medieaval Maharashtra helped the process of social, cultural and religious integration and how for its impact moulded the history of Maharashtra during this period. To understand the significance of the contribution of saint poets a little historical background is very much necessary. The 13th century A D marks the loss of political independence and sovereignty of the Marathas. The defeat of Ramdevrao Yadav at Deogiri (1318 AD) inaugurated a long and difficult period of darkness and chaos that continued upto the rise of Chatrapati Shivaji. During this period Maharashtra witnessed the lowest ebb of its fortunes. In every walk of human activity there had been a degeneration and dectine. Sudden loss of political power left the rulers and the ruled in the wilderness of uncertainty, confusion, frustration and humiliation. In the earlier periods there had been several invasions of India. The invaders attacked the country, registered victories and military triumphs but after a short spen of time got completely mixed up and assimilated in the main stream of Indian life. These invaders had brought vividity and comprehensiveness to Indian culture and civilization. But the story of Muslim inroads and occupation is distinctly different. The Muslims before storming the subcontinent had been a comparatively new force in world civilization, Within a short time they had succeeded in founding are the largest empires the world had over seen. When they knocked at the gates of India they were armed with vigorous monotheistic religion and most aggressive militant philosophy. Their entry marked an unprecedented crisis of identity between the idolworshippers and the iconoclasts, between polytheism and monotheism and between a tolerant peace-loving culture and the most aggressive nomedic hordes of the Arab world. The Indian princes were thoroughly unprepared to meet such a blatant fury and challange. They had seldom engaged among themselves into military combats of such a severity. The invasions of Muslims, not only uprooted political stability of the land but it totally disturbed socio-religious fabric that had been already worn out by passage of time. The iconoclast spirit made the invaders restless as they could find out vast lands and population offering them easy targets. They had scant regard for the culture and values of others. Their maddening fury prevented them from grasping the best characteristics of Indian civilization. They could not reconcile with fact that land which they had conqured had a superior culture and a glorious past. As a result whereever they had come across the semblance of politheism including magnificient temples, religious shrines and holy places, the devastation and destruction was ruthless, more or less complete, and beyond repairs. They could not tolerate the sages and seers as they could not appreciate spirit of understanding and co-operation. Their attitude was that of suppression, tyranny and destruction. The loss of political freedom, therefore, also marked the loss of personal freedom and individual initiative. It reflected not only in the destruction of outward symbols of culture out worse of it, the suppression of internal attitudes of the vanquished people. The only alternative that remained was either to perish or to reconcile with the new masters and their vigorous faith.

The impact of Muslim invasion in the Deccan had two significant aspects. Firstly, it revealed the political and military weakness of rulers and the ruled alike. It exposed the dire truth that none of the Maratha chiefs had the capacity to fight back against the invaders nor did they ever visualise a near or distant possibility of eliminating foreign rule and regaining freedom. It took more than three centuries till the rise of the Marathas under Chatrapati Shivaji to proclaim the war of independence. In stead, the nobility preferred to serve new masters and whole-heartedly helped to support and consolidate their rule. Political ambitions self assertion and love for freedom and dignity were lost. These chiefs failed to provide any programme or platform of national unity or patriotic feelings to the people at large. (3) They, meekly submitted to alien domination, their political system and government. Secondly, the loss of political freedom also sharply reflected on socio-religious conditions of the period. The society had already shown cracks in its rank and file due to degeneration of class and caste system and its inherent defects. It had been a divided apparatus having innumerable sects and their offshoots having opposit philosophies and practices. Socio-religious stagnation, ignorance and backwardness prevailed every where. This weakness was further accelerated because of tremendous hold of Brahmin priest-hood over the society which did not allow other castes and communities to take lead or initiative. (4) The priestly class kept people engaged in unnecessary rituals, ceremonies religious pilgrimages, observances and practices having no utility or purpose. Healthy traditions, open and free thinking was deliberately curd. Various restrictions were imposed on the people depriving them of free worship. Every aspect of religious or philosophical significance was brought under the monopoly of priesthood. Study of Vedas and Shastras was prohibited to other communities except the Brahmins. Class and caste exclusiveness and water tight social compartments were meticulously maintained. Although the varna system prevailed, in reality only two classes existed : the Brahmins and non-Brahmins. The shudras were completely eliminated from spiritual fold and were deprived of certain rites and entry into important religious shrines. The position of atishudras was worse than that of others. Women too, were treated with inequalities and had to suffer the most because of restricted attitudes of over bearing males and priestly class. The freedom and dynamism of vedic times was substituted with Pouranic philosophy that was based on excessive ritualism, ceremonies, and obervances. True spirit of religion was ignored and supersitions, dogmas and evil practices were allowed to prevail upon the people. Exclusion of shudras and atishudras from the fold of higher castes led them to take shelter to debased practices and worship of senseless lesser dieties. Thus the spiritual leadership of Brahmins failed to inculcate the sense of belonging and homogeniety within the society. The advantage of these weaknesses was umptinly taken by the Muslim ruling class. It allured lower communities to accept the new faith that not only promised jobs, position, wealth and land but most significant as it was—socio-religious equality. The downtroden communities and lower sections of society after accepting Islam found themselves in elavated status and prestige. They could claim parity with other Muslims and felt very sound and superior in comparision to their earst-while brothers. This proved to be a serious threat to Hinduism in the Deccan. With the help of new converts it became a much more easy task for the Muslims to consolidate their political authority. The Hindu society had been in such a disarray and confused state that it would have lost its identity and independence if the saints would not have come to its rescue. It was at this stage of extreme socio-religious deterioration the saint-poets in Maharashtra began their unique mission. Their main task had been to save the people from Muslim onslaught and secondly, to offer them such a path, Philosophy and channel that would foster spirit of reformation and awakening. (5) It is at this juncture the role of saint-poets as a means of cultural integration becomes very significant. They provided the most helpful and matured leadership to the people. Their activities opened flood gates of intense devotion, fellow feeling and personal warmth that was the greatest need of the time.

The contribution of saint poets and its impact on the society has a definite sequence and continuity. Their preaching and activies provided a solid ground to form a distinct ideology and a platform through which they could communicate with all sections of society. The departure of saint poets from the then set socio-religious order indirectly provided for regenerating healthy and purposeful trends. They preferred the path of devotion—Bhakti-Marga but it was to be associated with responsibilities attached to daily life of a common man. The saints synthesised intense devotion and respect for one's duty irrespective of caste, creed and set into one unit and one ideal. The amalgam of these ideals first resulted in turning Bhakti-Marga into Bhakti-Yoga and later on transformed it to the most popular and pragmatic philosophy—the Bhagawat-Dharma. (6)

Dnyaneshwar—the path-finder : Guide of common masses :

The credit of this unique transformation obviously goes to the greatest of the saints of Maharashtra—Dnyaneshwar. It was Dnyaneshwar who first realised the necessity of a break with the past traditions and fast degenerating theological and metaphisical wrangles and controversies. His departure from the age old spiritual attitudes turned to be the first effective step information of the Bhagwat—Dharma. Dnyaneshwar belonged to the early parts of the 13th Century A. D. when the Muslims were yet to cost their eyes upon the Deccan. But by the time their military compaigns had began the great saint had already realised and took note of the internal degeneration and decay that had set in the Hindu Society. He felt the need to redeem the masses from socio-religious bondage and especially from the cluthes of archaic Shastris and Pandits.

He was extremely eager to take the message of god to common masses and to enlighten them on pure and simple means through which proximity with god could be obtained. (7) The synthesis of Bhakti and karma i. e. devotion and duty became the most appealing force and cardinal principle of his teachings. Descarding the then prevailent practice of the Shastris and Pandits of wasting time on unnecessary debates and discourses on pauranic literature and dharma-shastras, Dnyaneshwar decided that the best means of enlightening the people would be through the most inspiring and convincing critique on the Bhagwat-Gita. He thought that the Gita would be the only medium that would lead the society to its emancipation and free it from stagnation and chaos. The great saint, therefore, decided to spread message of Vitthala through common language i. e. Marathi instread of Sanskrit. This event marked greatest turning point in the destiny of medieaval Maharashtra. A simple and lucid translation of the Bhagwat-Gita in Marathi known as Bhavartha Deepika—popularly known as Dnyaneshwari—become a gospel of reformation creativeness, dynamis and stood as a beakon of light that granted guidance and spiritual solace to his followers.

Dnyaneshwar and his followers :

The process of socio-religious integration was strengthened and popularised by a galaxy of saint-poets who had come across the spiritual influence of the great master. These saint-poets belonged to various castes and creeds but were sincularly attached to the principles of the Bhagwat Dharma. The most prominent among them had been Namadev, Eknath and Tukaram. In fact, all of them could be considered as pioneers of Bhakti Movement in Maharashtra. If Dnyaneshwar had prepared the intellectual and metaphysical ground of the Bhaktiyoga, Namadev, Eknath and Tukaram took the movement to the doors of the common man. (8) Along with their own devotional compositions they encouraged and participated in the Varkari activities thereby bringing the people together on solid ground of religious fraternity. The development of Varkari Sampradaya had been a remarkable achievement as it engulfed the people of all denomination and raised castes or sub-castes centred around the only principle—the intense devotion of Vitthal. In fact, in the absence of political unity and under constant fear of tyranny and oppression by the foreign rulers, the Varkaris intrinsically wove a pattern of fellow-feeling, and spiritual unity. The Varkaris, through annual pilgrimages to holy shrines of Pandharpur and Alandi indirectly created and fostered a deep sense of belonging and oneness not only among their followers but among hundreds of people who whole heartedly participated in this movement.

Legacy of Saint-poets : Foundation of Bhagwat Dharma :

The contribution of saint-poets resulted in co-ordinating and systematising socio-religious order of medieaval Maharashtra. It provided uniformity in the mode of worship and recognized religious equality. The rise of Bhagwat Dharma brought the people together on a common platform and provided them : (1) a movement in the form of Varkari Sampradaya which had more popular appeal compared to the Nath or Datta Sampradaya ;

(2) Marathi as a common medium of communication ;

(3) Centralization and symbolization of worship in the form of Vitthal and Rakhumai as the most revered duties.

(4) Annual pilgrimage to holy places such as Pandharpur, Alandi, Tuljapur and several others. While discussing the legacy of Bhagwat Dharma P. G. Sahasrabuddhe refers to six main points which transformed the entire living pattern in Maharashtra. These are (a) the use of Marathi, (b) Bhakti-yoga

—realisation of ultimate self through intense devotion, (c) Swadharmacharan—following one's profession dutifully and thereby render service to god, (d) preservation of sound social order and organization—Lokasanstha—by promoting spirit of unity co-ordination and equality, (e) upholding utility and dignity of worldly life instead of resorting to renunciation or Sanyasa and (f) discarding worship of debased dieties which had attracted the lower communities. (9) All the above features have been invaluable as a force of social integration.

Marathi—River of Spiritual Enlightenment. :

The significance of the use of Marathi could better be understood through the sayings and poetic works of the saints. From Dnyaneshwar onwards scores of other religious and literary personalities preferred to contribute their work in Marathi. It was through regional language one comes across spontaneous outburst of poetic inspiration, imagiration, lucidity of thought, emotions and feelings. The sweetness of Marathi could not be better understood if any one is not well conversant with its natural charm including poetic metre and style. It does not require difficult compositions as the Shastris and Pandits did earlier, but it could be expressed through simple constructions and utilization of meaningful words. Dnyaneshwar not only deported from age old tradition of using Sanskrit on matters of religion and philosophy but introduced simplest literary style in the form of ovee. His outstanding works such as Dnyaneshwari, Amritanubhava, and Changdev-Pasasthi are all composed in ovees. Tukaram was interested in the Abhangas while Samarth Ramdas has mostly used shlokas. These forms besides being simple have the gaity of music and could be easily song either alone or in congregations. Through these forms the other medium of expression such as Bhajans, Kirtans, Bharuds, Ballads and story telling have been exploited enriching Marathi. The use of Marathi also gave a serious jolt to the monopoly the

Shastris and Pandits enjoyed over Sanskrit. Dnyaneshwar had been very confident about his performance in the use of Marathi. He felt that he would write in Marathi in such a way that it would win any bait so as to differentiate between what was original and what was translated. (10) He further pointed out that just as a candle among the lamps or a shining full noon among the nights, Marathi is the most charming among the languages. (11) Father Stephens, a Christian missionery from Goa, reflects that just as jasmine among flowers, or the scent of Kasturi among fragrance, in the same way is Marathi attractive among the languages. (12) Eknath expresses his doubt on importance of Sanskrit. According to him— how could one say that the anthors of Sanskrit works be called great and that of Prakrit of lesser significance ? He felt that languages old or new are the same and are like flowers of gold. (13) However, Tukaram highlightens the meaning and purpose of words in the most apt way. 'In our abode (poets) the wealth is in the form of words (diamonds), are the essense of ourlife. We (poets) shall distribute the wealth of words to all (people). Look ! words are manifestation of god. It is with words like flowers we shall make their offering to the diety and feel proud.' (14)

Integration through the words of Saints :

Dnyaneshwar, Namdev, Eknath and Tukaram had been the main architects of Bhagwat Dharms. A popular verse of Bahinabai points out : By the compassion of Saints the edifice of Bhagwat Dharma has been constructed. Dnyandev laid its foundation, Namdev being his servant prepared the foreground, Janardhan—Eknath provided pillars and the pinacle was put on top by Tukaram. (15) The greatest gift of Bhagwat Dharma had been centralization of worship in the form of Vitthal and Rakhumai—the primer duties of Maharashtra. In addition to

16

other deities they became a symbol of spiritualism where all aspiration, emotions, feelings and desires were concentrated. The saints adorned these deities in most appealing and convincing poetic expressions. Entire philosophy of Bhagwat Dharma is based on appreciation and glorification of Vitthal and Rakhumai as benefactors of human race. The greatness of these deities was further emphasised when Varkaris began to pay their humble homage from distant parts of Maharashtra. The pilgrimage to Pandharpur formed an inseparable duty on the part of voteries of Vitthal and became a binding force that brought the people together irrespective of class or creed. It turned out to be a movement of the masses. It also marked socio-religious mobility. The people with intention of visiting holy places moved from different regious bearing hot sun, cold nights and inclement wether. These gatherings provided opportunities to people to share discussions on religious matters, social obligations, political upheavals, annual Larvests, personal sorrows and sufferings. One could visualize spiritual integration when the surroundings were resounding with the call of Vitthal and Dnyanoba Tukaram Vitthal Mauli. The dindis of Varkaris making in groups with safron flags completely engrossed in Bhajans and Kirtans used to be most memorable sights. The Dindis had been expositions of cultural life of medieaval Maharashtra.

Attributes of Bhagawat Dharma :

The worship of Vitthal and Rakhumai culminated the processes of Bhakti movement in Maharashtra. The devotional works of the saints and Varkaris gave a dozzling gloss to it. The greatness of the movement now depended on the Bhakta or devotee and his characteristics. In the words of Dr. Sahasrabuddhe the concept of Bhakti Marga emerged into a more appealing term—i.e. Bhakti Yoga. (16) About the Bhakta or devotee, Dnyaneshwar said that 'The greatest devotee and sire is in whose heart is located intense love of Vasudev— creator of the Universe. (17) According to Namdev' One who love everything living and non-living in the Universe and worships its creator he should be considered as a true devotee. He further pointed out that those who worship deities nade out of stove are likely to loose everything by their folly. (18) Eknath opined that any one who sincerely carries out his profession without any motive it should be considered as an offering to god. It is this concept of which is pure and without any blemish should be worshipped. This should be considered as pure Bhagwat Dharma. (19) In his most illustrious verse Tukaram said : The holy personages are born for the welfare of the world. They exert for the good of the people. They do not have any personal desires. Compassion towards the living is the capital of the Saints. Happiness of others is the happiness for all. This is the nectar that pours out through the hearts. (20) Tukaram further explained that one who has love and compassion towards those who are in distress and sorrow, he should be considered as a real saint and it is in whom one should find out the devine grace. (21) But at the same time he made it clear that the strength of saints should not be underminded. We the servants of god are softer than wax but if time comes we shall have no hesitation even in breaking the hardest possible stone.

The revealation of devine grace through simple devotional songs and expressions had been the key note of socio-religious amity advocated by the followers of Bhagwat Dharma. They highlightened the virtues of human character and emphasised the significance of love, piety compassion and mutual co-operation in day today life. The highest sense of brotherhood could best be understood (22) When the saints gave a call of mutual help and co-operation and to follow the best of the path i.e. Bhagwat Dharma.

If the great saints including Mukteshwar, Sopan, Mahipati and others had prepared foundation of Bhakti movement, the lesser personalities adorned the main edifice by their realistic expositions of worldly problems, human emotions and varied traits of human life. It is really heartening to observe that men and women belonging to the humblest of professions have contributed in fostering and caring humanism and human understanding during the days when socio-religious inequality and caste bias was at its highest. Their compositions deal with such subjects which are very dear to common man. They express the sentiments of the poor, the needy and the downtroden. They throw interesting light on the socio-economic life by bringing out details and intricacies of various professions and attitudes. Rarely in any literature we come accross the attempt of won to project proximity with god by faith holly carrynics out the duties and responsibilities attached to one's profession. Devotion and duty being the cordinal principles of the Bhakti movement. This resulted in freedom of expression and sense of unity for every man who wanted to find out true faith. It is for this reason the Bhagwat Saints earnestly appealed to maintain proper family relalions and there by preserve social harmony. Preservation of Lokasanstha and upholding of virtuous and moral life had been one of the chief objectives. The saints decried samyasa as a way of escapism. (23)

The saints following humble professions : Contributions : Such a Namdev, a tailor, his disciple Janibai, Gora Kumbhar a cobbler, Sawata Mali, a Gardener, Chokha Mahar a scavenger. Narhari Sonar a goldsmith and scores of others will ever stand as perenial source of inspiration and guidance to those who are thirsty of spiritual attainments and satisfaction. Even in the age of inequality and expoitation women saints too have played a unique role by their poetic talents. Mahadamba, Muktabai, Janabai. Bahinabai are the names which will always stand at the apex of process of integration in Maharashtra. (24) The imagination, expression, use of metres and selections of words and ideas shown by these poets in their devotional songs is extra ordinary and definately point out to devine inspiration. Namdev and Tukaram have often talked on their disposition of being a tailor or a grocer. Sena Nhavi had been a barber. Explains the devine worship through his profession in the most graphic and convincing manner He says :

We are barbers, we shall carry out close shave. We shall show the mirror of thought. When a hair is to be timmed we pluck it with forcep ofrenunciation. We shall apply water of peack and trangial to the head, but we shall twist the pigtail if selfishness prevails. We shall clean the armpits of worldly life and we shall cut finger nails of, desire and anger. (25) Savata Mali, a gardener compares his gardening tasks as a way of devotion. Gora kumbhar, a potter experiences proximity of Vitthal when working on a potter's wheel. Chokha Mela, Baka and karma Mela belonged to the lowest strate of society but find out freedom and solace when engrossed in the worship of Vithoba.

Saints as Social reformers :

While propagating the Bhagawat Dharma the saints exposed social evils and worship of debased form of dieties. They did not spare hypocrates as well as those who wasted time in rituals and useless observances. They felt that by outward show of rituals no one could realize devine grace. There was no need going to the tirthas. This is possible only by living good life and selfless devotion to Vithoba. The saints often warned and chastised people to ward off influence of evil-minded persons and quacks in society. Dnyaneshwar is very particular when he points out to his

devotees that they should not waste time in unwanted rites and
regulations nor trouble the body. They should not use such
language that way hurt others nor is the necessity of visiting
the tirthas. (26) Tukaram felt that how 'Kashi and Ganga
would be helpful if the devotee is not pure at heart ? What is
the use of application of gandha to forehead or garlanding
oneself if he does not have good disposition and character ?'
For Tukaram purity of heart and good living is the real faith.
According to him, whatever may be the family whether of high
caste or that of a chandala—any one who calls himself as
servant of Hari is nobler to Tukaram. (27) Eknath asks a
devotee as to what did he achieve by visiting holy place ? He
may look clean outwardly but inside his heart may be impure.
A dip in the holy waters is just useless if one's mind is not pure.
If the heart is pure be sure that god resides within oneself and
the devotee could see him flom any position where he sits. (28)
Eknath is very outspoken when he criticises the inequalities
created by the Vedas by forming varnas. He said that 'the
vedas brought three classes on a parity but doing so were
ignored women and the Shudras. The vedic words could not
reach their years. It is in this way the Vedas have devalued
themselves. (29)

Saints as Advocates of Social Equality :

Almost all saint poets believed in dignity of human life
and mobility of character. They felt that castes and birth
is no barrier for any one who wants to devote himself for the
service of god. They often lament that caste barniess have
destroyed true spirit of worship. In anguish and agony they
sometimes pose this problem to God and ask such questions the
answers to which one finds difficult to get.

Dnyaneshwar feels that simple devotion is enough, castes are
no standards for devotion. Status of family caste or warna are

all useless in the matter of devotion. As particles of salt have no purpose when dropped into the sea in the same way all devotees irrespective of caste or creed get completely assimilated with devine grace by their devotion. (30) For Namdev, caste and class or dictates of Vedas are of no use if the devotees sincerely meditate the name of god. By Recitation of god's name the soul gets satisfaction. What is required is pure feeling in the innerself by forgetting all differences—high or low. (31) Tukaram goes a step forward and claims right of worship to all inclusive of Brahmins, Kshtriyas, Vaishyas, Shudras and even Chandals. For that matter any one whether men or women, children and even prostitutes should also be entitled to carry out worship of their dieties. (32) The views expressed by the saints are not only progressive in spirit but point out the freedom of an individual to carry out worship according to their own choice. The saints did not advocate equality in the modern sense of term. In fact they had keen ardent supporters of varnashramdharma. They did not like any one transgressing the caste barrier as far as resigned and its social utility was concerned. They had simply submitted themselves to devine disposition for their birth. What they attempted was spiritual equality. Their aim had been equality or equal opportunity for all in the service of god. It is strange that inspite of the fact that saints like Dnyaneshwar and Eknath had been intellectuals par excellance. The meta-phisical and spiritual explanations which they often give will stand as a super pience of philosophy compared to the other religious luminiaries of medieaval world. Yet their field of activity had been immensely narrow. They pleaded for common status for all before god but had been to visionaries to spell out all pervading social life. Therefore, they were not immovaters or reformers in the strictest meaning of term. Same times, we even find contraditions in their statements concerning treatment of various castes and subcastes. The feeling of being born in a low family had been often agonizing to the saints of low denomination. Tukaram often feels about this but then convinces himself that it was better that he was low born otherwise he would have died of pride. (33) However, Karmamela a seavenger puts a direct question to god that why he was given low caste. Dosn't god understand repurcassions of that ? The whole life has been spent in eating leftover food (by higher castes). Dosn't god feel a-shamed of this act ? (34) No more eloquent words than this could be found when the saints express their distress and frustration over status by birth.

Impact of Bhagwat Dharma on other communities. :

Along with others, the impact of Bhakti-movement was also felt over Muslim, Christian and other communities including gains in Maharashtra. They too while highlightening extreme devotion to God expressed themselves in Marathi. Amongst the most prominent Muslim religious poets names of Shaikh Muhammad, Hussain Ambar khan, Alam Khan, Shaikh Sultan, Shah Muntoji, Bhahmani and Shah Muni stand prominentator their efforts towards religious and linguistic integration. What is remarkable is that being Muslims they were supposed to be nearer to contemporary Sufi saints, instead, they were very much under the influence of Bhagwat philosophy. The impact of Mahanubhawas, Dnyaneshwar and other holy personalities could be seen very often on their mystical and theological expressions. (35) The Islamic concept of unity of God and the Bhagwat philosophy of extreme and unqualified devotion have been beatingally synthesised and blended by the Muslim poets. So much so that religious orders in Maharashtra speak very highly of these saints. For example, famous Marathi poet Moropant had given a place of honour to Shaikh Muhammad in his work 'Sanmanimala'. (36) He is often described as an incurnation of Kabeer.

Among the literary contribution of Muslims Shaikh Muhammads' Yogasangram, Dawanvijava and Nishkalanka prabodh, Muntoji Brahaman's Siddhasanket Prabandha and Anubhavsara, Shah Muni's Siddhant both and Hussain Ambarkhani Gita Tika or commentory on Bhagwat Gita are extremely significant. While the Hindus and Muslims, especially new converts were settling themselves in the Deccan, the efforts of Muslim Marathi saints in bringing communial harmony and mutual understanding is definitely commendable. In fact, this requires urgent attention of both the present rulers and all those who are concerned with seriousness of communial disturbances of modern times. A new light on their contribution would be helpful in defusing communial hatred and tensions.

The Muslim poets were well aware of discord and differences of religious beliefs and practices. By opting Marathi as a means of expressing their feelings they did try to establish co-ordial relationship between the two communities. (37)

Emphasising use of Marathi Shaikh Muhammad wrote :

If the Muslim poet had Hindu gurus several Hindus had been disciples of the former. Shaikh Muhammad while pointing out the greatness of preceptor and teacher remarks : 'Great teachers guide their disciples such as the lamp burns itself but gives light to others. They take rest only when they forget theirself and do away with pride and ego of family or caste. (38) I would speak my thought in Maharashtra bhasha. Thereby I shall bring out the depth of my heart. I would analyse thoughts in vivid manners. The listeners should understand its hidden secrets. (39) Shah Mutabji Brahmani composed a book on Sanskrit-Persian Lexicon. While presenting it he informs that he wrote the book for bringing Hindus and Muslims together. (40) Amber Hussaini concluded his commentary on Bhagwat Gita by commendation to Ganpati. He stated that all people

(Hindus, Muslims) are obstinate over mutual differences. It is this huge group of obstacles that should be destroyed by Lord Ganesh. (41) Shah Muni, the celebrated another of 'Siddhant-bodha' pleaded to Hindu saints that although he born as a Muslim he was much more devoted to Lord Krishna and he should be taken within theirfold and accept him as a devotee. (42) Shaikh Muhammad referred to himself as a product of Hindu-Muslim harmony. He was bron in unacceptable family C Muslim. Started speaking about both the Quran and the Puranas, and honoured both Muslim Walis and Hindu Saints and holy personalities. This he did became the qualities were for self realization. (43) He also pleaded to his follower to open their eyes and find that whether one should call the saint as Sachapir or Sadguru there is no difference between them.

Father Thomas Stephens : Christa—Purana :

Among the Christian Missionaries who had came into contact of religious traditions of Maharashtra. Was Father Thomas Stephens. (1549-1619) He will ever be remembered for his outstanding contribution—the Christa-Purana or the life and message of Lord Christ. (44) An Englishman by birth he visited Goa as a priest and learned and obtained superb mastery over Marathi and Konkani (a dislect of Marathi). He wrote the doctrines of Christianity in Konkani and Christa-Purana in Marathi. The Christa-Purana acquaints Marathi speaking people on Christian traditions inciding Old and New Testaments. The reading of this master piece obviously points out suberb command of Father Stephens on various aspects of Marathi literature. The lucidity and simplicity of diction and his knowledge of contemporary Marathi works is worth appreciating. (45) Another Christian missioners, Father Creuwa was also a prolific writer. His work 'Mahapurana' is based on the life of St. Peters. However, his comparisons of Christian traditions with those of the Hindus and his uncharitable remarks on Hindu dieties is not in good faste. What is remarkable about the Christian missioneries is their real to spread Christian docrines in regional languages. Their had been the earliest attempts to bring Christian literature into Marathi. They added one more stream of semetic religion to the ever comprehensive cultural tradition of India.

Contemporary Jain Marathi Literature :

The Jain saints of medieaval Maharashtra have also contributed several works in Marathi. Pandit Meghraj had been perhaps the first poet to compose the life sketch of Yashodhara entitled 'Jasodharras' Kamraj Shah originally belonging to Gujrat contributed 'Sudarshan-Charitra' and 'Chaitanyaphag' Surijan had been a remarkable poet welknown for his Champa-kavya—'Pranhansakatha'. Nagoaya and Gunanandi had been other renowned poets to write on the themes of Mahavira and important personalities of Jainism. (46)

Samartha Ramdas : Call of Maharashtra Dharma :

The saint-poets till Samartha Ramdas were deeply involved in preacking people values of ethical life and parity of character. Their main aim was socio-religious reforms. Although they pleaded for sanctity of worldly life and importance of famility organization in social set up they were inclined more towards spiritual redumption. They preferred Lokasanstha based on grihasthashrama and upheld sociological importance of family institution. The process of reforms therefore had been of volantary nature and a time consuming one. More than three hundred years had passed between Dnyaneshwar and the rise of Samartha Ramdas. During these centuries the followers of Bhagwat Dharma did succeed in organizing the people on socio-religious platform but none of them had any ability to rouse the people on political and military front. As a result the socio-religious unity proved to be lusterless and barren. The saints created a sense of belonging for Vithoba or the holy places associated with Bhakti movement but they never thought of enkindling the spirit and love for motherland. Inspite of their best efforts, the results had always been negative. The task of inspiring people with burning passion of patriotic ferver and liberating their dear mother-land fell upon Samartha Ramdas. In time we came across the greatest visionary of the Marathas of medieaval times. His achievement had been the liberation of society from excessive inclination of Bhagwat Dharma towards nivrutti marga or passive look out of life and to inculcate ambitions based on active political struggle. He took up challenge of the time and gave a beacon call for people to rise and revolt against the foreign power in the Deccan. Indoing this he transformed Bhagawat Dharma to a strong and aggressive patriotic politico-religious philosophy i. e. Maharashtra Dharma. Ramdas offered a new dynamic political vision to dormant Maharashtra by enkindling in their heart the flame of Maratha patriotism. His war-cry had been : 'That all the Marathas should be united together and every one should exent to promote Maharashtra Dharms.' According to S. R. Sharma 'Ramdas was as much the instrument of this transformation as Shivaji. He converted the Varkaris (religious pilgrims) to Dharkaris (Warriars) Sampradaya ; as Rajwade puts it : the Sahishnu psychology was revolutionired into the Jagishnu. The God of this virile cult is not static Vithoba of Pandharpur, but the dynamic Maruti of Ramdas'. (47) Thus Ramdas through his Dasbodh and Manache Shloka shattered the mgth of political slavery and openly pronounced a rebellion against oppressive and tyrannical rule Maharashtra Dharma, as envisaged by Ramdas, was not merely a political gospel but it regenerated a tremendous explosive force that ultimately helped Shivaji to found Maratha Swarajya. He infused a firy spirit of insurgence among the dormant Marathas. Some of his verse would stand the test of time and have formed imperishable piece of patriotic form of Marathi literature.

Although a celebate, Ramdas vehementaly pleaded for well organised family life. He explained that man should first look after his duties towards the family and then get involved in spiritual penance. He felt that all people should rally around the safron flag. Along with roots of patriotism Ramdas fostered intellectual and rational qualities of the people to make them more organised and to consolidate their position. He further pointed out that ceaseless efforts for progress was vital for resurgence of a political state. According to him effort-Yatna-itself is god. 'One who endevours, himself is indeed a fortunate one. Life without an endevour is nothing but a sign of passiveness and poverty'. (48) Yet he went a great leap forward when he appealed to the people that in addition to Bhaktiyoga the Buddhiyoga or intellectual persuit was most essential. (49)

The rise of Chatrapati Shivaji and Samartha Ramdas marked the fulfilment of Maharashtra Dharma. If the sword of Shivaji succeeded in carring Swarajya the pen of Ramdas triumphed in giving a philosophy of religious patriotism to the people of Maharashtra. Ramdas gave a clear and comprehensive meaning to the term Maharashtra Dharma and strengthened it by a concrete programme of the destruction of the foreigners. Unlike negative approach of Bhagwat followers Ramdas enthused this people to exant for building new Maharashtra that would be nothing but 'Anandabhuvana' or paradise upon the earth. He regenerated a tremendous confidence among the dormant society and awakened it to accept challenges of time. He encouraged the people to resist tyranny and exploitation. In one of his famous addresses he wrote : 'Do not loose courage, do not get confused. Behave according to challenge of time. Do not have any fear. Be courageous as it is courage that counts. Impatience is of no use. Those who are impatient do not understand the crux of time'. (50) Ramdas destroyed uncertainty of time and infused people with political ambitions and dynamine. He decried fatalism and pleaded for positive and constructive outlook. He emphasised that action and positive approach was extremely significant for successful life. His clear and practical political thoughts and his intense appeal for patriotic sentiments have won him the title of Rajguru. Coincidence as it might have been, but Maharashtra had produced the greatest political chief and the greatest political preceptor, Shivaji and Ramdas respectively who integrated Marathi society on the basis of strong military footing and astonising political philosophy. Ramdas like Mazzini in Italy, created confidence and faith among peopl and revitalised Maharashtra with ideals of political resergence, self-respect and dignity. In his famous poem Anandawan he expressed hope for brilliant future for Maharashtra—envigorated with political freedom, courage of conviction, national pride and national honour.

Conclusion :

A brief survey of socio-religious upheaval in Maharashtra and subsequent rise of Bhakti movement in the form of Bhagawat Dharma points out a sustained sttempt on the part of the people and their saint-leaders to redeem themselves from archacic and bondage and to organise themselves on sound spiritul grounds. Looking at the opposition from Muslim powers, the saints maintained social and religious integrity of the region the task that was extremely difficult. The saints did succeed to a certain extent in liberating people from monopoly of priesthood and provided them with pure and simple means of devotion through Bhagwat Dharma. One of the most remarkable achievements had been popularity of Marathi. The saints enriched it in every respect giving it a gloss of style, fine vocabalary and a literature that could be termed as classic. It became a language of hearts binding people together with common affinity, love and fraternity. It provided avenues to express literary talents to all shades of people including Muslims, Christians, Jains and others. It revealed spancenous flow of devotion for more than three centuries after the composition of Dnyaneshwari that proved be the greatest integrating and unifying force.

Sametimes the role of saint poets of Maharashtra has been criticised as they did nothing but giving the people and philosophy of Bhaktibhav which was at once passive and uncreative. They did not take part in the amelioration of sorrows of the poor, the down-troden and women. They stuck to Varnashrama and worked within narrow frame work of caste and class. In later times they became excessively devotion prove thereby neglecting real values of life. The Bhagawat Dharma failed to regenerate required co-operation from society. These are some of the standard objections raised against the contribution of saint poets. However, one has to conclude that, the period during which the saints perseed their mission was not favourable to them. They had to face obstades from within and without. To speak about political freedom, as Samartha Ramdas did, was possible only when the Muslim powers in India began to loose their military and political grip and when the ruthless iron hard of authority was turning week and seable. Even in the hay days of Muslim rule, Namdev and Eknath did express their displeasure against excesses and atrocities perpetrated in the name of religion by Muslim masters. Namdev had the guts to move from places to places, from Maharashtra to Punjab bringing people together on emotional and spiritual grounds. The missions of saint poets had limited application. They wanted overall internal reformation and for that, they appealed to the heart and consciousness of the people. To them unting force was devotion ; became through devotion ehty dreampt to build up spiritual kingdom within. They sincerely believed that once this had been done, the other problems would end naturally. In this sense the progress achieved by the saints in

transorming Bhakti-marga to comprehensive Bhagwat-Dharma
and then to Maharashtra Dharma itself speaks of unprecedented
and outstanding phenomenon of medieaval times. For saint-poets
of Maharashtra they have carved out their place in the heart
of every Marathi speaking man and woman.

While paying my humble tribute to the Saint-poets for
their endevour to integrate and unite medieaval society and for
the spread of eternal light of wisdom, I gratefully recall the
benediction of Santa Dnyaneshwar :

दुरितांयें तिमिर जावो | विश्व स्वधर्म सूर्यें पाहो |
जो जे वांछिल तो तें लाहो | प्राणिजात || १५ ||

(Let the darkness of evil be destroyed, Let the sun of nobler
religion rise, Let every animate being get whatever that is
being desired).

REFERENCES

1.	Ranade M. G.	:	Rise of the Maratha Power. Publication Division, Delhi, 1961 p. 17.
2.	Sardar G. B.	:	Santa Vangmayachi Samajik Phalashruti. Pune 1970, pp. 12-14.
3.	Bhave V. K.	:	Peshwekalin Maharashtra Pune 1935. pp. 12-13.
4.	Inamdar H. W. & others.	:	Namdevanchi Abhangawani, Pune, 1979 pp. 2-3.
5.	Pendse S. D.	:	Maharashtracha Sanskritik Itihas. Pune 1933, pp. 156-158.
6.	Sahasrabuddhe P. G.	:	Maharashtra Sanskriti. p. 305.
7.	Pendse S. D.	:	Maharashtracha Bhagwat Dharma. Dnyandev Ani Namdev. Pune 1972. pp. 1-5.
8.	Sardar G. B	:	Ibid. pp. 159-160.
9.	Sahasrabuddhe P. G.	:	Ibid. pp. 318-319.
10.	Dandekar S. W. (Mamasaheb)	:	Sartha Dnyaneshwari, Pune. 1984. 6. 14- p. 138.
11.	Malshe S. G.	:	Santarpan, Pune 1986. Quoted from Yogavasistha 1. 294-99 p.
12.	Malshe S. G.	:	Ibid. Quoted from Christa-Purana 1. 1. 122-25 p.
13.	Pendse S. D.	:	Ibid. p. 160.
14.	Neurgaonkar S. K.	:	Shri Tukaram Maharajanchi Sarth Gatha. Pracharya Dandekar Prakashan Mandal, Pune. 1982. p. 1.
15.	Akashvani, Publication Division.	:	Maharashtra Dharmache Pranete : Bahinabaichi Gatha p. 266. Abhanga 229. 1 to 6 Lines.
16.	Sahasrabuddhe P. G.	:	Ibid. p. 318.
17.	Sahasrabuddhe P. G.	:	Ibid. p. 305.
18.	Sahasrabuddhe P. G.	:	Ibid.
19.	Pendse S. D.	:	Ibid Eknathi Bhagwat. z. 451. p. 161.
20.	Neurgaonkar S. K.	:	Ibid.
21.	Neurgaonkar S. K.	:	Ibid. A-2065. p. 456.
22.	Sardar G. B.	:	Ibid. p. 26.
23.	Sahasrabuddhe P. G.	:	Ibid. p. p. 308-309, 318.

24. Irlekar Suhasini   : Prachin Marathi Sant-Kaviyatrinche Vangmayin Karya, Aurangabad, 1980. pp. 317-319.

25. Pendse S. D.   : Maharashtracha Sanskritik Itihas p. 125.

26. Dandekar S. W. (Mamasaheb)   : Ibid. Dnyaneswari. 3-89-91.

27. Sahasrabuddhe P. G.   : Ibid. Eknathi Bhagwat pp. 312-313.

28. Sahasrabuddhe P. G.   : Ibid. Namdev. p. 323.

29. Sahasrabuddhe P. G.   : Ibid. Eknathi Bhagwat 41-21 p. 323.

30. Sahasrabuddhe P. G.   : Ibid. p. 322.

31. Sahasrabuddhe P. G.   : Ibid.

32. Bhave V. L.   : Maharashtra Saraswat Vol. p. 289.

33. Neurgaonkar S. K.   : Ibid. Tukaram—280. p. 66.

34. Sahasrabuddhe P. G.   : Ibid. p. 326.

35. Dhere R. C.   : Musalman Marathi Santakavi, Pune 1967.

36. Dhere R. C.   : Ibid. p. 85.

37. Dhere R. C.   : Ibid. 37

38. Dhere R. C.   : Ibid. 89

39. Dhere R. C.   : Ibid. 99

40. Dhere R. C.   : Ibid. p. 37

41. Priyolkar A. K.   : Marathi Sanshodhan Patrika. Jan. 1963.

42. Bendre V. S.   : Yogasangram. 16-66

43. Dhere R. C.   : Ibid. Siddhantabodha. 2. 129-132.

44. Bhave V. L.   : Ibid. p. 279

45. Malshe S. G.   : Ibid. pp. 46-48

46. Nashirabadkar L. R.   : Pachin Marathi Vangmayacha Itihas, Kolhapur. p. 116.

47. Sharma S. R.   : The Founding of Maratha Freedom, Bombay. 1964. p. 127.

48. Pendse S. D.   : Ibid. p. 187

49. Pendse S. D.   : Maharashtracha Bhagwat Dharma. Samartha Ramdas. II Edn. Pune 1980. p. 223.

50. Akashwani.   : Maharashtra Dharmache Pranete, Publication Division Delhi. p. 88.

SELECT BIBLIOGRAPHY

(1) Bhave V. L.   : Maharashtra Saraswat Popular Prakashan, Bombay, 1982.

(2) Bhave V. K.   : Peshwekalin Maharashtra, Anand Mudran Mandir, Pune, 1935.

(3) Bendre V. S.   : Shaikh Muhammadbaba, Shri Gondekarkrita Yogasangram, Bombay—1959.

(4) Dandekar S. W.   : Sartha Dnyaneshwari. Swananda
(Mamasaheb)   Prakashan, Pune 1984.

(5) Dhere R. C.   : Musalman Marathi Santakavi, Dnyanraj Prakashan, Pune 1967.

(6) Inamdar H. V.   : Namdevachi   Abhangawani.
& others.   Modern Book Depot, Pune 1979.

(7) Irlekar Suhasini   : Prachin Marathi Santa Kaviyatrinche Vangmayin Karya, Parimal Prakashan, Aurangabad, 1980.

(8) Malshe S. G.   : Santarpana, Mehta Publishing House, Pune 1986.

(9) Pendse S. D.   : Maharashtracha Sanskritik Itihas.

(10) Pendse S. D.   : Maharashtracha Bhagwat Dharma.
                               1. Rajguru Samartha Ramdas, II Edn. 1980.
                               2. Dnyandev Ani Namdev. II Edn. 1972.
                               3. Bhagvatottam Sant Eknath II Edn. 1982
                               Continental Prakashan, Pune.

(11) Neurgaonkar S. K.   : Shri Tukaram Maharajanchi Sarth-Gatha, Continental Prakashan, Pune 1982.

(12) Sardar G. B.   : Santa   Vangmayachi   Samajik
                             Phalashruti. Maharashtra Sahitya
                             Parishad, Pune-1970.

(13) Tulpule S. G.   : Panch Santakavi, Suvichar Praka-
                             shan Mandal, Pune 1984.

(14) Sahasrabuddhe P. G.   : Maharashtra Sanskriti. Continen-
                             tal Prakashan—Pune 1979.

(15) Akashwani   : Maharashtra Dharmache Pranete.
                             Publication Division, Delhi, 1959.

(16) Sharma S. R.   : The   Founding   of   Maratha
                             Freedom. Orient Longman's Ltd.
                             Bombay-1960 (1964)

(17) Ranade M. G.   : Rise   of   the   Maratha   Power.
                             Publication Division, Delhi 1961.

(18) Indian Institute of   : Shivaji and Swarajya.
     Public Administration. Orient Longman's, Bombay 1975.

PART—III

Modern Indian Lessons

HINDU-MUSLIM INTEGRATION IN HYDERABAD DURING SECOND HALF OF NINETEENTH CENTURY

Dr. (Smt.) Sheela Raj, Bombay.

The erstwhile Hyderabad State under Asaf Jahi rule during the first half of nineteenth century was a place of chaos and confusion. There was no peace and tranquillity among the masses. Even there was a threat to the lives of the people. The disturbance creating elements were mainly the Rohillas and Arabs. Hyderabad city was the abode of different castes and classes, speaking different languages and belonging to different ethnic groups.[1]

Nizam-ul-Mulk Asaf Jah I (1724-1748), the founder of the Asaf Jahi dynasty though separated Hyderabad from Mughal Empire, centralised the administration of the Deccan under his personal control but could not consolidate his Empire. His immediate successors were left to face the uncertainty and confusion which was prevailing at that time. They had to bow to French and English overlords who were trying to lay the foundation of their rule on Indian soil.

The period 1748-1781 was a period of intrigues and rivalries of the French and the English. By this time the English were able to establish their ascendancy over the French. The conclusion of number of treaties with the Nizam's from time to time strengthened British power and increased their influence in the Deccan. The study of these treaties revealed that all these treaties were signed by the Nizam under compulsion. In fact these treaties were more advantageous to the British compared to Nizams.

The treaty of subsidiary alliance[2] in 1798, by which the Subsidiary Force was made permanent and the Nizam was paying for it handsomely. Subsequently the development of 'Hyderabad Contingent', which belonged to the Nizam's army in name only. According to Henry Russell, the then Resident of Hyderabad, the force actually belonged to the British.[3]

The maintanance of these troops proved a heavy burden to the bankrupt treasury, and the Nizam was consequently in arrears in respect of the expenditure of the contingent. The Nizams were constantly under the pressure of contingent debt which began to accumulate rapidly. Pawning of State jewels and sum on high rates of interest was not sufficient to meet the growing demand. Lord Dalhousie, the then Governor General taking full advantage of the critical situation coerced the Nizam to conclude a new treaty.[4] As a result of this treaty, the Nizam was forced to assign the fertile cotton growing districts of Berar and the Raichur Doab, to the exclusive management of the British.[5]

The future of the Hyderabad State, which seemed to be evidently dark and definitely gloomy, particularly after the policies of Lord Dalhousie, changed. There appeared a silver lining. The newly appointed Prime Minister Sir Salar Jung I (1853-1883) declined to act as puppets like his predecessors. He laid the foundation of Hyderabad's future greatness from the chaos left to him. With remarkable assiduity, he reorganised every part of administration and effected phenomenal change in the conditions of the State. An orderly State with a balanced budget and introduction of modern administrative machinery. The socio-economic and cultural renaissance was brought in with great impetus to education. Restoration of peace and tranquility and the all round progress gave rise to integration and communal harmony.

The history of late nineteenth century Hyderabad, its administration, culture and fine arts present a true vision of Hindu-Muslim brotherhood, communal harmony and integra-- tion, an example of a unique relationship of these two communities, which was not found anywhere else in India. Peace loving and enlightened policies of Mir Mahbub Ali Khan Nizam VI (1869-1911) has won the hearts of the people.

During his reign friction between the Hindus and Muslims, the two major communities, was unheard, However, such friction between Hindus and Muslims were common in other parts of British India. The British found it advantageous to play one group off against others. The ruler as well as the aristocracy of Hyderabad played a very important role to prevent importa- tion of such discord from across the border and by outsiders in the State.[6]

Like Lucknow, Hyderabad was the second major city where Hindus and Muslims prosper together. They were profoundly influenced each other culturally. They had similari- ties in their customs and traditions, such as costumes, food, jewellery, marriage, birth and death ceremonies. They were mixed together as if sugar mixed with milk.[7] The integration of the heterogeneous society and especially the association of Hindus and Muslims gave birth to a mixed culture. This close association sometimes made it difficult to distinguish among Hindu and Muslim household.

The analysis of the study of Hyderabad nobility indicates that the Nizam Mir Mahbub Ali Khan made no distinction between Hindus, Muslims and other religions. He believed in communal harmony and integration. So did his nobility. The

Hindus and Muslims equally shared the awards, titles, jewels, robes of honour and other distinctions. The post of Prime Minister was not reserved for any particular community. It was occupied by Hindus and Muslims both. Religion was not the criteria for the selection and appointment of Prime Minister.[8]

The administrative machinery of the State was headed by both Hindus and Muslims. Sir Salar Jung I, Maharaja Narendra Bahadur and Maharaja Kishan Pershad, Sir Afsar-ul-Mulk, Shams-ul-umara and members of Paigah family and Raja Girdhari Pershad (Bansi Raja) held high positions. Bansi Raja as Sarishtegar Nizam's Regular Forces used to lead the Moharrum procession seated on elephant. Ramkishan, Balmukund, Raja Sheo Raj and Murli Manohar of renowned Kayasth families as well as Paigah nobility were close to Nizam VI.[9]

Mir Mahbub Ali Khan once told a British Resident that "he wanted the best men from outside the State. No matter what their religion. Sir Salar Jung was a Sheo Muslim, but among his trusted employees were Candaswamy, a Tamilian and Bansi Raja, a Kayastha".[10]

The Nizam not only showed a religious tolerance towards different religions but he gave assistance towards the promotion of all religions. Jagirs, inams, grants of land and money were not only given annually for the support of mosques and temples but also to Christian Missionaries and others. He was of the view that Hindus and Muslims are his two eyes. If one of the community is damaged, he deemed it as damage to his eye. He considered these two communities as the pillars of the State and for the progress of the State if they are strong, the Government would run efficiently.[11]

In Hyderabad, Darbars were held to mark the significance of festivals like Holi, Basant, Dasserah, Ramzan, Bakr-Id and Nauroge, which provided occasions for the nobles and other dignitaries to attend.

The colourful festival of Holi was celebrated on a large scale at the Nizam's Palace either at Aftab Mahal or Purani Haveli in which Hindus and Muslims both were invited by the Nizam.[12] On the occasion of Basant Panchmi customary requisites like yellow silk robes, yellow flowers, jars of yellow colour water with sprays sent to the Nizam by the Hindu nobles.[13]

Besides these festivals there used to be the traditional Dhan Lakshmi Puja every year at the Government treasury and on behalf of the Nizam the Accountant General of the Treasury used to present shawls to the Treasurer and others. The Superintendent of the treasury used to distribute alms to the poor and turbans to the Bankers.[14]

Religious processions are generally the starting point of the communal conflagrations. The Government of Hyderabad did not lag behind to maintain communal harmony and integration. A separate department of Religious Affairs was set up. The most important function of this department was to grant permission for such religious processions in consultation with the representative through which the procession was to pass. In 1883, Dassarah festival coincided Moharrum. The Nizam's Government appointed a committee consisting of Raja Sheo Raj Bahadur, Raja Girdhari Pershad (Bansi Raja), Raghunath Rao from Ray Rayan State and Rasul Yar Khan Bahadur to maintain law and order and harmony in the city.[15]

At the time of the disastrous floods of 1908, the grief striken Nizam never hesitated to perform puja on the advice of

Brahmin Pandits in traditional Hindu way to extinguish the fury of angry river Goddess.[16]

The nobility of Hyderabad did not lag behind in following the footsteps of their ruler and setting up an example to the common man on the street to maintain the communal harmony and integration. On the occasion of Til Sankranti the kite flying festival, the then Prime Minister Sir Asman Jah Basheer ud-Daulah Bahadur (1887-1896) used to invite both the Hindus and Muslims for Kite flying.[17] The festival of Basant was celebrated at Bashirbagh palace by Basheer-ud-Daulah Bahadur. On this occasion, he used to distribute clothes among the poor.[18] Similarly, other Hindu festivals like Nag Panchmi was celebrated at Baradari, the palace of Nawab Khursheed Jah Bahadur.

In the same manner large number of Hindu nobles joined in the observance of Moharrum. Maharaja Kishan Pershad, Raja Rao Rambha, Maharaja Sheo Raj Bahadur, Raja Ray Rayan Bahadur, Bansi Raja and other Hindu jagirdars contributed considerably for the Moharrum.[19] The Nizam used to visit the palaces of some of these nobles during Moharrum.[20]

Hyderabad city had been a centre of different cultures and religions. It is evident from the history that right from the inception of Hyderabad city, the Nizam aristocracy and jagirdars had an active part in the celebration of Moharrum festival, when Alams and Tazias were installed in their palaces on the first day of Moharrum. Special Majlises were held in the houses of Hindu nobles. Daily forty seers of khichdi and on the 8th of Moharrum biryani was distributed among the poors at Ashurkhana on behalf of the Nizam.[21]

The most striking aspect of the Moharrum festival in Hyderabad was of Hindu participants coming from the rural areas to the city during this month. They had great and staunch belief even more than the Muslims.[22] Similarly celebrations of Moula Ali Urs, or fair, with the traditional pomp and respect was of a picturesque kind. The usual crowds making the unusual pilgrimage to the tomb of this Saint was made up more largely of Hindus than Muslims.[23]

Ganapati Utsav, the ten day long festival of Lord Ganesh, the God of wisdom, was celebrated by the Hindu community of the city with traditional gaiety. It was Bal Gangadhar Tilak who made Ganesh Puja a public festival in Maharashtra. His main objective was to use the forum of this religious function for propagating the message of freedom from British imperialism. This instigated the people of Hyderabad who started the celebrations of Ganesh utsav on a public scale in 1895.[24]

Thus the celebration of Moharrum, Ganesh utsav and Moula Ali Urs in Hyderabad originated as a socio-political mela in which people belonging to different castes and creed had participated. These religious festivals represented a real atmosphare of integration. No other city in India can present such an atmosphere of integration as Hyderabad, where the enlightened and liberal policies of Mir Mahbub Ali Khan were very significant.

Hyderabad during second half of nineteenth century was a city in which many cultural strains were intermingled, Persian and northern Islamic, with the Hindu culture of South, itself a blend of Marathi, Telugu and Tamil influences, and last of all a little of the western world. During Asaf Jahi rule, Hyderabad had carried on its tradition of learning and literature. The pioneers of Persian and Urdu literature were not only inherited but were encouraged by the Nizam for keeping the lamp of learning alive, and making Hyderabad a centre of scholarship. The liberal patronage offered by the Nizam and the aristocracy attracted a number of poets and scholars not only from India but from distant places, who devoted their lives to literature and became ornaments to the court.

Literary institions from all over India were the permanent recepients of aid from the Nizam's Goverment.[25]

Though Persian was the official language, Marathi, Telugu and Kannada were also encouraged. During the Prime Ministership of Salar Jung II (1884-1887), Persian was replaced by Urdu as the official language. The change was beneficial, particularly in the realm of education. Urdu was developed due to the association of Hindu and Persian languages, Hindu, Muslims and various other communities brought up this language. Being a common language, Urdu words were used in other languages, such as Marathi, Kanarese, Gujarati and Hindi.[26.]

During late nineteenth century, under the patronage of Mir Mahbub Ali Khan, Urdu progressed rapidly and Urdu literature flourished to a great extent. Hyderabad became a resort of the scholars after their dispersal from Delhi, Luchnow, Rampur and other places. A number of scholars like, Dagh Dehlvi, Altaf Hussain Hali, Shibli Nomani, Pandit Ratan Nath Sarshar, Sherar and many others were employed in Hyderabad State at one time or other who enjoyed court favours, hospitality and royal patronage.[27.]

Literary activities started flourishing in prose, poetry fiction and drama. The literary circles of Hyderabad were most enthusiastic in opening literary associations and clubs and also take pleasure in arranging literary discussions and poet's gatherings. Maharaja Kishan Pershad the then Prime Minister (1900-1911), a noted poet of urdu and persian language used to arrange such types of gatherings at his palace. Likewise nobles, jagirdars and other officials, both Hindu and Muslims used to arrange such literary and poet gatherings inviting poets from outside Hyderabad.[28]

Music and dance in parties of high dignitories of both Hindus and Muslims was not objectionable. Parties in Hyderabad whether big or small were always entertained by Qawwals and professional singers.

Naubat and Roshan chowki were the musical instruments used in Hyderabad. Naubat is a set of kettle drums, struck at stated hour, before the palace of a King or a dignitory. It was also one of the rare awards bestowed by Nizam on both Muslims and Hindus. Naubat and Roshan chowki are a must on the occasion of marriage and other auspicious occasions. Muslims were always the players of naubat and the Hindus of Roshan chowki.[29]

In conclusion "these are the memories of an older Hyderabad scarcely touched by modern influences, which retained the glamour and grace, the colour and splendour of a bygone age, the Hyderabad of Mir Mahbub Ali Khan whose name enshrined in the hearts of his people, whose fame is deathless, secure in the songs and legends of the Deccan over which he so graciously ruled." These were the feelings expressed by Mrs. Sarojini Naidu to the beloved ruler 'Mahbub'.[30]

Unfortunately, in this republic India, communal riots have become a common phenomenon. After independence India progressed in every walk of life and we are successfully marching ahead towards twenty-first century. But the real vision of integrity and harmony seemed to be disappeared. A handful of greedy politicians who love their position more than their countrymen are initiating and encouraging communal riots, thus hampering country's development. The history of Hyderabad had proved that integration and communal harmony were the two weapons through which the ruler had won the hearts of millions. People could live in peace and state progressed. Now the time has come to revive the sweet memories of the bygone days of late nineteenth century Hyderabad.

REFERENCES

1. A Claude Campbell, Glimpses of the Nizam's Dominions, Bombay and London, C. B. Barrows William Watson & Co., 1898. pp. 181-182.

2. C. U. Aitchison, A Collection of Treaties, Engagements and Sanads, Vol. IX., Calcutta, Superintendent Government Printing, 1909, Treaty No. VIII, pp. 51-56. The subsidiary Alliance Treaty was concluded on the 1st September 1798 between the Nizam and British on the following terms :—
   (a) Permanent Subsidiary Force at Hyderabad.
   (b) Disbandment of French Corps by Nizam.
   (c) British Government to arbitrate between the Nizam and Peshwa.
   (d) To protect the Nizam from any urgent and unreasonable demands of the Marathas.

3. R. G. Burton, A History of the Hyderabad contingents, Calcutta, 1905, p-35.

4. Aitchison, op-cit, Treaty with the Nizam, dated 21st May, 1853, pp. 93-97.

5. Abul Ali Moudoodi, Daulat-e-Asafia Aur Hukumat-e-Hyderabad, Syed Ali Bashar Hatmi, 1928, pp, 10-20.

   Inspite of repeated endeavours on their part, the Nizam could not get back the Berars, and ultimately Lord Curzon imposed a new Treaty upon the Nizam VI, on Nov, 5, 1902, by which the districts of Berar were leased in perpetuity to the British.

6. Dr. Sheela Raj, Communal Peace during the Nizams, Deccan Chronicle, English daily, Secunderabad, 6th February, 1983.

7. Jeevan yar Jung, My Life, Autobiography of Nawab Sarwar-ul-Mulk, London, Arthur H. Stockwell Ltd., pp. 110.

8. K. Krishnaswamy Mudiraj, Pictorial Hyderabad, Vol. I, Hyderabad, Chandrakantha Press, 1929, p. 174.

9. K. Chandraiya, Communal Disturbance, A challenge to Hyderabad City, Siasat, urdu daily.

10. Vasant K. Bawa, A Meeting of two Minds, Indian Express, Hyderabad, dated August 19, 1984, p. 4.

11. Syed Mohiuddin Habibi Hafeez, Shahan-e-Asafia aur Firqah Varana Hum Ahangi, Subras, Monthly Journal, Sept, 1967, Hyderabad, National Fine Printing Press, p. 28.

12. Siasat, urdu daily, Hyderabad Holi K Tewhar, March 1972 Hyderabad.

13. Chronology of Modern Hyderabad, from 1720-1890 A. D. Hyderabad, Central Records Office, Hyderabad Government, 1954, pp. v-viii.

14. Musheer-e-Deccan, urdu daily Hyderabad, dated 24th October 1903.

15. Manik Rao Vitthal Rao, Bostan-e-Asafia, Vol. III, Anwar-ul-Islam Press, Hyderabad, 1909, pp. 560-561.

16. Begam Bilkees Latif, Times of India, dated August 15, 1982, Bombay, Excerpts from her book The Fragrance of Forgotton years.

17. Raja Girdhari Pershad, Private Collection, Invitation from the Prime Minister.

18. Siasat urdu Daily, Basant celebrations at Bushirbagh, 1891, Hyderabad, dated 18th Sept. 1978, p. 5.

19. Census of India, 1971, Series-2, Andhra Pradesh, A Monograph on Moharrum in Hyderabad city, by J. Vedantam, Hyderabad, pp. 34-36.

20. The Evening Mail, June 17, 1899, Hyderabad, p. 3.

21. Rahat Azmi, Hyderabad Ka Moharrum, Siasat daily, dated 21st December, 1977, p. 2.

22. Census of India, 1971, op-cit, pp. 34-36.

23. The Deccan Budget, 18th January 1895.

24. Freedom struggle in Hyderabad. Vol. III, Published by the Hyderabad State Committee, 1957, Hyderabad, p. 60.

25. Mumlikat-e-Asafia, Vol. I. Karachi, Idara-e-Mohiban-e-Deccan, 1978, p. 33.

26. Islamic Culture, The Deccan's contribution to Indian Culture, Vol. V, Hyderabad, Islamic, Culture Board, Hyderabad, 1936, p. 431

27. Saksena, Ram Babu, A History of urdu literature, Allahabad, Ram Narainlal, 1927, p. 199.

28. Nasir uddin Hashmi, Deccani culture, Lahore, Aliya Printers, 1963, pp. 208-212.

29. Nasr Ullah Khan, Tarikh-e-Deccan, Lucknow, Nawal Kishore Press, 1865, p. 126.

30. Mrs, Sarojine Naidu, Foreword for Zahir Ahmed, Life's yesterday, Bombay, Thacker and Co. Ltd., 1945 pp. XI-XII.

HINDU RELIGION AND THE PROBLEMS OF SOCIAL AND EMOTIONAL INTEGRATION IN INDIA :

A Case Study of the Swaminarayana Sect in the 19th Century Gujarat

Dr. Mangubhai R. Patel
Reader in History
Gujarat University
Ahmedabad

The problems such as social and emotional integration, and modernization cover a wide range of views interpreting human development. Until recently the dominant view emphasized a unilateral approach equating modernization with Westernization. It undermined tradition as obsolete and even antithetic to the process of emotional integration and change. This assumption viewing progress in the context of "past versus present", and "tradition versus modernity" tended to overlook the experience of non-European societies like India which had developed their own mechanism of adjustment and adaptation in the course of their long histories. In fact, the Hindu religious system consisting of innumerable gods and godesses and a large number of temples and rituals still continues to be an integral part of the Hindu mores and behaviour. This paper, thus, attempts to analyse the role of the indigenous institutions and traditions in the process of socio-religious integration. It is a case study of the Swaminarayana sect which emerged in Gujarat as an off-shoot of Vaishnavism in the nineteenth century.[1]

II

The Gujarati Society passed through various phases of social integration and transformation in the course of its long history. In medieval period the saint-poets like Narsinh Mehta, Akho, and Bhalan had protested against the currupt practices of religious heads, superstitions, social evils, and rituals. They had also faught against the caste hierarchy and had preached the ideals of human equality.[2] So was the case with the Sufi poets and saints. In this way they had made efforts to bring about an emotional integration among the people belonging to different castes and communities, and social groups.

But inspite of the protest movement, the caste system and social evils continued to parsist in Gujarat. The social life in Gujarat (as indeed, in the other regions of India) at the turn of the eighteenth century was dominated by centuries-old traditions. Briefly summerized, the society was superstious and caste ridden upholding ascriptive social status norms, and tolerating social evils like child marriage, sati, femals infanticide, ban on foreign travel, ban on widow-remarriage, dowry system, and marriage and death dinners. The social structure permitted little scope to an individual, except occasionally, through the disapproved of some sects to express the "deviant" behaviour.[3]

III

Swami Sahajanand (1781-1830), a contemporary of Raja Rammohan Roy, was a product of this cultural ethos. Born in Chhapaiya, near Ayodhya (U. P.), Sahajanand left his home in 1793 in search of a *guru*. The contemporary accounts show how, in the course of his wandering, he visited a number of places of pilgrimage, came in contact with the *sadhus*, and attained a high proficiency in the *yoga*. He changed his original name from Ghanshyam Pande into Nilkantha Brahmachari in 1793. Around 1800 he settled down in Gujarat and founded a sect.[4]

At the time when Sahajanand came to Gujarat, this region was passing through the transition stage in political sphere. The British were then fighting with the Marathas for their political supremacy.[5] Although Gujarat was divided between the Gaekwads and the Peshwas, there existed a large number of petty independent ruling chiefs particularly in the Kathiawad and the Kutch regions. For example, the Garasias, the Kathis, the Boils, and the Kolis had never fully submitted to the Mughals and the Marathas. They had also thwarted the attempts of the British intruders to collect land revenue. The official accounts of the English East India Company in the first decade of the nine-teenth century describe them as illiterate, mistrustful, proud, haughty, and revengful.[6] Apart from these militant people, a large number of peasants and artisans, the *shudras* in the hierarchical casts parlance, lived in Gujarat. Because of their producing goods and services they occupied low social status. The condition of the untouchables was worst. They had to bear some sorts of symbolic marks in order to reveal their identity.[7] The Brahmins and the banias, small though in numerical strength, were the real gentry of the social order. They were well-entrenched in their respective castes and religious sects.

How did young Sahajanand perceive this situation ? In what way did he appeal and attract the people ? How did the people belonging to the various castes and even sects become the disciples of Sahajanand ? And what was the significance of this phenomenon in terms of social and emotional integra-tion ? These are some of the questions which need to be explained. To begin with, we should bear in mind that Gujarat was an abode of sects like the Madhavgar, Bijmargi, Pranami,

Vallabh, Shaiva, Kabir and Ramanandi sects at the time when Sahajanand started his career in Gujarat.[8] They were competing among themselves to strengthen their following. It was, therefore, not easy for a young man of twenty to snatch away the cake belonging to leaders of the well-established sects. Nevertheless, he succeeded to a considarable extent, for, as we shall see, he made himself acceptable to the poorer masses and also the brahmins and the feudal chiefs by creating an emotional and organizational infrastructure.

Sahajanand started with the miracles, the age-old game of the 'profets'. The contemporary sectarian works like *yamadanda* (1804), *Ghanshyamlilamrut* and *Haridigvijaya* (1820's) contain a number of miracles which he is said to have performed bringing his subject to a state of trance.[9] To some he showed *vaikuntha* or the heavenly abode of Lord Vishva, and some were saved from fire or from shipwreck ! The lame men were made to run and the blind were made to see !

But this was not the only thing. The Swami declared himself as an incarnation of Lord Krishna and propagated it through his *chelas* to such an extent that Vitthalrao Diwanji, the Gaekwad's *Kamavisadar*, imprisoned him in Ahmedabad in 1808. But he escaped from the prison, went to the nearby village, Jetalpur, and performed a magnificent *maharudra* with the help of the brahmins. A large number of men and women and children from the nearly villages gathered together to watch this religious sacrifice.

This single event increased Sahajanand's prestigs.[10] The crowds started flocking towards him. His followers predominantly came from the lower castes. The artisans such as the tailors, weavers, goldsmiths, carpenters, and cobblers and the peasants, particularly the Kava and the Leva Kanbis of North and Central Gujarat, were amongst his earliest followers.

Also various types of Rajputs like the Jadejas, Jethwas, Khachars, and Kathis joined the sect. They hailed from Kathiawad. Some of them were the feudal chiefs.[11] One Dada Khachar of Gadhada (in the present Bhavnagar district), a feudal chief, was the most loyal follower of Sahajanand. The Swami also saught his followers from Kutch.

After mustering the strength of about 20,000 followers, Sahajanand started preaching them. He toured indefatigably in the towns and villages and developed personal contacts with the people. He exhorted the people to live simple and pious life. Although Sahajanand was essentially a religious leader, he took up a few issues like female infanticide and *sati* and fought vehemently against these cruel practices. At the same time, he made attempts to change the life of the notorious robbers like Joban Pagi and Verabhai. The following incident throws light on Sahajanand's approach with regard to the social problems :

"At Bandhia several Rajputs among whom there were some men of prominence paid a visit to the Maharaj who, after receiving them properly and talking on general matters for some time, said to them : 'It is not right to commit infanticide, because thereby is committed a threefold sin, viz., one of murder of one's own family member, another, of a child murder, and the third, a murder of one belong to the female'. To this they replied that the marriage of daughters cost a great deal of money, and so they had to take recourse to such a practice. The Maharaj replied : 'We shall defray all such expenses by raising money from the Satsang. But under no circumstances you shall kill your infant daughters'. At this some one said : 'We do not want to lower our prestige by marrying our daughters to all and sundry'. Hearing this the Maharaj became angry, and dashing his hand against the floor said : 'Not only will you give your daughters to barbarians, but you will have to fulfill the word of God. Such a ruler (English) is coming as will make it impossible for you people to live by robbery and outlawry. He will make you live all such ways, and you will have to take rosary in your hands, and that won't save you then. But if you do that as my disciples, that will be the saving of you".[12]

Sahajanand's sect won great popularity in the course of time. The Kolis and the Kathis, the Garasias and the Bhils, the Jadeja and the Jethwas Rajputs, the peasants and the artisans, the Brahmins and the Vaishnava Vanias joined the sect. Some Muslims, particularly the Khojas and the followers of the *Pirana Panth* also joined Sahajanand's following called *satsang*. The Khojas and the *Piranapanthis* were on the boarder line between Hinduism and Islam. Even though the Khojas looked upon the Aga Khan as their divine *guru*, they still had a reverence for Hinduism and followed Hindu customs. The Pirana sect had also a following from the Muslims and the low-caste Hindus. Sahajanand preached the tenets of his sect in such a simple language and forceful manner that these Muslims got attracted towards his sect. The Census of the Bhanvagar State mentions that in 1931, thirty-four Khoja families followed Swaminarayana sect out of 32,202 Hindu followers in the State.[13] But the process had started during the life-time of Sahajanand himself. The *Buddhiprakash*, a monthly published from Ahmedabad, recorded in 1878 that the Khojas were originally the Hindu Bhatias before their conversion, and "many of them in Bombay and Bhavnagar follow the Swaminarayana sect".[14]

When Bishop Reginald Heber met Sahajanand Swami in Nadiad (Kheda District) on 26 March 1825, he was received initially by four peasants, a Muslim, and a servant in the services of the Ghodasar State. At that time the total strength of the Swaminarayana sect in Gujarat was 50,000. The Bishop was surprised to see that the Swami's followers were all loyal to him. Heber has observed that although his own body-guards were better armed and better disciplined in the art of warfare, they were, nevertheless, the paid servants who neither knew him nor cared for him. On the other hand Sahajanand's body-guards and followers were his own disciples who were ready to sacrifice their lives for him.[15] Although Sahajanand supported the caste hierarchy, he taught his disciples to treat each other like brothers. In the course of conversation, Sahajanand had told Haber that it was immaterial whether the people of different castes dined together or not. People could co-operate with each other maintaining at the same time the norms of their own caste.[15]

The caste system has come to be seriously attached by sociologists and historians. Most of them have pointed out that the caste system and emotional integration are antethetic. But things were different in Sahajanand times. People in those days were never seriously bothered about the caste problems. They seldom discussed these issues. Even the Western-educated Gujarati elites in the latter half of the nineteenth century, while giving a lip-service to the casteless-society as an ideal still maintained the caste system as a "necessary evil". Most of them believed that caste would remain intact and it was better for them to fight against the social evils by introducing reforms in the castes themselves.[16] Sahajanand's activities should, therefore, be viewed in the nineteenth century perspective. Really speaking, it should be seen in the light of the social norms prevailing in the first half of the nineteenth century when the Western impact in Gujarat was only at a marginal level.

The way in which Sahajanand brought people of diverse castes and sub-castes under the same umbrella was typical of a charismatic mass leader. This requires a brief discussion, for he fully utilized the skills of the Bhats and the Charans and the Barots whose profession was to popularize and strengthen the Hindu traditional mores and behaviour pattern.[17] They built up geneologis, sang patriotic songs during battles and wars, and entertain the princes and the courtiers. Of course they were not concerned with historical facts. Their clients were also not concerned with the *facts*. They were more interested in how these "facts" were narrated in the mythological garb.[18] These Bhats, Barots, and Charans were the traditional historians of Gujarat and they gave meaning to the society by narrating, reciting, and interpreting the past and projecting thereby their concerns and images of the *present* social reality. They entertained and educated their listeners and perhaps shaped their attitudes and behaviour towards nature, world, and society. Consciously or unconsciously they served as the agents of what M. N. Srinivas has called the "Sanskritization process."

Some of the Swaminarayana Sadhus and poets like Nishkulanand (1766-1848), Brahmanand (1772-1832), and "Premsakhi" Premanand (1779-1863) hailed from the Bhat and the Charan castes. They were not only great scholars but also versatile poets. Earlier they had served the princely courts and entertained the princess and the courtiers. They now used their craft in amuzing the larger and diverse gatherings. The fact of their being good vocalists and instrumentalists helped popularising the sect. These poets along with other saint-poets like Muktanand (1761-1831), Manjukeshanand (1790-1863), Bhumanand (1796-1852), and Devanand (1803-1854) toured numerious villages and towns in order to preach the teachings of their *guru,* that is, Sahajanand Swami, They also wrote prolifically and created a large bulk of literature.[19]

All these factors made an impact in bringing together disciples from various castes and walks of life. The tailors, the cobblers, the Kanbis, the peasants, the Kolis, the garasias, and the brahmins identified themselves with the Swaminarayana sect. The *satsangis* or the followers of the sect had to take vows such as "not to commit adultery, not to consume liquer and intoxicants, not to eat animal food." A large number of followers who had been previously flesh-eaters now turned to Vegetarianism. Many bands of robbers adopted peaceful persuits. Most of them turned to farming and became the pillars of the sect.

Sahajanand Swami was not only a spiritual leader but also a man of practical wisdom. He was convinced that unless the people from the various parts of Gujarat were brought together his sect would remain isolated. Thus, in order to bring the diverse sorts of people together he introduced an innovation. He decided to hold conventions at Vadtal (Kheda District) and Gadhada (in the Bhavnagar State, Kathiawad). Known as *samaiyas* in the sectarian literature, these conventions became an annual feature. To begin with, the *samaiyas* were restricted to the sadhus only. But eventually, the scope was broadened and this turned to be a great popular festival. Large numbers of disciples gathered together from different quarters, which itself was a source of inspiration and strength to the common man.[20] As the movement grew, numbers of people belonging to the lowest castes, untouchables, and the tribal peoples came to participate in the *mela* and the festivities, and the *Kathas* which became an integral part of the *samaiyas*. Here they were drawn away from a world of oppression and injustice, and brought into a new world where they tended to forget their social and economic limitations and mixed freely as *satsangis*. However temporary or escapeoriented this might seem to us, this was certainly a significant device at that period of time. The Swaminarayana sect brought the "high" and the "low" on the common platform in this fashion.

Sahajanand gave serious thought to the problems of women. An innovation in his organization was the creation of a class of *Sadhavis* or female preachers. They were known by the name of *Sankhayoginies* and enjoyed the status equivalent to a Sadhu. The *Sankhyayoginies* preached to the female gatherings.[21] It was under his influence that the widows and other women started receiving training as preachers. They had to study Sanskrit and dovote their time in reading and writing. On a number of occasions Sahajanand had exhorted his disciples to be kind and affectionate towards women. At the same time he had advocated severe restrictions on women. This was in view of the fact that the Swami had himself attacked the sexual corruptions of the heads of the rival Vallabh sect. The Vallabha priests had made themselves notorious by indulging in sexual relations with their female followers.[22] No wonder, therefore, that Sahajanand launched a crusade against the Vallabha sect on the one hand, and put severe restrictions on the widows and married women on the other hand. The temples constructed by Sahajanand had two separate entrances for men and women. Sahajanand was not strict with the women-folk alone. He had also advised his male followers to lead moral and pious life and not to cast, an evil eye on a woman. The preachings of the Swami and *Sadhus* and the *Sadhvis* did not go in vain. The following of the sect increased from 50000 in 1825 to 175000 in 1849. In 1872 it was 3,20,879. Jagendra Nath Bhattacharya made following observations in the closing years of the nineteenth century :

"The Vallabha sect is a great competitor of the Swaminarayana sect. It was so firmly set in Gujarat that it was difficult for the Swaminarayana to supercede it. The Swami, therefore, proceeded very carefully and cautiously, and the same spirit characterizes his followers (*acharyas*) at Vadtal and Ahmedabad. The result is that though the Vallabhacharyas have not yet lost much of their ground gained by them, and are in full possession of the middle classes including the Banias and the Kanbis, yet the superior morality of the Swaminarayana sect has seriously undermined the power of the Maharajas, and these are signs that their influence is waning. The Swaminarayana sect, on the contrary, is in the full vigour of youthful growth. The middle classes being in the possession of the Vallabhites, the Swami, from the necessity of his position, was obliged to admit to his faith the low castes such as the Dhobis, Mochis, Darjis, etc., rejected by the Vallabhites".[23]

This phenomenon points to the fact that the Swaminarayana sect actually started as a protest movement and this set in motion the unifying forces deep-rooted in the traditional Hindu ethos. H. G. Briggs' observations are relevant in this regard since he wrote only seventeen years after Sahajanand's death. He wrote :

"The genius of Sahajanand Swami was not confined simply to the rigid re-establishment of Hindu worship in virgin integrity. He worked also among the lawless persons, dacoits and robbers. Of his success in this respect there is abundant testimony, from the vast hordes who have been reclaimed to honest and industrious pursuits. If we keep in mind the turbulent period during which he worked to improve the morals of these dacoits, we have to say that he justly earns the appalation of reformer. The wide latitude to which his doctrines comprise, permitting men of all classes to become his followers, so long as they are faithfully observed—has materially tended towards kolis, kathis, Grasias, Rajputs, and a vast variety of castes and classes of men, to rally under his banner". Briggs described Swami Sahajanand as "the most remarkable Hindu of the present century".[24]

To sum up, Sahajanand Swami generated the indigenous forces of emotional and social integration. This was as much due to his organizational skills as to the doctrines of knowledge, devotion, and non-violence. But here, what he said was not new. How he said it was new at that period of time. He preached in simple Gujarati. He used popular symbols and ideoms citing examples from the day-to-day experiences of the common people. In this way he created new imageries of social reality even though they were moulded exclusively in the Hindu theological framework. In this respect Swami Sahajanand was very much different from his great contemporary, Raja Rammohan Ray ; the latter had also cherished the Western secular and rational values among other things. Sahajanand drew his inspiration exclusively from the Hindu theological doctrines. Obviously these had limitations. But like the Raja, he also tried to synthesize the various Hindu cultural strands in attempting to generate emotional bonds among the people. Sahajanand's focus was, of course, limited, but his genius lay in his ability to interpret and bring down the scriptural ideals and injunctions to the realm of personal and social morality. Unlike Raja Rammohan Roy, Sahajanand was basically a religious leader.

REFERENCES

1. For details see Manilal C. Parekh, *Sri Swaminarayana* (Rajkot, 1960).

2. Umashankar Joshi et. al. (ed.), *Gujarati Sahityano Itihas*, Vol. 1 (Ahmedabad, 1976), K. M. Munshi, *Gujarat and its Literature From Early Times to 1852* (Bombay, 1952).

3. Neera Desai, *Social Change in Gujarat : A Study of Nineteenth Century Gujarat Society* (Bombay, R. L. Rawal, *Socio-Religious Reform Movements in Gujarat during the Nineteenth Century* (Ph. D. thesis, Gujarat University, 1983), pp. 16-30.

4. Parekh, *op. cit.*, pp. 46-75.

5. Mangubhai Patel, *Rao Bahadur Becherdas Ambaidas Laskari (1818-1889) : A Biographical Study of the Social and Industrial Leader of Gujarat* (Ph. D. thesis, Gujarat University, 1985), pp. 147-227.

6. Bombay Government, *Selections from the Records of the Bombay Government*, New Series, no. 37. (Bombay, 1856), pp. 16-22.

7. Bombay Government, *Gazetteer of the Bombay Presidency : Gujarat Population : Hindus*, Vol. 9, Pt. 1 (Bombay, 1901), p. 341 ; A. K. Forbes, *Ras Mala*, 2 Vols, II (London, 1856), pp. 235-37.

8. Bombay Gazetteer, Vol. 9, Pt. 1, *Ibid.*, pp. 336-47.

9. Parekh, *op. cit.*, pp. 164-78 ; 254-67.

10. H. G. Briggs, *The Cities of Gujarashtra* (London, 1849), p. 237.

11 Makrand Mehta, "The Swaminarayana Sect A Case Study of Hindu Religious Sects in Modern Times", *Quarterly Review of Historical Studies*, XVII, No. 4, 1977-78, pp, 225-30.

12. Parekh, *op, cit.*, pp, 114-15.

13. R. K. Trivedi (ed.) *Bhavnagar State Census 1931*, Pt. 1 (Bhavnagar, 1932), p. 253.

14. *Buddhiprakash*, September 1878, pp. 195-97.

15. Reginald Heber, *Narrative of a Journey Through Upper Provinces of India*, 2 Vols., II, pp, 146-48.

16. Makrand Mehta, "From Sahajanand to Gandhi : Role Perception and Methods", in S. P. Sen (ed.), *Social and Religious Reform Movements in the Nineteenth and Twentieth Centuries* (Calcutta, 1979), pp. 229-48.

17. A. M. Shah and R. G. Shroff, "The Vahivancha Barots of Gujarat", in Milton Singer (ed.), *Traditional India Structure and Change* (Philadelphia, 1959), pp. 40-70 ; Neil Rabitoy, "Administrative Modernization and the Bhats of British Gujarat 1800-1826",

The Indian Economic and Social History Review, xi, No, 1, March 1974, pp. 46-73.

18. Ashis Nandy, *Alternative Sciences* (New Delhi, 1980), pp. 4-5.

19. Parekh, *op. cit.*, pp. 254-67.

20. For details see Kishorlal Mashruwala, *Swami Sahajanand* (Ahmedabad, 1923).

21. Bombay Gazetteer, *op. cit.*, pp, 537-40.

22. For details see Annonymous, *History of the Sect of Maharajas or Vallabhacharyas in Western India* (London, 1965),

23. Jogendra Nath Bhattacharya, *Hindu Castes and Sects An Exposition of the Origin of the Hindu Caste System and the Bearing of the Sects Towards Each Other and Towards other Religious Systems* (Calcutta, 1896), pp. 373-75.

24. Briggs, *op. cit.*, pp, 237-39.

SOCIAL REFORM MOVEMENT IN THE 19th CENTURY TAMIL NADU AND ITS CONTRIBUTION TO NATIONAL INTEGRATION

Mr. C. Paramarthalingam M. A.,
Lecturer in History,
Institute of Correspondence Course,
Madurai-Kamaraj University,
Madurai—625 021, Tamil Nadu.

Introduction :

Problem of integration is common to any country where people belonging to varied cultures live. India is no exception. In the Independent India, national integration is the crying need as disintegrating forces are discernible in certain quarters. But compared to the present position, in the nineteenth century, India had a semblance of unity, thanks predominantly to the Social Reform Movement. In this paper, an attempt is made, in a brief compass to study the contribution of the Social Reform Movement that touched the fringes of Tamil Nadu, to National Integration.

India known for its geographical unity has continued to maintain it right from the ancient period. Dr. Zakir Hussain, the late President of India, compared India's unity to a "Boquet of flowers of different hues, shapes and sizes in which each flower maintains its uniqueness and blends into the whole".[1] Saints and sages have proclaimed the oneness of Bharadvarsha and Bharad Khanda. Poets had sung the glories of this ancient land stretching from the Himalayas in the North and Cape Comorin in the South. In the second century B. C. Prakrit became the court language of the rulers and in

19

the subsequent period Sanskrit replaced it. Sanskrit influenced the regional languages of India including the Dravidian tongues which helped to promote integration. The Ramayana and the Mahabharata have been read with avid interest by all Indians alike. They were read with as much interest in the South as in the North. They became the common heritage of the people irrespective of the language in which they were written. Valmiki and Kamban, Tulsidas and Potana, Kalidasa and Bharavi, Rabindranath Tagore and Bharati were not only national poets but also world poets. Adi Sankara promoted the unity of India by founding monastic orders in the four borders of the country such as Badrinath in the North, Sringeri in the South, Dwaraka in the West and Puri in the East. He underlined the relation between Jivatma and Paramatma as being one. He aimed to bring the entire India under one umbrella of spirituality. In the 12th century A. D. Ramananuja-charya propounded the theory of Visishtadvaita proclaiming that man was a limb of god. It spread to other parts of India also. In the 13th century A. D. Madhvacharya spread among the people the philosophy of Dvaita. In the modern period Swami Vivekananda had emphasized the significance of National Integration by making constant tours in the country. Indians had demonstrated their unity of strength when the Chinese and the Pakistanese attacked India in 1962 and 1965 respectively.

Religion has also promoted unity. As Hinduism is not dogmatic, it advocates many paths for the realization of the Ultimate Reality. In the Rig Veda, we find sages declaring "Reality is one, the wise call it by various names, 'what is one, they envisage in different modes." The same idea is expressed in subsequent literature, not only in Sanskrit, but also in other languages. The similies of the differently coloured cows yielding the same white milk, of the different rivers flowing towards and dissolving in the same ocean, are given to illustrate the non-duality of religion.[2]

Languages also had contributed to National Integration. Those who were conversant with more than one Indian language had been struck with wonder that almost all sayings and proverbs in one Indian language had reverberations in the other Indian languages, including Dravidian tongues.

Pilgrims and merchants who travelled various parts of India made cultural contacts with the people of the respective regions.

Festivals also had helped integration. The Durga Pooja of Bengal had been celebrated as Navaratri in the South. Shivarathri, Ramanavami, Gokulakshmi, Vinayaka Chaturti, Deepavali and a host of other festivals have been common to all Indians for thousands of years. Pilgrim centres like Kashi and Rameswaram, Dwaraka and Puri have helped the evolution of a common culture for the whole of India throughout ages. The celebrations of Independence, Republic and Gandhiji's birthdays have also been the contributory factors in this direction. Christian and Muslim festivals are also celebrated throughout India. In the opinion of K. A. Nilakanta Sastri, "From the prehistorical times to the present day, there has been no period when the two regions (North and the South) did not influence each other politically and culturally and on at least three occasions before the advent of British rule both the North and the South formed parts of a single empire embracing nearly the whole of India."[3]

Thus right from the remote past, a fundamental unity of culture developed in India transcending region, religion, race, language and environment. It is against this background only that we will have to study the contribution of Tamil Nadu to National Integration.

Contribution of Tamil Nadu to National Integration :

Tamils. imbued with broader vision, considered the whole world as one family. Kanian Poonguntanar, a Sangam Tamil poet, declared that "all regions are our own and all people are our kinsmen" (யாதும் ஊரே யாவரும் கேளிர்). Thirumoolar another Tamil poet who lived in the 5th century A.D. held that "god is one and all people belong to one human family." (ஒன்றே குலம் ஒருவனே தேவன்).

The fusion of the Aryan and the Dravidian cultures could be seen from the Sangam literature roughly ranging from 4th century B. C. to 4th century A. D. Sangam poems refer to Vedic gods like Indra, Yama, Vishnu, Siva and Balarama. The Dravidian God Muruga was identified with Subramanya, the son of Siva. In fact, Hinduism did not divide the Indians into Dravidians and Aryans. It laid the foundation upon which the superstructure of the common Dravidian—Aryan consciousness was built. Tamil kings like Pandiyan Nedunchezhian and Rajendra Chola went upto the Himalayan and Gangetic regions. They attempted to bring about a united India by means of conquest. The Tamil kings, the Cheras, the Cholas and the Pandyas had promoted cultural unity among themselves.

The Bhakti Movement started in the 7th century A. D. by the Saivite and the Vaishnavite saints spread to North India also. Chaitanya in Bengal and Ramananda in Maharashtra became the votaries of the Movement.

When India came under the control of the British in the 18th century, India in a sense became politically united. The English language kindled the flame of nationalism. In the opinion of R. C. Majumdar, "this unity was undoubtedly nurtured in the nineteenth century by a uniform system of administration, easy means of communication and the spread of education on modern lines".[4] When the English introduced reforms, the natives resented it which resulted in the Social Reform Movement. Thus the Social Reform Movement in India was the brain-child of Indian renaissance that took its advent in Bengal in the nineteenth century. It was partly due to Western education and partly due to indigenous factors. The Indian leaders absorbed whatever that could be taken from their ancient culture and synthesized it with the thoughts and ideas of the West. Hence, the Indian Renaissance Movement is a synthetic restatement containing the best of the Indian and Western thoughts. Thus, it is called revivalism encompassing modern values and ideas needed for the times, along with reviving the great seminal ideas of the old Indian thoughts.

Christian Missionaries converted many Hindus into Christians. They levelled scathing attack on Hindu religion, its customs and traditions. Charles Grant, a Missionary described the Hindu religion as "idolatory with all its rabble of impure deities, its monsters of wood and stone, its false principles and corrupt practices, its delusive hopes and fears, its ridiculous ceremonies and degrading superstitions, its lying legends and fraudulent imposition".[5] Alexander Duff, another Missionary wrote in his book, "India and Indian Missions" that "Of all the systems of false religion ever fabricated by the perverse ingenuity of fallen men, Hinduism is surely the most stupendous".[6] At this critical juncture in India's history, a new middle class group consisting of landlords, businessmen and intellectuals emerged in Bengal. Though small in number, they wielded tremendous influence over the Bengali society. They aimed to remove the disabilities that encrusted the Hindu society such as Sati, infant-marriage and enforced—widowhood and slavery. Thus, the wholesale condemnation of the Christian Missionaries against the Hindu religion and its institutions led to the emergence of the Social Reform Movement. It was said that fear of Christian Missionaries was the beginning of much social wisdom among Indians. Educated youths of Calcutta were fired by unbounded enthusiasm which manifested itself in the birth of mighty socio-religious reform bodies like the Brahmo Samaj (1828), the Prarthana Samaj (1867), the Arya Samaj (1875), the Theosophical Society (founded in New York in 1875, shifted to Bombay, India in 1879) and the Ramakrishna Mission (1897), * The educated Youths of Bengal published two journals, "Parthenon" and "the Bengal Spectator" which became their mouth-piece. These journals made a vehement attack on the Hindu religion and its customs. This spirit of enquiry and free-thinking led to the protest against orthodoxy. Some even went to the extent of repudiating Hinduism. It was against this background that Indian Social Reform Movement took its advent in Bengal. Raja Ram Mohan Roy, the founder of the Brahmo Samaj has been rightly called the Father of Modern India. Western education, Western science, astronomy, surgery and social sciences came to be percolated into India through Bengal. Thus, Calcutta became the springboard of Indian Renaissance. Yet it could

---

* Though every century in India witnessed the emergence of Social or Religious Reform Movements, it became an organised movement only in the nineteenth century. Thus, R. C. Majumdar observes that "The Nineteenth Century was the great dividing line and these hundred years changed the face of India." R. C. Majumdar (Ed.), *The History and Culture of the Indian People*, Vol. X, *British Paramountery and Indian Renaissance*, Part II, (Bombay, Bharatiya Vidya Bhavan, 1981), p. 96. Thus a United India, socially conducive, became the fertile field for promoting National Integration. The social legislations passed to wipe out the excrescences such as Sati, infant-marriage and slavery came to be introduced into Tamil Nadu also. Moreover, social reform associations which were started in the Madras Presidency during this period became the corollary to the Indian National Social Conference founded in 1887. Thus, the Indian National Social Conference, like the Indian National Congress founded in 1885, promoted forces of National Integration. A co-mingling of people and the resultant cultural cohesion came into being in the wake of the founding of Social Reform Associations in various parts of the country.

not be called renaissance in comparison to the one that took place in Europe during the Medieval period. It was only revivalism, for as N. Subrahmanian has pointed out, "...the past has always been with us : we have never parted company with it. We are trying to see if certain new values coming to us for the first time now can be fitted on to the corpus of the old."[7]

In order to realize their objective, the social reformers therefore began to start associations with a view to creating a consciousness among the people so that these evils might be gradually eradicated".[8] References may be made to the Indian National Social Conference founded in 1887 and the Madras Hindu Social Reform Association founded in 1892.

Tamil Nadu and The Social Reform Movement :

India being a country of cultural unity, the social disabilities that prevailed in other parts of the country, existed in Tamil Nadu also. The Christian Missionaries converted thousands of low caste Hindus to their fold. Societies like the Society for the Propagation of the Gospel, London Missionary Society, Wesleyan Mission, the Free Church Mission of Scotland and the Church Missionary Society undertook the task of spreading the Gospel in Tamil Nadu. As in Bengal, there took place a clash between the two cultures, resulting in the birth of Social Reform Movement in Tamil Nadu. Educated Tamils, with a view to preserving the purity of the Hindu religion, effected changes in social institutions such as infant-marriage and enforced-widowhood, infanticide, devadasi system, slavery and untouchability. These, measures were the offshoot of the Social Reform Movement that took its advent in Bengal in the nineteenth century.

Sati :

It is said that Social Reform Movement in Modern India started with the Anti-Sati Movement, for Sati was the first social evil to be discussed by the social reformers. Sati prevailed in Vedic period. In Tamil Nadu it existed during the Sangam period. During the nineteenth century numerous instances of Sati took place in Tamil Nadu. Sati stones are to be seen in various parts of Tamil Nadu bearing testimony to the prevalence of Sati. Its chief centres were Tanjore, Pudukottai, Coimbatore and Salem. C. M. Lushington, the Acting Magistrate of Tanjore reported to the Madras Government in 1813 that one hundred widows were feared burnt alive in various parts of the Tanjore district between 1806 and 1813.[9] He recommended that "prohibition of this practice would give universal satisfaction." Raja Ram Mohan Roy, published his Tracts on Sati in 1818 and 1820. In his Tracts Ram Mohan Roy held that the widows did not become satis of their own accord, but they were induced by their relatives to do so.[10] Lord William Bentinck who took over charge as Governor-General in July 1828 made his motto as "British Greatness founded on Indian Happiness".[11] He prepared a Minute which stated that "To consent to the consignment year after year of hundreds of innocent victims to a cruel and untimely end when the power exists of preventing it is a predicament which no conscience can contemplate without horror".[12] Based upon Ram Mohan Roy's Tracts and Bentinck's Minute, Act no. XVII was passed on December 4, 1829 declaring that, "the practice of Suttee, or burning or burying alive the widows of Hindus, is hereby declared illegal, and punishable by the Criminal Courts".[13] This Act came into force in the Madras Presidency in 1830. In the opinion of R. C. Majumdar, the abolition of Sati gave a fillip to the movement for social reform.[14] Reformers could now concentrate on other problems such as infant-marriage and enforced-widowhood, restriction on temple entry and slavery.

Infant-Marriage and Enforced Widowhood :

The abolition of Sati led to the problems of the widows. Widowhood consisted of two types—infant-widowhood and adult widowhood. It was the problem of the infant widows that caused concern to the social reformers. In the Madras infant-marriage prevailed among Brahmins, Kshatriyas and Chettis. Brahmins had their children married between the ages of 6 and 7 which increased the percentage of widows.[15] In 1881 the total number of Hindu girls married in the Madras Presidency was 157,466 and the number of widows in the same year was 5,621.[16] Similarly, an estimated number of 434 girls below 10 years of age were married out of whom 16 became widows.[17] Thus, the problem of widow marriage engaged the attention of social reformers who made the Widow Re-Marriage Movement popular in the Madras Presidency.

Ishwar Chandra Vidyasagar (1820-1891) of Bengal spearheaded the Widow Re-Marriage Movement which gained momentum. His hard efforts bore fruit when the Widow Re-Marriage Reform Act No. XV was passed in 1856. This Act declared that no issue should be declared illegitimate on the ground that the woman had been previously married or betrothed to another person, who was dead at the time of such marriage.[18] The grateful women of Calcutta perpetuated his memory by imprinting on the borders of their sarees the first line of a song "May Vidyasagar live long".[19] As a follow-up action, the first widow marriage was celebrated in Calcutta on December 7, 1856 under the auspices of Vidyasagar. During that period, seventy widow marriages took place at Calcutta.[20]

In Tamil Nadu, the first widow re-marriage took place at Salem in 1858, Widow re-marriage associations were established in various parts of the Presidency. Mention may be made of the Widow Re-Marriage Society (1873) at Nagercoil, the Madras Hindu Widow Marriage Association (1874), the Hindu Women's Re-Marriage. Association (Madras), (1882), the Madras

Hindu Social Reform Association (1892) and the Rajahmundry Widow Marriage Association (1897).

Social Reform becoming a National Movement : Birth of the Indian National Social Conference, 1887.

When the Indian National Congress was founded in 1885, its leaders felt the need for giving importance to social reform also. With this end in view, Mahadev Govind Ranade delivered a lecture on social reform at its first session at Bombay in 1885. In its second session held at Calcutta in 1886, its leaders such as Dadabhai Naoroji, Budruddin Tyabji and W. C. Benerji emphasised the need for discussing social matters as part of the Congress programme. In its third session held at Madras in 1887, it was finally decided by leaders like Raghunatha Rao, M. G. Ranade, Narendranath Sen and Janakinath Ghose that a separate conference should be held for the social progress of the country.[21] Thus as a parallel association to the Indian National Organisation, the Indian National Social Conference came into existence in 1887. Madras had the honour of hosting its first session in December 1887. T. Madhava Rao was its President, Raghunatha Rao, its General Secretary and M. G. Ranade, its Vice-President. It was decided to hold annual conferences in different parts of the country to discuss matters such as sea-voyages, inter-caste marriages, enforced-widowhood and ill-assorted marriages.[22] It was also decided to hold provincial conferences to expand the scope of social reform. Thus, by founding the Indian National Social Conference, M. G. Ranade made the Social Reform Movement a national movement. At its third session in Bombay in 1889, the Indian National Social Conference under the Presidentship of Justice Telang, passed a resolution to prevent early consummation of marriage and fix fourteen as the age of marriage for girls.[23] However, the age-limit was fixed at 12 when the Age of the Consent Act was passed in 1891, thanks to the efforts taken by B. M. Malabari, a social reformer from Western India. Charles H. Heimsath has justified that with the passage of the Age of the Consent Act, the "...social reform movement achieved national recognition and henceforth the social reform question was inescapably a part of national ideologies."[24]

In 1903 N. Subba Rao and his fellow Theosophists founded the Madras Hindu National Association[25] as a splinter group from the Madras Hindu Social Reform Association founded in 1892 by G. Subramania Iyer. Its main object was to introduce social reform on national lines.[26] It was decided to train Pandits, Priests and Preachers so that reform could be effected by way of removing social disabilities.[27]

Temple Entry :

The fulcrum of the Social Reform Movement shifted its centre of activities from the welfare of women to that of the Depressed Glasses. Low caste Hindus in Tamil Nadu particularly the Nadars, a community known for its hard work and industry, were not allowed to enter the temples to worship gods and goddesses. They agitated for temple entry at Tiruchendur in 1872, at Madurai Meenakshi temple in 1874, at Thiruthangal in 1876/78, at Gollapatti in 1885, at Tiruchuli in 1890, at Ettaiyapuram in 1895, at Kamudhi in 1897 and at Sivakasi in 1899. Of all these agitations, the agitation at Sivakasi in 1899 was the most important one. The Nadars desired to enter the local Viswanathaswami Temple which action was objected to by the Maravas (a marauding tribe) and the Vellalas, a land-owning community. On June 6, 1899 the Nadars faced the opposition of anti-Nadar combination of 10,000 men. The battle ended in favour of the anti-Nadar combination. 886 Nadar houses were destroyed[28] and 25 Nadars were killed.[29] In 1910 the Nadars to promote their welfare, founded an organisation, Nadar Mahajana Sangam, at Madurai.

At the dawn of the 20th century, the Temple Entry Movement gained all-India status. It was first started in Travancore in 1919 by the Ezhavas, a low caste community in Kerala. The Congress made Temple Entry Movements a vehicle for the promotion of the welfare of the Depressed Classes. Thus, the Temple Entry Movement was appended to the national movement which made it an all-India movement. In 1923 the Indian National Congress at its Kakinada session passed a resolution favouring the entry of the Harijans and other Depressed Classes into temples. In 1924 E. V. Ramasami Naicker (1879-1973) popularly known as "E. V. R." or "Periyar" (Great Soul) spearheaded an agitation at Vykom, Travancore, seeking the rights of Harijans to use the road leading to the temple. E. V. R. succeeded in his mission when the temples in Travancore were thrown open to Harijans on November 12, 1936 by Chittrai Tirunal Maharaja. All temples in Travancore were thrown open to all Hindus irrespective of their castes. In the opinion of K. K. Pillay, it marked an "...epoch in the History of Hinduism, and has set an inspiring example to the rest of India."[30] Following this, a few temples were thrown open to all Hindus in Tamil Nadu in 1939 by means of Act No. XXII known as the Temple Entry Act.[31] Finally, all the temples were thrown open to all sections of the Hindu community in 1949 by means of the Madras Temple Entry Authorization (Amendment) Act.[32] Thus, Temple Entry formed an important phase in National Integration.

Slavery :

Those Depressed Classes who were allowed to enter temples, still could not get social status. They were groaning in the rock bottom of the society. Being economically poor, they remained as slaves. Slavery consisted of two types : Domestic slavery and Agricultural slavery. Slavery abounded in Tanjore,

Madura, North Arcot, South Arcot, Salem, Coimbatore Trichinopoly and Tinnevelly. In 1819 at North Arcot, a mother sold
her two sons for two pagodas, one rupee and nine fanams
(approximately 9 rupees).[33]

Unlike the abolition of Sati, infant-marriage and temple
entry for which private individuals like Raja Ram Mohan Roy,
Ishwar Chandra Vidyasagar, B. M. Malabari and Mookka
Nadan took up the initiative, the initiative for the abolition
of slavery was taken up by the Government itself. The social
environment in which the slaves languished motivated the
Government to improve their condition and emancipate them
from the fetters of serfdom.

In Bengal, the first attempt to abolish slave trade was taken
by Warren Hastings in 1774 who prohibited slave trade. Lord
Cornwallis who succeeded him, continued the policy till 1789.
In 1811 the Bengal Government passed a legislation prohibi-
ting importing of slaves. In 1832, the sale and purchase of
slaves from one district to another was prohibited, but their
sale within the district, was allowed. Following the Bengal
Government, the Government of Fort St. Georges prohibited all
traffic in slaves in 1790.[34] In order to enforce the law effectively, a reward of 30 pagodas was offered for the discovery of
every offender.[35]

The dawn of the nineteenth century witnessed a series of
enactments curbing slavery. Following England, which abolished
Slave Trade in 1808, the Government of India enacted the Slave
Trade Felony Act doing away with slave trade. It declared
slave trade in the British Empire a great offence. In 1809
another Act was passed (Act No. XI of 1809) which declared
slave trade to be unlawful. In 1811, the exportation of slaves
was made on offence.[36] In 1812 slave trade was punished with

a fine.[37]   But these legislations were of little effect. Consequent on the ineffectiveness of the statutes, the Supreme Government at Calcutta, empowered the Magistrates to arrest any person dealing in human trade and send them up for trial.

The Anti-Slavery Movement which gained momentum in England during the 1830's and the subsequent passing of the Act of 1833 to abolish slavery in India[38] the Act V of 1843 which statutorily put an end to slavery in India,[39] the recommendation of the Select Committee, 1837 and the Indian Penal Code Act of 1860[40]—all these developments were responsible for the abolition of slavery in India. In the opinion of R. C. Majumdar, the abolition of slavery formed one of the causes of the Sepoy Mutiny of 1857 as it deprived the Masters of their slaves.[41] The anti-slavery laws passed by the British Government in India indirectly promoted national integration as it was applicable to all the slaves existing in the country.

St. Ramalinga :

Saints also played a notable role in promoting national integration. St. Ramalinga (1823-1874) was one such saint who aimed to integrate all souls. His concept of integration transcended region, religion, nation, caste or colour. Such an integration alone could thrive long. Wars came because of national interests and so the saint felt that the best remedy for the malady that afflicts the mankind is the Universal Integration.

Ramalinga's philosophy mainly consisted of four aspects : Jeevakarunya (compassion for all souls), Anmaneya Orumaippadu (Oneness of soul in love) and Suddha Sanmarga (Unity of all religions).

Imbued with the spirit of humanism, Ramalinga put into practice his ideals of compassion and love to all living beings.[42] With this end in view the Saint founded in 1865 the Samarasa

Suddha Sanmarga Sanga.[43] People were admitted into it irrespective of caste and creed. As Tagore did in Calcutta, he found the entire universe as one entity. He sought to build upon Jeevakarunya, the brotherhood of all men which he gave the name Anmaneya Orumaippadu (Oneness of soul in love). He appealed to all people to free themselves from caste and religious sentiments "and practice Jeevakarunyam which is the only prerequisite for entering into Suddha Sanmarga or the True Path for attaining grace."[44] It was the time when Tamil Nadu was in the grip of religious tension. There was a constant fight between the Saivites, Vaishnavites, Jains, Buddhists and Muslims. He therefore aimed at creating a society without caste and religious feuds which he named Suddha Sanmarga (Pure Path). According to him, religions are path-ways to reach God and so there should be no religious fanaticism. He says :[45]

"Every religion is sustained by the grace of God,
I have understood this truth,
Hence all religions have my acceptance,
Have I ever thought of discriminating religion

and religion.

He felt that religion, instead of uniting men, had sown the seeds of discord. Therefore, the Saint aimed at the integration of all religions.

In his great Appeal the Saint says that religions and castes are positive hindrances to the realization of God.[46] He prays that God should grace humanity with love and unity.[47] All human beings were manifestations of God and so it is improper to distinguish them as high and low. The Saint felt deep sorrow for the miserable lot of the people as they were divided by caste system. He condemned it as a bondage to be broken.[48] All the treatises on four-fold castes and orders of life are but childishness.[49] Instead of uniting men, the four-fold castes divided them as poles apart which hinders social cohesion of

people. He declared in a forthright manner that blind faith and
superstitious beliefs enjoined by false scriptures should be
discarded so that they could never raise their head.[50] He had
no respect for those scriptures which brought about confusion in
the minds of men and thus sowed disunity in their ranks. He
pleaded that everyone should have a pure approach for understanding things in their perspective. He held the view that no
social reform could be beneficial to the society without
cleansing the religious base. So he added a very significant
adjective 'Suddha' (Pure) to the already existing Sanmarga Path
with a view to cleansing Hindu religion of its narrow outlook
and sectarian behaviour. He evolved his 'True Path' rid of out-
worn dogmas and meaningless ritualisms which have deluded
the minds of the people. Says he :[51]

> "Discarding all distorting faiths and beliefs,
> to evolve a common 'True Path'
> that would vouchsafe to all afresh
> the nectar of immortality."

The Saints also condemned the superstituous beliefs of the
Vedas and the Puranas. To him, therefore, the four Vedas, the
Agamas and the Shastras did not form the true and the only
wisdom :[52]

> "The four Vedas, the Agamas, and all these Shastras
> Do not become our own wisdom
> But remain only outside ourselves as our wisdom for the
> > market."

The Saint attacked the lop-sided structure of the society in
which the rich became richer and the poor became poorer.
Seized with compassion, he was unable to stand the tedium of
sufferings and distress of the people. He cried in agony :[53]

> "I cannot for a moment put up with the trials,
> and tribulations of the people in this world,
> I cannot any longer see or hear anybody in distress."

He felt aggrieved at seeing poor people being suppressed by the rich people who squeezed the blood of the poor. Unable to bear the pangs of agony, he shed tears which mingled in the sea.[54] He aimed to create a society in which all people would lead a happy, prosperous and contented life. It should have no economic inequality.[55]

> "Middle class, poor, rich, everyone should
> through harmony ensure social happiness."

In this context he resembled Karl Marx and Mahatma Gandhi who aimed at creating a society free from economic exploitation. Such a society alone could thrive long.

To put into practice his teachings, Ramalinga founded at Karunguli in 1865 the Satya Sanmarga Sanga in which people were admitted irrespective of caste or religion. The objectives of the Sanga were : Teaching and Jeevakarunya, abolition of meat-eating, animal sacrifices and superstitious beliefs and casting away off 'Jati' (Caste) and 'Varuna' (Colour) differences and bring about *unity* among people of all creeds by making them realise the oneness of all souls in love. In 1867 the Saint founded the Satya Dharumachalai (Feeding Centre for the poor) for the purpose of feeding the poor which tradition is still maintained. In 1872 the Saint established the Satya Gnana Sabai (Hall of Wisdom for Universal Worship). He felt that God could be worshipped in the form of Light. The temple was designed in the shape of a full-blown lotus flower representing the human body, the temple of God. A five-foot high mirror and an oil lamp were installed in the sanctuary. Seven curtains (black, indigo, green, red, yellow, white and mixed colour) representing seven illusions, were placed in front of the glass. Each screen indicated an illusion that the Suddha Sivam or Para Sivam (Pure Siva) could be attained only after passing

20

through these illusions. The implication of the Light worship is that God is in the body of every human being.

In order to realize an integral view of religions, the Saint created the concept of one God who was given the name Arutperunjothi. To him, the whole mankind is a single body, single 'jothi' (Effulgence of God). The whole world was one family. The United Nations whose aim is to form the World Government may be said to be the manifestation of the Saint's dream.[56] If everyone tried the True Path of Sanmarga, it was possible for one world to emerge—a world based upon social and economic equality. His message was of Universal nature, to Universal man for Universal peace, harmony and happiness through simple practice of love.[57] When people fought against one another on caste or religion, Ramalinga introduced a new way of worship to bind them together with love and spirituality.[58] In his philosophy, ignorance is metaphysically represented as darkness whereas the illuminating spiritual knowledge is represented as Light.[59] He gave the concept of "Arutperunjothi" (Supreme Grace of Light) to the form of new God who was not only the True Reality but also the manifestation of compassion. He yearned to promote unity among many cults, creeds and sects by giving them the true spiritual vision. He aimed to create one Religion, one Reality and one Society.[60] Thus Ramalinga formed an integral part of the renaissance movement in Tamil Nadu in the nineteenth century and contributed to spiritual unity of the country.

Hindu Revivalism :

St. Ramalinga was not the only voice of revivalism in the nineteenth century Tamil Nadu. Revivalist ideas which were gradually awakening in Tamil Nadu came from all over India and even from the West. Revivalism was the reinforcement of Hindu religious tenets in Social Reform. It also meant the revival of the Hindu tradition and also modifying some aspects of Hinduism in the light of the changing conditions. As observed by Sri Aurobindo, it satisfied the "...old mentality and the new, the traditional and the critical mind. This in itself involves no mere return, but consciously or unconsciously hastens a restatement".[61] The Indian leaders absorbed whatever that could be taken from their ancient culture and synthesized it with the thoughts and ideas of the West. Hence, the Indian Renaissance Movement is a synthetic restatement containing the best of the Indian and the Western thoughts. In other words, the sould of the old civilization was to be preserved in all its essential nature and at the same time, it was to be adaptable to new situation that emerged in the wake of the Western education.[62]

Revivalist ideas changed many of the out-worn traditional outlook, especially with regard to religion, the position of women and the Depressed Classes in the Tamil Society. These changes sprang up when traditional society was breaking down and the modern Tamil society was fast emerging. The main torch-bearers of the Revivalist Movement were the Brahmo Samaj (1828), the Prarthana Samaj (1867), the Arya Samaj* (1875), the Theosophical Society (founded in New York in 1875, shifted to Bombay, India in 1879) and the Ramakrishna Mission (1897). The Brahmo Samaj was the first attempt to found a new spiritual religion based upon original Hindu theism. It was a protest movement of the educated elite against the dogmas and superstitions of Hindu religion. In 1864 a branch of the Brahmo Samaj was opened at Madras by Sridharlu

---

* A branch of the Arya Samaj was opened in Madras in 1920 by Rishi Ram. It had a girls' school, a primary school, homoeopathic and Ayurvedic dispensaries and the Dayanand Anglo-Vedic School in Madras—S. P. Sen (Ed.), *The North and the South in Indian History : Contact and Adjustment,* (Calcutta, 1976), p. 153,

Naidu.[63] The first Brahmo marriage was solemnized by Sridharlu Naidu on 29 December, 1871. Branches were opened at Coimbatore (1880), Cuddalore (1905), Tinnevelly and Trichinopoly. It performed widow marriages in the Madras Presidency. In the social field, besides lessening the intensity of the caste system, the Brahmo Samaj did constructive work for ameliorating the condition of the Depressed Classes. In Viresalingam Pantulu's Theistic High School, several Harijan students studied. The great achievement of the Brahmo Movement lies in the fact that it arrested convession to Christianity in Tamil Nadu.

The Theosophical Society was one of the foremost revivalist bodies that came to Tamil Nadu in the nineteenth century. It was founded in 1875 by Col. Olcott and Madame Blavatsky in New York.[64] It was shifted to Bombay in 1879 from where it was shifted to Adyar, Madras in 1882. Its objective was to diffuse knowledge of the laws which govern the Universe.[65] Branches were opened all over the Presidency. By 1884, the Theosophical Society had 80 branches in South India, with its members and sympathisers running into thousands. Olcott and Blavatsky started Sanskrit schools at Triplicane, Mylapore and Black Town[66] to promote Vedic learning. In 1884 at the annual conference of the Theosophists at Adyar, a resolution was passed to the effect that an "Aryan League of Honour" should be established in all centres to promote the cause of regeneration.[67] Col. Olcott started schools for Pariah children in 1894 at Adyar.[68] By 1901, 384 boys and 150 girls studied in these schools. Annie Besant (1847-1933) who came to India in 1893 wielded greater influence over the Theosophical Society. She reminded Indians that they should get back to their past glory. She goaded the Indians to get them mentally prepared to play an important role in national life. In her first lecture delivered at Tuticorin, she said that India's past glory could be got back only by the revival of her philosophy and culture.[69]

She advocated abolition of caste system. She believed that the caste system had injured the national spirit and also the nation's unity. She advocated abolition of child-marriage also.[70] She emphasized the fact that common people should be educated so that they could rebuild the nation. She also held that there should be no racial distinction between peoples of various countries. She wanted that people of all walks of life should join together under one umbrella—the Indian National Congress for allround progress.[71]

In 1904 Annie Besant and her associates, N. Subba Rau and Rangacharya founded the Madras Hindu Association with a view to raising the age of betrothals for boys and girls.[72] In 1917-18 she founded the Women's Indian Association at Adyar for the promotion of women's welfare, which, in 1927 blossomed into the All India Women's Conference. The formation of the Madras Hindu Association was a landmark in the Revivalist Movement in Tamil Nadu as it, in the opinion of Heimsath, "...admirably reconciled revivalist and social reformers".[73]

In 1886 the Saiva Siddhanta Sabha was established at Tuticorin for the promotion of Saivism. In 1887 Sivasankara Pandiah started the Hindu Tract Society in Madras to spread the philosophy of Hinduism.[74]

The Ramakrishna Mission, a religious and charitable institution, founded by Ramakrishna Paramahamsa and reshaped by Swami Vivekananda in 1897, held that service to man was service to God. It emphasized that change of heart was essential for social change. It defended Hinduism from the onslaughts of Christianity. A branch of the Ramakrishna Mission was opened at Mylapore in March 1897 "for the attainment of one's own liberation as well as to get equipped for the amelioration of the world in all possible ways by following the path laid down by Bhagavan Sri Ramakrishna Deva".[75] Its main objective was to promote the study of Vedanta as propounded by Sri Ramakrishna Paramahamsa and was practically illustrated by his own life and of comparative theology in its widest form.[76] Branches were also opened at Nattarampalli, Arasampatti, Barur, Krishnagiri and Dharmapuri. It did commendable educational and social work to Tamil Nadu.

Thus, as a result of the Revivalist Movement, Hinduism began to acquire new strength. Farquhar has rightly said that "...everything oriental was glorified as spiritual and ennobling, while everything Western received condemnation as hideously materialistic and degrading."[77] It created a new social awareness that kept itself above narrow religious, caste consciousness. For example, the Theosophical Society rejected caste system and encouraged the marriage of virgin widows. Vivekananda restored Hinduism to its purity and heralded a new era. For the first time, the country projected a United Social Movement. It also changed the Tamils' style of thinking. It introduced new concepts, rejuvenated ancient ideals and injected new blood. It disseminated spiritual knowledge to the people irrespective of their castes and religions and set up educational institutions for imparting secular education.

By the end of the nineteenth century, revivalism became the major principle of the Indian Social Reform Movement. In 1897 Narendranath Sen, the President of the Indian National Social Conference, declared in unequivocal terms that social reform meant nothing more than a return to the social structure that was built up in ancient India.[78] With N. G. Chandavarkar's succeeding M. G. Ranade upon the latter's death in 1901 as President of the Indian National Social Conference, a new blood was injected into social reform[79]. In 1904 Candavarkar declared that if social reformers were to follow Western ideas instead of proceeding on "national lines," he would repudiate their Movement. He also maintained that reform should be aimed at restoring India's ancient ideals which alone should form the programme of the reformers. To quote him : "I am one of those who cling to the belief that all reform to be productive of good and lasting must begin by taking into account the past history of the people for whom it is meant and it ought to regulate itself on lines which do not conflict with their highest and noblest ideals."[80]

At the Indian National Social Conference held in Benares in 1905, it was decided that the principles of social reform should be linked with Sanatana Dharma. At the Conference held in 1907, the Chairman of the Reception Committee noted that "Reform is not revolution, it is not innovation, or an apish imitation of foreign ideals. To be effective with the general masses it must aim at ideals which we call our own."[81] Accordingly, local and provincial social reform associations were formed throughout the presidency with the objective of "advance along national lines."

Conclusion :

With the dawn of the twentieth century, two opposing trends were discernible in the political domain of Tamil Nadu. One was the Congress-dominated Indian Nationalism. The second one was the Dravidian Movement which was diametrically anti-Aryan Movement. With the coming into existence of Annie Besant in the Tamil Nadu politics in 1916 and with her Home Rule Movement, the Non-Brahmin Movement gained momentum. Leaders like P. T. Chetty and T. M. Nair felt that the Non-Brahmin communities were subservient to Brahmin domination which prompted them to start the South Indian People's Association in 1916, subsequently to be renamed as the

South Indian Liberal Federation and the Justice Party. Its chief objectives were "to create and promote the education, social, economic, political, material and moral progress of all communities in South India other than Brahmins."[82]   The Dravidian Movement became anti-God Movement when E. V. R. started the Dravidar Kazhagam (Dravidian League). Soon after Independence, it became even anti-Indian Political Movement under C. N. Annadurai. However, the Chinese invasion of India in 1962 sounded a warning to the disintegrating forces and the subsequent action taken by the Government of India to promote national integration changed the psychology of the Dravidian Movement which began to work for the first time since then for a federal set-up.

The division of India on linguistic basis has become a bane rather than a boon. Language disputes, border disputes, water disputes and communal disputes have become irritants to the nation's solidarity. Though, after Independence, castes have lost their rigours, they are yet a force to reckon with. National Integration is a pre-condition to social and economic integration.

The velocity with which our freedom fighters were motivated with the feeling of oneness to gain political freedom had been totally absent among their successors after Independence, to gain social and economic freedom. Regional rivalries and frustrations regarding the pace of economic development and establishment of public sector undertakings are undermining national unity.[83] Consensus on a national language is still eluding. Making all the 14 Indian languages as the official languages, as in Sweden, with English as the link-language, may be one of the ways through which the gordian knot could be cut. Emotional integration of various sub-nationalities is the cherished goal of the Government but it remains a distant dream. The linking of waterways from one part of the country to another will be of little avail, unless it is cemented by a sense of commitment for unity on the part of the people. Mere economic planning, or social achievement, science or technology could not guarantee national unity, unless they are tinged with patriotic fervour and fellow-feeling. The tragedies of two Germany, two Korea and two Vietnam should be the grim reminders. Thus, unless a fundamental community of interests and fellow-feeling come to be shared by the people and differences are settled amicably on mutual consent as if they cropped up in a family, there could be no real national integration.[84] A just social order based upon equality of opportunity should be ensured.[85] People should strive hard to understand each other more intimately and unitedly work for the cherished goal[86] keeping in view the dictum of Poet Tagore :

> "Where the mind is without fear,
> And the head is held high,
> Where knowledge is free,
> Where the world has not been broken up into fragments
> by narrow domestic walls,
>
> ...   .
>
> Into that Heaven of Freedom,
> Let my country awake."

Thus, compared to Free India's problem of National Integration, the nineteenth century India was relatively united, thanks predominantly to the Social Reform Movement and Tamil Nadu in no less a degree contributed to India's integration —a legacy to be followed for future guidance.

REFERENCES

1. T. S. Avinashilingam (Ed.), *Education for National Integration* (A Symposium), (Coimbatore, Sri Ramakrishna Mission Vidyalaya, First Edition, 1967), p. 86.

2. *Ibid.*, p. 132.

3. K. A. Nilakanta Sastri, *A History of South India*, (Madras, Oxford University Press, 1966), p. 34.

4. R. C. Majumdar, H. C. Ray Chaudhuri and Kalikinkar Datta, *An Advanced History of India*, (London, Mac Millan, Third Edition, 1967), p. 7.

5. Cited by V. K. R. V. Rao, *Swami Vivekananda—The Prophet of Vedantic Socialism*, (Builders of Modern India Series), (New Delhi, 1979), p. 2.

6. *Idid.*, p. 3.

7. N. Subrahmanian, *History of Tamilnad*, 1565-1956, (Madurai, 1982), p. 294.

8. S. P. Sen (Ed.), *Social and Religious Reform Movement in the Nineteenth and Twentieth Centuries* (Calcutta, Institute of Historical Studies, 1979), p. 347.

9. *Judicial Consultations*, Vol. 226, Cons. dated 2 Feb. 1830, p. 325 ; *Judicial Despatches to England Year* (Sic. Years) 1811 to 1815, Vol. III dated 1 Mar., 1815, p. 307.

10. Deena Nath Ganguli, *Memoir of Rajah Ram Mohan Roy*,(Calcutta, 1884), p. 29.

11. Cited by Demetrius C. Boulger, *William Bentinck*, (Rulers of India Series), (Oxford, 1897), p. 22.

12. *Minute by Lord William Bentinck*, dated 8 Nov., 1829 ; cited by Demetrius C. Boulger, *op. cit.*, p. 96.

13. *Papers Relating to East India Affairs* Viz., *Regulations passed by the Government of Bengal, Fort St. George and Bombay in the Year 1828*, (Calcutta, 1829), Regulation XVII, p. 45

14. R. C. Majumdar, *History of the Freedom Movement in India*, Vol. I, (Calcutta, 1971), p. 270.

15. *Papers on Indian Reform—The Women of India*, (n. p.), dated 4 June, 1889, p. 56.

16. *Report of the Fifteenth National Social Conference held in Bengal* dated 29 Dec. 1901, (Poona, 1903), Appendix H. p. 94.

17. Lewis Mc Iver, *Imperial Census of 1881—Operations and Results in*

the Presidency of Madras, Vol. I, *The Report—Madras*, (Madras, 1883), p. 69.

18. W. Theobald, *The Legislative Acts of the Governor—General in Council*, Vol. II, *1852-1858, Hindoo Widow Marriage Act No. XV of 1856*, p. 501 ; William Pilumbridge Williams, *The Acts of the Legislative Council of India Relating to the Madras Presidency*, (1848-1858), (Madras, 1859), p. 460.

19. Cited by Bipan Chandra, *Modern India—A Text-Book of History for Secondary Schools*, (New Delhi, 1971), p. 131.

20. Subal Chandra Mitra, *Isvar Chandra Vidyasagar—A Story of his Life and Work*, (New Delhi, Reprint, 1975), p. 318.

21. C. Yajneswara Chintamani (Ed.), *Indian Social Reform*—in Four Parts—Being a Collection of Essays, Addresses, Speeches & c. with an Appendix, (Madras, 1901), p. 365.

22. Ibid.

23. Ibid., Part IV, Appendix, p. 368.

24. Charles H. Heimsath, *Indian Nationalism and Hindu Social Reform*, (Princeton, 1964), p. 173.

25. N. Subbarau Pantulu Garu, (Ed.), *Hindu Social Progress*, (Madras, 1904), p. 1.

26. Ibid.

27. *Ibid.*, p. 3

28. *Judicial Department* (Press), G. O. No. 2017-2018 (Confdl.) No. 176, dated 12 Dec. 1899, Vol. I, p. 26.

29. *Report on the Administration of the Madras Presidency during the Year 1899-1900* (Madras, 1900), p. 1.

30. K. K. Pillay, *The Sucindram Temple*, (Madras, 1953), p. 266.

31. *Acts passed by the Madras Legislature in the Year 1939*, Government of Madras, Legal Department, Madras Act No. XXII of 1939, p. 2.

32. *The Madras Temple Entry Authorization* (Amendment) Act, 1949 (Madras Act XIII of 1949), p. 27.

33. *Proceedings of the Board of Revenue*, Vol. 844, dated 27 Dec. 1819. p. 11874 Letter No. 23.

34. Henry Davison Love, *Indian Records Series—Vestiges of Old Madras*, Vol. I, (London, 1913), p. 546.

35. *Ibid.*, Vol. III, p. 382.

36. *Judicial Despatch to England 1826-28* Serial No. 5, General No. 7465—*General Letter to England in the Judicial Department* dated 23 Jan. 1827, p. 108.

37. Ibid.

38. Dharma Kumar, *Land and Caste in South India—Agricultural Labour in the Madras Presidency during the Nineteenth Century,* (Cambridge, 1965), p. 73.

39. *The Unrepealed General Acts of the Governor—General in Council with Chronological Table* in Three Volumes, Vol. I, (1834 to 1863), (Calcutta, 1875), p. 53.

40. *Ibid.*, p. 480 (Section 371 only).

41. R. C. Majumdar (Ed.), *The History and Culture of the Indian People,* Vol. X, *British Paramountcy and Indian Renaissance.* Part II, (Bombay, 1981), p. 281.

42. T. Dayanandan Francis, *Ramalingaswamy*, (Madras, First Edition, 1972), p. 10.

43. Ibid.

44. *Ibid.*, pp. 25-26.

45. *Tiruvarutpa,* Sixth Canto (Ramalinga Mission, Madras, Second Edition, 1981), Line 3639, Tr. by S. R. V. Arasu, *Voice of Vallalar* A Modern Critique on the Tiruarutpa, (Madras, 1974), p. 24.

46. Uran Atikal (ed.), *Tiruvarutpa Urainadaipakuthi* (Tamil) (Tiruvarutpa Prose work), (Vadalur, First Edition, 1978), p. 444.

47. *Ibid.*, pp. 444-445.

48. *Tiruvarutpa, Third Canto,* Line, 1972.

49. *Ibid.*, Sixth Canto, Line 4174, (Tr.) by S. R. V. Arasu, *op. cit.*, p. 29.

50. *Ibid.*, Line 3768.

51. *Ibid.*, Line 3696 (Tr.) by S. R. V. Arasu, *op. cit.*, p. 27.

52. *Ibid.*, Line 4955 (Tr.) by S. R. V. Arasu, *op. cit.*, p. 28 ; Also Lines 5515-5516.

53. Cited by S. R. V. Arasu, *op. cit.*, p. 31.

54. *Fourth Canto,* Line, 2750.

55. *Sixth Canto,* Line 4082 (Tr.) by S. R. V. Arasu, *op, cit.*, p. 19.

56. A Subramania Pillai, *The Philosophy of Saint Ramalingam with Special Reference to its Basic Concepts,* (Unpublished Ph. D. Thesis), (University of Madras, 1971), p. 195.

57. *Ibid.*, n. p.

58. M. Shanmugam, *Philosophy of Saint Ramalingam,* (Madurai, First Edition, 1983), p. 62.

59. A. Subramania Pillai, *op. cit.,* n. p.

60. *Ibid.*, n. p.

61. Sri Aurobindo, *The Renaissance in India,* (Pondicherry, Reprint, 1982), p. 27.

62. N. Subba Rao Pantulu Garu (Ed.), *Hindu Social Progress,* (Madras, 1904), pp. 21-22.

63. *The Asylum Press Almanac and Compendium of Intelligence for 1882,* (Madras, 1881), p. 688.

64. Henry Steelte Olcott, *Old Diary Leaves : The History of the Theosophical Society—Second Series, 1878-1883,* (London, 1974), p. 392.

65. *The Golden Book of the Theosophical Society,* (Pamphlet), p. 23.

66. R. Suntharalingam, *Politics and Nationalist Awakening in South India* (Arizona, 1974), p. 303.

67. *Supplement to the Theosophist,* Vol. 6, No. 5 (Madras, Feb. 1885), No. 65, p. 1.

68. Henry S. Olcott, *The Poor Pariah,* (Pamphlet), (Adyar, 1902), p. 17.

69. Annie Besant, *Ancient Ideals in Modern Life,* (Adyar, 1925), p. 95.

70. Annie Besant, *Wake Up, India : A Plea for Social Reform,* (Adyar, 1913), p. 50.

71. Annie Besant, *The Besant Spirit, India : Bond* or Free, Vol. 5, (Adyar, 1939), Appendix, p. 227.

72. N. Subba Rau Pantulu Garu (Ed.), *op. cit.,* Appendix, B, p. 55

73. Charles H. Heimsath, *op. cit.,* p. 329

74. Suntharalingam, *op. cit.,* p. 304

75. *Ramakrishna Math and Ramakrishna Mission Convention, Souvenir,* 1980, December 23-29 (Howrah, 1980), p. 3

76. Swami Ranganathananda, *The Ramakrishna Mission—Its Ideals and Activities*—Institute Booklets : 12 (Calcutta, 1960), pp. 21-22

77. J. N. Farquhar, *Modern Religious Movement in India* (New York, 1919), p. 430

78. C. Yajneswara Chintamani (Ed.), *op. cit.,* Part III, (Madras, 1901), f. n. p. 192.

79. Charles H. Heimsath, *op. cit.*, p. 337.

80. L. V. Kaikini (Ed.), *The Speeches and Writings of Sir Narayen G. Chandavarkar*, (Bombay, 1911), p. 125.

81. Cited by Charles H. Heimsath, *op. cit.*, pp. 337-338.

82. Cited by K. Nambi Arooran, *Tamil Renaissance and Dravidian Nationalism, 1905-1944*, (Madurai, Koodal Publishers, 1980), p. 49.

83. K. Santhanam, *Transition in India*, (Bombay : Asia Publishing House, 1964), p. 13.

84. *Ibid.*, p. 14.

85. T. S. Avinashilingam, (Ed.), *op. cit.*, p. 14.

86. Ibid.

Social Reform Movement in the 19th Century Tamil Nadu and its Contribution to National Integration

C. Paramarthalingam

(SYNOPSIS)

Introduction :

The nineteenth century was a great landmark in the history of India as it witnessed the emergence of the Social Reform Movement. The contribution of Social Reform Movement to National Integration is unique. The various legislations passed to remove the social disabilities came to be applied to the whole of India. They gave the people a sense of unity. Compared to the lot of the 20th Century India which is torn asunder by disintegrating forces from various quarters, the 19th century India projected a United country, which was predominantly due to the Social Reform Movement. Tamil Nadu also contributed to the main stream. The legislations passed to abolish Sati, infant-marriage and enforced-widowhood, restrictions to temple entry and slavery and also the emergence of Hindu Revivalism had been extended to all parts of India and made the country socially one. These reforms were extended to Tamil Nadu also.

Sati :

It is said that Social Reform Movement in India in the 19th century started with the Anti-Sati Movement. Sati prevailed in India right from the Vedic period. In Tamil Nadu, it existed in Sangam period. During the nineteenth century, numerous instances of Sati took place in Tamil Nadu. The chief centres were Tanjore, Pudukottai, Coibatore and Salem. C. M. Lushington, the Acting Magistrate of Tanjore reported to the Madras Government in 1813 that one hundred widows were burnt alive at various places in Tanjore between 1806 and 1813. Raja Ram Mohan Roy in his Tracts published in 1818 and 1820 stated that the widows did not become Satis of their own accord, but they were induced by their relatives to do so. William Bentinck who took over charge as Governor-General in July 1828 prepared a Minute based upon which Act No. XVII was passed on December 4, 1829 doing away with the practice of Sati. The Act came into force in Tamil Nadu in 1830. In the opinion of R. C. Majumdar, the abolition of Sati gave a fillip to the Social Reform Movement in India. Social, reformers now began to concentrate upon other problems such as infant-marriage and enforced-widowhood, restrictions on temple entry and slavery.

Infant-Marriage and Enforced Widowhood :

The statutory abolition of Sati added more problems to widows. They underwent untold ordeals. Widowhood consisted of two kinds—infant-widowhood and adult widowood. It was the infant-widowhood that caused concern to the social reformers. In the ¡Madras Presidency, infant-marriage prevailed among Brahmins, Kshatriyas and Chettis. Brahmins had their children married between the ages of 6 and 7 which inevitably increased the percentage of widows. In 1881 the total number of Hindu girls married in the Madras Presidency was 1,57,466 out of whom 5,621 were widows in the same year.

Ishwar Chandra Vidyasagar (1820-1891) of Bengal spearheaded the Widow Re-Marriage Movement. Thanks to his efforts, the Widow Re-Marriage Reform Act No. XV was passed in 1856 which made the widow re-marriage legal and also made the issue born out of the widow marriage, legitimate. In Tamil Nadu the first widow re-marriage was celebrated at

Salem in 1858. The grateful women of Calcutta perpetualed Vidyasagar's memory by imprinting on the borders of their sarees the first Couplet of a Bengali song : "May Vidyasagar live long."

Following the Widow Re-Marriage Reform Act, Widow re-marriage associations were founded in various parts of the Madras Presidency. Mention may be made of Widow Re-marriage Society (1873) at Nagercoil, the Madras Hindu Widow Marriage Association (1874), the Hindu Women's Re-Marriage Association (1882) at Madras, the Madras Hindu Social Reform Association (1892) and the Rajahmundry Widow Marriage Association (1897). The widow re-marriage associations started in various parts of the country made the widow re-marriage issue a national issue.

The Birth of the Indian National Social Conference 1887 :

Then Indian National Congress having been founded in 1885, its leaders felt the need for discussing, social issues also at the session. With this end in view, Mahadev Govind Ranade delivered a lecture on social reform at its first session held at Bombay in 1885. In its second session held at Calcutta in 1886, its leaders such as Dadabhai Naoroji, Budruddin Tyabji and W. C. Banerji emphasised the fact that social matters should form part of the Congress programme. In the third session held at Madras in 1887, it was finally decided by leaders such as Raghunatha Rao, M. G. Ranade, Narendranath Sen and Janakinath Ghose that a separate conference should be started with the sole objective of achieving social progress. Thus, there came into existence in 1887 the Indian National Social Conference as an offshoot of the Congress. Madras had the honour of hosting its first session in December 1887. T. Madhava Rao was its President, Raghunatha Rao its General

Secretary and M. G. Ranade, its Vice-President. It was decided to hold annual conferences in different parts of the country to discuss matters such as sea-voyages, inter-caste marriages, enforced-widowhood and ill-assorted marriages. It was also decided to hold provincial conferences to expand the scope of social reform. Thus, by founding the Indian National Social Conference. Mahadev Govind Ranade, made the Social Reform Movement a national movement.

At its third session in Bombay in 1889, the Indian National Social Conference under the Presidentship of Justice Telang passed a resolution urging the Government to prevent early consummation of marriage and fix fourteen years as the age of marriage for girls. However, the age-limit was fixed at 12 when the Age of the Consent Act was passed in 1891 thanks to the efforts taken by B. M. Malabari, a social reformer from Western India. Charles H. Heimsath has justified that with the passage of the Age of the Consent Act, the "...social reform movement achieved national recognition and henceforth the social reform question was inescapably a part of national ideologies."

In 1903 N. Subba Rau and his fellow-Theosophists started the Madras Hindu National Association as a splinter group from the Madras Hindu Social Reform Association founded by G. Subramania Iyer in 1892. Its objective was to effect social reform on national lines.

Temple Entry :

The fulcrum of the Social Reform Movement shifted its centre of activities from the welfare of women to the welfare of the Depressed Classes. Low-Caste Hindus in Tamil Nadu, particularly the Nadars, were not allowed to enter the temples to worship gods and goddesses. They agitated for temple entry at Tiruchendur in 1872, at Madurai Meenakshi Temple in 1874, at Thiruthangal in 1876-78, at Gollapatti in 1885, at Tiruchuli in 1890, atEttaiyapuram in1895, at Kamudhi in 1897 and atSivakasi in 1899. Of all these agitations, the agitation at Sivokasi in 1899 was the most important one. The Nadars were denied entry into the local Viswanathaswami temple at Sivakasi. On June 6, 1899 the Nadars faced the opposition of anti-Nadar combination of 10,000 men, mainly Maravas (a marauding tribe) and Vellalas, a cultivating caste. The battle ended in favour of the Maravas. 886 Nadar houses were destroyed and 25 Nadars were killed.

In the twentieth Century, the Temple EntryMovementgained all-India status. The Congress made Temple Entry for the Depressed Classes as its main plank. Thus, the Temple Entry Movement was appended to the national movement that made it an all-India movement. In 1923 the Indian National Congress at its Kakinada session passed a resolution favouring the entry of the Harijans and the Depressed Classes into the temples. In 1924, E. V. Ramasami Naicker (1879-1973) popularly known as "E. V. R." or "Periyar" (Great Soul) spearheaded an agitation at Vykom in Travancore, seeking the rights of Harijans to use the road leading to the temple. E. V. R. succeeded in his mission when the temples in Travancore were thrown open to all Hindus irrespective of their castes. In the opinion of K. K. Pillay, it marked an "...epoch in the history of Hinduism, and has set an inspiring example to the rest of India." Finally, all the temples were thrown open to all Hindus in 1949 by the Madras Temple Entry Authorization (Amendment) Act. Thus, Temple Entry formed an important phase in National Integration in the nineteenth century.

Slavery :

Those Depressed Classes who were allowed to enter the temples, still could not get the status of equality in the society. Being economically poor, they remained as slaves.

Slavery consisted of two types : Domestic slavery and Agricultural slavery. Slavery abounded in Tanjore, Madura, North Arcot, South Arcot, Salem, Coimbatore, Trichinopoly and Tinnevelly. In 1819 at North Arcot, a mother sold her two sons for two pagodas, one rupee and nine panas (approximately 9 rupees).

Unlike the abolition of Sati, widow re-marriage and temple entry for which private individuals like Raja Ram Mohan Roy, Ishwar Chandra Vidyasagar, B. M. Malabari and Mookka Nadan took up the initiative, the initiative for the abolition of slavery was taken up by the Government itself.

In Bengal the first attempt to abolish slave trade was taken up by Warren Hastings in 1774 who prohibited slave trade. Lord Cornwallis who succeeded him, continued the policy till 1789. In 1811 the Bengal Government passed a legislation that prohibited importing of slaves. In 1832 the sale and purchase of slaves from one district to another was prohibited, but their sale within the district was allowed. Following the Bengal Government, the Government of Fort St. George prohibited all traffic in slaves in 1790. Following England which abolished slave trade in 1808, the Government of India passed the Slave Trade Felony Act doing away with slave trade. It made slave trade in the British Empire a great offence. In 1809 another Act was passed (Act No. XI of 1809) making slave trade to be unlawful. In 1811 the exportation of slaves was made an offence. But these legislations could not cut the ice. The Anti-Slavery Movement in England in the 1830's, the Charter Act of 1833, the Indian Slavery Act V of 1843 and the Indian Penal Code Act of 1860 were responsible for the abolition of slavery in India. The anti-slavery laws passed by the British Government in India applicable to all the provinces in British India promoted national unity.

St. Ramalinga :

Saints also played a notable role in promoting national integration through social reform. St. Ramalinga (1823-1874) was one such saint who went one step further and stood for Universal Integration of souls—an integration transcending region, religion, nation, caste or colour. Nations divided on nationalism had been the cause of many a war. Thus, the Saint aimed to integrate the human souls by means of love which alone could endure long. His philosophy consisted of compassion for all souls (Jeevaklarunya), oneness of soul in love (Anmaneya Orumaippadu) and unity of all religions (Suddha Sanmarga).

Ramalinga was the true spirit of Renaissance Movement in Tamil Nadu in the 19th century. In order to realize an integral view of religions, the Saint created one God who was given the name Arutperunjothi (Supreme Grace of Light). The United Nations whose aim is to form the World Government may be said to be the manifestation of the Saint's dream. If everyone tried the True Path of Sanmarga, it was possible for One World to emerge—a world where there will be no political instability, economic inequality and social disparity. His message was of universal nature, to universal man for universal peace, harmony and happiness through simple practice of love.

To put his precept into practice, Ramalinga founded the Satya Sanmarga Sanga in 1865 in which all people irrespective of caste or creed were admitted. In 1867 he established the Satya Dharumachalai (feeding centre for the poor) to feed the needy and the hungry. In 1872 he established the Satya Gnana Sabai (Hall of Universal Worship) to worship God in the form of Light. To him, the whole of man kind was a single 'Jothi' (Effulgence of God). Thus Ramalinga, a contemporary of Ram

Mohon Roy remained the harbinger of renaisance in Tamil Nadu in the 19th century and effecteds a spiritual integration in the country.

Hindu Revivalism :

St. Ramalinga was not the only voice of revivalism in the 19th century Tamil Nadu. Revivalist ideas which were gradually awakening in Tamil Nadu came from all over India and even from the West. The revivalist bodies included the Brahmo Samaj (1828), the Prarthana Samaj (1867), the Arya Samaj (1875), the Theosophical Society (founded in New York in 1875, shifted to Bombay, India in 1879) and the Ramakrishna Mission (1897). The revivalist bodies stressed the revival of India's past glory. As a result of the Revivalist Movement, Hinduism began to acquire new strength. In the opinion of Farquhar, "...everything oriental was glorified as spiritual and ennobling, while everything Western received condemnation as hideously materialistic and degrading." It created a new sense of social awareness that kept itself alone narrow religious, caste consciousness.

In 1897 Narendranath Sen, the President of the Indian National Social Conference noted that social reform meant nothing but a return to the social structure that was built up in ancient India. When N. G. Chandavarkar succeeded M. G. Ranade upon the latter's death in 1901 as President of the Indian National Social Conference, a new blood was injected into social reform. Chandavarkar made it clear that if social reformers were to follow Western ideas instead of proceeding on "national lines," he would repudiate their Movement. He declared in unequivocal terms that reform should be directed to restore India's ancient ideals. In the Indian National Social Conference held in Benares in 1905, it was declared that the principles of social reform should be linked with Sanatana Dharma. In the Conference of 1907, the Chairman of the Reception Committee stated that "Reform is not revolution, it is not innovation, or an apish imitation of foreign ideals. To be effective with the general masses it must aim at ideals which we call our own." Accordingly, local and provincial social reform associations were started throughout the country with the avowed objective of "*advance along* national lines."

Conclusion :

With the dawn of the twentieth century, Congress-dominated-nationalism and Dravidian Movement were discernible in Tamil Nadu politics. The Dravidian Movement became anti-national and anti-caste movement. With Independence, the Dravidian Movement became more anti-national. However, the Chinese invasion of 1962 sounded a warning to disintegrating forces and the subsequent action taken by the Government of India with regard to National Integration changed the political psychology of the Dravidian Progressive League (Dravida Munnetra Kazhagam), an offshoot of the Dravidian Movement, which began to work for the first time since then for a federal set-up.

Though politically united, India is divided both socially and economically. After Independence, there has been a dilution of patriotism. The division of India on linguistic basis is a bane rather than a boon. A consensus on a national language is still eluding. The making of all the 14 Indian languages as the official languages, as in Sweden, with English as the link language is one of the ways through which the gordian knot could be out. Emotional integration is the cherished goal of the Government, but it remains a distant dream. Unless problems are settled amicably by peaceful moans and unless the hearts of all the Indians are integrated with a spirit of fellow feeling and patriotic fervour, the linking of waterways from one part to the other would serve very little purpose.

Thus, in comparison to Free India's problem of national integration, the 19th century India was relatively united, thanks predominantly to the Social Reform Movement—a legacy to be followed for future guidance.

THE PARSEES : A Study in Integration

by Dr. Mani Kamerkar
S. N. D. T. Women's University—Oct. 1986.

The Parsees are today perhaps the smallest minority in India (90,000) but also with the highest rate of contribution to modern Indian history in the fields of industry, science, arts, and particularly in music and administration. In fact, there is no field in which a Parsee is not to be seen in Indian life. Zoroastrianism, their religion, has influenced the thinking of Muslims, Hindus, Jews and Christians and we find many of the Zoroastrian tenets incorporated in these religions. (1)

Today, the Parsees are concentrated by and large on the west coast of India. They are of Iranian descent. The word Parsee means the 'man from Pars' or Fars (Persepolis) in southern Iran, the centre of the ancient Iranian Empires of Cyrus and Darius. The present day Parsees are the descendents of those persons who left their homeland some 1200 years ago to save their religion, Zorostrianism, from forcible conversion to Islam. Here in India they have identified themselves with the Indian ethos and have become an integral part of the Indian nation.

In fact, historically, culturally and in their religion, the Parsees are closely allied to the people who developed the Vedic culture. Some-time in the remote past, tribes speaking an Aryan language descended from high mountains, probably the Pamirs, into Greece, Persia and India (this theory is now disputed). Zend Avesta, the language of the Gathas and Sanskrit have many common strands and many similarities are to be found in the rituals, sacrifices and worship of both. The Gathas of the Zend Avesta find their echo in the mantras of the Rig Veda.

In Iran these people gradually developed many distinct characteristics and by about 1000-700 B. C. accepted the religion of Zarathustra, who is perhaps the first prophet in human history to preach about one God, Ahura Mazda, Lord of life and wisdom, a God of the spirit and truth, of righteousness, of justice, of love and compassion, who is to be grasped in the purest essence and vision. Zarathustra proclaimed the existence of a sole, absolute, omnipotent eternal God, Ahura Mazda (wise Lord). Ahura Mazda desires all men to come to him of their own free will, in knowledge and love. Freedom of choice is, therefore, a cardinal doctrine in his teachings. (2) As Tagore puts it (Religion of Man) Zarathustra was the greatest of all pioneer prophets who showed the path of freedom, the freedom of moral choice, the freedom from blind obedience to increasing injunctions, and the freedom from the multiplicity of shrines.

To make free will a reality, man has the choice either to do good or indulge in evil. Zarathustra explains this in terms of the twin spirits, the twin 'Maiyu' the better and the bad, who are in opposition to each other in thought, word and deed. They mingle in the mind of man to form his dual nature. When man exercises his better mind he creates 'gaya' or life and draws Ahura Mazda and his divine power towards himself. When man exercises his evil mind, he enters the state called "Ajvaiti" or nonlife i.e. spiritual death. Confusion descends upon him and he rushes towards 'Aeshma'—wrath and bloodshed, by which actions human existence is poisoned. To protect his true believers from the onslaught of wrath, Ahura Mazda sends them his four great powers ; Asha-the divine law, 'Vohumanu'

—the good mind, 'Kshathra', the Lord's might and majesty and 'Armaiti'—divine devotion. (3) These four powers are the just man's constant companions through life, guiding and sustaining in all his undertakings. The here and now is thus not an earthly vale of tears, but a battleground of good and evil. Parsee ethics corresponds with this call to battle for the good, which is optimistic and active, and includes truthfulness, faithfulness, purity, diligence and charity. (4)

The wicked also are not abandoned by Mazda. When the evil person repents, he is shown the way to salvation by 'Vohu Manu'. Thus happiness and misery are the outcome of man's good and evil deeds. A life of active good towards his fellowmen is, therefore, at the base of Zarathustra's teachings. Hence the simple motto 'Humata, Hukata, Huvarshta' or 'Manashni, Gawashni, Kumashni ; goods thoughts, good words and goods deeds. The three are integrated and none of the acts is useful without the other. As the Pahlavi texts maintain, good thoughts dwell in the starry heavens, for if not translated into action, its influence is as remote as that of the stars. Good words dwell in the moonlit Heavens, for if sweet speech does not lead to right action, it is as ineffectual as the silvery light of the Moon. Good deeds which flow out of these two dwell in the mansions of the Sun, for good deeds shine in their own lustre and do not need any one to proclaim their existence. After man's death reward and punishment are distributed as earned and clemency is not practised. The individual is thus responsible for his own actions and the fate of his soul. Rites in Zoroastrianism are mainly for purification. Great care is expected of a Zoroastrian in keeping his body and the natural elements, i. e. earth, fire, and water, pure and free from pollution.

The two great emblems of the religion are 'Hvare Kshaeta' : the glorious sun, and 'Atar 'Khvareh' : the radiant fire. Ahura

Mazda's body is said to be clothed with the Sun. His very being is said to be of one accord with the Sun. Fire is an emblem of the divine and so is called 'Son' of Ahura Mazda. Just as physical fire burns up any filth flung into it and remains pure, retaining its quality, so is the lie burnt up in the heart and mind, so that, thought, word and deed may be dedicated to the truth.

Therefore, the sacred fire is kept alive day and night in the Parsee fire Temples, fed with sandal-wood and incense, to reach as if to the heavens. Zarathustra, thus focused attention almost exclusively on man's behaviour and its moral drives. (5)

From About 1000 years before the Parsees landed in Gujarat, Indo-Iranian relations had been in existence and it is obvious that both were aware of the existence of the other, and probably influenced one another in various ways. We find mention of Hindus four times in the Avesta, and in turn Iran is mentioned many times in the Rigveda, Mahabharata Vishnu Puran, Bhavishyapuram. Mention is also made of visits by Iranian Kings to India in the Shahnama. These may be remembrances of a common past of the two strands of Aryan people. More important contacts came with the conquest of north west India by Darius in 512 BC. This started a continuous exchange between the two peoples. For a number of years, Iran sent its Governors to look after its provinces in India. Many Zoroastrians must have settled in these provinces, as a fire temple and a dokma (tower of Silence) has been found in Taxila. (6) Some Asokan inscriptions have also been found in 'Kharoshti' script in these regions. (7) Probably because of the many similarity in ritual and worship, not much comment is to be found regarding these early settlements. Neither did the Iranians forcibly impose their way of life on the indigenous people. After the weakening of Iran, the Governors-the Mahashatrapas—

became independent and seem to have lost contact with their homeland. The Zoroastrain settlers merge in the Mauryan age as Magha Brahmins (320BC—200AD) (8) and as a result of these influences, a Surya Mandir was built in Multan. These communities of Zoroastrians seem to have lived amicably with the local population till the advent of the Hindus in N. W. India, who under Timur in 1398, annihilated the 'fire-worshipping' Zoroastrians. (9) Whoever escaped seem to have merged themselves with the Hindus and lost all signs of a separate identity.

Following the Arab invasion of Iran in 641 A. D., many Zoroastrians fled to remote parts of Iran and then, about 145 years later, in about 756 A. D. groups left for the western coast of India. They arrived on the shores of Gujarat at Sanjan (10). They were met with consideration, and were able to establish some sort of communication in spite of the barrier of language. A legend current in Parsee folk songs (rarbas) is that king Jadhav Rana (Jadi) was persuaded to permit the refugees to stay in his kingdom when the leader of the group convinced king of their good intentions by putting two grains of sugar into a bowl of boiling milk, thus indicating. The 'sweetness' that would be added to the kingdom by the presence of the refugees. According to these traditions, the king Jadhav Rana on his part granted the Parsees the following concessions :

(1) freedom of worship (2) freedom to bring up their young according to their own traditions and (3) some land to cultivate. One of the songs gives an illustration of the Parsee determination to accept the above mentioned terms by portraying the refugees as prostrating themselves before the king and kissing the earth of Gujarat.

Apart from this oral tradition, most of the information regarding the migration and settlement of these people is found in the Persian chronicle, Kissen-Sanjan, written in 1600 A. D. by Behmam Kaikobad Sanjan. Obviously, the writing is based on oral transmission of tradition and may have many inaccuracies but this is the only historical material available.

According to this chronicle Jadhav Rana (Jadi Rana) allowed the Parsees to settle in Sanjan on the follwing five conditions :

(1) the Parsee high priest would have to explain their religion to the king ;

(2) the Parsees would have to give up Persian and adopt the language of the Kingdom i. e. Gujarati ;

(3) the women would accept Indian dress i. e. sari and discard their Iranian ones ;

(4) the men should surrender their weapons ; and

(5) the Parsees should hold their wedding processions at night. This may have been a request from the refugees to protect themselves. It is reported that all these conditions were accepted.

The Parsee priests explained their religion, particularly bringing out the similarities between the two groups. Later in the tenth century the tenets of their religion were composed in Sanskrit and explained to their neighbours wherever they went. The schlokas, are as follows :

(1) We are worshippers of Ahura Mazda, (Supreme Being) and the Sun and the five elements.

(2) We observe silence while bathing, praying and making offerings to five and eating.

(3) We use incense, perfume, and flowers in our religious cremonies.

(4) We are worshipper : of the cow.

(5) We wear the sacred garment, the **Sudra** or shirt, the Kusti and the cop of 2 folds.

(6)   We rejoice in songs with instrument of music on the occasion of our marriages.

(7)   We ornament and perfume our wives.

(8)   We are enjoined to be liberal in our charities and especially in excavating Tanks and wells.

(9)   We are enjoined to extend our sympathies towards males as well as females.

(10)   We practice ablutions with gaomutra, one of the products of the cow.

(11)   We wear the sacred girdle when praying and eating.

(12)   We feed the sacred flame with incense.

(13)   We practice devotion 5 times a day.

(14)   We are careful observers of Coujugal fidelity and purity.

(15)   We perform annual religious ceremonies for our ancestors.

(16)   We place great restraints on our women during and after their confinement. (12)

As will be seen, the scholars had stressed the common factors in the forms of worship such as use of fire, flowers, ablutions, incense, Particular attention was drawn to the Zorastrian respect for the sun and other elements of nature all common to the Hindus. The 'worship' (actually respect) of the cow and the use of gaomutra added to the similarities. Thus from the very beginning, both from necessity and conviction the Parsees were eager to integrate with the Indian society.

The other conditions accepted by the immigrants also show the some tendencies. The Parsees complied without restriction on the question of clothing and language. Gujarati became the native language of the community to the extent that Zend,

Pahlavi etc very soon became forgotten languages. In clothing also both men and women adopted the native Hindu dress. The men even kept a lock or top knot on the crown of the head (13). Language and clothing are two very essential channels and indicators of socio-cultural change in which the Parsees proved very adaptive. In fact in the 18th & 19th centuries the leaders of Gujarati Journalism and literature were Parsees. By the clause promising to surrender their weapons, the Parsees showed their loyalty towards the ruler wherever they went By becoming one with the ruler of their adopted country they hastened the process of integration.

The Parsees seem to have settled peaceably and amicably in Sanjan for several hundred years without any serious dissensions with the local populations. Probably because they did not come in the way of the economic development of their fellow citizens and contributed to the prosperity of the state by paying their dues. In the early centuries they settled as farmers, fruit-growers, today planters, carpenters and weavers-vocations in which obviously they did not prove to be competitors, but were probably supportive.

They are not to be found, however as blacksmiths as that vocation involved blowing of five. In fact no work connected with five was done by them. Their peaceable existence in Sanjan was broken in the fifteenth century by an attack by muslim invaders. From available sources it seems the attack was from Mohmad Begada between 1481 and 1521 (14). The loyalty of the Parsees and their genuine integration into the state was demonstrated by the King calling upon them along with his other subjects, to help defend his territories. The Parsees, Sanjana states, full heartedly took part in the defence of Sanjan. They demonstrated that the cause of the King was their own. Sanjana reports that a force of 1400 Zoroastrians joined the Sanjana forces, and it is claimed that they were instrumental in routing the enemy. The muslims, however, regrouped and counter-attacked, this time defeating the Sanjan forces. The Parsees had to flee Sanjan, hiding in the mountains with the their fire, till at last they reach Bansda, 12 years later. (50 miles N. E. of Navsari).

The Parsees had settled during the two centuries after reaching Sanjan in various parts of Gujarat, mainly in the coastal regions. As early as the 10th century, they seem to have reached near Bombay, as two inscriptions on the Kanheri Caves (44 km from Bombay) are found in pehlavi, giving the names of Parsee visitors to these caves. The Silhara Grants are another evidence of early Parsee activity. They refer to various land grants given by the rulers of Konkan to Parsee Anjumans (assemblies). They had small settlement also in Thana, Bassein, and Kalyan by the 12th century.

Settling in Gujarat, they lived peacefully and contributed to the economic and social well-being of their adopted country. They had settled as farmers and agriculturists, fruit-growers, today-planters, carpenters and weavers. The last group has given Gujarat her most ancient and beautiful textiles ; the Surti Ghat (Soft Satin Silk), the garo and the tanchoi.

Weaving during the early days was a primary source of income both for the men and women of the community. As time passed they developed special skills in this and produced 3 excellent varieties of cloth—the Surti Ghat, the Garo and the Tanchoi. These styles were the offshoot of their economic enterprises in trading with the far east. As early as the 1750's Parsee merchants were trading with China and the new weaving styles were an outcome of these contacts.

The Surti Ghat is a soft silk with a Satin finish on one side. In the past, the thread was woven by little children aged 4-6 years, in damp, half-lit cellars, after which the thread was slowly exposed to the light. The handwoven silk was then dyed in vegetable dyes. The favourite colours were red, tyrian purple, bright pink, dove grey and saffron. The material thus woven was so strong that it was known as Surti Ghat—the Surat mountain-since the weavers were mostly from that town. (16)

The garo and the tanchoi are both crafts originally imported from China. The garo is a fine silk with elaborate chinese embroidery all over the sari. The word garo means to strain through a cloth or sleve. (17) The tanchoi is a fine silk brocade with floral designs woven in. Three Parsee brothers (tan chois=3 chinese) learnt the secret of its weaving after a long stay in China and started a weaving centre of their own in Surat. Today, this craft has spread throughout India through the efforts of one of their descendents-Kaikushrau Sorabji Joshi.

The Parsees had thus become a part of the socio-cultural and economicscience of Gujarat by the fourteenth century, without disturbing the tenor of life of the local inhabitants. They had been careful not to raise the jealousles of their fellow citizens. However, in their settlements at Varia and Cambay, economic rivalries had led to the massacres of the Parsees in the 10th and 11th centuries, (15). In Cambay, the Parsee settlers had become very prosperous and overbearing. They had obviously taken over the trader professions earlier practiced by the local people. Kallianrai, a local bania (trader) secretly plotted against the Parsees and organised an attack on them through a band of kolis and Rajputs. The Parsees it is reparted were put to the sword and their homes were set on fire. Those who escaped fled the city with the sacred fire. Another incident occurred towards the end of the 11th century in Variv. Here also the parsees had prospered, probably at the expense of the local inhabitants, and became overbearing and refused to pay an excessive tribute demanded by the chieftam. Again they became a target for attack and it is reported that they faced the attack bravely, but lost and had to flee. These 2 instances seem to have taught the Parsees some important economic lessons. We now find them pursuing avocations which do not challenge the vested interests out right and which were particularly suited to them.

In order to avoid such economic and social conflicts, the Parsees seem to have chosen areas of economic activity best suited to their ethos in the context of the general Indian situation at that time.

Surat attracted the Parsees as the most important sea port on the west coast of India, as it was the centre of trade for both the Mughal Empire and the European trading companies.

By the 18th century, the sea-port of Surat had the largest Parsee settlement. Parsees became brokers for the Europeans and played an important role in import and export trade. The Portuguese, French, Dutch and English factories all employed Parsees as their chief brokers. After the East India Company shifted its head-quarters to Bombay we find large scale migration of Parsees to Bombay, first from Surat and then from other Gujarat settlements. Today 90% of the Parsees are to be found in Bombay. Parsees had, from the beginning, settled in the cities of Gujarat and were more urban-oriented. Today they are the most westernised community in India, and have contributed to the growth of Indian economy and trade wherever they have gone. In the towns, they are mainly to be found in trade, banking, secretarial work, accountancy and, up to the middle of the 19th century, as master-shipbuilders and furniture-makers. The peculiar factor which made the Parsees the premier 'traders' of those regions was their socio-religions makeup—which did not conflict with their social environment, but rather filled in the vacuum created at a certain stage. The advent of the European traders and adventurers from the 14th Century onwards opened a vaste area for the Parsees. In the absence of caste restrictions, with very little concept of 'pollution', which was ever present with the Hindus, the Parsees became the first to act as agents, mediators and intermediates to these foreigners : Portuguese, Dutch, Danes and English. Unfettered by any socio-cultural barriers to these occupations they eagerly entered these fields of economic activety.

The economic behaviour of the Parsees, as well as their adaptation of modern rational economic attitudes, in contrast to the Hindus and the Buddhists, was the result also of their ethical and religious norms. In the Parsees, there is no trace of denial of life or of asceticism or contemplation. On the contrary, the affirmation of life and the appeal to be active in shaping the world are expressed in no other religion as clearly as in the 'Parsian'. As shown, Zarathustra asks man to stand up of his own free will for the good principle and to help the good to its final victory. This is made impossible by a denial of worldly life, or an ascetic life-style, both of which are considered a betrayal of the good powers.

Thus Parsees positively reject asceticism or resignation of life. Whoever fights against lies, misfortune, illness, discord, poverty and immorality, the offsprings of evil in this world, is supporting the good in its cosmic battle (Vendidad). Thus man makes an essential contribution to the victory of the good by working. Great importance is attached to self-reliance and self-help. This explains the Zoroastrian work ethics and the general value for work. This affirmation of life and work in the Parsees explains their success to a great extent. They have an active approach to life, a will-power, urge to work and are achievement-oriented. Zoroastrianism means work, duty, business and industry.

By the middle of the 19th Century this tendency towards trade increased. Rural youths began to migrate to Bombay in large numbers and after working under European firms, they set up their own establishments and amassed enormous fortunes within a single generation. (18) This surplus capital thus produced was ploughed into the new industrial opportunities opening up to Indians in the form of Textile Mills and culminated in J. N. Tata starting the Jamshedpur Steel Mills.

The Parsees, for the same reasons cited above, adapted early to the new western education and were the first and formost to enter the new professions of lawyers, technicians, doctors and professors. Some idea of their preminence in these fields is given in the 2 Apendix' attached herewith (19). They were also the first to accept white collar and administrative jobs in the 19th century in the Bombay Presidency. They filled the posts of Assistant Collectors, translators at Courts, Subassistant surgeons and postmasters. (20)

In the field of politics, also, the Parsees have, in spite of a section of the Community keeping aloof, generally played an important role in the growth of Indian nationalism. Because of the forward movement of the community, unrestricted by traditional brakes, the Parsees are more westernised, but no less Indian today. In fact the beginnings of Indian political associations in Bombay was made by Parsees who also contributed the largest amount of money for this. The role played by the Parsees in the Bombay Association, the Bombay Municipality affairs, the Indian National Congress was spearheaded by unforgettable people like Sir Jamshedji Jeejeebhai, Dadabhai Naoroji, Phiroj Shah Mehta, Dinshaw Wacha, Madame Cama and a legion of others whose work cannot be described in detail here.

The participation of Parsees in this field clearly indicates the complete integration of the Parsees into the Indian national stream. The Parsees were by now merging into an Indian identity at the same time retaining their own Parsee identity, as much as say a Christian or Buddhist. Dadabhai Naoroji and other leaders therefore always stressed the aspect of 'secular' nationalism to facilitate the emergence of a modern all-Indian nationalism. This idea of secular nationalism was a definite contribution of the Parsee intellectuals and helped to build a healthy nationalism and was a counter to the later strands of 'neo-Hindu renaissance in politics introduced by Tilak, Lala Lajpat Rai Vivekananda, Smt. Aurobindo and Annie Besant.

Language is always a very important link toward integration of people. As told earlier, the Parsees had accepted Gujarati as their mother tongue when they took refuge in Sanjan. This, however was not done half-heartedly. The Parsees demonstrated great adaptability in this field and have became great literaturs of Gujarat great novelists, poets, essayists and journalists. The first gujarati newspapers, even before a marathi newspaper was started, were initiated by Parsees in Bombay. In 1822 came the Bombay Samachar, in 1830 the Mumbai Vartman, in 1832 the Jame-e Jamshed, in 1832 the Mumbai Chabuk, in 1844, the Samachar Durpan and in 1848 the Chitranjan Durpan, to name only a few (21). These papers did a great deal in integrating the Gujarati speaking elite in these regions. They also helped in developing a linguistic syslthesis between Parsee Gujarati and Sanskritised Hindu gujarati. (22)

With integration, the Parsees have kept their identity, and it is this identity that is today threatened for good or evil, depending on how one looks at it. If variety adds to the richness of a nation, it will be a sad day, when the Parsee community disappears, as it may.

A distinctive identity was achieved by the Parsees through their passionate adherence to their religion and the exclusive character which the Parsees in India attributed to their religion, by not allowing any converts to their religion (which in fact is contrary to Zorathustra's teaching). Tradition has it that this was an out come of a promise given to some early rulers, during their period of immigration. A Zorastrian can be one only through birth and this was recognised only through the paternal line. A sense of ethnic exclusiveness seems to have been present in their refusal to accept any outsiders. Another factor giving them a separate feeling may be the consciousness of a common enemy, the Arab invaders of Iran, and of having gone through a common persecution. This gave the community a closed feeling. They alone, they felt, saved Zoroastrianism and are preserving it. A consciousness of elite status has developed in the community through their economic achievements and success, especially during the 19th century, adding to their exclusiveness.

Alarmed at these trends, Parsees and non-Parsees have sounded warnings and suggested remedies to prevent the total loss of identity of a group which has contributed much to the development of modern India. Many steps are advocated to stem this tide, such as opening the doors of the Parsee community to children of women, who intermarry, and conversion of others wish to embrace the Zoroastrian faith. It is pointed out that every prayer in the khordeh Avesta (daily book of prayers) ends with the invocation calling upon the knowledge and commandments of Zarthustra to be spread to all regions of the world.

Leaders of the community are trying to revive a deep and full understanding of the teachings of the Prophet. By doing so, Parsees will be able to continue their contribution to this great land of ours, and remain a distinct people with their own driving force. It is difficult to foreasee the future but chances are that Parsees may take up this new challenge and survive as a small but strong group in modern India.

FOOT NOTES

1. P. Nanavutty, The Parsees, National Book Trust N. D. 1977 p. 15

2. F. A. Bode and P. Nanavutty, Songs of Zarathushtra, London. 1952 pp. 30-35

3. Erach J. S. Taraporewala 'Gatha Metre and chanting,' in Bulletin of Deccan College Research Institute, Vol. III, pp. 219-224

4. Eckehard Kulke. The Parsees in India. Vikas Publishing House Pvt. Ltd. N. D. 1978 Ch 2

5. P. Nanavutty, Op. Cit. p. 21

6. J. Marshall. A Guide to Taxila p. 87

7. V. Smith, An early history of India. p. 175

8. Bhavishyapuram 31 p. 139

9. Pallonji B. Desai. Tankhe Shahane Iran (Gujerati), Vol. II p. 416-418 & Fircze—K Davar—Iran and its culture. Bombay, 1962

10. This date has been disputed by several scholars, who claim that the Parsees arrived in 936 A. D. This cannot be accepted as an inscription dated 926 A. D. has been found in Dahanu Taluka, recording a Grant given to a Parsee Anjuman in 926 A. D. by the Rashtrakuta Raja Indrava. An inscription has also been found in the Kanehri caves, near Bombay, recording a visit by Parsees in 936 A. D. The 1st date is more credible as records have been found showing that the Jadav Mandliks were feudatories of the Rashtrakutas and were ruling over Sanjan. (Maitrakal Ane Anu Maitrakal. Vol. 3 Gujeratno Rajkiye ane Sanskritic itihas, B. J. Vidya Bhavan Ahm, 1974,)

11. The folk songs, the traditional Gujarati garbas (group songs and dances) composed by the Parsees are sung at festive occasions.

12. D. F. Karaka, CSI, The History of the Parsees, Macmillan & Co. London 1884 p. 31

13. See descriptions of travellers. Sir Thomas Herbert & Mr. Lord in Churchill's Voyages Vol. VI p. 520 ff

14. B. K. Sanjana in Kisse Sanjan has mentioned Champaran as the capital of the invaders, Description of the battle is given detail,

15. Gazeteer of the Bombay Presidency Vol. IX P. II. Govt. Central Press, Bombay, 1899 pp. 185-187

16. P. Nanavutty Op. Cit. p. 45-46

17. Ibid

18. D. F. Karaka. Op. Cit. Vol. II pp. 38, 132, 247
19. App. 1 & 2 From Kulke Op. Cit. pp. 56-57
20. Bombay Civil list, 1864, pp, 53-83
21. Gujerati Prtrakartva no Itihas Dr, Rattan Marshall, Gadiv Sahitya
     Mandir, Surat 1950 p, 1-94

22. R. P. Karkaria—The Oldest Paper in India—in Calcutta Review
     Vol, CVI Apr 1898 p, 223

NATIONAL INTEGRATION IN HISTORICAL PERSPECTIVE :

A Cultural Regeneration In Eastern India *

Dr. Binod S. Das
Indian Institute of Technology,
Kharagpur.

The myth of cultural disunity and political diversity of India was harped by the British imperialist writers which assumed a menacing dimension within a period of thirty years after independence of India from the foreign yoke. Despite her stunted capitalist development, India today is on the verge of sociopolitical disintegration since her numerous ethnic groups each with its glorious heritage are on the breaking point due to its asymmetrical economic development and regional imbalance. It is high time that our research scholars should direct their attention to discover the essential cultural unity in the Indian way of life under the historical perspective. The object of study is to explore the trends of unity binding eastern India since geographical location and ethnic settlements evolved the unity in wet paddy cultivation and bamboo based industry bringing uniformity in the way of life of the people, in their value system and supplying uniformity in the evolution of socio-economic institutions from a long glorious past. Again changes and continuity in agrarian life, in surplus value of labour leading to surplus exchange brought homogeneity in trade and commerce. With this object in view the study was

* I am indebted to Dr. R N Chakravorty, my research scholar for data collection and from his thesis I have extensively drew my conclusions.

undertaken within the time-frame of the tenth through the sixteenth centuries, viz, within the time-frame of five hundred years.

I

The author in this paper proposes the basic question : was there any fundamental unity in the socio-cultural life of Bengal and Orissa from the tenth to the sixteenth centuries ? There was a wide diversity in dynasties, administrative units, language and dialects, customs, life style and religious value systems in eastern India. Out of this diversity, geographical location and ethnic homogeneity had brought in socio-cultural unity to the people of eastern India. Despite this undercurrent flow of cultural unity because of the internecine warfare among the successive rulers, feudalisation of the economy and militarisation of civil offices the political diversity cropped up and brought about disintegrating forces in the political institutions culminating in the collapse of the martial spirit of the people and end of the occeanic trade. The result was the Muslim conquest of eastern India without any strong millitary resistance. But why this military defeat despite its past glory of military adventure and maritime ascendancy, despite its abundant raw resources and a big idle population with an annual spiral growth rate ? The questions, is it something inherent in the bio-physical environment and life style of the people, ingrained in its tropical climate and food habits or was it caused by the inevitable decline in socio-economic institutions and value systems, wait for their solutions.

The answer to this probing on the causes of the decline of socio-economic institutions of Bengal-Orissa could be found in two models. One, that the British rule was responsible for the colonial exploitation of the people of Bengal and Orissa and two, the other model tend to define the economic backwardness of eastern region in terms of a continuous process of degeneration ·starting from the decline of the imperial Ganga and the Sena dynasties in the thirteenth centuries. To the author this analytical model seemed necessary for the present day crisis in the agrarian economy leading to regional imbalance and stunted growth of industrial developments in eastern India which made the present day political disharmony a fact of life. In this paper attempts would be made to explore the cultural homogeneity of the people in eastern India which coloured her way of life.

II

The geographical location of eastern India made her the terminating point of the Mahanadi-Ganga-Brahmaputra and numerous other streams and susceptible to climatic depressions during the rainy and autumn seasons. The existence of the Himalayas in the north as a collosul father-figure, its vast expansion of river valleys making possible water management necessary for deep wet paddy cultivation and its broken, long coast line making possible the coastal trade, helped to mould her cultural heritage with a strong agrarian base and made possible the emergence of isolated clusters of tiny village kingdoms with strong sense of individuality which could not be broken by the Vedic culture. On the backdrop of the solid base of the isolated, tiny kingdoms with wet paddy cultivation and jute, bamboo based industry the early christian era witnessed the expansion of coastal trade and riverian inland commerce in eastern India since the north Indian trade routes along the riverian route of the Ganga-Mahanadi and Brahmaputra were terminating with the coastal ports of the Che-li-ta-lo, Polura, Tamralipta and later on of Saptagram. The contempt about the ferocity and cultural independence and migratory tendency of the peoples finds expression in the Vedic and the Jaina literature. Thus the Jaina and Ajivika Sramanas and Vikkus could never entrench themselves in this region. But it was Ashoka Maurya who ruthlessly broke down this socio-economic isolation and tagged her destiny with the north Indian socio-economic developments.

Any discussion on the unity in religious-cultural life of eastern India even within the time-frame of tenth to sixteenth centuries would start with the religious beliefs and rituals which originated in the pre-historic period and in course of time influenced the course of invading currents of religious beliefs and rituals from outside through different phases of history. The fundamental difference between the pre-historic religion and the invading Aryan belief system was that the pre-historic rituals were worship based (Brata) where women played a dominant role with folk art forming an inseparable part. While the Indo-Aryan religion was mainly hymnbased fire worship (Jagnya) where butter oil was offered to the fire god by the dominant priest class on behalf of the community of devotees.

The worship of mother cults of the nomadic inhabitants of the region centered round all seasons of the cultivation process starting from gestation and seedling of crops and climaxing with the harvesting season of the agrarian community indicating thereby the role of religon as a catalyst for transforming a food gathering nomadic community to a settled food producing people. Thus its folk religion was not temple based institution dominated by the Brahmins or a priest class enjoying the topmost position in the Varna hierarchy. The folk cults were invariably dominating deities of tools of production connected with the village cultivation process and artisans crafts and each deity was the protecting power of a particular unit of production in villages reflected in the village Deothan under the shade of a banyan or a bel tree. But the deities were invariably worshipped along with their carriers (Vahan) either birds or animals. But side by side anthropomorphism was also a dominating force in their religious value system since the hill tops, trees and large block of stones were worshipped as protecting deities of a particular community of cultivators in a particular village. But the worships associated with singing, dancing, partaking of common food from common kitchen and magical hymn chanting could continue for days together as passion and miracle plays and colourful processions to allure the piety of the whole community under the garb of holy get-together for attaining a never attainable utopia. 'Jatra' or processions to allure popular participation through charm, magic and continuous festivities were absorbed into the religious cross-currents invading from outside. But Brata led by the fasting women, rituals connected with folk art, singing and dancing were dominated not by the priest class but by the women folk. This phenomenon illustrates the remnants of a matriarchal pastoral society gradually absorbing the dawn of agricultural mechanism ensuing male domination and priest superiority in the Varna hierarchy. In course of time a happy balance was maintained within the role conflict between women folk in ritual singing and the priest class for hymn chanting rituals. The origin of the hindu religious pantheon, magic and rituals, invariably centered round the mother cult for protecting the cycle of birth and death and to win over the inescapable phenomenon of death. The worship of the fertility cult was invariably associated with the germinating and harvesting seasons of nature and the idea of conjunction of male and female power, the elements of Purusa and Shakti in nature to keep the cycle of gestation going, gained ground. Behind the magic and miracle plays the discovery of the truth of creation through the unitary process of conjunction of male and female power of an unperceivable god gave way to the first dawn of a philosophical idea of the primitive folk a religious belief system discovered through the endless cycle of birth and death, seedling, germination and harvesting. This manifestation of a supreme power combining female and male roles into one to keep the cycle of creation going as a continuous process was ultimately absorbed into the successive folk-Tantric, Buddhist and Vaisnava religious thought processes. Despite continuous process of transformation these phenomena of female role in the folk brata rituals, domination of the idea of male-female conjunction to attain the final bliss and the discovery of a continuous life cycle through birth and death, gestation and harvesting in nature and the superiority of certain sound symbols to realise the glory of the Almighty in a rather sound-less universe dominated the successive religious value system of the period and gave rather a unitary character to diverse currents and cross-currents of religion, art forms and litera-ture in eastern India. Thus it would be wrong to compart-mentalise the different manifestations of a dynamic culture of the community within the time frame of this study expressing through the societal changes with the changing mode of production and production relation in the social hierarchy.

III

With the decline of the later Guptas small political units emerged in eastern India and each unit worshipped the Hindu cults as a mark of their reassertion of the Hindu faith and from the seventh century onwards there continued the regrouping of powers. In Bengal Sasanka, a lone figure, a devotee of the Saiva cult had to fight with the Sailodbhabas of Orissa, initially a Saivite dynasty, for territorial expansion towards the west. And initially Siva was the dominating deity of agricultural operation, learned in the knowledge of life cycle in nature starting with gestation and seedling and ending with harvesting of agriculture. He was the ruling deity of a settled kingdom of the nomadic pastoral community. Ultimately the Pala supremacy led to the tripartite struggle in the rice producing Ganga-Mahanadi valley marking the impact of resurgent Buddhism in the socio-political life while the rise of the Ganga imperialism in Orissa gave political cohesion to that state signalled by the emergence of the cult of Jagannatha as Rastra Devata. After the decline of the Pala dynasty the Senas from the Karnata became sovereigns in Bengal while the Gajapati Chiefs from Andhra held sway in Orissa and the two empires in turn came into military conflict with each other leading to socio-political readjustments. While in Bihar the Karnata rulers starting with Nanyadeva claimed descent from Karnata and patronised Saivism and revival of Hinduism. Karnata, according to folk myth, became the store house of the Khatriyas and after the Muslim invasion Rajput myth came into sway in this region to replace the Karnata myth to trace the origin of the royal houses.

These political changes in Bengal, Bihar and Orissa in the shape of rise and decline of dynasties synchronised with the spectacular social and economic changes in the shape of enhancement of agricultural productivity by reclaiming virgin soil and prosperity in the inland and coastal trade ultimately influenced the dynamics of changes in the religious value systems and ritual practices. As an answer to the possible growth of population in the wake of expansion of economic activities and to the political aggrandisement of the rulers and caste rigidity in the society, flourishing trade and commerce acted as a social safety valve till the eighth century AD. But between the tenth and the sixteenth centuries this social safety valve for releasing the surplus agrarian produce and population, languished and the contact with the outside world seems to have been snapped. Thus the Pala-Sailodbhaba period marks the climax of eastern India's contact with the outside world leading to migration of values and population from Orissa and Bengal to the far eastern countries in Asia.

This decline in trade and commerce ultimately led to the increased emphasis on agriculture as the only means of production as well as petty commodity production in village level industries mainly used by the elites and temple clergies in the society became another alternative occupation. The rise of regional political groups heralded the expansion of territories through military adventures. The emergence of Bhaumakara and Somabamsi imperialism in Orissa and later on of the Palas in Bengal led to the ascendency of a military-feudal hierarchy in the agrarian society. A corollary to expansionism was sub-infeudation of landed property, militarisation of civil offices and feudalisation of the administrative machinery. Under the stress of Pala-Ganga-Pratihara imperialism local political units succumbed. This sub-infeudation of political hierarchy led to the splitting of castes and classes into innumerable pressure groups as a challenge to the Brahmanical and Ksatriya ascendancy. There was also the upward mobility of the lower stratum as each dominating group claimed Brahmin and Ksatriya castes for itself resulting in splitting of numerous sub-caste groups, each claiming higher status on the basis of newly acquired landed estates with the extension of the area for rice cultivation and bamboo-jute based artisan crafts.

Moreover, decline of trade and commerce and feudalisation of land tenure system led to the process of migration of population as a socio-economic safety valve towards the migrating zones at the periphery of the Pala-Ganga empire of Bengal-Bihar-Orissa towards the uncultivated forest tracts (atavika countries mentioned in Harisena Prashasti of Samudra Gupta) and Chattisgarh division. The period witnessed the twin process of peasantisation of the tribals and the Hinduization of the aboriginals leading to the state formation in the periphery of the Hindu empire of Bengal-Orissa and extension of the area of rice cultivation and salt manufacture and bamboo, jute based crafts in the Ganga-Mahanadi-Brahmaputra valley as the only means of commercial agriculture. The sub-castes of the Raju and Khandait communities as new landed aristocracy now claimed Ksatriyahood and the Brahmins as their Kulapurohits spun successively the so-called Karnata and Rajput myths to award them solar-lunar Karnata and Rajput lineage to legitimise the new regrouping of powers. This upward social mobility and the new sanctification of the Sudra Stratum against the Brahmanical caste rigidity could be found in the emergence of the cult of Jagannatha where the Sabara Daitapatis became the neo-Brahmins. There are also instances to show that the tribal goddesses in the forest tracts in between Bengal and Bihar became Hinduised mother goddess of creation and protection and the new landed aristocracy, the so-called Rajput Ksatriyas, the Singhs and the Majhis, turned to be the greatest devotees of the popular cults. These types of socio-political changes affected religious institutions and ideas which mirrored socio-political changes. The value system of religious institutions acted as the catalytic agent to the dynamics of changes in the vehicles of expression, i. e., changes in the language structure and changes in the mirrors of expression,

i. e., literature coloured with religious overtones which are obviously natural in the middle ages. Changes in language and emergence of indigenous literature had their reflection in the emergence of new cults and ritual practices since the beginning of Jainism and Buddhism.

THE CONCEPT OF INDIANNESS IN THE RELIGIOUS
Historiography of Akshaya Dutta
And Kshitimohan Sen

Smt Krishna Samaddar
Institute of Education,
Chandernagar, West Bengal.

Introduction :

This paper deals with The concept of Indianness—In The Religious Historiography of Akshaya Dutta and more particularly of Kshitimohan Sen. As we all know, Akshaya Dutta and Kshitimohan Sen are two most important landmarks in the development of a liberal religious historiography in Bengali language—one belonging to the middle period of the 19th century, the other belonging to the first half of the 20th century. The idea behind this paper has been to show the impact of a liberal rationalistic outlook upon the Bengali middle class even in this sphere of religions thinking. Frankly, I am not an expert on religious literature. My interest in the present paper has been to note the impact of Bengal renaissance upon the religions outlook of the new middle class of Bengal. Already in the first half of the 19th century, we saw that the Brahma religion had been born which was in a sense a revolt against medieval Hindu—orthodoxy—a revolt which was properly speaking a protest along rationalist line that was different and distinct from the popular disacceptance of the orthodox time and culture. Though we cannot be sure of the impact of popular religion and culture upon Rammohan, the later impact of Rammohan's rationality was undoubtedly strong upon the

religious outlook of Bengal middle class. The most noted
religious historians combined both the rationality of Rammohan
as well as the populist nature of the mass culture of a previous
age. In this way I shall show with examples of Akshaya Dutta
and Kshitimohan Sen, the educated middle class tried to shift
their earstwhile 'sanatan' outlook to a more populist one that
looked for the sources of culture and religion among the people
of the whole country. Essentially then, this religions search
had to be concerned with the whole nation and none of these
two could remain satisfied with probings confined to a sect,
caste, religion etc. This could be the ideological—historical
roots of the writings of Akshaya Dutta and subsequently
Kshitimohan Sen.

Akshaya Dutta as we know, was closely related to the
Brahma literati of his times. He was the founder of 'Atmiya
Sava' in 1852. Ten years back in 1843 on 21st Dec, he had
accepted Brahma religion[1], and even in his Brahma faith he
was never an obscurantist and always reasoned regarding the
infallibility of even the Vedanta.[2] Kshitimohan Sen was also
a Brahma. This suggests that both used the liberal and rational
influence of Brahmoism to good effect in searching for the roots
of our religions culture. Neither did they confine themselves
with a parochial outlook to Bengal only nor did they remain
within the Holy scriptures. With their rationality the searched
into the popular past of our composite culture. The folk religion
and folk culture were the religion and culture of the whole
country. It was an assimilated one. The people meant to them
the people of India and though they did not have occasion to
define Indian nation as a political concept, spiritually they had
approached and reached the idea in their writings from an
ideological-cultural quest. I would argue, this was a complemen-
tary part to the awakening of liberalism and nationalism among
the Bengal middle class.

(2)

Akshaya Dutta—and his Bharat Barshiya Upasak Sampradaya—(2 volumes, 1870 and 1883) (The Mendicant Communities of India)—

To understand the remarkable nature of Akshaya Dutta's venture in religious historiography, we have to make a brief note of the development of Akshaya Dutta's rational bent of mind. As his biographer Nakur Chandra Biswas informs us, Akshaya Dutta had a very spontaneous affinity with science through his very early acquaintance with German, English, Physics, geography, geometry, Algebra, trigonometry, higher Mathematics and psychology. The conventional 'sanatan' religion held no fascination for him. Along with his rational temper he was perhaps initiated to the popular culture of the land through his association with Iswar Gupta, though of that we cannot tell anything with certainty. In the "Tattabodhini Pathsala", he used to teach Physics and Geography. With the help of "Tattohodhini Sabha" his two books on geography and physics were published in 1841 and 1856. In his preface to the Bengali periodical "Vidyadarshan" in 1842, he said that the periodical aimed at publishing Bengali translations of English writings on history and science.[3] His efforts at popularising a rational attitude were widely acknowledged during his editorship of "Tattobodhini Patrika". I have already said that meanwhile Akshaya Dutta had accepted Brahma religion. But this was nothing like the religiosity of Debendra Nath who caustically commented in his autobiography that under Dutta's leadership, the 'Atmiya Sabha' sessions used to decide upon the nature of God by vote of hands. Further, Akshaya Dutta was all along associated with the social reform movements led by Vidyasagar, Kishori Chand Mitra, Rajendralal Mitra, Harish Mukherjee, Radhanath Sikdar etc. Even the rationality of Brahma type could not satisfy Akshaya Dutta for long and before his death he had turned into a agnostic. His famous equation about the irrelevance of prayer may be known to you—wherein he said :

$$Labour = Crop.$$
$$Prayer + Labour = Crop.$$
$$Prayer = Zero.$$

His friend Rajnarayan Bose had discerned this agnostic turn of mind in some of his passages on Hindu sects. Thus it is clear that in his chronicle on the Hindu sects, Akshaya Dutta never lost his cool and rational mind. As we shall see now, he went on narrating the various sects of the whole country without even for once being emotionally involved in them. This approach of covering the whole country and concertrating on the popular religious sects without even for once falling into obscurantism or emotional involvement was truly the product of a long trained rational mind.

Benoy Ghosh makes a similar comment in his editorial introduction to the 1969 edition (Beng. 1376) of 'Upasak Sampradaya'. Benoy Ghosh comments, a century ago there was no worth tradition of scientific historiography particularly in cultural field. Yet Akshaya Dutta due to his scientific temper could resist emotionalism in his discussion on such a sensitive matter like the religious sects of the country. To quote Benoy Ghosh "Even in modern days of science, discussion on the religious communities is always clouded by medieval obscurantism. Considering that, Akshaya Kumar's book would still stand as an unparallel and essential reader in to-day's age of scientific historiography".[4]

Akshaya Dutta's observation was very keen and pages always seem even to-day directly leaping out of the narrator's own experience. Akshaya Dutta surveys the entire length and breadth of the country, accurately observes the cultural rites of different communities—like scriptures, marriage, food habit, caste structure etc. But he never makes any subjective evaluation of these communities. In a passage on the 'Dasanamis' Akshaya Dutta derides the urbanised babu culture of his contemporary middle class Hindus and finds that a vigorons potentiality and a strong Indian character was much more evident among the popular sects.[5] Then again with an astonishing boldness relative to his timc, he tells us that the toiling common people whom we see everyday in gardens, fields and public roads are the real original people of the country. The Hindus or the Aryans had cruelly tortured them and evicted them from their homeland—but these and such other communities were the original dwellers, of the country.[6] In this way if one goes through both the volumes, one would find that Akshaya Dutta's attention has been less on the high caste Hindus—but more on the low caste popular communities, the hybrid cultural groups, the Bhakti sects etc., of the eastern northern as well as the southern parts of the country. He even quotes their principal hymns. To give a few illustrative examples from his two volumes (1st vol. on 1870 and 2nd vol 1883) on the religions sects, we find, Akshaya Dutta surveying the Ramanuj sect of south India, the Ramananda sect of North India the Kabir sect composed of both Hindus and Musalmans, the Dadus of Jaipur the Ballavacharis of West India. Similarly, Akshaya Dutta Surveys the saivas also in details—the Dasanamis, the Paramahansas, Abadhults etc.

But these are the only welknown sects. So many obscure and lesser known sects like Dangali, Urdhamukki Jogi etc. are also mentioned by him.

Suffice it to say, that when we consider Akshaya Dutta with later works of historiography, his keen, liberal and an all India outlook comes out in bolder relief. For example, Jogendranath Bhattacharya (on Hindu castes and sects, 1898) gave a greater emphasis on evolution of Hindu-Jati-Varna. Even the very famous work of Bhanderkar did not give such a searching attention to the popular communities, though Bhanderkar's method was much more scientific. Hem Chandra Roy Chowdhury's discussion on the Vaisnaba sect is more scholarly. Yet Akshaya Kumar's variety is missing there. One can say Akshaya Dutta was the pioneer in the field of a liberal and a nationalist religious historiography which later on prduced such eminent men like Bhanderkar, Ramaprasad Chanda or Hem Chandra Roy Chowdhury.[7]

(3)

Kshitimohan Sen :

The liberal and the social outlook that led Akshaya Dutta to probe into the popular religious solidarities of the country, finds a full flowering in the works of Kshitimohan Sen. As we shall see an all India outlook was implicit in Akshaya Dutta, but in Kshitimohan Sen this is explicit. His search into the synthetic culture of the lower classes is deliberate. On numerous occasions Kshitimohan writes that the various social stratification in Indian culture have placed an obstacle in the path of national unity.[8] In "Hindu Sanskritir Swarup" ; he comments ; to know the religious culture of the popular societies of India, we can have little help from demography or ethnology. We shall have to be really culture conscious to make a prove into that. He concludes the same book with the line, "Those who wish to import parochialism in this country are out to divide their mother land".[9]

In Kshitimohan's search for an all India identity in our popular culture, Tagore has noted a dominant concern for lower classes. He appreciated Kshitimohan with these Words—"We can discover in the writings of Kshitimohan, the natural capacity of the Indian people for a spiritual pursuit (on sadhana)". Earlier in the same comment which he made as a preface to Kshitimohan's magmum opus "Bharatiya Madhya Yuge Sadhanar Dhara" (Pub in 1930 from Cal. Univ), Tagore writes"......this pursuit of a spiritual culture has never been constrained by a high caste erudite consent in the form of scriptures. It there is any influcnce of erudition that is negligible. A large part of this pursuit has been beyond the realm of scriptures and unfettered by social regulations. The source of such a pursuit has been the innermost heart of the people and has come out with case overcoming the boulders of inhibitions and prohibitions. Those who have given expression to the spontaneous flow have almost all been people of the low classes ; what they have received or expressed have not been due to learning nor from an imitation from other......my friend Kshitimohan in this book has followed this flow of heart, which has gone on within the country for long in its various meanderings and branches.[10] This was possible for Kshitimohan, for, like Akshaya Dutta, in his case also, we find, a unique combination of rationality and the appreciation of the mystic aspect of the religions culture of our country. This was as well the typical Tagore's stamp upon his contemporary religions historiography. Kshitimohan born in Kashi, had his classical learning there. Then from 1908 starts his long association with Tagore. He joined Santiniketan in 1908 and ended his teaching career there in 1953. From an early age he was attracted towards the popular religions pursuits of our country in the middle ages. He wondered to collect the 'Donhas' (   ) or Kabir and published them for a wider mass recognition of the medieval Synthetic culture. After coming to Santiniketan he was engaged in collecting the Baul Songs and concentrated upon a study of the spiritual significance of

the Baul cult. For a long half century, he was engaged in
that pursuit and Tagore too enthused by the religions historiography of Kshitimohan, edited and published in English—"One
Hundred Poems of Kabir "in 1914 along the line of Kshitimohan's 'Donha' collection. For a wide national survey
Kshitimohan was particularly equipped, for besides Sanskrit
and Bengali, he knew other Indian languages too and had
written in Gujrati and Hindi also.

(4)

Bharatiya Madhya Yuge Sadhanar Dhara :

Now what in essence has been the topic of "Bharatiya
Madhya Yuge Sadhanar Dhara" ? As we all know, the medieval
India had two alter-egoes in the demain of ideology which
constantly, grappled with one another : One was the conservative Brahmanical culture with its castism and idolatry, the
other was the popular folk religion and culture with its
mystique, humane and earthly nature. Kshitimohan Sen in
trying to give due recognition to the contemporary popular
culture, delved into its past and showed that India was the
land of not only rajas, priests and the lords, she was essentially
the land of her common people who inspiteof andtranscending the
various barriers and diversities between them showed a oneness
in their religion and culture. He mentions repeatedly in the
pursuits have rarely been recorded in the formal social annals
have not been given recognition by the idiological god-fathers
of Society which was rather natural and many of these noble
attempts at articulating popular culture have been lost for
posterity, which is why, we to-day get a distorted picture of
our country's past. The task of religions historiography is
then to unravel the past and trace out the lost flows of popular
culture.[11] The uniformity in these attempts at articulating
popular religion, Kshitimohan observes, is striking. What he
omits in saying is that there is a uniform pattern in the material

life and the thought proces of the lower classes of Society, which could be the reason behind the uniform nature of the various popular spiritual culture of our country. They have been synthetic, spiritually broad as well as never disdainful of the material reality among the lower classes below.

"Bharatiya Madhya Yuge Sadhanar Dhara" was delivered as Adhar Chandra Mukhopadhya Lecture in Calcutta University in 1929. The whole lecture deals with the popular mystic preachers who could defy the scriptural rigidity and absurdity of the middle age. The coming of the Muslims in India was not treated by Kshitimohan as a foreign invasion upon his country ; but it was analysed mainly in cultural terms. The Muslim culture, he found, had a direct and powerful liberating impact upon the lower classes of Hindu Society. The most forceful among the new breed of thinkers were not the, purits of Islam religion but the mystic preachers known as 'Sufis'. In his words, "the awakening of India in the middle ages owes first to the Sadhana of the Muslims. Hence, that should be recognised first".[12]

He recorded the roles of many pioneer Sufis of India like— Saiyed Ali Al Huzariri, the chisti Sufis like Main-ud-din Chisti, Farid chisti, Nizam-ud-din Aouliya, Sekh Salim chisti, what appealed to Kshitimohan was the Catholicity of these Sufis and he noted that the Hindu Brahmins had become disciples of a great mystic like Main-ud-din. The Synthetic culture of Agra or Rajputana impressed him. The sufis of Gujrat like Jamal-ud-din, Shah Karim, Enayet and Shah Latif were recorded with reverence by Kshitimohan, who said that the common people of western India still vividly remember the Sufi culture and find consolation in their hour of grief. In Sind, in Kangra, in Kashmir or in Amethi, he noted that, the lower classes below rarely fought amongst themselves over religious identity. Many communities rarely thought in terms of pure Hindu or pure Muslim culture. Just as the broad Hindu masses found solace and comfort in Muslim mystics, reversely, many Muslim thinkers like Nur Mahammad, Pirzada, Hafiz-Hussain-Nizami drew inspiration from Hindu popular culture and had incorporated Hindu religions figures Ram, Krishna, or Budha in their own sermons, Kshitimohan Sen noted the existence of such popular culture even in Bengal, like Baul and Jik is, of the tantriks, he particularly mentions the low-Caste and the under-caste preachers of south India who were the Pariahs. He has covered similar communities of Assam also. When the Social degradation of the middle ages had reached its nadir and the cultural rites of the Tantriks and Ballavacharis had become too much confused, Kshitimohan noted, there were popular efferts again at bringing into reality a people's religion that would bring heaven into the earth. The Farajis were for example, a reaction to too much Catholicity and Sahajananda's pure religion in late 18th century was a reaction to Ballavacharis. What however Kshitimohan did not mention was that these popular attempts at pure religion were, just like the earlier synthetic attempts, the mirror of the aspirations of the lower order for a free and happy Society. Sen refers to Kirtibas and Kasiramdas as well and particularly of Kasiramdas, he said it was an evidence of how popular culture transcended the barrier of language, for he had seen Kasiramdas even in the home of a half literate or almost illiterate Hindusthan peasant of Bihar, Raipur and Bilaspur of Central India.

However, the most appreciative reference is to Guru Ramanand and his 12 disciples which included Rabidas and Kabir. Popular religion could never be preached in the language of Qristrocrats. So Ramanand, Rabidas, Kabir—all preached in Hindi and not in Sanskrit, To quote Kabir.

(সংস্কৃত কূপজন কবীরা ভাষা বহতা নীর ।)

(Oh Kabir, Sanskrit is the water of the well ; but language is the flowing water). As Kshitimohan noted, the articulation of popular religion gave birth to popular Hindi literature. It is not possible here to mention all the glittering references to Kabir. He had infact edited Kabir's 'Donhas'. He respected Kabir more because Kabir in his preachings had never demeaned labour, even while a preacher he remained a 'Jola'. Sadhana did not mean being a parasite. This was truly the hall mark of a popular culture as Kshitimohan refers to Kabit.

কহেঁ কবীর অস উত্তম্ কীহৈ
আপ জীয়ে ওরণ কো দীজৈ ॥

(All would earn bread by labour all would help each other. No body would earn unjrestly—that is the advice of Kabir).
Kabir attacked the Scriptural Superstitions too even to extent of defying the death rites.[13]

We need not mention here all the Communities that Kshitimohan referred to. It easily crosses 200 ; it Surveys various parts of the country, it refers to various currents and cross-currents. It uncovers the link between these communities and popular life. In short, Kshitimohan's "Bharatiya Madhya Yuge Sadhanar Dhara" can be termed as the high priest of Bengalee liberal progressive religious historiography.

I have already mentioned earlier that while Akshaya Dutta was not consciously nationalist in outlook-strictly in a political sense, Kshitimohan is the reverse. Perhaps because that was the gift of the time, for within 50 years of Akshaya Dutta, the national movement reached a peok in India. This conscious nationalist outlook is best revealed in Kshitimohan's "Hindu Sanskritir Swarup" In his concluding remarks to this book

Kshitimohan writers : "Our music has diversities and the advocates of pure classical music had to accept popular strains. Similarly our aesthetic culture is full of variety. Yet it has a whole. So, why should we be suffering from the disease of parochialism ? The people of India have migrated in the past from one part to another. So, who could be termed as the original inhabitant of any part ? "Sarcastically, he says about Social radicalism"—"We remain centent with echoing Balshevik declarations. But we can perform all evils with Khadi as dress and Ramdhun on lips. We have to renounce in all ways communalism, parochialism or class distinction".[14]

Armed with a historical attitude, Kshitimohan has traced this tradition of a popular culture to the early ages of Indian Society. To him Indian culture is a combination of Aryan and Non Aryan elements. The Vedic religion was too not a Brahmonical culture the priests would like us to believe. In his words—"In the Vedas we find the desire for wealth and desire to live in the material world, instead of a desire for heaven to live in the world beyond......In the Atharva Veda there is a deep link between Vedic and popular culture of indigeneous origin. Thus we find the unparallal example of an attraction towards man in lieu of paradise".[15]

To buttress his point, Kshitimohan has explained many myths and stories and has laid particular emphasis upon the ancient culture of India. He has mentioned the 64 arts which were a combination of popular as well as aristocratic performing arts. He has made particular reference to Buddhist "Donhas" as the next important landmark in the making of a composite national culture of India. His observation on Caste system is also penetrating. While deriding the Caste system Kshitimohan remarked that mere platitudes would be of avail. What was required was fearlessness of those popular Sayings. He quoted Dadu—

সূরা চড়ি সংগ্রামে কৌ পাছা পগ কৌ দেই।

(দাছু সূরজ্ঞান অঙ্গ ১৩)

(This is the path of Sadha of the heroes—the meek has no place
here)

কাইর কাম ন আবই যছু সূরে কা খেত (ঐ ১৫)

(This is the battle in form of Sadhana, centinuing throughout
the 24 hours of the day. It is a battle without arms.)

This general attitude of Kshitimohan in religions historiography is correctly exemplified in his study of Bengal culture.
In his book "Banglar Sadhana", Kshitimohan has written that
the plural nature of Indian Society is fully manifested in the
history of Bengal too. Bengal's culture has been a combination
of both aryan and non aryan elements. Bengal had the
capacity to assimilate plural elements. The Saiva, the Jaina,
the Budha—all had been assimilated in a popular culture that
found its greatest expression in the Baisnava, Bhakti movement
in the middle ages. Even the later Baul religion centinued
this popular humanist tradition. Kshitimohan has called it
the "Prakrit" humanism of Bengal. What I wish to emphasise
here is that his comments on Bengal did not prove to be an
occasion for parochialism to Kshitimohan. Bengal to him was
but a case of manifesting a wide national culture.[16]

Conclusion :

To conclude—the liberal humanist religions historiography
of Bengal does not consist only of Akshaya Dutta and Kshitimohan Sen. They are only two great representatives of it. As I
said at the beginning, this religions liberalism was a part of the
general Social awakening of the Bengal middle Class. True,
such a religions historiography did not consciously unearth the
material roots of a popular culture—its enquiry remained at a
cultural level. But that limitation was a reflection of the general
limitation of the broad Social awakening of the middle class.
Notwithstanding that, it proved to be a direct accopaniment of
a national awakenig in India.

24

REFERENCES

1. Brajendra Nath Bandopadhyay—"Akshaya Kumar Dutta"—in Sahitya Sadhak Charitmala, Vol I (Bangiya Sahitya Parisad, Cal.).
2. Sibnath Sastri*—"Ramtanu Lahiri O Tatkalin Banga Samaj." P 200 (New Age) (Cal).
3. Brajendra Nath Bandopadhyay—Op. cit, pi p. 17.
4. Benoy Kumar Ghosh's introduction—to Akshaya Dutta's—Religious Sects Of India, Patha Bhaban, Cal, Beng 1376.
5. Akshayay Dutta—pp. 213-214 op cit.
6. Ibid, p. 340.
7. Ibid, Benoy Ghosh's introduction, pp. 4-5.
8. Kshitimohan Sen—Hindu Sanskritir Swarup, pp. 51-60. (Visva Bha Bharati Beng 1354).
9. Ibid,—p. 60.
10. Introduction by Rabindra Nath Tagore to Kshitimohan Sen's*— "Bharatiya Madhyayuge Sadhanar Dhara" (Lekhak-Samabaya—Samiti, Cal. 1965.)
11. Kshitimohan Sen—Ibid, pp. 127-128.
12. Ibid,—p. 79.
13. Sen, Hindu Sanskritir Swarup, pp. 52-58, Visva Bharati, Beng, 1354.
14. Sen, Bharater Sanskriti, p 10. Visva Bharati, Ben, 1350.
15. Ibid, p. 81.
16. Sen, Banglar Sadhana, Visva Bharati Ben, 1352.

KAZI ABDUL ODUD (1894-1970) :
Ministrel of a forlorn hope

Mr. Dhurjati Prasad De.
Gobordanga Hindu College,
Gobordanga, West Bengal.

The impact of Wahabi movement on socio-religious life of Bengal Muslims was rather remarkable. It not only helped to nurture a sort of anti-British attitude among them but also led to the development of a hyper-consciousness among all the strata of the community regarding the need of Islamisation. Under its influence a long chain of reformist missions was carried out by different missionaries of different social categories with the common aim of freeing the Islam of all syncretic tendencies. While among the subalterns the leadership of Titu Mir and Dudu Miyan gave a religious reactionary movement the shape of a mass upsurge against economic exploitation, in a higher echelon, among elites and lesser elits, it gave birth to a vaunted sense of pre-eminence.[1] The Wahabi spirit, especially its anti-British stand soon died down with the more mundane realisation that material benefits accruing from co-operation and collaboration with the colomialists were more fruitful than futile hostility. Led by a more pragmatic sense the Muslim leaders like Nawab Abdul Latif and Justice Ammer Ali preferred to become more resilent in their sociopolitical overtures, making discernible efforts to make their community's existence and aspirations felt. Their ideas and imaginations got a fillip from the Pan-Islamic movement which was already in advanced stage in different quarters outside India. Pan-Islamism as aparticular brand of thought put emphasis on close links with the larger world of Islam, implied a quest for trans-Indian Identity. In fact to establish an exclusive identity this approach was extremely helpful for the reformers but strict adherence to the doctrine led to a real break-away from the social framework giving birth to a sharp polarisation between Hindus and Muslims. That the threat was of real potency it had been expressed by Bipin Chandra Pal who in his memoires pointed out how the Pan-Islamic leader Djemal-ed-Din came to Bengal, particularly in Calcutta, held talks with the front-line leaders like Abdul Latif and Ammer Ali and so thoroughly indoctrinated them that they drew themselves away from joint socio-political ventures of the Hindus and Muslims, soon a wide gulf of misunderstanding was created between the intellectuals of both the communities.[2] The Indian Muslims particularly those of Bengal were so much caught with the Pan-Islamic fever that by 1902 the enthusiasts among them set up a Demasque-Hejaj Railway Fund Committee with its office at 7 Rowdon Street, Calcutta to finance the project,[3] while between 1919 and 1920 different Mofussil towns and business centres of Bengal witnessed holding of numerous 'Khilafat' meetings.[4] Eventually on 15th Oct. 1922 the Calcutta Muslims invited the famous leader Jalaluddin Al-Hosseini who delivered lecture on Pan-Islamism at the Town Hall.[5] It is a fact that the raison d'etre of separatism was provided by Pan-Islamism but the Bengal Renaissance culminating into the emergence of a 'neo-Hinduism'[6] contributed largely to division and the Muslims of this province having been put into the melting pot of political and social conflicts with the Hindus was rather confounded to take the right course. This prevarication of Muslim mind became more apparent in the process of their identification with the Bengali Socio-cultural milieu. That the Bengal Muslims were unmistakably a part of the Bengal society and were closely interwoven in its fascinating cultural texture could be well appreciated from the instances of mediaeval or late mediaeval

Bengali literature which bore quite a distinguishable imprint of the literary genius of the Muslim prose writers and poets who not only enriched but also added a colourful variety to the burgeoning World or Bengali literature. But this Pan-Islamic pull which resulted in the creation of an unprecendented fascination in Urdu and Arabic, considered to be courier of Islamic ideas, totally alienated a major section from the composite Bengali culture and literary tradition. The social reformer of early 20th Century Muslim Bengal thus reminded his co-religionists 'Mind it'. You are entirely a different race and profess a different religion (other than the Hindus).[7]

(মনে রাখিও—তোমরা সম্পূর্ণ ভিন্ন জাতি এবং ভিন্ন ধর্মাবলম্বী)

and they could well afford to say that 'Bengali is never our National language, since Bengali is our mother-tongue we have gradually been losing our national identity'.[8]

(বাঙালা কখনও আমাদের জাতীয় ভাষা নহে। বাঙালা আমাদের মাতৃভাষা হওয়াতে আমরা ক্রমেই জাতীয়ত্বহীন হইয়া পড়িতেছি)

Even an intellectual of first rate like S. Wajed Ali chalked out a fairly acceptable scheme of inducting few Urdu alphabets into the Bengali variety for the Islam hungry Bengali Muslims.[9]

The cumulative effect of all this was that inspite of a feeble resistence offered by a conscious group of intellectuals the majority among them began to think in the way which was far from the spirit of unity while their ideas on nation, nationhood and nationality had come to be interpreted in terms of Islamic scriptures which hardly contained any cogent expostulation on those modern concepts. The conviction that Muslim sense of nationalism was religion based hence the geo-political boundary of India or Bengal and the cultural traits so far attained could not prevent a Bengali Muslim from getting identified with the international feeling of Islam which transcended all accepted notion of nation and nationality had begun to gain currency and been proclaimed with much gusto.[10]

The thinkers of the day were so thoroughly affected with the spirit that they went so far as to declare "We (the Mussalmans) are Bengali in the sense that we live in the land of Bengal but we do not belong to Bengali race[11]

(আমরা বাঙালা দেশের অধিবাসী বলিয়া বাঙালী বটে, কিন্তু বাঙালী জাতি নহি ।)

While this had a profound impact on Muslim thought there was some kind of hesitation in accepting it, but this attempt to Islamise the highly secular issue of culture and nationality obviously shaken the Muslim belief in the credibility of a national integration.

At that crucial moment while the Muslim mind was quite at a loss to choose the right track at the discovery of an international Islamhood fostering the conviction of a separate identity there appeared in the social scene a group of thinkers who, professing the Mutazila doctrine of 'Ilm Ul Kalam' (law of reasoning)[12] tried to solve the problem. Headed by two stalwart thinkers kazi Abdul Odud and Abul Hussein this group laid foundation to 'Muslim Literacy Society' in Dacca.[13] Their principle became emancipation of intellect which implied scientific thinking and an endeavour to promote a very positive approach towards the problem of disunity and disintegration.[14] Kazi Abdul Odud as the leader of the group highlighted the liberal aspects of the faith and offered suggestions for broadening of social perimeter of the Bengal Muslims so that it could include extra-Islamic elements.[15] The most articulate of Odud's thought regarding unity and intergration was expressed in 'Hindu Musalmaner Birodh'. (হিন্দু-মুসলমানের বিরোধ) which at the request of Rabindranath was delivered as Nizam Lectures in 1935 at Viswa-Varati.[16] In this superbly written essay the author with all earnestness tried to go to the root of the problem and in his own liberal way offered suggestions so that the two

communities, at least socially could find out a modus vivendi.
According to him the reason of mutual mistrust lied partially
in Hindu ignorance and lukewarmth to understand the problems
of his neighbour particularly the sea of change which affected
his social outlook after the Wahabi movement and partially to
Muslim intransigence to understand the social forces and to
shun orthodoxy and obscurantism. The origin of this particular
attitude of both the communities could be traced back to 19th
Century "aggressive Hinduism" as also to the Wahabi reaction
which in a equal way were indicative of their frustration on
social and political aspirations.[17] For the Muslim community
as a whole this "aggressive Hinduism" spelled out danger ; it
even gripped the attention of a positive thinker like Iqubal who
declared that nationalism as preached and practised by the
Hindus was but a veiled attempt on their part to establish
Hindu supremacy all over India, to which the Mussalmans
could not possibly agree without detriment to the great
civilisation and ideal they represented.[18] For this reason the
Indian Muslims including those of Bengal had not only been
trying to strengthen their religious community within the
boundary of their exclusive social norms and particular ideology
but also were becoming conscious of an uncharitable socio-
political environs verging on undisguised belligerency.[19] To
get rid of this situation Odud's formula was a novel one. The
remarkable aspect of his approach lied in the fact that while
other contemporary thinkers and reforms clamoured primarily
for a political solution of the problem of disunity and
disintegration and subsequently preferred to descend to cultural
level it was Odud and his group, on the contrary thought it
prudent to unify Hindus and Muslims particularly of Bengal,
in a cultural whole and thereafter the possibility of political
unification was given credence. Odud, therefore, entreated both
Hindus and Muslims to shun fondness of the past and traditions
which could harmfully affect a Hindu or a Muslim to evaluate

the social issues endangering their mutual relation. Secondly it was his considered opinion that Hindus and Muslims as communities should have comfortable understanding of each other within a given cultural environment resting within a given society. It is within that perimeter that socio-culural aspirations of both the communities would coalesce to form a single whole. Odud in this connection drew attention to the populist cult of Marfatis, Baul, Darvesh, Pir and Guru among the subalterns in which the much sought for synthesis had been achieved.[20] In other words the essence of Odud's thought was creative humanism to develop it as a social philosophy which would assign to each individual the ultimate responsibility for active participation in the process of dealing with social problems—particularly separatism.[21] Odud therefore brought forth a panel of suggestions expected to resolve the issue. In his opinion, firstly every ritual of either community should be treated with respect unless it got anything reprehensible ; secondly members of both the communities should understand that any old and traditional socio-religious ritual or practice should be accepted on its merit, specially considering its social utility ; thirdly there should remain no distinctive difference between Hindu and Muslim names, nor in their sartorial practices ; fourthly social intercourse including marriage between the two communities should be more free and frequent and fifthly rule of law should be imposed on both the communities with equal emphasis without any sort of discrimination.[22]

Odud and his group proclaimed themselves 'Kemalists' due to the reason that Kemal's brand of nationalism and his ways of approaching the age-old problems of Islamic society of Turkey earned their respect and attention.[23] For the time being this group (nicknamed as 'Sikha' group) had been able to influence

Muslim Youths towards a distinctive line of thinking, but soon due to much opposition from a very powerful quarter its operational area got restricted. Even the promoters of the group were castigated as anti-Islamic. Braving all odds Odud and his team lingered on their activities for a fairly long time imploring the intellectual section among the Muslims to think de novo the problems of disintegration. It is important to note in this connection that however earnest had been Odud in his appeal to come to a social understanding with the Hindus the process which he suggested in effecting a fusion in cultural and ideological level between the two communities did not of course signify erosion of the distinct social identity of the Muslims. Even politically he went so far as to accept Hindu Nationhood as a corrupt from of Indian Nationhood to which, he believed, the Muslims belonged. But he strongly felt that the composite character of the Indian nationhood need not be disturbed and all the component parts, he maintained, must combine effectively to create the grand Indian harmony.[24] Odud in this respect, was certainly influenced by the theory of a cultural cringe which got currency long before his appearance. Cultural Jingoism of the majority which had its origin in the "Neo-Hinduism" had a profound negative impact on the early Muslim thinkers and reformers who were under a constant fear of losing their own Cultural identity under the looming shadow of a more dominant Hindu language and literature. The result was that instead of getting closer to the Hindus who were more a cultural entity than political the bewildered Muslims began to draft apart and toyed with the idea of creating a separate socio-cultural zone of their own, the result being the formation of separate cultural institute like "Bangiya Mussalman Sahitya Samity" and initiation of a long drawn battle between Urduphiles and vernacularists. Odud as a fairly conscious person did not subscribe to the idea of a total segregation nor subjugation under Hindu influence, he rather had an inherent belief in the existence of a separate literary tradition bearing a distinct Muslim Cultural imprint which could comfortably co-exist with its Hindu component, both contributing significantly to the creation of a grand cultural heritage. He therefore maintained "The realm of the Bengali literature has been enriched by two streams of literature one of the Hindus and other of the Muslims ; but each of it is distinct from the other like the streams of Ganga and Yamuna."[25]

(বঙ্গ সাহিত্যে হিন্দু ও মুসলমান এই দুই ধারা সম্মিলিত হয়েই রয়েছে, কিন্তু গঙ্গা-যমুনা ধারার মতো)

This psychosomatic fear of losing a socio cultural identity while in a broader way explains the Bengal Muslims" tilt towards Pan-Islamism and an unaccounted love of Urdu, in the same way it provides cogent reasons for the upward thrust of the Julahs of Northern India, reflected in greater use of Arabic and Persian names including boycott of non Muslim festivals and obsurvance of 'Sajjada nashins', an example of Islamisation, by the Punjab Muslims. In short throughout the late 19th and early 20th Century similar Islamising movements can be discerned among numerous Muslim communities in different parts of India. However, in the back-drop of such social and lingual movements Odud's feeble voice to maintain unity in diversity drowned amidst bitter political struggle between the two communities accelerated by strained agrarian relations affected by communalism.[26] and rat-race for jobs and opportunities among the professional middle class of either community. The possiblity of integration and subsequent freedom from colonial exploitation was less preferred than sectarian politics feeding to various class and community interests. The ideal had gone to winds. It was a coup manque for the adventurist who waged an intellectual war against disunity and disharmony.

REFERENCES

1. For detailed discussion See : Rafiuddin Ahmed—The Bengal Muslims, 1871-1906, A Quest for Identity, Oxford 1981 ; Marahari Kaviraj—Wahabi and Faraizi Rebels of Bengal, New Delhi, 1982 ; Hossainur Rahman—Hindu Muslim Relations in Bengal, 1905-47, Calcutta 1974 ; Muin-Ud-din Ahmed Khan—Research in the Islamic Revivalism of the 19th Century and its effects on the Muslim Society of Bengal, Social Research in East Pakistan, edited by Pierre Bessaignet, Asiatic Society of Pakistan, Publication No. 5. 1960.

2. B. C. Pal—Memories of My Life and Times, Calcutta, 1932. Ch. XXI, P—417.

3. Demesque—Hejaj Railway—Islam Procharak, Jan-Feb, 1902, P-283.

4. The Mussalman 1919 and 1920,

5. Pan-Islamism—Speeches of Jalaluddin Al Hosseini (translated from original Fassee into Bengali by Abdul Hafez Sharifabadi, Calcutta, 21st Feb. 1923).

6. term used by Bipin C. Pal in his memoires Op. cit ; See Nihar Ranjan Roy—Unish Sataki Bangalir Punurujjiban Sambandhe Kimchit Punarbibechana, Jijnasa, 1st year 1st issue, Baishakh 1387 (B. S) P-6-33.

7. Esmail Hossain—Sahitya Shakti O Jati Sangatan, Nabanoor, 1st year No. 3 1310 B. S. Asada.

8. Editorial comment by Reyazuddin Ahmed, Islam Procharak, 5th year No. 1, January, 1903.

9. S. Wajet Ali—Bangla Barnamala, Sahityika 1st year 9th issue Sravana 1334 (B. S.).

10. Prisidential address of Maulabi Md. Akram Khan in the Chittagang Muslim Literacy Conf. 1325 (B. S.), quoted in 'Bangla Bhasa O Mosalman Sahitya'—Md. Wajed Ali, AL Eslam, 5th issue Part 11-12th Falgun-Chaitra, 1325 (B. S.) P. 591-99.

11. Ibid.

12. Encyelopaedia of Islam ; Syed Ameer Ali—The Spirit of Islam, London, 1955.

13. Dhurjati Prosad De—Muslim Sahitya Samaj O Buddhir Mukti Andolan, Bangiya Sahitya Parishad Patrika, 88th year, 2nd issue, Sravana—Aswin, 1388 (B. S.) ; Banglar Chintanayaka Abul Hussein O Muslim Samskriti, Parichaya, 52nd year, 5th issue, Dec. 1982.

14. Ibid.

15. Kazi Abdul Odud—Samaj O Sahitya, 1341 (B. S.) Calcutta.

16. Kazi Abdul Odud—Hindu Musalmaner Birodh (Nizam Lectures, Viswa Varati, 1935) Sawswata Banga, Calcutta 1358 (B. S.)

17. Kazi Abdul Odud—Creative Bengal, Calcutta, 1950.

18. Ibid.

19. Ibid.

20. Kazi Abdul Odud—Milaner Katha, Swaswata Banga Op. Cit.

21. Kazi Abdul Odud—Griha Juddher Prakyale, Swaswata Banga, Op. Cit.

22. Kazi Abdul Odud—Samskritir Katha, Swaswata Banga Op. Cit.

23. Kazi Abdul Odud—Creative Bengal Op. Cit. ; Mustafa Kamal Samparke Kayekati Katha, Swaswata Banga Op. Cit.

24. Ibid.

25. Kazi Abdul Odud—Bangala Sahityer Muslim Dhara, Swaswata Banga, Op. Cit.

26. Partha Chatterjee—Agrarian Relations and Communalism in Bengal, 1926-1935, Subaltern Studies—I,| Edited by Ranajit Guha, Oxford—1982.

THE VANGUARDS OF NATIONAL INTEGRATION :
The Working Class of Bengal (1937-47)

Dr. Nirban Basu
Department of History
Kalyani University. (W. B.)

India is a land of diversity, in points of communities, languages, religions, castes and culture. The question of national integration tends to be crucial at present times and the experiences and lessons of Indian History can be of great use in this regard.

The industrial working class of Bengal is an apt illustration in the study of national integration. The heterogeneous character of the working class of Bengal in points of communities, languages, religions and castes maks it a miniature edition of the All-India Scenaric.

I

In the first section of our articls, we will narrate the growth and formation of the labour force in the major industries of Bengal—their origin, composition and recruitment. Their living conditions in Bengal will also be discussed.

In spite of a considerable amount of research regarding the industrial labour force, our understanding of their *historically specific evolution* in Eastern India remains incomplete and fragmented. Few attempts have been made to collect and systematise the information available as well as to investigate the process.[1] Given the constraints imposed by the limited data availability, a somewhat connected account of growth and composition of labour is possible by using quantitative information wherever it has been available (mainly in the Census Reports) supplemented by stray and sketchy statements available in some other decuments.

With the growth of industries in Bengal at a comparatively more rapid pace towards the closing years of the 19th Century, the employers increasingly felt an acute shortage, particularly of the unskilled labour. There were several migration streams of labour towards Bengal. The labour "catchment area" in the Western districts of Bihar (Gaya, Patna, Shahabad, Saran and Muzaffarpur) and the adjoining Eastern districts of the U. P. (Azamgarh, Balia. Ghazipur, Benares and Jaunpur) had different common destinations—the Jute Mills and other factories in Calcutta and surrounding areas and the tea gardens in Surma Valley area. Again, both the Dooars tea gardens and Coal mines of Ranigunj depended heavily on tribal and semitribal elements from the Chotanagpur and surrounding areas.

The shift from Bengali labour to non-Bengali labour, mostly from Bihar, U. P. and Orissa had probably became conspicuous by 1905, when it was found that about two-thirds of the labour in Bengal were immigrants.[2] In 1929, the Royal Commission on labour noted[3] the prodominantly, non-local character of the factory labour in Calcutta. It seems that in all the industries of Bengal, in general, a powerful influx of non-local labour took place from the beginning of the 20th Century. This trend continued since then. By the 1920's, the labour force became, more or less, settled in composition.[4] By this time the wage-earning industrial labour-force in Bengal became quite large in absolute number, though not in proportion to total population. It further increased during the inter-war and the World War II years. The proportionats composition of different social, ethnic and religious groups, however, underwent little change.

The broad features of the Working Class of Bengal, industry by industry, are as follows :

Jute Industry—Of the major industries of Bengal, the Jute mills stood first. The whole of the Jute mill area in Bengal, was located on either side of the river Hooghly, within a radius of 30 miles around Calcutta from Bansberia in the north and Budge Budge in the south. Even within this radius, there are certain areas in which one finds considerable concentrations of Jute mills. The total number of Jute mills was nearly 100. The number of Jute labour reached its peak in 1929-30 (3,39,665). Between 1929 and 1937, the number of labour decreased by about 60,000 primarily due to the World Wide Great Depression. The situation improved since 1934-35 and became stable since 1937-38, but it never reached the 1929-30 level.

Along with the rapid development of the Jute industry in the late 19th and early 20th Centuries, Jute mill workers began to be drawn from an ever-widening area. Labour from Bihar and U. P. were first to come in the Jute mill areas. Labour from Orissa was also employed quite early. Still later on, labour came from the Bilaspur and Raipur districts of the Central Provinces and from the Telugu speaking areas of Ganjam and Berhampore in Madras Presidency.

As for the area of origin of the Jute labour, the 1921 census shows that Bihar contributed (36.81 p. c. and 30.78 p.c.,), U. P. (22.56 p.c. and 23.77 p.c.), Orissa (7.5 p.c. and 14.92 p.c.) and Madras (1.66 p.c. and 6.93 p. c.), while Bengal (31.31

p.c. and 18.32 p.c.) of the skilled and unskilled labour force respectively. This proportion remained basically unchanged in the subsequent years. It is, however, wrong to think that this proportion was applicable in all the mills. For example, in several mills of Budge Budge area (24-Parganas, South, District) and some mills in Uluberia Sub-division of Howrah district Bengali labourers constituted at least a sizable proportion, if not a majority.

It is also significant that each mill had formed connections with certain districts although these connections were not deleberately formed by the managers. The Labour Investigation Committee (1946) also found workers from a particular province working in a particular department.

As for the Communal Composition, from the 1911 census we get the information that the Muslims contributed 31. 81 p. c. of all Jute mill operatives. The proportion remained more or less unchanged in 1921. The census reports of 1911 and 1921 also provide detailed information regarding the Jute workers. Caste-wise distribution of the Jute Mill operatives among the two broad categories of workers, skilled and unskilled, shows that while 17 p. c. of all unskilled workers, was composed of Chamars and Muchis, their contribution was only 5 p. c. of the skilled workers. All the low castes, taken together, made up more than 30 p. c. of all unskilled workers. As against this, they made just 9 p. c. of the total skilled workers. Another large group, the Muslims, mainly Sheikhs and Jolahas, constituted 41 p. c. of the skilled workers, its proportion of the unskilled workers being 26 p. c.

As for the recruitment, the Jute mills of Bengal did not want any special measures. In fact, the supply of labour to the Bengal Jute Mills was part of the much larger eastward stream of labour migration to the Coal Mines, plantations and factories. The labour themselves came to the mill gates for employment. Till 1937, virtually all recruitment of Jute Mill labour was done solely through the jobbers, locally known as 'Sardars'. Even after the appointment of Labour Officers and the opening of Labour Bureaus in some mills in 1937, the Sardars continued to maintain their pivotal position in recruitment.[5]

The Sardars' activities included not only recruitment of the workers, alloting of work, granting of leave, enforcing of work-discipline, punishment, etc., but also housing the workers (in private 'bustees' often run by the Sirdars themselves) and lending them money, in time of distress at high interest. Much of the basis of the Sardar's social control of the workforce lay in community, kin of other primordial relationships and in the ideas and norms associated with them.[6]

The heterogeneous origin and the prevalence of the Sardari system tended to compartmentalise the workers for long.

Cotton Mills—The Cotton Mills of Bengal also were situated mostly in the Calcutta metropolis area, almost in the same localities where the Jute Mills were situated. Only a few of them, however, were situated in the districts of Dacca and Nadia.

The patterns of workforce in the Cotton Mills in the Calcutta metroplis area, more or less, conform to the patterns prevailing in the Jute Mills though exact figures are not available for the continuous period. The local labour was gradually replaced by the immigrants. The only detailed source, the census of 1921, shows comparatively a higher percentage of Bengali and Oriya labour than the Biharis.

Bihar provided 7. 68 p. c. and 6.01 p. c. ; Oriss 33.01 p. c. and 24.65 p. c. ; U. P. 32.16 p. c. and 18.07 p. c. ; and Bengal 18.20 and 36.24 p. c. of the unskilled and skilled labour respectively. As for the religious composition, the Muslims constituted nearly 20 p. c. Regarding the caste-wise composition, at least 10 p. c. came from Hindu Weavers castes (i. e. Tantis and Jugis) and approximately same percentage of labour came from the Muslim handloom manufacturers. In the mills of Kusthia and Dacca, the local Bengali labour, both Hindus and Muslims, maintained a much higher percentage compared to the cotton mills of Greater Calcutta.

The method of recruitment was just like in the Jute Mills. The workers presented themselves before the mill gates for recruitment. The Sardars, as in the case of Jute mills, had a predominant say in the appointment, control and dismissal of workers.

Apart from the Jute Mills and Cotton Textils, two other important labour-employers in the Calcutta area were the Calcutta Tramways Company, at that time the most important source of road transport and the Calcutta Port and Dock, then the largest terminal in South Asia.

Tramways—The number of employees in the Calcutta Tramways rose from 5,750 in 1939 to 8,411 in 1947. The majority of the workers were from Bihar and U. P. Drivers were recruited mostly from illeterate up-country men. Literate men were taken in for the posts of conductors. In the Engineering Section and Permanent Way Department, only the unskilled workers were recruited through Sardars and Chargemen. Of the up-countrymen, the Muslims formed a huge percentage. According to an estimate of 1947, they numbered about 2,000. Among the Hindu workers, the upper castes including Brahmins had a predominant share. This was in sharp contrast to Jute or Cotton Mills.

Port—In the Calcutta Port, there were about 22,000 workers under the direct control of the Calcutta Port Commissioners in the 1930's and '40s. In the dock, the number of workers were about 14,000, most of whom were unregistered and employed on a piece-work basis under the stevedors. Both the port labour and the dock labour belonged to the same class of men and came from the same areas. The principal regions from which labour was recruited were Bihar and U. P. A significant section of the dock workers, however, came from Orissa. No detailed statistical data are available about the communal, regional or casts composition of the workforce. According to a very rough estimate, out of the total 14,000 dock workers, about 9,000 were Muslims and 5,000 were Hindus. Of them, the Winchmen (or, the skilled labour) were mostly Muslims, hailing from U. P. The gangmen (or, the unskilled labour) were both Oriya Hindus and Muslims, mostly from Bihar.

Apart from the industries situated in the Calcutta metroplis area, there were three other major industries in Bengal—Iron and Steel, Coalmines and Tea Plantations.

Iron and Steel—All the three major Iron and Steel factories, the Indian Iron and Steel Co., the Steel Corporation of Bengal, and the Indian Standard Wagon Co., were situated in the Burnpur-Kulti area of Burdwan district. Since the mid—1930's, the total number of employees working in these concerns was approximately 20,000. There are no reliable sources of information regarding the composition of the labour force. Only some broad generalisations can be made. As the Steel works required a huge number of skilled labourers, the local labour was of little use. The skilled workers were obtained from almost all the provinces in India—Bengal, U. P., Bombay, Madras, Punjab and even the North Western Frontier Provinces.

Coal Mines—In the coalmines of Bengal about 56·5% were drawn from the Coal districts, 7·5% were drawn from districts of Bengal other than Coal districts ; about 33·9% were imported from the contiguous districts of Bihar and only 2·1% came from provinces other than Bengal and Bihar. Most of these Bengal mines were situated in the Asansol-Ranigunj fields of the Burdwan district. The number of mines employed rose from 57,882 in1939 to 64,491 in 1944.

The mining labour force was predominantly composed of the Santhals and the Bauris, a caste on the lowest wrung of the Hindu hicrarchy. According to the census of 1921, of the total labour force, the Santhals comprised 36.1 p. c. and the Bauris 21.4 p. c. in the Bengal Collieries. Most of the remaining percentage was provided by the socially lowest castes like the Muchis, Kamars, Rajwars and a small percentage of Muslims. In spite of the growing heterogeneous composition, a distinct pattern of occupational specialisational remained. The Santhals and Bauris readily took to underground work from the beginning, other castes also had their fixed preferences.

The Coalmines adopted an almost bewildering variety of methods of recruitment supervision and control of labour. Still, the fact remained that the miners remained half agriculturist and half labourer.[7]

Tea-plantations—Bengal stood second in the tea production, the principal plantation industry in India. Its tea producing areas included the Dooars in the Jalpaiguri district, the hill areas and the plains of Terai in the Darjeeling District ; and Chittagong. By 1947, the number of gardens was about 158 in the Dooars, 77 in Darjeeling and 30 in Chittagong employing nearly 2½ lacs plantation—workers.

In the Darjeeling hills, the immigrants or descendants of immigrants from the neighbouring country of Nepal furnished almost the whole of the labour force. In the plains of Terai (excepting some Nepalis), the Dooars and Chittagong, the composition of the labour-force was almost the same. Chotanagpur and Santhal Parganas were the main recruiting grounds of labour and the aboriginal tribals like the Santhals and the Oraos provided the bulk of the labour force.

Unlike Assam, the labour was technically free. A worker could leave whenever he pleased. But whatever might be the exact form of recruitment, everywhere the garden-workers were reduced to a semi-servile status. Here were a mass of illiterate people, living far away from their original homes with which practically all relations had been cut off, scattered in the tea gardens, segregated from outside influence and unorganised while the employers had formed themselves into one of the most powerful and well organised associations in the country.

An overall survey of the composition of workforce in different industries of Bengal shows that over the years, the non-Bengali workers outnumbered the Bengalis, most of whom came from Hindi speaking areas. Others like Telugus and Oriyas also were not rare. In certain industries, the aboriginal tribes predominated. The Muslims also formed an important segment. The caste-wise analysis shows the preponderance of the socially low castes. Higher caste workers, however, were also found in certain types of jobs.

II

Form the narrative in the foregoing section, it is quite easy to find out the main constraints in the working class solidarity. By the 1920's, the labour force in Bengal became, more or less, settled in composition. They were mainly non-local and heterogeneous in composition. They remained as a class apart and had little connection with the Bengali-speaking masses of the province.

But with the beginning of the mass oriented politics since the 1920's, the working classes posed a serious problem. For the national political leadership, the question was how and to what extent they should be drawn in the mainstream of national movement. Particularly with the mass movement, having reached a new height since the mid-30's, a militant and vigorous trend came also in the ranks of the working class movement of Bengal. But at the same time, their forces of disintegration also raised their heads.

The concentration of one group of labour, in point of regional origin or casts, in particular one department, or even their living in one bustes—all compartmentalised the workers. But the greatest danger was Communalism. The then powerful Muslim League and its allies tried to keep out the Muslims, who formed a significant percentage of the labour force of Bengal, out of united struggle. The Trade Union Congress and different leftist organisations were painted as Hindu organisations. With direct government patronage and the tacit support of the employers, these communal organisations gathered considerable strength.

Things took a new turn with the establishment of the Muslim League—Praja Party coalition in 1937.[8] There were a series of strike in the Jute miles and other factories in and around Calcutta. All sections of Congressmen, then in opposition came to support these agitations. This impressed upon the Muslim League the necessity of devising a tactful labour policy. The Muslim labour organisers, being supporters of the new Ministy, turned to such industries where there were a substantial number of Muslim labour such as Port and Dock ; Jute Mills, and other factories in and around Calcutta. The labour Minister of Bengal, Suhrawardy took early steps to set up a labour organisation, in the name of Bengal National Chamber of Labour (B. N. C. L.) which was loyal to the Ministry and in particular to himself. It was formed to begin with these trade union of which he was either the President or General Secretary for a number of years, previous to his appointment as the Minister for Labour. In these years, he tried to organise and control a number of unions in the eastern bank of the Ganges, particularly in Jagaddal and Tittagarh with the help of a band of energetic organisers. Suhrawardy not only took keen personal interest in the organisational matters of the B. N. C. L., but also gave regular financial assistance. He also arranged the money earmarked for the Labour Welfare fund in the Government budget for these white unions.[9]

That the Communalists could muster considerable strength among the labourers was clearly illustrated by the massive demonstrations organised by the Bengal National Chamber of Labour on August 8, 1938 in protest against the no-confidence motions tabled in the Legislative Assembly. The organisers claimed that even the Hindu Workers had joined in the hartal and demonstration.[10] But the police reports clearly said[11] that one of the most remarkable after—effects of these demons trations in support of the Ministry had been an almost clear-cut division between the Muslim and Hindu members in large number of unions. It became evident that great majority of

Muslim workers in Greater Calcutta came to genuinely believe that Islam was in danger and they were too much agitated over no-confidence motion to care for trade union.

But once the Muslim League went out of power the official patronage of the white unions came to a stop. Even when a new Muslim League Ministry under Nazimuddin was formed in 1943, in the labour policy of the new government, the stress was definitely on the formal government machineries rather than on the informal reliance on the favourite trade union organisations as in the 1938-'41 period.

The end of the World War II (August, 1945) was followed by unprecedented upsurge of the working class in almost all industries everywhere in India. Cutting across all barriers of caste, religion and language—the workers jumped into the struggle.[12] Under these circumstances, the forces of Communalism had to make a retreat. In the provincial assembly election, held in early, 1946, the B. N. C. L. put up four candidates from Calcutta, Howrah, Hooghly and Barrackpore labour seats, all of whom suffered humiliating defeats. However, the fact that their candidates in Calcutta and Howrah could poll about 10 p. c. and 8 p. c. of the total votes cast show that still the Communalist unions had some pockets of influence.

The election of 1946 resulted in the formation of a new Muslim League Ministry in Bengal now unders Suhrawardy himself. This was soon followed by almost a continuous spate of communal violence and riots on an unprecedented scale. Starting from Aug. 16, 1946, this state of affairs continued intermittently for about a year. It seems that during the communal disturbances started since the great

Calcutta killing all sections of population were affected. The uneducated and poor labouring classes of both the communities were the worst—hit. But it goes to the eternal credit of the workers of organised industrial sector of Bengal that they, by and large, could keep themselves away from the mad communal orgy ; did not join the riot ; and there were numerous reports that workers of one community and viceversa. So, it may be concluded that in spite of inherent communal feelings, the organised industrial workers had reached that level of maturity to realise that the game of division would not serve the interests of the either community.

However, it is wrong to think that the industrial workers came out untouched from the communal holocaust. Rather, it was they who had to bear its brunt most in the weeks following the disturbances. With hundreds of bustees gutted or looted, thousands of workers were made homeless. Many workers left for their native places in Bihar, U. P. and Orissa as they could not go to their work and were actually starving. Nothing had been done by the government or employers to help them. On the contrary, in a large number of cases, the bosses took resort to huge scale retrenchment on communal basis—dismissal of one community here and another community there to break the communal unity of the working class shown during the riot.[13]

In spite of all these, however, the organised working class could not be induced into fatricidal warfare. It is also noticeable that in spite of the fact that a Muslim League Ministry under Suhrawardy himself had been in office, the Bengal National Chamber of Labour had not much activities during the period. Some attempts, however, were made to organise the labour openly on communal lines such as in the Calcutta Tramways or in Bata Shoe Factory. But communal sentiments could not be solidly crystallised around organisational bases and such ventures mostly made during the course of some strikes hardly succeeded.

Particular reference may be made of four historic strikes, all in the early months of 1947—in the Calcutta Tramways, in the Calcutta Port ; in the Indian Iron & Steel Works, Burnpur ; and in the Dooars Tea Garden. Everywhere, the workers made a valiant and united struggle in the face of all divisive, reactionary and oppressive forces.

Tramways—The Tramway Workers in Calcutta are considered to be the vanguards of tade union movement in Bengal. The Calcutta Tramway Workers' Union, (C. T. W. U.) established in 1927, came to be dominated by the Communists since 1938-39, although it represented all sections of workers having different political ideologics. The Calcutta Tram Workers included mostly up-countrymen, workers from Bihar and U. P., both Hindus and Muslims.

The termination of the World War II witnessed the beginning of the post-war upsurge of working class actions in India. The Calcutta Tram Workers were the first to break the ice in Bengal. Their strike continued for nine days (Sept. 19—Sept. 27, 1945) and ended in a great victory of the tram workers. It appears that the workers gained practically all their points and it encouraged the workers in other industries too.

But the increasing communal tension seriously affected the position of the union. Matters came to a head during the Direct Action Day. A body called the Calcutta Tramway workers' Muslim League had already been formad. The C. T. W. U., in a meeting on the 14th August, passed a resolution expressing its neutrality on the Direct Action Day and appealing for national unity. In a press-statement, Sayedur Rahman, Secretary of the above-mentioned, C. T. W. M. L. "on behalf of over 2,000 Muslim Tram Employees" alleged[14] that the resolution of the C. T. W. U., regarding the Direction Action Day was a bogus resolution. He spoke of the deepest resentment and disillusionment of the Muslim workers with the Communists immediately and "stand on their own legs." Alleging that the Communists never worked for the redress of the injustices done on the Muslim Workers, the statement demanded 56 p. c. Muslim representation on all branches of the tramservices, commensurate with the percentage of Muslims in the total population of Bengal, clearly, the allegations and demands were both fantastic, but significant in context of general communal holocaust. On the 15th August, 1946, the Muslim League called a separate conference of the Muslim Tram Workers.

The C. P. I.'s firm held over the C. T. W. U. was considerably affected, at least temporarily, by the communal riots which shook Calcutta for a number of days following the Direct Action Day. A large number of Muslim employees joined the Muslim League. As a reaction, a considerable number of Muslim Workers took shelter in the Congress-led Hindusthan Mazdoor Sevak Sangha.[15]

It was perhaps rightly believed by the C. T. W. U. leadership that a call for movement on economic issues would help to close the ranks of the general workers. The communal holocaust temprarily put a stop to the advance of the movement. As soon as there was some improvement of the situation the C. T. W. U. took initiative in achieving their demands. After making initial preparations throughout Dec. 1946, the C. T. W. U. served a strike notice on the management on Jan. 7, making the following demands, which included, a rise of basic wage, reintroduction of gratuity system, free quarter, two months' wages as bonus etc.

Even at this stage, the Communalists pursued their divisionary tactics. T. Ali, Deputy Speaker, Bengal Legislative Assembly, accompanied by the Secretary, Muslim Tramway Workers Assocation met the Agent of the C. T. C. on Jan, 4, to complain about the paucity of Muslim officers and sub-ordinate staff in every branch of the Co. and reportedly got the assurance that preference would be given to Muslims in future in every department.[16] Such gesture, however, could not influence the workers.

As all attempts of conciliations failed, the 7,000 Tram Workers of Calcutta, Hindus and Muslims, unitedly started their strike from January 21, 1947 which continued for 86 days. In the course of the strike, an alternative union cropped up. The Calcutta Tramways Employees' Union, which was established in 1943, but lay dormant during all these years, was now suddenly activised.[17] While the Communist controlled C. T. W. U. Executive was composed of a large number of middle class Bengali political organisers, from the beginning the leadership of this new union was provided by the workers themselves, hailing from Bihar and U.P. They made propaganda among the up-countrymen against the "Bengali-controlled", Communist union and their strategy of prolonging the strike which had been affecting the workers. Such propaganda could make little impact upon the workers.

The strike ended on April, 17, after a settlement was finally reached in a tripartite meeting of the union, the Company and the Labour Commissioner. No doubt, the workers gained little from this prolonged strike directly. Subsequently, some of their demands were fulfilled through the award of the Tribunal formed under the Industrial Disputes Act of 1947.

Calcutta Port—Almost simultaneously with the Tram Strike of 1947, Bengal witnessed another protracted struggle of the working class. It was the strike of the Port Workers of Calcutta. Like the Calcutta Tramways, the Calcutta Port, which employed nearly 22,000 men, had Muslim and Hindu workers nearly in equal |numbers.

Since 1938, two competiting unions were mainly in the picture. The Calcutta Port Trust Emloyees' Association (CPTEA) had been established in 1920. In 1922, the union was revived by Nepal Bhattacharya, a nationalist—later turned—into a non-Conformist Marxist. In 1929, it was registered under the Indian Trade Unions Act of 1926. After its recognition, during the years when it had no rival, it achieved through negotiations a great deal on such matters as Provident Fund, leave and other fringe benefits.[18] After H. S. Suhrawardy became the Labour Minister in the Muslim-League—Praja Party coalition that came into power in 1937, under his inspiration, the National Union of Port Trust Employees (NUPTE) was formed in 1938. With its inception, rivalries started between two unions. From the beginning, NUPTE, indirectly appealed to the sentiments of the Muslim Workers against the C. P. T. E. A., which so far represented Hindus as well as Muslim workers.

Certain developments during the World War II affected both the unions. The exterrment of Nepal Bhattacharya from Calcutta and the arrest of some its Executive members temporarily crippled the activities of the C. P. T. E. A. and gradually its leadership passed into the hands of the Communists who began to control its Executive. By 1945, the leadership of its rival union, the NUPTE, had also been changed.[19] A section of the pro-Congress labour leaders came to dominate the union. A new Executive Committee was formed with Humayun Kabir (President) ; Ahmedullah (General Secretary) and Dr. Maitreyi Bose (Treasurer). The NUPTE entered into a fight with the Communist dominated CPTEA and drew a sizeble part of their members over to its own ranks. Since his release, Nepal Bhattacharya after some hesitation rejoined the CPTEA and was re-elected President of the union.

With a view to close the ranks among the workers, the CPTEA sought to resort to agitation on economic grounds. Towards the end of the year, 1946, the CPTEA gave strike notice to the authorities demanding among others no retrenchment ; fixation of the minimum wage, grade system and Dearness Allowance. As all attempts of conciliation failed, the CPTEA started the strike from Feb. 5, 1947. The NUPTE joined the following day and thus, the entire workforce was involved. A Joint Council of Action of the Port Workers had been formed with Jolly Mohan Kaul (CPTEA) and Moulevi Ahmedullah (NUPTE) as Joint Convenors. The Congress leaders like Maitroyi Bose and Humayun Kabir, the C. P. I. leaders like Indrajit Gupta and Jolly Kaul, Dr. A. M. Melak of the Muslim League and Nepal Bhattacharya of the Workers' League —leaders of different political groups, connected with these rival unions, worked side by side within this Joint Council.

The strike lingered, neither the open Interim Government, under the Indian National Congress, nor the Provincial Government of theMuslim League, took any initiative for ending the strike. Rather they put the blame on the representative of the workers. But in spite of all political pressure, the striking workers remained firm. Different sections of public in Bengal came in support of the strikers. The B. P. T. U. C. President, Mrinal Kanti Bose, in a statement strongly criticised the attitude of the Calcutta Port Commissioners and the Central and State Governments congratulating the Port Workers for their united struggle and maintenance of communal harmony, he said.[20] "The Port workers are to be congratulated on the solidarity they have shown and on the remarkably affective work done by the joint Hindu Muslim squads in keeping peace in the Kidderpore area during the present communal disturbances. On this ground alone : if no other, they deserve generous contribution from the public to their funds."

Ultimately, the Calcutta Port Commissioners had to climb down from their previous uncompromising stand, A settlement was reached between the Port Authorities and the workers. This ended the eighty-seven day old strike and the workers resumed work from May, 3. The workers gained significant concessions.

While the Tram and Port workers scored significant victories through their united struggle in the heart of Calcutta, there were two other incidents of the workers' united struggle in the far-off areas of Bengal. One was in the IISCo and the other in the Dooars gardens.

Iron and Steel—The three main iron and steel producing concerns—The Steel Corporation of Bengal, The Indian Iron And Steel Company and the Indian Standard Wagon Company, under the same Managing Agency of M/s. Burn & Co., were all situated in the Burnpur-Kulti area in the Asansol sub-division of Burdwan district.

Here, the Labour Union was first established in 1937, under the leadership of Manek Homi, an opportunist labour agitator of Jamshedpur. During the war-time, however, the Communists came to the forefront and formed the Asansol Iron & Steel Workers' Union. But after 1945, the Communists lost their

control and the leadership passed into the hands of Prof. Abdul
Bari, the renowned Congress labour leader from Jamshedpur.
From the middle of August, 1946, the workers union started a
historic strike which lasted till the first week of December
1946. To continue the strike successfully which involved
about 14,000 workers of hetrogeneous origins, in a period of
such communal stress and strain was no small achievement.

It may be noted that the strike coincided with an unprecedented wave of communal violence that swept Bengal and
other parts of India starting with the Muslim League's call
for Direct Action. So, the Labour Union's main concern was
to maintain solidarity in the ranks of the workers composed
of diverse linguistic and religious elements. At a public
meeting at Burnpur on Aug, 28, Abdul Bari urged upon the
workers to avoid communal disturbance and remain peaceful.[21]

As the strike continued for indefinite period, indications of
a division of opinion among the general labourers became
clearly visible. A large number of workers were eager to
return to work. In October, a Settlement Committee was
formed whose supporters included almost all the Sikh employees
and a few Biharis and Bengalis. These persons were prepared to
resume work immediately on the terms already offered by the
Company. Feelings between the Sikh members of the Settlement
Committee and the Punjabi Muslim members of the union
became strained. Bari openly declared that the union would
retaliate if assaulted by the supporters of the Company and
that the unionists were prepared to enter the company premises
by force, if necessary, and to destroy the plants.[22]

Again on Nov. 4, at a public meeting, the leaders of the
union, who included Sikhs, Bihari Hindus and Punjabi Muslims,
urged the labourers to encourage communal amity and thus to
prevant the spread of communal disturbances to Burnpur.

They warned the labour against the agents of the company-authorities who were allegedly endeavouring to foment communal trouble in order to split the workers' organisation.

The strike was eventually settled on Dec. 9, 1946, when both sides agreed to refer the disputant points to an Adjudication Board. It is, however, wrong to think that the communal feelings died so easily. Even after the end of the strike, a discordant note within the workers' union leadership itself on the issue of communalism was noticeable. At a workers' rally on January 17, 1947, one speaker Samandar Khan, an important official of the union, openly protested against Prof. Bari, speaking ill of the Muslim League at Public Meeting. He said that this had caused resentment among Muslim members of the volunteer corps, some of whom wished to resign and that he warned Bari to refrain from making such indiscrimate remarks in future.[23]

As the Labour Union was composed of labour of different political ideologies, Prof. Bari, inspite of being the undisputed supreme leader of the union could not thurst his avowed anti-Muslim League sentiments on the workers. To maintain the unity of the union was the formost thing and it was not always possible to be the official Congress line.

The Dooars : The trade union movement among the tea garden labourers of the Dooars in North Bengal had a late start. Not only that, the Dooars for long remained unaffected by the national movement which had engulfed the rest of the country. The weak organisation of the nationalists in the district, the immense difficulty of making contract with the labourers in the tea gardens, which were literally "forfresses" of the European owners, and also the lack of will on the part of the nationalist workers, who were a middle class educated high-caste Bengalees, towards organising the tea-workers, most of whom were immigrant tribals or discendants of immigrants—all these led to the non-starter of the trade union movement in the Dooars.[24]

Only after 1945-46, the trade union organisation had a start in this region. The great increase in the economic hardships of the workers in the immediate post-war period due to the rise in prices of food commodities and scarcity of cloth compounded their discomtent. It was in such an economic background that the overall political development in the country as a whole and also the election-campaign undertaken by the Communists in the neighbouring areas e. g., Darjeeling Tea—labour and Jalpaiguri Rural scheduled—Reserved Constituencies began to affect the Dooars Tea Garden labour. For the first time, the message of the Red Flag was carried to the labour in the sprawling tea-belt of the Dooars.

While all these provided a favourable background for organising the tea labourers, the Dooars Tea-Workers showed signs of collective action only after the trade union organisers of the Bengal-Assam Railroad Workers' Union (BARRWU) most of whom were active Communist workers made an attempt to organise them since early, 1946. The role of the leaders and unionised B. D. R. workers in spreading movement among the tea garden labour was most important.[25] Their work was facilitated by the fact that the railway lines went by the side or even through the tea gardens, that the big railway stations had around them several tea gardens and that the lowest-ranking railway workers—the unionised gangmen and pointsmen came into frequent contract with the sprawling labour population. This was also partly facilitated by the fact that many of the gang Khalasis and pointmen themselves were tribals. The pioneer organisers, however, had to do their work in a clandestine fashion and often under the cover of darkness of night.

After the middle of 1946, strikes became frequent in a number of gardens in spite of all oppressive measures by the management. By the end of the year, the situation became tense. And the first few months-from the end of January to April, 1947 saw the peak of unrest. Now, the labour revolted on masse in a large number of gardens and left work to join with the Peasantry. They had been roaming in the countryside in many cases armed with lathis and spears with the object of raiding paddy stocks in support of general demand of the share-croppers for a two-thirds share (tebhaga).[26]

This was a unique struggle in the annals of the working class movement of Bengal in many respects. What was most crucial was the interaction between three sections of workers—the unionised railway workers and employees having a hetero-geneous composition—men coming from Bihar and U. P. ; Nepalis, upper caste Hindu Bengalis, Muslims, tribass etc., the overwhelmingly tribal tea-garden labour in the midst of a process of being organised ; and the immigrant tribal peasents (with the exception of sprinkling of Rajbansis and Muslims). Peoples of all these castes and religions were united by a spirit of mass upheaval.

CONCLUSION

Thus, on the eve of national independence and partition, only the industrial working class of Bengal could make united mass movements while almost all other sections of society were engrossed in deep fatricidal quarrels. In this way, they played a vanguard's role in the movement for national integration. It is true that it was beyond their power to check the communal tension, which was the result of wider social and political factors. But they left a glorious legacy of a solidarity. They proved that the heterogeneous linguistic, social and religious groups could be united only through a militant mass struggle against oppression.

REFERENCES

1. The most brilliant work so far done in this field is of Dasgupta, Ranajit—Factory Labour in Eastern India : Sources of Supply (1855—1946), Indian Economic and Social History Review, Vol. XIII, No. 3, July-Sept. 1976.

2. Report on Labour in Bengal by B. Foley (1906)

3. Report of the Royal Commission on Labour in India (1929)—Main Report.

4. Census of India, 1911, Vol V, Bengal, Bihar and Orissa, Pt. II ; Census of India, 1921, Vol. V, Bengal Pt II.

5. Dasgupta, Ranajit—Structure of the Labour Market in Colonial India (Economic and Political Weekly, Special Number, Nov. 1981)

6. Chakravarty, Dipesh—Conditions for knowledge of Working Class Conditions : Employers, Government and the Jute Workers of Calcutta, 1890-1940 in Guha, R. (ed)—Subaltern Studies (Vol II)

7. For details, see Simmons, C. P.—Recruiting and Organising an Industrial Labour Force in Colonial India : The case of the Coal Mining Industry, 1880-1939 (I. E. S. H. R., Vol. XIII, No. 4, Dec. 1976)

8. Ahmed, Kamruddin—Labour Movement in East Pakistan (Dacca, 1969) P. 25

9. Intelligence Branch, File No.—506/38 ; Reports dated 8.4, 9.4, and 4. 5. 38.

10. *Star of India*—15. 8. 38

11. Special Branch, Calcutta, File No. 516/38, Report dt. 15. 8. 38.

12. For details, see, Chattopadhyay, Gautam—The Almost Revolution, in S. C. Sarkar Felicitation Volume (Delhi, 1976)

13. *Amrita Bazar Patrika*—3. 9. 46 ; *Peoples' Age*—20. 10. 46

14. *Morning News*—15. 8. 46 ; *Azad*—15. 8. 46

15. Intelligence Branch—Review of the Revolutionary Matters by the D. I. G. I. B. dt. 5. 9. 46, 19. 12. 46.

16. *Morning News*—6. 1. 47.

17. Mitra, Sisir—A Public Facility, Its Management and the Workers, (New Delhi, 1980) P. 136.

18. Bogaert, Michael Van Den—Trade Unionism in Indian Ports : A Case—Study at Calcutta and Bombay, P. 29.

19. Ibid.

20. *Amrita Bazar Patrika*—13. 4. 47

21. Intelligence Branch, Bengal Police Abstract dt. 7. 9. 46

22. Intelligence Branch, Bengal Police Abstract dt. 19. 10. 46

23. Intelligence Branch, Bengal Police Abstract dt. 8. 2. 47

24. Dasgupta, Ranajit—Nationalist and Left Movements in Bengal : Jalpaiguri, 1905-47 (unpublished manuscript)

25. Bhowmick, Sarit—Origins of Trade Unionism among Tea Plantation Workers of Bengal (in Marxist Miscellany : No. 4, June 1976).

26. Dasgupta, Bimal—"Dooars Tebhaga Andolan : Krishak Sramiker Rakhi Bandhan in Bengali (Tebhaga Andolaner Rajat Jayanti, Cal, 1971) P. 105.

THE PROBLEM OF THE INTEGRATION OF COOCHBEHAR STATE WITH INDIAN UNION.

Dr. Ananda Gopal Ghosh
Department of History
North Bengal University.

I

The Primary objective of the present paper is to make a comprehensive study of the problem of Integration of Cooch-Behar State with the Indian Union. This small but strategically important native State of the North-East India created a serious problem to the newly born Independent Government of India. Though unofficially and personally Maharaja Jagaddipendra Narayan Bhup Bahadur agreed to join the Indian Union,[1] but officially he signed the Instrument of Accession (known as Merger Agreement) only after two years on 28th August, 1949.[2] Naturally, the first question which draws our attention is why was the Maharaja of CoochBehar killing so much times to sign the Instrument of Accession ? Was there any motive behind this delay ? Or were there any groups or sections in CoochBehar State who did not want integration with the Indian Union ? All these vital questions will be investigated in this paper.

II

Having an area of 1307 sq. miles and a population of 5,90,866, CoochBehar was smaller than many other native states of Northern and Western India. The State of CoochBehar earned a revenue of Rs. 22,20,000[3] and the Maharaja of CoochBehar was entitled to 13 gun salutes.[4] It is to be noted here that only 118 rulers of native states were entitled to gun salutes.[5] As a matter of fact the British Indian Government had classified the Indian States into two groups. The States like CoochBehar which belonged to group 'A' were honoured with gun salutes for their Maharajas.[6] When is 1921 the Chamber of princes was formed, CoochBehar became its member.

It is true that in size, area and population CoochBehar was a medium-sized native state like Bhopal and Jaipur. But owing to her close relations with the British Royal family since the time of Maharaja Nripendra Narayan, CoochBehar had been gaining much political importance in different ways. Maharani Sunity Devi, the wife of Maharaja Nripendra Narayan, was the first Indian Lady to obtain the title C. I. E. in 1887. Queen Victoria agreed to offer herself as the god-mother of prince Nityendra Narayan, the son of Maharaja Nripendra Narayan.[7] Because of this bond with Queen Empress the young prince was named Victor Nityendra Narayan. Maharaja Nripendra Narayan attended the Coronation ceremonies of Edward VII and George V in his capacity as A. D. C. to the King-Emperor. Out of 562 Indian states, the Maharaja of Patiala, Gwalior and Cooch-Behar achieved this rare distinction.[8] When the Constituent Assembly was formed in 1946, CoochBehar was represented by Himmat Singh Maheswari, the prime-Minister (Dewan) of the State.[9] On the eve of partition in India in 1947, 284 Royal Houses were allowed the privilege of privy purse. The Maharaja of CoochBehar was entitled to a privy purse amounting to Rs. 8 lakhs and 50 thousands.[10]

III

With the lapse of the British paramountcy on August 15, 1947, the relations of the newly born Independent Government of India with the native states was determined by the Stand still Agreement which meant the maintenance of status quo. The result was that except in matters of foreign policy, defence and communication the, Indian states rulers enjoyed the fullest autonomy over their internal administration like the pre-independence days.

In fact, the Stand still Agreement was a stop gap arrangement between the lapse of the British paramountcy and the Instrument of Accession. It is to be mentioned here that the Instrument of Accession also provided the same powers to the Indian states rulers. This extra-ordinary internal autonomy whetted the political ambition of some of the Indian states. In the name of internal autonomy, some states even indulged anti-India Unity conspiracy. This situation further deteriorated when Jinnha announced that Pakistan is ready to concede the demands of each state separately, not in a common way which India had done. CoochBehar was one such states which entangled herself with this type of Anti-India unity conspiracy.

IV

Initially, Maharaja Jagaddipendra Narayan was a supporter of Indian Unity. Even the Royal family of CoochBehar nourished the concept of Indian Unity. Maharani Gayatri Debi (Princess of CoochBehar) wrote "Ma, I remember, had always told us that India's future lay in all the small kingdoms merging their identity into one strong nation. Even as children in CoochBehar we had supported the idea of independence ......and we often shouted Congress slogans about a free and united India".[11] In a letter to Sardar Patel on 12th August, 1947, Maharaja wrote "The policy of fair play and sympathetic understanding which you have initiated towards the States is,......a very happy augury for the future of our Country. The ready respons that policy has evoked from a very large body of Rulers is proof of its signal success".[12] Maharaja also agreed in principle to accede to the India Union.[13]

In fact, the problem of Integration was really created by the members of the State Council, CoochBehar. In Cooch-Behar States administrative and political framework, the State Council enjoyed enormous powers. The Maharaja was a constitutional head of the State. All the powers of the State had been vested upon Maharaja-in-council since the administrative reforms of 1883. The State Council was dominated by the members of the Hitasadhani Sabha, a regional party. The Hitasadhani Sabha consisted of both the Hindu and Muslim Rajbanshi jotedars (Landlords.) It is interesting to note that ethnically, culturally and linguistically both the Hindus and Muslims (Rajbanshi) belonged to the same stock. The Hindu sections of this ethnic group are known as Rajbanshi Kshatriya. This Rajbanshi People enjoyed the benefit of the scheduled caste community. However, the Hitasadhani Sabha as a whole and particularly its Muslim members pro-Pakistani feelings created the problem of Integration.[14]

To understand the Hitasadhani's Muslim members role, we will study the demographic pattern of the CoochBehar State. In CoochBehar, there were 40% Muslims, 46% Rajbanshi Kshatriyas and the remaining were Caste Hindus and others.[15] The last category of people had come from the districts of East and South Bengal to CoochBehar in different times. The Hitasadhani Sabha called this people as 'Bhatias' which means outsiders,[16] However, though the Muslims were 40% of the total population of the state, they had occupied 50% of the State's higher services and 50% of the State's total land.[17] In the village social and economic life, the Muslims were very much influential. But what is strange enough is that there was no branch of the All India Muslim League in Cooch-Behar State. Some crities opined that the Hitasadhani Sabha acted as the counter-part of the Muslim League in Cooch-Behar State.[18] Some others compared the activities of the Hitasadhani's with the Rajakars of Hyderabad State.[19]

The origin of the Hitasadhani Sabha is still shrouded in obscurity. The exact date of its foundation is not known. The Government's documents are very scanty. But recently some writings have been published by the participants of the Merger Movement on the activities of the Hitasadhani Sabha.[20] They opined that the Hitasadhani Sabha was the brain-child of Nawab Khasru Jung of Hyderabad who was a personal Adviser of Maharani Indira Devi during 1922-1936.[21] They also opined that the British Resident at the Durbar of CoochBehar patronised the growth of the Hitasadhani Sabha. In fact, the British Government had some definite political objectives behind this patronisation. Firstly, they wanted to free CoochBehar from the influence of the Tebhaga Movement of the neighbouring districts of Bengal. The Land Holders' Association of CoochBehar was the Chief defender of the Hitasadhani Sabha. They became alarmed at the rapid growth of the Tebhaga Movement in the border area of the Cooch-Behar State which greatly fanned the peasant unrest in Mekhliganj and Haldibari, Secondly, in order to check the communists infiltration in CoochBehar State, the British Government also encouraged the foundation of the Hitasadhani Sabha.

The role of the Maharaja in the formation of the Hitasadhani Sabha is unknown. He, however, was a patron of the Hitasadhani Sabha. He addressed the meetings of the Hitasadhani Sabha.[22] A scion of the Royal family, Kumar Indra Jitendra Narayan also addressed the Hitasadhani Sabha's meeting at Mekhligaj.[23] Abbas-Uddin Ahmed, a leader of the Hitasadhani Sabha and an eminent international folk singer wrote in his memoirs that the Maharaja was sympathetic to the cause of the Hitasadhani Sabha.[24]

What were the objectives of the Hitasadhani Sabha ? Yet now we could not collect any precise information about this.

matter. It is known that the Hitasadhani Sabha started the movement with the slogan "Bhatia Hatao".[25] But what is interesting is that they considered the Bengalis of East and South Bengal as outsiders, not the other people i. e. the Marwaris. Abbas-Uddin Ahmed again remarked that the predominance of the outsiders or the Bhatias was the main reason behind the formation of the Hitasadhani Sabha.[26]

The outsiders have really enjoyed a predominant position in the higher services of the State. In fact, the conflict was between the CoochBeharis[27] (Original inhabitants) and Non-Cooch-Beharis (Outsiders). The Ministers of CoochBehar State who were also the Hitasadhani spokesmen, had introduced several communal and repressive measures against the Non-Cooch-Beharis in the field of service, education and land distribution.[28] Sir Akbar Hyderi, the Governor of Assam and in-charge of the CoochBehar State, wrote to Sardar Patel that there was a strong anti-Bengali feeling in the State.[29] This communal activities of the Ministers had vitiated the social atmosphere of the State. The Hitasadhani Sabha had also launched a political movement. The Muslim followers of the Hitasadhani Sabha wanted merger with Pakistan. A section of the members of the State Council, a clique exercising considerable influence, actively worked few the merger of the State with Pakistan. The Revenue Minister of CoochBehar State, Amanatullah Khan Chaudhury, who was a pro-Muslim League political figure and a Leader of the Hitasa-dhani Sabha and his Colleague Satish Chanda Singha Roy, the Education Minister of the State expressed in a meeting held at Mekhliganj that they wanted CoochBehar to remain indepen-dent of the Union of India.[30] They called for the destruction of the State Congress. They accused the State Congress as rebel.[31] Amanatullah Khan Choudhury, individually demanded plebiscite to solve the problem of integration.[32] Another official of the State namely Hakim Ahmmad Hossain, while serving as a S. D. O. of Mathabhanga delivered a speech on the occasion of a Muslim religious festival supporting the cause of merger of CoochBehar with Pakistan.[33] The Indian National Flag was dishonoured at Mathabhanga.[34] The CoochBehar State Government had also obstructed the celebrations of Independence day on 15th August 1947 at CoochBehar Organised by the Civil Liberties Committee.[35] Similar type of Independence Day Celebration was also held at Tufanganj. But the Organisers did only hoist the Indian National Flag. The CoochBehar State Government authorities had therefore arrested and subsequently externed the leader of the Celebration from the State.[36] This anti-Indian feelings of the members of the State Council and the Hitasadhani Sabha complicated the integration problem of CoochBehar State.

The political environment of the State was further complicated by the indifferent attitude of the Maharaja to this anti-Indian activities of his Ministers. It was argued that without his tacit approval it would not have been possible for his Ministers to make such assertive and clear-cut statements.[37] It was also alleged that the Maharaja had become a puppet into the hands of the members of the State Council and wanted to maintain the separate identity of CoochBehar State.[38]

VI

Barring the Hitasadhani Sabha, there was no organised political group at CoochBehar in the pre-independence days. Some Communists and Forward Block activists had been working there secretly since 1940's.[39] But they had no regular official party office there. In fact, the different political parties opened their office only after 1947. The Indian National Congress opened their branch at CoochBehar in 1947.[40] Even the foundation of the Praja Mandal (States peoples' conference) was a belated event. It was founded in July 1946 when the State Military Police had severely beaten some students and teachers of the Victoria College, CoochBehar.[41]

The Praja Mandal was a secular organisation. The President of the Praja Mandal was Umesh Chandra Mandal, a Gandhite Rajbanshi Pleader of the Dinhata Bar and the Secretary was Ramesh Roy, a C. P. I. Worker.[42] The Praja Mandal Leaders and followers actively supported the cause of joining with Indian Union. They cautioned the people about the dangerous communal politics of the Hitasadhani Sabha. They also tried to remove CoochBehari—Non-CoochBehari animosity. The Praja Mandal was very much aware of the anti-India activities of the Hitasadhani Sabha. In a membrandum dated July 26, 1948 addressed to Vallabhai Patel, the Vice-Premier of India, the Praja Mandal Samiti alleged that the Maharaja and his Pro-League Muslim Ministers as well as the Ministers who belonged to the scheduled caste were hobnobbing with Pakistan.[43] It has also been said that the Maharaja himself met Suhrawardy, the Prime Minister of Bengal and invited his opinion about the question of merger refering to the fact that his State was surrounded on three sides by territories of Pakistan.[44] Besides, the State authorities had forced the people to sign against merger with Indian Union.[45]

To draw the attention of the Government of India, some workers of the Praja Mandal convened a convention at Calcutta under the banner of CoochBehar Peoples' Association, Calcutta.[46] Because all such anti-Indian activities of the Hitasadhani Sabha, Members of the State Council and Ministers of Cooch-Behar States was a less known affairs to people outside CoochBehar. The Calcutta based daily news papers could not ventilate all these news of CoochBehar State.[47] Besides, there were some restrictions upon the press in CoochBehar State. There was no newspaper in CoochBehar State except the State financed "CoochBehar Darpan". These anti-Indian activities of the Hitasadhani Sabha was first published in the "Janamat" Patrika of Jalpaiguri.[48] Dr. Charu Chandra Sanyal, the Editor of the Journal was an eminent local Congress Leader and Physician. He sent all the copies of "Janamat" which carried news about CoochBehar to Sardar Patel through Dr. Bidhan Chandra Roy, the Chief Minister of West Bengal.[49]

VII

The political atmospher of CoochBehar State rapidly turned into a turmoiling condition. Nari Rustomji, Adviser to the Governor of Assam noted that pro-Pakistani element were very active in CoochBehar State.[50] The Governor of West Bengal, K. N. Katju also alleged that a plan was afoot to infiltrate huge number of Muslims into the State of CoochBehar thereby strengthening the cause of merger with Pakistan.[51] In a letter to Sardar Patel, Dr. Bidhan Chandra Roy, the Chief Minister of West Bengal wrote that the obnoxious developments of CoochBehar State will not only affect the security of West Bengal but also of the Indian Union.[52] Sardar Patel himself informed Jawaharlal Nehru that the Hitasadhani Sabha had sympathy for Pakistan.[53]

This topsy-turvy political development of CoochBehar State alarmed the Government of India. Meanwhile the Government had solved the integration problem of the major States of West and Southern India.

The Government now turned their attention to this troubled State in the North Eastern part of India.

It was after prolonged deliberation that the treaty of merger of CoochBehar with India was finally signed on August 28, 1949.[54] In accordance with the treaty, the Government of India took over the administration of CoochBehar on September 12, 1949 and placed it under a Chief Commissioner.[55]

The man who had played an important part behind this merger was, Maharaja Swai Man Singh II of Jaipur, the botherin-law of Maharaja Jagaddipendra Narayan. The role of Maharani Gayatri Devi was also significant. The contemporary high officials of the State opined that Swai Man Singh II and Gayatri Devi had tremendously influenced Maharja Jagaddipendra Narayan to accede to India.[56] Yet, I could not explore any primary documents about the role of Swai Man Singh II.

Thus ended the rule of the historic royal family of Cooch-Behar Sardar Patel highly appreciated the Maharaja's gesture and spirit and expressed his gratefulness to him.[57] Cooch-Behar was merged with the national stream of Indian Union and strengthened India's North East Frontier. Had Cooch-Behar acceded to Pakistan, the course of history of the North Eastern part of India might have been different ? Fortunately, that did not happen.

REFERENCES

1. Durga Das (ed.), Sardar Patels' Correspondence, Vol. 5, Letter No. 470, 17 August, 1947.
2. Asoke Mitra, District Census Hand Book, CoochBehar, 1951, P. I.
3. The CoochBehar gazetter for the year 1940, p. 3
4. Ibid, p. I
5. P. L. Chudgor, Indian princes under British Protection, p. 3
6. Ibid—Appendix. "A".
6a. Ibid.
7. Meredith Brothrick. Keshub Chunder Sen, p. 201
8. Larry Collins and Dominique Lapierre, Freedom at Midnight, p. 142.
9. Shibani Kinkar Chaube, Hill politics in North-East India, p. 78.
10. Durgadas Majumdar, West Bengal District Gazetteer—Cooch-Behar, p. 41.
11. Gayatri Devi and Santa Rama Rau, The Princess Remembers, p. 204.
12. Durga Das (ed.) Sardar Patels' op. cit. Letter No. 469, 12 August, 1947.
13. Ibid. Letter No. 470.
14. Personal Interview with Tarapada Chakraborty, Calcutta. He is 76 years old. An organiser of CoochBehar Peoples' Association.
15. Dr. Charu Chandra Sanyal (ed.), "Janamat" (A Bengali Weekly) 12th January, 1948, Jalpaiguri.
16. Personal Interview with Dr. Sib Shankar Mukherjee, CoochBehar. A Researcher and Writer.
17. Jiban Dey, Octoberer Aloke Alokita ; p. 133-134.
18. Personal Interview with Dr. Sib Shankar Mukherjee, CoochBehar.
19. Personal Interview with Sree Prabhat Kumar Basu, CoochBehar. An eminent student leader and political worker of CoochBehar and Jalpaiguri in the 50's.
20. Jiban Dey and Birendra Chandra Dey Sarkar's articles in different local journals.
21. Dewan Jarmani Das and Rakesh Bhan Das, Maharani, p. 80.
22. Personal Interview with Binit Kumar Mukherjee. He is a Secretary of CoochBehar Naba Bidhan Brahmo Samaj.
23. Personal Interview with Paritosh Datta, Calcutta. A former resident of Mekhliganj and was an Worker of I. P. T. A., Jalpaiguri.
24. Abbas-Uddin Ahmed, Amar Silpi Jibaner Katha, p. 118.

25. Personal Interview with Prof. Krishendu Dey, CoochBehar.

26. Abbas-Uddin, Op. cit. p. 118.

27. CoochBeharis included Rajbanshis, Muslims and Kamrupi Brahmans.

28. Durga Das (ed.) Sardar Patels' op. cit. Vol. 7, letter No. 461 ; Janamat, op. cit. 15th Kartick, 1355. B. S.

29. Ibid : Letter No. 459.

30. Janamat, op. cit. 31st Bhadra ; 1355, B. S.

31. Ibid.

32. Personal Interview with Dinesh Dakua, M. L. A. Mathabhanga. He was a member of the B. P. S. A. during 1948-50.

33. Janamat, op. cit 31st Bhadra, 1355 ; B. S.

34. Ibid.

35. Personal Interview with Sree Durga Kinkar Bhattacharya, Principal, Malda College. Formerly he was a lecturer of Victoria College, CoochBehar. He was externed from CoochBehar in August 1947.

36. Jiban Dey (ed.) Jhar-Tufan (A Bengali Fortnightly), 30th April, 1986, Tufanganj, CoochBehar.

37. Dr. B. P. Misra (ed.), North Bengal University Review, Vol. 7, Anticle ; Indian Nationalist Movement and the Maharajas of the CoochBehar State. By Ananda Gopal Ghosh and Malay Shankar Bhattacharya.

38. Banga Sahitya Sammilan, 1381, B. S. Article ; 'Upekshita Cooch-Behar Kitchu Katha''. Jiban Dey, p. 34 ; Hiren Mukherjee, India's Struggle for Freedom, p. 294.

39. Personal Interview with Jiban Dey, Tufanganj, CoochBehar. An Ex-M. L. A. of C. P. I. Founder Member of the Praja Mandal Samiti, CoochBehar.

40. Durga Das Majumder, op. cit. p. 199.

41. Personal Interview with Sree Pulakesh Dey Sarkar, Calcutta. He is 78 years old. He was the Secretary of the CoochBehar Peoples' Association.

42. Jhar-Tufan, op. cit.

43. Durgadas, (ed.) op. cit. Vol. 7 ; Letter No. 461, 26 July, 1948.

44. Abbas-Uddin, op. cit. p. 204.

45. Durgadas, (ed.) op. cit. Vol. 7 ; Letter No. 462, 4 August, 1948.

46. Personal Interview with Prof. Sauren Bhattacharya ; He was the Joint-Secretary of the CoochBehar Peoples' Association.

47. Personal Interview with Sree Sekhar Sarkar, Principal, Cooch-Behar College, CoochBehar.

48. Asoke Das Gupta et. el. (ed.) Uttardesh, January 1984 Article, CoochBeharer Bharat Bhukti Addolan : Ekti Bangla Saptahiker Bhumika—Dr. Ananda Gopal Ghosh.

49. Durgadas, (ed.) op. cit. Vol. 8, Letter No. 408, 13 April, 1949.

50. Nari Rustomji, Enchanted Frontiers—Sikkim, Bhutan and India, p. 88.

51. Durgadas, (ed.) op. cit. letter No. 464, 4 October, 1948.

52. Ibid Vol. 8, Letter No. 408.

53. Ibid Vol. 9, Letter No. 27, 28 December, 1949.

54. Asoke Mitra, op. cit. P. I.

55. V. P. Menon, The Story of Integration of the Indian States, p. 294.

56. Dr. Sib Shankar Mukherjee has heard it from Late Bimal Ghosh, A. D. C. of the Maharaja and Late Asnuman Dasgupta, Accountant of Royal Household. And I heard it from Dr. Mukherjee.

57. Durgadas, (ed.) op. cit. Vol. 7 Letter No. 463, 11 september, 1949.

* I finish my paper by expressing my gratitude to those who have helped me in preparing it. In this conection I specially mention the names of profesor D. P. Sinha, Smt. Ratna Roy, Sree Kamalesh Das and Sree Malay Shankar Bhattacharya.

THE POLITICAL INTEGRATION OF THE KHASI STATES INTO THE INDIAN UNION

Dr. D. R. Syiemlieh
Lecturer Department of History
North-Eastern Hill University
Shillong 793014

I

Much has been written on the integration of Indian states into the Indian Union. However, the process of integrating Manipur, Tripura and the twenty-five Khasi states has hardly caught the attention of researchers, despite the new geographical situation in which these states were located from mid 1947 with many of them abutting on East Pakistan (now Bangladesh). This was a concern for the Indian authorities then, who saw that their integration should be with India and not Pakistan and that the states should not be permitted to exist as islands between the two new Dominions. There appears to be a tendency among historians and social scientists to overlook developments in the north-east as not significant enough to warrant attention, or they see little in the region that fits into the mosaic of a broader Indian ethos. This state of things is clearly reflected in the near total omission of the political integration of the states mentioned into India. Their 'story' is as interesting as is the 'story' of the integration of other Indian states. For want of time and space this paper will relate to the Khasi states alone, thereby giving an account of a little known episode in contemporary history.

II

The transfer of power from Britain to the Dominions of India and Pakistan was laid in the Cabinet Mission Plan of 16 May 1946 in which the Cabinet Mission and the Viceroy, in consultation with the British Government issued a statement embodying their suggestions and recommendations towards a solution of the Indian political question. The most important constitutional issue then was to determine the position and future of the 550 odd Indian states. Referring to these states the Cabinet Mission said that with the attainment of independence by British India the relationship which had existed between the states and the British Crown would no longer be possible, though it was expected of the states to co-operate with the new governments in building up a new constitutional structure.[1] The position of the states was further elucidated by the Cabinet Mission in its Memorandum on State's Treaties and Paramountcy of 22 May 1946. The Memorandum stated that with the transfer of power His Majesty's Government would cease to exercise paramountcy. This meant that the rights of the states in relationship with the Crown would no longer exist and that all rights surrendered by the states to the paramount power would return to the states. The void that would arise from the lapse of political arrangements between the states and the Crown was to be filled in either with the states entering into federal relationship with the succeeding governments or enter into political arrangements with or without them. States were, therefore, free to associate with one or the other Dominions, to federate among themselves or to stand alone. The British Government emphatically stated that it would not put the slightest pressure or influence in deciding which Dominion the states should accede to.[2] Realizing that the states would find it difficult to exist independently, the Secretary of State for India underscored the importance of states to find their appropriate place within one or the other of the two new Dominions.[8]

On 15 August 1947 British rule in India ended and erstwhile British India was partitioned into independent India and Pakistan. Earlier an Interim Government was sworn in on 2 September 1946 and this body was to fill in the time gap pending the framing of a new constitution for India. The responsibility of negotiating with the states to accede into India was entrusted to the States Department of this Government. To remove all possible fear and suspicions in the minds of the Indian rulers, Sardar Vallabhbhai Patel who headed this Department issued a statement underlying the paramount necessity of maintaining the unity of the country by the states joining the Indian Union for defence, foreign affairs and communication. He admitted "it is an accident that some live in the States and some in British India." Although with the transfer of power, paramountcy would lapse, he urged that it was in the interest of India and the Indian states that the working of the treaties and agreements entered by the states with the British Government should continue to operate until new agreements were made.[4]

III

In their relations with the Khasi states the British recognized twenty-five states categorised as semi-independent and dependent states. These states had from the third decade of the nineteenth century entered into relations with the East India Company and the Crown's Government of India through *sanads*, engagements and *parwanas* which clearly laid down the principles of relations between the two parties. Juxtaposed to and interspersed with these states were thirty-five Khasi villages that had either been annexed by the British after the Anglo-Khasi war of 1829-1833 or by Khasi villages voluntarily becoming British areas.

With the Jaintia Hills that had been annexed in 1835, these villages formed the Khasi and Jaintia Hills District, the Deputy Commissioner of which held the dual function of Political Officer in relation to the Khasi states. The Government had before the turn of the century established its control over the states, demanding a share of their natural resources, intervening in their internal affairs over questions of maladministration, disputed succession and having criminal cases in the states tried in the district court. It was not too difficult for one officer to perform this added function because the Khasi states were small. Malaisohmat covered only one village, Khyrim the largest of the states had a population in the 1870s of a little over 20,000.

Only in the 1920s did political activity start in the Khasi Hills. The Khasi chiefs—*Syiems*, *Lyngdohs*, *Wahahdadars* and *Sirdars* influenced by the growing political consciousness in the British areas, and encouraged by official circles, established the Federation of Khasi States in 1934.[5] The hope that the Indian princely states would cooperate in the proposed Federation envisaged in the Government of India Act 1935 and the failure of this plan must have in a way resulted in the Khasi states, like many other Indian states, losing the political momentum that had aroused an interest in their future. The offer of transfer of power to India and Pakistan once again aroused the interest of the Khasi chiefs who revived the Federation, with which, the Indian Dominion had to negotiate for their integration into independent India.

Even as early as April 1945 it was reported that the tribal people were beginning to take a more vocal interest in their own future. A meeting in Shillong which contained most of the more prominent men opposed emphatically their inclusion in either Pakistan or India.[6] But the future of these hills was not to be decided at that point of time by this body but by the Khasi chiefs. Sometime in July 1947 an agreement was reached between the states and Sir Akbar Hydari, the Governor of Assam on the three terms that Patel had asked the states to accept.[7] On 9 August the Khasi states signed the Standstill Agreement. They agreed that with effect from 15 August 1947 all existing arrangements between the Province of Assam and the Indian Dominion on the one hand and the Khasi states on the other should continue to be in force for a period of two years or until new or modified arrangements should be arrived at between the authorities concerned. The agreement was subject to certain exceptions which gave the federated states judicial, administrative, legislative and revenue powers. It was also agreed that all Khasi (British) villages in the district which decided to rejoin states of which they formerly formed a part should be allowed to do so.[8]

The Government of India found a problem when it came to the question of getting the Khasi states to sign the Instrument of Accession. On 2 December that year Hydari informed the Khasi chiefs that he had brought with him from Delhi the Instrument of Accession and that they should sign it. It was accordingly agreed that all the twenty-five chiefs should assemble at the Governor's residence in Shillong on 15 December and individually sign the Instrument. Twenty chiefs signed the Instrument that day, among the remaining five states the chiefs of three were ill and would sign at home, while two refused to sign, it being assumed that summons had not reached them.[9] Hydari reported to Patel :[10]

> That various underhand forces had been at work between 2 December and 15 December is shown by the fact that this morning's proceedings seemed likely to break ; for, three of the principal Siems ; i. e. those of Mylliem, of Khyrim and of Cherra... refused to sign and wanted more time "to consult their people." I made them realise what the conse-

quences of not signing would be, and after nearly an hour's confabulation among themselves they signed. The rest was easy.

Generally the Khasi states had no desire to join Pakistan. The *Syiem* of Cherra did flirt with the local authorities in Sylhet before signing the Instrument of Accession but was warned by Hydari against playing that game. The *Syiem* was attached to Pakistan for the simple reason that some part of his personal land lay in Sylhet. Hydari had exerted his authority during these negotiations by intimidating the chiefs that the fact of mere accession was not a guarantee of a particular person continuing as a chief and that if there was substantial amount of feeling in a particular state that its chief was not doing his duty, he would have an enquiry conducted by the Deputy Commissioner. If it was found that allegations against a chief were true fresh elections would be ordered. This undertaking by the Governor reconciled the people of the Khasi states at large to accepting the Instrument of Accession. The statement annoyed the chiefs who found their tenure thereby insecure. The Federation considered it as a diminution of their influence.[11]

Among the states that had not signed the Instrument of Accession in December, Nobosohphoh and Nongspung states signed on their own accord on 11 January 1948 followed by Mawlong on 10 March 1948.[12] There remained Rambrai and Nongstoin which procrastinated. Hydari then sent G.P. Jarman, the Deputy Commissioner/Dominion Agent and his Assistant, R.T. Rymbai, one of the few Khasi civil servants, to these states with instructions that failure to sign the Instrument would be followed by pressure of various kinds and in the last resort to deposition.[13] At one time it looked as if Jarman might encounter armed opposition from Nongstoin and so a platoon of the Assam Rifles was sent into the state "whose presence and Jarman's tact did the trick."[14] The *Syiem* signed on 19 March

1948. Rambrai had signed two days earlier.[15] Hydari who felt that the policy should be one of conciliation and patient adjustment of difficulties is said to have told Rymbari before the Assistant Dominion Agent left for Nongstoin "Let Junagadh not be repeated."[16] Behind a tough exterior Hydari had a concern that there should be no violence in the integration process.

More material is now available about how Nongstoin acceded into India. R. W. Selby, the British High Commissioner to India had come across a curious reference in the *Sunday Statesman* of 28 March 1948 to an alleged appeal by the *Syiem* to the United Nations Organization Security Council against the unlawful aggression of the Indian Government into his state. The *Syiem* was also understood to have sent a note to Jawaharlal Nehru requesting the withdrawal of Indian troops "in order to avoid further complications." Wickliffe, the *Syiem's* nephew and likely successor to the *Syiemship* who disclosed this was then preparing to leave for Lake. Success to take the matter with the United Nations Organization.[17] Selby's enquiries made in official quarters confirmed that the *Syiem* had in fact sent a letter to Nehru. There was however no reference in the *Syiem's* letter to an appeal to the United Nations Organisation.[18] Further enquires revealed that on the day the *Syiem* signed the Instrument of Accession certain parties, official reports say, were sending out false telegraphic reports to the effect that the Government had sent military forces into the state and that the chief had appealed to the U. N. O.[19] That Nongstoin and Rambrai were pressurised into acceding into India there is no doubt. The appeal to the world body and its reaction must still be verified. Wickliffe does not appear to have gone to the U. N. O. to take up the case. It is believed that Wickliffe soon after the Instrument of Accession was signed by his uncle crossed the new border. He remains till this day in Sylhet district of Bangladesh.

The Khasi states had acceded into India but refused to merge[20] on the ground that the chiefs were elected heads of their respective states. Their refusal caused Patel to visit Shillong on 1-2 January 1948. His meeting with the chiefs ended in a stalemate over the merger issue, for the Khasis said that only a duly constituted *durbar* of the states could decide on such an issue.[21] Accordingly rules were drawn up by the Dominion Agent for the nomination and election of members to the Khasi States Constitution Making Durbar.[22] This took almost sixteen months. The Durbar was inaugurated on 29 April 1949.

While the Khasi States Constitution Making Durbar had just been convened the Indian Constituent Assembly was preparing its final draft of the Constitution. J. J. M. Nichols-Roy who was a member of both the Constituent Assembly and the Khasi States Constitution Making Durbar and a minister in the Assam Government urged the members of the latter to accept the broad framework of the Sixth Schedule of the Constitution. The Schedule was the product of the North East Frontier (Assam) Tribal and Excluded Areas Sub-Committee headed by Gopinath Bordoloi, the Assam Prime Minister. Its report submitted to the Constituent Assembly on 28 July 1947 pointed out that the Khasi states had comparativey little revenue or authority and seemed to depend for a good deal of support on the Political Officer in their relations with their people. It believed that there was a strong desire among people of the states to "federate" with the people of nonstate villages. It was also noted that some of the *Syiems* favoured amalgamation but their idea of the Federation differed from that of the people in that the chiefs sought greater power for themselves than what the people were prepared to concede to them.[23] By then factionalism had raised its head in the Khasi Hills with two political bodies viewing with each other to voice the demands of the people.

The Federation we have already noted. The more popular body was Nichols-Roy's Khasi-Jaintia Federated State National Conference. By then Nichols-Roy was much disliked by the chiefs for the official stand he was taking.

Matters came to a head over the question of the future administrative arrangement for the Khasi and Jaintia Hills. On 21 July 1949, Dr. Homiwell Lyngdoh, the Chairman of the Durbar read Nichols-Roy's resolution which suggested the formation of an autonomous unit of the Khasi and Jaintia Hills within Assam province. This was followed by the *Syiem* of Jirang's amendment demanding one united administration for the Khasi and Jaintia Hills outside Assam, provision for which was possible under the terms of the Instrument of Accession and the draft Constitution of India. Though Nichols-Roy and his supporters had a majority of members in the Durbar, the vote over the resolution and its amendment went with a 40-46 victory for the chiefs. At this Nichols-Roy and his 39 supporters walked out of the proceedings of the Durbar. The remaining members then elected a sixteen member Negotiating Committee which sent a resolution to the Drafting Committee of the Constituent Assembly for a reconsideration of the future status of the Khasi states and non-state villages.[24]

The twenty-five Khasi states were too small, even collectively to get a representation in the Constituent Assembly. The eminent anthropologist, G.S. Guha was made the representative of the Khasi states, Tripura and Manipur. The Khasi chiefs suffered two disadvantages. Guha does not appear to have said anything on their behalf ; Nichols-Roy did all he could in the Constituent Assembly to undo the defeat he had suffered in the Durbar. On 7 September a resolution was adopted in the Assembly creating the United Khasi-Jaintia Hills District comprising the territories which before the commencement of the

Constitution were known as the Khasi states and non-state areas.[25] There was still no mention in this third reading of the draft Constitution of whether the district would form part of Assam. Nichols-Roy was particularly happy that the Khasi states had been incorporated in the Sixth Schedule for it would enable the same people (apart from being a personal triumph) to have one adminstration for the two types of areas.[26]

Oddly enough it was Mohammad Saadulla one of Assam's earlier premiers who pointed out an anomaly over what had been accepted. "Sir", he addressed the Chairman of the Assembly,[27]

> the Khasi Hills have been relegated to the Sixth Schedule for which Rev. Niclols-Roy is very thankful, but there is a constitutional anomaly. Although the Constituent Assembly is not to find a remedy for that, yet I must sound a note of warning that this small district of Khasi Hills embrace 25 Native States most of which had treaty rights with the suzereign power in Delhi. They were asked to join the Indian Dominion in 1947. Instruments of Accession accompanied by an Agreement were executed by these Chiefs and they were accepted by the Central Goverment. But even though this area has been included in the Sixth Schedule, up till now no agreement or settletment has been arrived at between the Constituent Assembly of the Federation of the Khasi States and the Assam Government or the Government of India.

Saadulla added that Olim Singh, President of the Federation of Khasi States had led a delegation early in November to press their grievances before the States Ministry and the Drafting Committee, but "they are late in the day" he said, "and nothing can be done at the third reading".[28] The Draft Constitution was adopted on 26 November 1949 and the Assembly was adjourned till 26 January 1950.

A year earlier an interesting suit was filed in the Federal Court of India by Sati Raja, *Syiem* of Mylliem, against the Dominion of India and the Assam Government. Carefully worded the case reviewed the developments between Mylliem state and the Indian Dominion since the Standstill Agreement and the arbitrary manner of the Assam and Indian Governments in continuing to exercise the rights, privileges and jurisdictions that the former Government had exercised. Among others, the *Syiem* wanted a declaration that his state had recovered or was entitled to recover sovereign rights, power, functions and jurisdiction over his state.[29] This must have been quite an embarrassment for the Governments of India and Assam. Sri Prakasa, the Governor of Assam meeting Sati Raja and others on 31 December 1949 was able to make the *Syiem* withdraw his case.[30]

Something of the irregular manner of administering the Khasi Hills that the *Syiem* of Mylliem had sought clarification in his suit may now be explained. On 15 August 1947 the Governor-General issued a Provisional Constitutional Order abolishing all references to "tribal areas" and the distinction between "India" and British India. This was followed on 27 August by the Extra-Provincial Jurisdiction Ordinance re-establishing retrospectively the severed links which resulted from the first order. Two notifications were issued under this Ordinance. The first promulgated the Assam Tribal Area Order, 1947, confirming and giving effect to every instrument that is, every notification, order, bye-law, rule, regulation or directive made or issued under Section 313 of the Government of India Act, 1935. The second notification authorized the

Assam Governor to continue to discharge his former functions in or in relation to the tribal areas in Assam as the Agent of the Governor-General,[31] Under provisions of the Extra-Provincial Jurisdiction Order, 1947, a special notification, the Khasi States Federation (Administration of Justice) Order, 1948 was made applicable from 1 July. This notification defined the civil and criminal powers allocated to the Federation of Khasi States and the Khasi States under the supervision of the Assam High Court.[32] A Khasi Federation Court and Executive began exercising the judicial and executive functions formerly vested in the Deputy Commissioner, who however remained in that capacity and as Dominion Agent.

This arrangement continued till the end of 1949. One may surmise that very little control was actually transfered to the chiefs and their courts because their future hung on a balance. More surprise was in store for the Federation and its chiefs. One day before the Constitution of India was adopted the Governor of Assam passed an order cancelling the Khasi States Federation (Administration of Justice) Order, 1948 and its supplement of the same year. The Khasi States (Administration of Justice) Order, 1950 which came into force on 25 January 1950 entrusted civil and criminal justice to the Deputy Commissioner, Khasi and Jaintia Hills District, his Assitants and the Courts of the *Syiems*, *Sirdars*, *Lyngdohs* and *Wahadadars* in a manner similar to the pattern that existed during British administration. That same day another notification was issued changing the designations of the Dominion Agent, Additional Dominion Agent and the Assistant to the Dominion Agent and the Court of the Khasi States Federation as referring respectively to the Deputy Commissioner, Additional Deputy Commissioner, Assistant to the Deputy Commissioner and the Court of the Deputy Commissioner, United Khasi and Jaintia Hills District.[33] All this was done without taking the Khasi Chiefs into confidence.

Apparently this was done to suit the Constitution, for Part A of the First Schedule of the Constitution read that the territory of the State of Assam "shall comprise territories which immediately before the commencement of this Constitution were comprised in the Province of Assam, the Khasi States and the Assam Tribal Areas. "Thus the Khasi states became part of Assam without any agreement of merger and disregarding the provisions of the Standstill Agreement. It was in the Constitution of India, in the drafting of which the chiefs played no part, that the integration of the Khasi states into India was made complete. The final process may have been done arbitrarily, but this was only possible because of the divergent views among the Khasis, their indecision to merge and the inordinate delay in working out an arrangement.

REFERENCES

1. N. Mansergh (ed), *The Transfer of Power 1942-1947*, Vol. VII, (N. Delhi, 1978) No. 303, p. 586.

2. *Ibid.*, No. 262, pp. 522-524.

3. B. S Rao (ed), *The Framing of India's Constitution*, Vol. I, (N. Delhi, 1968), p. 534.

4. S. L. Poplai (ed), *India 1947-1950 : Select Documents on Asian Affairs*, Vol. I (Bombay, 1959) No. 39, p. 170.

5. K. Cantlie, *Notes on Khasi Law*, (Reprint, Shillong, n. d.), pp. 176-186 ; H. Bareh, *The History and Culture of t e Khasi People*, (Calcutta, 1967), p. 235.

6. Mansergh, *op. cit.*, Vol. V, (London, 1974), No. 397, p. 912.

7. D. Das (ed), *Sardar Patel' Correspondence*, Vol. V (Ahmedabad 1973) No. 43, pp. 42-43.

8. LL. D. Basan, *The Khasi States under the Indian Union*, (Shillong, 1948), pp. 1-3.

9. Das, *op. cit.*, pp. 42-44. These five states were Nobosohphoh, Nongspung, Mawlong, Rambrai and Nongstoin.

10. *Ibid.*, p. 43.

11. Das, *op. cit.* Vol. VI (Ahmedabad, 1973), No. 74, pp. 101-103.

12. Poplai, *op. cit.*, No 55, p. 236 ; *White Paper on Indian States* (N. Delhi, 1950), p. 216.

13. Das, *op. cit.* Vol. VI, No. 74. p. 103.

14. *Ibid.*, No. 76, p. 105 ; Das, *op. cit.*, Vol. VI, No. 76, p. 105.

15. *White Paper on Indian States*, p. 216 ; Poplai, *op. cit.*, p. 236.

16. Das., *op.*, *cit.*, Vol. VI, No. 74, p. 103 ; Interview with R. T. Rymbai, 8 July 1979.

17. India Office Records, London, L/P&J/7-106 35, R. W. Selby to H. A. F. Rumbold, 13 April, 1948 ; *The Statesman*, 28 March 1948. Khasi *Syiemship* is not hereditary in the strict sense. It usually passes from *Syiem* to nephew.

18. *Ibid.*

19. *Ibid.* Selby to Rumbold, 10 May 1948. V. P. Menon, Secretary of the States Department gave the impression to Selby that he considered the whole affair as having no importance at all. The Governor-General accepted these Instruments of Accession on 17 August 1948. I. O. L. London, L/P & J/7-106 35, Selby to Rumbold, 10 May 1948 ; *White Paper on Indian States*, p. 216.

20. Poplai, *op. cit.*, p. 266, shows that 15 Khasi states with an area of 3788 square miles and a population of 213,000 (what was the fate of the remaining ten states since all 25 states had eventually signed the Instrument of Accession ?) had merged with Assam. This is an incorrect statement as there was no merger among the Khasi states, nor was there any merger with Assam.

21. Bareh, *op. cit.*, p. 241.

22. Basan, *op. cit.*, pp. 29-35.

23. Rao, *op. cit.*, Vol. III, (N. Delhi, 1969), p. 68?.

24. L. G. Shullai, *Ki Hima Khasi*, (Shillong, 1975), pp. 11-13.

25. *Constituent Assembly Debates*, Vol. IX (Reprint N. Delhi, 1967), p. 1008.

26. *Ibid.*, p. 1009.

27. *Ibid.*, Vol. XI (Reprint, N. Delhi, 1967), p. 735.

28. *Ibid.*

29. Case No. V. of 1949 in the Federal Court of India, N. Delhi.

30. L. G. Shullai, *Ka Ri Shong Pdeng Pyrthei* (Shillong, 1979), p. 15.

31. S. Chaube, *Hill Politics in North-Eash India*, (Calcutta, 197?.), pp. 80-81 ; J. N. Choudhury, *The Khasi Canvas* (Shillong, 1978), pp. 362-363.

32. Basan, *op. cit.*, pp. 12-28. On 4 October 1948 the Ministry of States issued a Supplemental Notification to the Khasi States Federation (Administration of Justice) Order, 1948.

33. Shullai, *Ki Hima Khasi*, pp. 27-36.

NATIONAL INTEGRATION AND THE UNION TERRITORY OF PONDICHERRY : A CASE STUDY

Dr. E. DIVIEN, M. A., M. Litt., Ph. D.,
Reader
Department of Indian History
University of Madras.
Madras-600 005

History makes men wise and the truth of History is that 'No Man is an island and everyman is a part of the mainland. In today's India this truth is forgotten and people think interms of State, District, Taluk, Panchayat Union politically and caste, creed, colour, religion and community socially. Historically India has often been described as an ethnological museum, in which number of races of man kind may be studied.

Unity in Diversity :

A correct reading of History, particularly the cultural history of India will prove that despite the differences in race, language, arts, religious and crafts, there runs a deep thread of unity, as the undercurrent of an ocean. Herbert Risely observes : 'Beneath the manifold diversity of physical and social type, language custom and religion, which strikes the observer in India, there can still be discerned a certain underlying uniformity of life from the Himalayas to cape comorin.'

Superficial observers of India, used to standadisation and dull uniformity, are likely to be impressed very much by the variety and diversity and men the unity of India. Vincent Anthur Smith in his Oxford History of India, rightly points out that "India beyond all doubt possesses a deep underlying funda-

mental unity, far more profound either by geographical isolation
on by physical suzerainty. That unity transcends the innumerable
diversities of blood, colour, language, dress, manners and sect."

India had never been a 'geographical expression.' India has
total geographical unity. References to the North and the South
as distinct units goes to show the mis-understanding of the
history of India.

Religious unity forms the very soul of Indian history. India
is a land of many religious. Temples, mosques, churches syna-
gogues viharas, and mantaps lie scattered throughout the length
and breadth of India. We find many of them in the same street
in several parts of the country. But when political considerations
interfere it results in religious animosities filled with hatred and
violence.

A South Tamil Poem runs thus—
    'Into the bosom of one Great Sea
    Flow all streams that came from Hills on every side
    Their names are various, as their springs
    And thus in every land do men bow down,
    To one, Great God ; There is no God but He.
    O, Lord—The Christ way
    La Illahi Illalah—The Muslim way
    Our Brahmam—The Hindu way.

Thus above the clouds, the sky is clear but the clouds below
provide a different vision to the physical eye—not to the inward
eye.

The people of India have had a fairly long common history,
they inhabit a compact territory, and under British imperialism
as well as after independence they have had a common economic

life. But the Indian people do not have a common language on a common culture. On the other hand, there are in India a number of peoples inhabiting compact territories, speaking a common language and having a common culture, a common psychological make-up and economic life. They comprise the various nationalities of India, many of whom today are organised in linguistic states of their own within the Indian union.

The Indian people may, therefore, be said to consist of a group of developed nationalities and certain tribes in various stages of development, some of them aspiring to have states of their own. To stop short at this point, however, would be giving a very incomplete and unreal picture. The Indian people are not merely a group of nationalities just as, say, the African people comprise a group of nationalities or the European people can also be said to form a group of nations.

It has to be noticed that as far as the Indian people are concered there is a for greater sense of unity, a far deeper sense of oneness, many more common bonds than exist of the whole process of historical, political and economic development that has taken place in India. Beginning from ancient times there has been this feeling of unity in India.

The most important factor cementing the unity of the Indian people was the two century long common struggle against British imperialism. This struggle began the moment the British set foot an Indian soil. The revolt of 1857, the numerous peasant revolts such as the Moplah revolt in ralabar, the national movement led by the congress, the heroic struggle of revolutionary young men called 'terrosists' by the British, the mass movements of the peasantry and the working class, the naval revolt and other army revolts, all combined to the British finally from the Indian soil.

This long struggle gave all Indians a feeling of being one great people, instilled a common Indian patriot that continues till this day.

Moreover, the development of a common economic life, the introduction of capitalism into India by the British, and after independence the further development of a common Indian market and the further strengthening of capitalism at a pace too slow for our needs but rapid as compared to the British rule, brought into being economic bonds and ties and helped to swell the rising tide of nationalism.

Thus the Indian people have developed a common Indian patriotism and a feeling of Indian unity not withstanding their differences of language and culture.

This is perhaps a speculior development to which an exact parallel would be difficult to find elsewhere. Something resembling it might be found in the Soviet Union of today where now, after several decades of a common struggle against imperialist intervention and fascist invaders and in the course of the unified endeavour of all the various nationalities of the Soviet Union to build a socialist society, the various Soviet nationalities, vastly different from one another, have nevertheless developed a common feeling of Soviet patriotism that is to be found amongst the Tajiks, Uzbeks, the Ukranians, the Russians, and so on for all the nationalities in the Soviet Union.

A parallel may also be found in the example of Switzerland where a feeling of being Swiss exists amongst the different nationalities of Switzerland. The same could probably be said also of Yugoslavia, Czechoslovakia, etc., countries with different nationalities where at the same time a sense of being one people with common ties has developed through various historical and other factors.

If we ignore on slur over one on the other facet of this dual reality we are likely to go wrong. Unity in diversity, that is how the problem of India has been described. The diversity has to be borne in mind and a correct attitude towards this has to be evolved if we wish to maintain and strengthen the bonds of unity.

Having determined the general line of approach let us now try to address ourselves to each of the problems that face. The aim of this paper is to make a comparative study between the British and French rule in India and the situations prevalent in the Union Territory of Pondicherry and in the rest of India.

Union Territory of Pondicherry

The Union Territory of Pondicherry constituted out of the four erstwhile French establishments of Pondicherry, Karaikal, Mahe and Yanam (excluding Chandernagore) is not merely a creation of the Seventh Amendment of the Indian Constitution, but an outcome of a three—hundred year long history.

Pondicherry and Karaikal regions are embedded respectively in the South Arcot and Thanjavur Districts of Tamil Nadu. Yanam is a small area encircled by the East Godavari District of Andhra Pradesh. Mahe region is enclaved within the confines of the Cannanore District of Kerala. Chandernagore merged with the Union of India in 1949 and is now part of West Bengal. While Pondicherry, 162 km south of Madras and 22 km north of Cuddalore is the Territorial headquarters, Karaikal, Mahe and Yanam are the regional headquarters of the respective regions-Karaikal lies about 150 km down south and Yanam about 840 km north-east of Pondicherry on the eastern coast of the Indian Peninsula. Mahe lies almost parallel to Pondicherry 653 km away on the West Coast.[2]

The French first established their 'loge' in Pondicherry in 1974. In 1963, it was captured by the Dutch but restored in 1699 following the Treaty of Ryswick. As for Karaikal, the tussle between the native rulers and the English continued from 1739-1817. The French took final control of the region on 14 January 1817. Regarding, Mahe, this region come under the complete control of the French on 22 January 1817. As for Yanam, like all other French Yanam too fell thrice into the hands of the British. After the Napoleonic wars, Yanam was finally returned to the French early in 1817.[3]

The destiny of the French settlement of Chandernagore is unique in the annals of colonialism in India.

In a referendum held on 19 June 1949 the people of Chander nagore (99%) voted for merger with India. On August 1949 on the eve of the second anniversary of India's independence. France agreed to transfer Chandernagore to the Indian Union. The 'de facto' transfer of Chandernagore took place on 2nd May 1950. On 2 February 1951 the Indo-French Treaty for the cession of Chandernagore to India was signed in Paris and an Indian Administrator was appointed to take charge of the town on 2 February 1951. Under the Chandernagore merged with West Bengal and was declared the headquarters of a subdivision of Hooghly District with effect from 2 October 1954.

The reasons for the swift merger of Chandernagore with West Bengal are mainly due to the fervent sense of patriotism of the people of Chandernagore and also due to the influence of the nationalist leaders of West Bengal.

Communalism

That the communal problem or Hindu-Muslim antagonism was a creation of the British rulers is now a commonly accepted fact. However, in French India we had no such problem either during the French rule or after the merger of the settlements with the Indian Union on 1 July 1954. The total population of the Pondicherry Union Territory as per the 1971 census is 4,71,707. Hindus from the largest religious community in the Territory. In all, 84.32 percent of the Territory's population belong to the Hindu religion. The percentage of Hindus varies from region to region i.e., **94.74** per cent in Yanam, 87.70 percent in Pondicherry, 75.37 percent in Karaikal and 74.31 percent, in Mahe. Yanam records the highest and Mahe the lowest. At the Territorial level Hindus account for 89.57 percent in the rural areas. Region-wise, Pondicherry has the highest percentage of Hindus in the rural sector with 92.23 percent and Mahe has the lowest percentage with 77.29 percent. In urban areas Hindus constitute 67.83 percent of the total population. This varies from 94.74 percent in Yanam to 54.38 percent in Karaikal region.[5] This difference between the rural and urban percentages indicates the consomopolitan nature of the urban population, persons belonging to different religious communities living together as contrasted with a single religious community predominating the rural areas.

The Caste Complex

It cannot be denied that there were caste disputes even under the French rule, but this can in no way be compared to what prevailed in British India. Of late, in the Union Territory the caste feelings have come to surface. The reasons for this being the role of the political parties who far up these sentiments.

Linguism

In the Union Territory of Pondicherry, the following languages are spoken—Tamil, Telugu, Malayalam and French.

The percentage of people speaking Tamil is the largest, since this comprises the areas of Pondicherry and Karaikal. Telugu is spoken in Yanam, and Malayam in Mahe. One should appreciate the fact, that none of these areas in the Union Territory of Pondicherry have clamoured for merger with the respective contiguous linguistic states.

In the real of education besides the respective regional languages, English and French is also taught. Recruitment to Government Services is not based on the 'sons of the soil' principle.

CONCLUSION

Having stated the above mentioned facts are tends to opine that in the Union Territory of Pondicherry a sense of national integration does prevail. The question arises as to why this small territory did not have recourse to fissifarous tendencies. Perhaps this can be explained away by the influence of the French system of administration, the system of education and above all the results of the culture contacts which the people of the French settlements had enjoyed.

REFERENCES

1. V. A. Smith—Oxford History of India, OUP 1958
2. Gazetteer of India—Union Territory of Pondicherry—Vol. I, p. 1. 1982.
3. Ibid.,—p. 86.
4. Ibid.,—p. 10.
5. Ibid.,—p. 329.

INDIGENOUS ROOTS OF THE CURRENT PANJAB PROBLEM :
A Case Study in National Integration

Dr. B. B. Srivastava
(Sagar University)

The present agitation in the Panjab by the Sikhs demanding religious concessions and greater political autonomy is a covert movement for a Sikh state. The latter is intimately related to Sikh resistance to being absorbed by Hinduism. The story of the twin processes of Sikh homogenity and its protest to aggressive Hinduism is an account of the present complexities in the Panjab and presents an interesting illustration in dimensions of national integration in modern India.

The Sikh religion was born in the latter half of the fifteenth century with Guru Nanak initiating a religious movement emphasising what was common between Hinduism and Islam and preaching the unity of these two faiths. By the beginning of the seventeenth century it crystallised into a religious body consisting of the disciples or Sikhas of Nanak and the Gurus who followed him. Its tenets found expression in the anthology of their sacred writings, the 'Adi Granth', comprising the writings of the Sikh Gurus as well as of Hindu and Muslim saints. The next hundred years saw the growth of a political movement alongside the religious, culminating in the call to arms by the last Guru, Gobind Singh. Within a few years after the death of Gobind Singh, the peasants made the first attempt to liberate the Panjab from Mughal rule. Under the leadership of Banda they defied the authority of Mughal governors and kept the imperial armies at bay for full seven years. Although Banda and his followers were slaughtered, it gave an impetus to the Sikhs sectarianism which was furthered by Ahmad Shah Abdali's invasions of the Panjab. Sikh sectarianism enabled organisation of peasants in bands (misls) which harrased and ultimately expelled the invaders.The 'Sikh sectarianism achieved its consummation with the setting up of the first independent kingdom of the Panjab under Ranjit Singh during 1799-1839 A.D. This kingdom collapsed in a clash of arms with the British in 1848-9. The Sikhs, having evolved a faith, or outlook and a way of life which gave semblance of homogenity or collectivity had to fight against the forces of dissolution to preserve their identity during the British rule. The fate of the Sikhs in the partition of their homeland in 1947, their position in independent India, and the demand for an autonomous Panjab State within the Indian Union are distinct stages in the development of Sikh consciousness.

The chief factor in the growth of Sikh consciousness was the evolution of one common tongue from a babel of languages once prevalent in the Panjab, the main gateway into India. The spirit of Sikh consciousness first manifested itself among the Jat peasanty of the Central plains of the Panjab, although the founders and many of the leaders of the movement were not agriculturists. The Jat's spirit of freedom and equality refused to submit to Brahmanical Hinduism and in its turns drew the censure of the privileged Brahmins. Many innovations of the Sikh Gurus broke the affiliations of the Sikhs with Hindus. The new forms of ceremonial for birth and deaths, in which the recitation of hymns of the Guru replaced the chanting of Sanskrit 'Slokas' the attempt to do away with the practice of 'purdah', encourgement to monogamy, inter-caste alliances and remarriage of widows, prohibition of 'Sati' etc. are measures which aroused the hostility of the Brahmins, who saw the size of their flock and their incomes diminishing. They began to persecute the Sikhs and, when their own resources failed, they bribed local officials to harass the Sikhs. This was the beginning of the oppression of Sikhs, which subsequently compelled them to take up arms, and the first break with Hindu social polity.

In course of time Sikh socio-religious movements emerged. The importance of the Nirankari which emphasises formlessness of God—'Nirankar' (hence the futility of worshipping idols or saints) lies in the fact that it initiated ceremonial rites which inculcated among the Sikhs a sense of separateness and thus checked the process of their absorption into Hinduism. The difference between orthodox Sikhism and the Nirankaries are limited to the latter's worship of Gurus other than the ten recognised by the Sikhs. They also disapprove of the militant Khalsa.

The Radha Soamis of Beas propounded a doctrine which contained elements of both Hinduism and Sikhism. The Beas Radha Soamis have some basic differences with orthodox Sikhism. They believe in a living Guru, who initiates the disciples. Radha Soami temples do not have the Granth Sahib but only a raised plateform where the Guru sits to deliver a discourse. Although the Radha Soami Gurus of Beas as well as their Sikh adherents remain 'Kesadhari', they do not believe in 'pahul' (baptism, nor in the militant vows of the Khalsa.

The Beas Radha Soamis have close resemblance to the 'Sahajdharis'. The 'Sahajdharis' nominally accept the teachings of all the ten Sikh Gurus and keep up the fiction that in due course they will be baptised as the Khalsa. The Radha Soamis only accept the teachings of the first five Gurus contained in the 'Adi Granth' and reject the rest. The Radha Soamis present a new version of 'Sahajdhari' Sikhism. Their faith has considerable attraction for the religiously inclined educated classes, for the Hindu-oriented Sikh, and the Sikh oriented Hindu.

The Namdhari sect or Kuka movement has been inspired by the religious discourses with a political flavour. Whatever little sympathy the Sikhs may have had with the revivalist aspect of the Namdhari movement was forfeited by resort to violence and the defiance of the administration. Nonetheless, the Kukas have a place in the history of the freedom movement in India.

The Nirankari, Radha Soami, and Namdhari movements made shall impact on the Sikh masses. The first was confined to the urban community in the north-west ; the second was largely concerned with theistic problems ; while the third was temporarily blasted out of existence. All three developed into schismatic coteries owing allegiance to its particular guru and practicising its own esoteric ritual. The evils they had set out to abolish continued unabated.

The inherent weakness of the Sikh body politic was only one factor of disintegration ; there were three others : the activities of Christian missions, the rationalism that came with the introduction of scientific concepts, and the proselytisation by a new Hindu organisation known as the Arya Samaj.

Four years before the setting up of the Arya Samaj (1877) the Sikh gentry organised themselves in a society which described itself as the Singh Sabha to protest against the speeches of a Hindu making scurritous remarks against the Sikh Gurus. The Singh Sabha's objects included the revival of the teachings of the Gurus, production of religious literature in Panjabi, and a compaign against illiteracy. The founders also sought to ensure the patronage of the government for the educational programme of the Sabha. Hence, the Sabha sought to cultivate the loyalty of the crown. The government extended its patronage to the educational programme of the organisation.

The Singh Sabha, with its multifarious educational, literary and religious activities, soon evolved its own politics as well. These crystallised in the formation in 1902 of the Chief Khalsa Diwan pledged to safeguard Sikh rights vis-a-vis the other communities, and to fight for adequate representation of Sikhs in services, particularly the army.

The Singh Sabha movement not only checked the relapse of the Sikhs into Hinduism but retaliated by carrying proselytising activities into the Hindu camp. Large number of Hindus became 'Sahajdhari' Sikhs and they were in due course baptised to become the Khalsa.

The rise and expansion of Arya Samaj in the Panjab had a decisive bearing on the course of Hindu-Sikh relations and on the pattern of anti-British political movements in the province. The 'Sudhi' crusade launched by the Samaj were fiercely resisted by the Sikhs. The more Samajists claimed Sikhism to be a branch of Hinduism, the more the Sikhs insisted that they were a distinct and separate community. This action and reaction broke up the close social relationship which had existed between the two sister communities. Although the Singh Sabha movement petered out in the 1920's it left a legacy of a chronically defensive attitude towards Hinduism.

The domination of the Indian National Congress by Arya Samajists gave the freedom movement an aspect of Hindu resurgence and was chiefly responsible for the aloofness of the Muslim and the Sikhs.

Enthusiasm for the British Raj, which had reached its climax during the first world war (1914-18), rapidly declined. The government's refusal to protest against Canadian and American maltreatment of Sikh immigrants, disappointment over constitutional reforms, the shooting at Amritsar (April, 1919) followed by the repression of the movement to gain control of shrines from hereditary priests etc. created resentment against British rule. From these movements political parties emerged contending for power ; much the most influential of them being the Akalis.

Political parties reflected common economic interests. Land Alienation Act, 1900, was designed to protect the agriculturist from the clutches of the moneylenders. But, it sowed the seeds of racial separatism. It broke up the population on a new racial basis. The question as to who was or was not an agriculturist was not decided by actual occupation but by caste. In certain districts Brahmins were declared agriculturist, in others, non-agriculturist. Muslims, amongst whom caste considerations mattered little, were not particularly affected, nor, for precisely the opposite reason, were the Hindus. The community most adversely affected was the Sikhs. They had gone a long way in breaking the barriers of caste. The Land Alienation Act severed the links between the Jat Sikh farmers and the non-Jat Sikh farmers and put them in opposite camps. As a result, while the Jat Sikh was drawn closer to the Jat Mussalman and the Jat Hindu, the Khatri and Arora Sikh drew closer to the Khatri and Arora-Hindu.

Economic and political differences ultimately affected social life as well. Sikh Jats preferred to marry into Hindu Jat families rather than into non-Jat Sikhs. And Sikh Khatries and Aroras preferred to inter-marry with corresponding Hindu castes rather than with Jat Sikhs. Finally, there was the third racial group among the Sikhs—the untouchables. Sikh untouchables found that they had more in common with Hindu untouchables than with higher caste Sikhs. They sought the statutory privileges accorded to "Scheduled Castes." In short, with the Land Alienation Act, race came to matter more than religion. The Sikh community split into three racial divisions—the Jats, the non-Jats (which included Brahmins, Kshatriyas and Vaishyas),

29

and the untouchables (Mazhabis, Ramdasias, Siklighars, Kabirpanthis, etc.)

The socio-economic factors led to the founding of the Ghadr party by the Indian immigrants in the beginning of the 20th century. Though the vast majority of the Ghadr party was Sikh (and therefore its literature were printed in Gurumukhi and its meetings held in Gurdwaras), it had nothing whatever to do with the revival of Sikhism. It aimed to drive out the English from India ; but no Englishman lost his life at the hands of the Ghadrites, nor at the time did it pose a very serious threat to the British raj. Nevertheless, the movement is of considerable importance. It attracted Hindus and Muslims to its fold and later influenced other revolutionary groups in the country to shed their religious bias. The conversion of the Ghadr party from Xenophobic nationalism to communism came after the World War I. Communist infiltration split the Ghadr party.

The impatience generated by the Ghadr party and the nationalist movement coupled with the awakening brought about by the Singh Sabha movement had made the Sikhs conscious of their rights. While the educated began to press for their due in services and administrative bodies, the masses were more anxious to gain control of their 'gurudwaras'. There were no rules for the administration of Sikh shrines and over many of them priests ('Mahants'), who were Hindus as often as Sikhs, had asserted proprietary rights. The incomes of some of the 'gurdwaras', such as the Golden Temple in Amritsar and the birth place of Guru Nanak at Nankana, ran into several lacs per year. For many years, Sikh associations carried on futile civil litigation against the 'mahants'. Then, the Sikh masses adopted the non-cooperation and passive resistance of the newly formed party the Akalis (Immortals).

On November 15, 1920, a proclamation was made from the Akal Takht, Amritsar, to the effect that a committee of 175 to be known as the 'Shiromani Gurudwara Prabandhak Committee' (Central Gurudwara Management Committee—thereafter referred to by the initials S. G. P. C.) had been set up for the management of all Sikh Shrines. The more radical elements organised a semi-military corps of volunteers known as the 'Akali Dal' (army of immortals). The Akali Dal was to raise and train men for 'action' in taking over the gurudwaras from recalcitrant 'mahants'. A Gurumukhi paper, the 'Akali', was started. All this brought them into conflict with the Panjabi Hindus, many of whom unwittingly sided with the 'mahants' as well as the administration, which felt impelled to support the priests who were in possession of the temples. However, under pressure of Sikh opinion backed frequently by demonstrations of strength, the 'mahants' began to yield control over 'gurudwara' properties to elected committees and agreed to become paid 'granthis'.

By 1921 the pace of Sikh agitation quickened due to political repression and economic distress caused by famine conditions prevalent in the Panjab. Radical leadership which came to the force reflected different shades of political opinion and religions enthusiasm. There were also fanatics believing in the militant tradition of the Nihangs who wanted to meet force with force. This group organised itself into bands of terrorists known as 'Babbar Akalis' (immortal lions). The new leaders exploited the religious sentiments of the people to the full. The number of Akalis rose considerably high. Its result was the Sikh Gurudwaras and Shrines Act of 1922, which the Sikhs preferenced to ignore. The Akali demands were met the Sikh Gurudwaras Act of 1925. The Act provided for elected bodies to replace the 'mahants'. The central body, S. G. P. C., was to consist of 151 members, of whom 120 were to be elected, 12 nominated by the Sikh states, 14 to be coopted, and 5 to represent the four chief shrines of the faith. Local 'gurudwaras' were to have their own elected bodies of management with one nominee of the S.G.P.C.

on its committee. The Act also indicated in what way the incomes of gurudwaras were to be utilised. The most important part of the Act was to define a Sikh as one who believed in the ten 'gurus' and the 'Granth Sahib' and was not a 'patit' (absolute). This last proviso was particularly odious to the Hindus.

Akalis had thus won their bitter struggle against the 'mahants' and the government over control of their shrines. The most significant outcome of the four years of intense agitation (which procured the Sikh Gurudwaras Act of 1925 and in which the Hindus supported the Udasi 'mahants' against the Akalis) was to widen further the gulf between the two communities. The breakaway from Hinduism was even more emphatically stated. Whether the Sikhs were a separate people or a branch of Hindu social system became a major issue in the years that followed.

The S. G. P. C. became a sort of parliament of the Sikhs : its decisions acquired the sanctity of the ancient 'gurumata', its Dal became its army ; and the income from 'gurudwaras' (over ten lacs of rupees per year) gave it financial sustenance. Disbursement of this income in the management of shrines, patronage in the appointment of hundreds of 'granthis', sewadars (temple servants), teachers, and professors for schools and colleges which were built, arrangements for the training of 'granthis' and for missionary activity outside the Panjab, all made the S. G. P. C. a government within the government. Its control became the focal point of Sikh politics. The Akalis automatically took over control and have never relinquished it. The struggle for power has been between different factions of the same party.

The Akali movement was indirectly responsible for the political awakening in the princely states, After the settlement of disputes over the 'guradwaras', the Akalis from the states began to agitate against the autocratic misuse of power by the 'maharajas.'

In 1928 Akalis from the states joined with Hindu nationalists and founded the 'Praja Mandal' (States People's Association), the 'mandal' was later affiliated to the All India States People Congress (in its turn associated with the Indian National Congress). The 'Praja Mandal' movement in all princely states of the Panjab gained momentum in times to come.

Nonetheless, Panjabi Sikh was indifferent towards politics. The Panjab was the most reluctant state to respond to the schemes of self-government : and of the three communities of the Panjab, the Sikhs were the least responsive. Panjabi Hindus and Muslims had the benefit of the guidance of enlightened Hindus and Muslims from other parts of India. The Sikhs had no political teachers.

The formation of the Indian National Congress in 1885 and Sir Syed Ahmed Khan's United Patriotic Association in 1887 began a ferment in the Indian body politic. At the same time communal bodies became active. Educated members of the Chief Khalsa Diwan felt that they should also press for the rights of the Sikhs such as separate representation, special privileges and safeguards in services and facilities for developing their language and pressing their way of life. The Akalis, the party that really mattered, consisted largely of 'jathedars' incapable of grasping the niceties of constitutional practice, the Akalis tacitly acquiesed in the partition of India and their aspiration for a Sikh homeland still remained unfulfilled creating various compexities leading to the current situation in the Panjab.

Nonetheless, the twin processes of the continuing "homogenisation" of the Sikhs and the breaking down the barriers are simultaneously taking place. They are consistent with the principles of dialectical materialism of thesis, anti-thesis and synthesis. The first is the process of self-assertion by Sikhs, Hindus and other castes, sub-castes, linguistic groups, religions, region, zones etc. each wishing to maintain their separate identity and showing active hostility to others. The other is the process of assimilation whereby these very Sikhs, Hindus and other castes, sub-castes and linguistics group merge into each other to form more viable associations. Obviously these two forces are mutually antagonistic and have become source of violent disturbances. But, they are the inevitable concommitant of historical development and have to work themselves out at their own natural pace. There is a search for identity and security by each of them out of which will emerge the true Indian shorn of caste, creed and language appellation. From early nineteenth century, when a group of rationalists established themselves in Calcutta, to near end of twentieth century has been a long and steady journey of Indian progress lending strength to the hope that ultimately we will reach the goal of national unity, sans caste, sans creed, sans chauvinism.

REFERENCES

1. Adhikari, G. : *Sikh Homeland through Hindu-Muslim-Sikh Unity* (Bombay, 1945)

2. Ahluwalia, M. M. *Kukas : The Freedom Fighters of the Punjab* (Bombay, 1965).

3. Archer, J. C. : *The Sikh in relation to Hindus, Muslims, Christians and Ahmadiyyas : A Study in Comparative Relation* (Princeton 1946).

4. Benerjee, I. B. : *Evolution of the Khalsa*, 2 vols. Mukerjee & Co. (Calcutta, 1947).

5. Banerji, S. N. : *Ranjit Singh* (Lahore, 1931).

6. Basham, A. L. : *The Wonder that was India*, Grove Press (1954)

7. Browne, Major James : *History of the Origin and Progress of the Sikhs* (London, 1788)

8. Chatterjee, G. C. : *The Punjab Past and Present* (1939).

9. Chhabra, G. S. : *Advanced Study in the History of the Punjab.* 2 vols. Sharanjit (Ludhiana, 1961).

10. Singh, Chhajju : *The Ten Gurus and their Teachings.* (Lahore, 1903).

11. Chopra, Gulshan Lall : *Punjab as a Sovereign State, 1799-1838* (Lahore, 1928).

12. Court, Henry : *History of the Sikhs* (Lahore, 1888).

13. Cunningham, J. D. : *History of the Sikhs* (1853).

14. Dardi, Gopal Singh : *Translation of the Adi Granth*, 4 vols. Guru Das Kapur (1960).

15. Dowson, J. : *Classical Dictionary of Hindu Mythology and Religion*, Kegan Paul (1928).

16. Farooqi, B. A. : *British Relation with the Cis-Sutlej States 1809-1823*, P. G. R. O. (1941).

17. Field, Dorothy : *Religion of the Sikhs* (London, 1914)

18. Ganda Singh : *Banda Singh Bahadur* (Amritsar, 1935).

19. Gordon, J. H. : *The Sikhs*, Blackwood (London, 1904)

20. Griffin, Lepel, H. : *Ranjit Singh* (Oxford, 1905).

21. Griffin, L. H. : *Rajas of the Punjab* (Lahore, 1870).

22. Gupta Hari Ram :

    (a) *Studies in Later Mughal History of the Punjab* (Lahore, 1944)

    (b) *History of the Sikhs, Vol. I, 1739-1768* (Calcutta, 1939)

    (c) *Cis-Sutlej Sikhs*, Vol. II, 1769-1799, Minerva (Lahore, 1944)

    (d) *Trans-Sutlej Sikhs*, Vol. III, 1769-1799, Minerva (Lahore, 1944)

    (e) Marathas and Panipat, Punjab University (Chandigarh, 1961)

23. Hutchison and Vogel : *History of the Punjab Hill States*, 2 vols. Govt. Printing Press (Lahore, 1933).

24. Ibbetson, D. C. :
   (a) *Punjab Castes*, Govt. Printing Press (Lahore, 1916).
   (b) *The Religion of the Punjab* (Calcutta, 1883).

25. Kartar Singh :
   (a) *Life of Guru Nanak* (Amritsar, 1937).
   (b) *Life of Guru Gobind Singh* (Amritsar, 1933).

26. Khazan Singh : *History and Philosophy of the Sikh Religion*, 2 vols. (Lahore, 1914).

27. Kacker, Hansraj : *The Punjab*, 1792-1849. Moon Press (Agra, 1916).

28. Khushwant Singh : *The Sikhs* (London, 1953).

29. Latif, Syed Mohammed : *History of the Punjab* (Calcutta, 1891).

30. Ma Cauliffe, M. A. : *The Sikh Religion*, 6 vols. (Oxford, 1909).

31. Malcolm, Sir John : *A Sketch of the Sikhs* (London, 1812).

32. M'Gregor, W. L. : *History of the Sikhs*, 2, vols. (London, 1846.

33. Murray, W. M. : *History of the Punjab*, 2 vols. (1846).

34. Narang, Sir Gokul : *Transformation of Sikhism*. 3rd ed. (1960)

35. Payne, C. H : *A Short History of the Sikhs* (London)

36. Prinsep, H. T. : *The Origin of the Sikh Power in the Punjab* (Calcutta, 1834).

37. Scott, G. B. : *Religion and Short History of the Sikhs* (London, 1930).

38. Singh, Khuswant : *History of the Sikhs*, 2 vols. 1963-64.

39. Sinha, N. K. :
   (a) *Rise of the Sikh Power* (Calcutta, 1946).
   (b) *Ranjit Singh* (Calcutta, 1933).

40. Tara Chand : *Influence of Islam on Indian Culture* (Allahabad, 1954).

41. Teja Singh & Ganda Singh : *Short History of Sikhs* (1950).

42. Teja Singh : *Sikhism—its ideals and institutions*. (Bombay, 1938).

43. Thornton, T. H. : *History of the Punjab*, 2 vols. (London, 1846).